Computers as Cognitive Tools, Volume Two: No More Walls

✼ ✼ ✼

THEORY CHANGE, PARADIGM SHIFTS, AND THEIR INFLUENCE ON THE USES OF COMPUTERS FOR INSTRUCTIONAL PURPOSES

Computers as Cognitive Tools, Volume Two: No More Walls

✳ ✳ ✳

THEORY CHANGE, PARADIGM SHIFTS, AND THEIR INFLUENCE ON THE USE OF COMPUTERS FOR INSTRUCTIONAL PURPOSES

Edited by

Susanne P. Lajoie
McGill University

2000

LAWRENCE ERLBAUM ASSOCIATES, PUBLISHERS
Mahwah, New Jersey   London

Lawrence Erlbaum Associates, Inc., Publishers
10 Industrial Avenue
Mahwah, NJ 07430

Cover design by Kathryn Houghtaling Lacey

Library of Congress Cataloging-in-Publication Data

Computers as cognitive tools: no more walls/ edited by Susanne P. Lajoie.—Vol. II.
   p. cm.
Includes bibliographical references and index.
ISBN 0-8058-2930-X (cloth: alk. paper)—ISBN 0-8058-2931-8 (pbk.: alk. paper)
   1. Computer-assisted instruction—United States. 2. Artificial intelligence. I. Lajoie, Susanne.

LB1028.5 .C5722 2000
371.33'4—dc21   99-088271

Books published by Lawrence Erlbaum Associates are printed on acid-free paper, and their bindings are chosen for strength and durability.

Printed in the Untied States of America
10 9 8 7 6 5 4 3 2 1

Contents

✳ ✳ ✳

PART II: COGNITIVE TOOLS THAT FOSTER NEW FORMS OF REPRESENTATION

PART III: EPILOGUE

PART IV: DISCUSSION

Preface

✳ ✳ ✳

Since the publication of *Computers as Cognitive Tools* in 1993, rapid changes have been made in the uses of technology for educational purposes and the theories underlying such uses. The introduction to this book, "Breaking Camp to Find New Summits," addresses my reconceptualization of the camp analogy used in Volume 1 to stimulate thinking about how researchers situate themselves within specific theoretical perspectives and to guide the development of computer-based learning environments based on such perspectives. Although many of these perspectives still exist, the analogy may have outlived its purpose. The introduction addresses this issue with regard to the influence of learning paradigms on the design of computers as cognitive tools.

Changes in perspectives on thinking and learning are guiding the instructional design of computer-based learning environments. Learning theorists are considering the nature of individual learning as well as how knowledge is constructed in social situations. The chapter authors in this book demonstrate some variability in their choice of guiding learning paradigms; consequently, readers have an opportunity to examine how such paradigms are operationalized and validated. Some of the paradigms represented are information processing, constructivism, and situativity.

This book has four parts. Part I addresses issues of individual knowledge construction and learning in social situations through the use of technology. Akhras and Self (chap. 1) specifically address ways in which situated learning theory can be operationalized computationally. They provide examples of situations and how learning can be assessed within situations. Examples of technologies for supporting knowledge building in distributed learning contexts are presented by Sugrue (chap. 5); Derry, Gance, Gance, and Schlager (chap. 2); Greer, McCalla, Cooke, Collins, Kumar, Bishop, and Vassileva (chap. 3); and White, Shimoda, and Frederiksen (chap. 4). Sugrue examines uses of the Internet from several theoretical perspectives that support cognition: information processing, situated learning, collaborative learning, and student modeling. This review synthesizes and exemplifies instructional uses of the World Wide Web (WWW), providing both researchers and developers with a valuable resource.

The chapters by Derry et al., Greer et al., and White et al. describe ways in which research can be conducted in the area of distributed learning contexts. Knowledge building is a difficult concept to grasp, especially in the context of distributed learning. Derry et al. begin to demystify the concept by outlining specific indexes for assessing knowledge building in technology-mediated workplaces. Greer et al. explore instructional mechanisms for knowledge building through a combination of human peer support and an intelligent computer matching program, described as the Intelligent IntraNet Help-Desk facility. By modeling both the individual learner and peers, this facility is able to find appropriate matches between partners that can facilitate appropriate assistance. White et al. combine a computer-pedagogical agent approach to enhancing collaborative knowledge construction with inquiry tasks where humans can alter and test the effectiveness of pedagogical advisors with other students. This is a hybrid computer and human agent approach to enhancing instruction. Part I provides examples of instructional strategies and assessments for collaborative learning situations that are mediated by cognitive tools.

In Part II, researchers describe cognitive tools that foster new forms of representation. Jonassen and Carr (chap. 6) outline the various ways in which computers can provide the tools for multiple forms of knowledge representation and how such representations can be used for assessment purposes. They describe how different classes of mindtools, i.e., semantic organization tools, dynamic modeling tools, information interpretation tools, knowledge construction tools, and conversation tools enable learners to represent what they know in different ways, thereby engaging them in a range of cognitive activities.

Many of the chapters in Part II refer to novel forms of representation that are enhanced through the use of technology. Erickson and Lehrer (chap. 7), for example, have defined a new way of documenting transitions in the hyperauthoring design process. They examine the student as hypermedia author and how that the author's conception of a hypermedia link and the function it serves during composition affect the use and design of links. In essence, the hypermedia link is a new form of representation that is specific to the hypermedia design process. Documenting transitions in proficiency in the design process through this new language of rhetorical links is unique to this computer tool.

Harper, Hedberg, Corderoy, and Wright (chap. 8) demonstrate ways in which multimedia tools provide opportunities for students to express themselves through alternative forms of representation. Exploring the Nardoo is a multimedia computer environment that teaches students about ecology through authentic learning situations. Students prepare multimedia reports that address specific ecology problems, and cognitive tools are embedded within the multimedia tools that scaffold the problem solving and support the writing process. The embedded tools enable successful multimedia reporting and support the manipulation of complex ideas, which can be represented in different forms, such as text, video, and audio. In addition to simply viewing or listening to video or television and radio shows, students can manipulate these images and sounds into their own notebooks and present a multimedia project presentation that represents their problem-solving activities in ecology.

Lajoie and Azevedo (chap. 9) describe several computer-based learning environments in the area of medical informatics that encourage reflection and self-assessment. Each of these systems is unique in terms of the types of mental representations that are externalized and scaffolded within the learning situations. For example, the Bio-World system embeds evidence and argumentation tools into a problem-based learning environment where students reason about diseases. These tools provide external placeholders for groups to collect, post, categorize, rank, and discard evidence pertaining to hypotheses about specific diseases. Many of the chapter authors illustrate how computers can be used to highlight mental representations that are not apparent to learners. Learning and assessment become intertwined such that the learners can check their problem-solving processes while solving a problem.

Schwartz, Biswas, Bransford, Bhuva, Balac, and Brophy (chap. 10) describe a computer tool, STAR.Legacy, that organizes assessment and instructional resources into an inquiry cycle. Their approach takes the learning and assessment connection to two new dimensions: readiness to learn and transferability to new problems. Instead of assessing what type of problem a student can or cannot solve, they address whether a student is ready to learn and what format of instruction is most appropriate based on that readiness. They coin the phrase *domain learnability* and describe this as examining what students know, what misconceptions they have, and whether they can transfer what they have learned to new situations. STAR.Legacy has been researched in the context of instruction about electrical circuits, but it shows great promise for generalizing to new domains of learning.

One of the more ingenious cognitive tools for fostering new forms of representation is Decompose, Network, Assess (DNA), a tool for knowledge elicitation described by Shute, Torreano, and Willis (chap. 11). DNA helps experts externalize their domain expertise online. Many computer-tutor designers have used cognitive task analysis as a methodology for identifying the cognitive processes and strategies underlying individual differences in a specific domain. Although cognitive task analysis is a rich methodology, it is labor intensive in that it requires the analysis of complex verbal protocols to document the domain knowledge. Shute et al. provide insights into how one might automate the knowledge-elicitation phase and reduce the burden of analysis. DNA extracts and organizes knowledge and skills from subject-matter experts. These structured curriculum elements are fed into another computer tool (Student Modeling Approach for Responsive Tutoring, or SMART) as the basis for assessment, cognitive diagnosis, and instruction. DNA is used to discover what to teach, and SMART decides when and how to teach it. Together these tools feed into the development of intelligent tutoring systems. It is apparent from Shute et al.'s research and that of many of the other chapter authors that an emerging trend in the research on computers as cognitive tools is the reusability and modularity of tools to be used together with new supertools. It is also apparent that the empirical testing of such tools is a first step in the development of these supertools.

An epilogue and discussion are provided in Parts III and IV, respectively. Du Boulay (chap. 12) adds an international perspective to this book by providing a summary of research done in Europe in the field of artificial intelligence and education. Issues arising in this area pertain to both the individual construction of knowledge and knowledge building within a community. A central theme at a recent EuroAIED conference, for example, was on learning as a process in which affect, dialogue, context, knowledge organization, representation, and learning style play key roles. This synopsis can serve as a stepping-stone to identifying fertile areas of study in the field of computers as cognitive tools.

Whereas Du Boulay presents a conceptual representation of the field, Mandinach and Cline (chap. 13) provide a pragmatic look at the barriers or obstacles to the successful implementation of technology-based constructivist approaches in classrooms. They identify three major obstacles: a lack of adequate evaluation research designs, inappropriate measures of cognitive activity, and an abundance of financial and practical problems.

Attending to some of Mandinach and Cline's concerns can lead to better research and success at encouraging educators to incorporate technology in classroom settings.

Lesgold (chap. 14), as discussant, places the use of tools in education in a historic context and in so doing elucidates the reasons for developing the theme of computers as cognitive tools. He sagely points out that tools are created for a purpose and often by those who see the need for innovation. Provisions must be made for cooperative efforts by teachers, educational researchers, and information scientists to build and revise tools that can be used with successful outcomes in classrooms.

Computers as Cognitive Tools, Second Edition: No More Walls: Theory Change, Paradigm Shifts, and Their Influence on the Uses of Computers for Instructional Purposes provides examples of state-of-the-art technology-based research in the field of education and training. These examples are theory driven and reflect the learning paradigms that are currently in use in cognitive science, ranging from information processing perspectives to situativity theories. An array of instructional and assessment approaches is described along with new techniques for automating the design and assessment process. New considerations are offered as possibilities for examining learning in distributed situations. A multitude of subject matter areas are covered in this book: scientific reasoning and inquiry in biology, physics, and medicine; electricity; teacher education; programming; and hypermedia composition in the social sciences and ecology. This book reconsiders the initial camp analogy posited in 1993 and presents a mechanism for breaking camp to find new summits.

ACKNOWLEDGMENTS

I thank the chapter authors for their diligence and patience in making this book a reality. Some of them were also chapter authors for volume 1. These original contributors provide continuity between the two volumes and provide opportunities to see transitions in the types of research in this field that has emerged. The authors new to this volume provide international balance, as well as new theoretical and computational perspectives regarding the theme of computers as cognitive tools. An interdisciplinary group of researchers is represented: computer scientists, cognitive scientists, educational psychologists, and instructional psychologists.

I acknowledge the support of the Social Science and Humanities Research Council in Canada for supporting my own research in the area of computers as cognitive tools and thereby assisting in making this book possible.

—Susanne P. Lajoie

Introduction: Breaking Camp to Find New Summits

❊ ❊ ❊

Susanne P. Lajoie
McGill University

Since the publication of *Computers as Cognitive Tools* in 1993, rapid changes have been made in the uses of technology for educational purposes and the theories underlying such uses. The most apparent technological changes have been in the growth of educational and training vehicles on the Internet, in communication technologies that allow for such activities as videoconferencing, and multiuser interfaces, where people work together synchronously in joint problem-solving endeavors or in chat rooms. One recognizable shift in how technology is used is that computers can support both the individual and groups of individuals who are working together toward a common goal. In parallel, learning theories are considering the nature of individual learning as well as how knowledge is constructed in social situations. More broadly, learning is being examined in terms of environmental factors, such as what is available to the learner in a concrete sense (books, tables, computers, instructional materials, or apparatus), as well as in a social sense (how individuals influence each other in the total learning experience). I address these changes as a way of highlighting the paradigm shifts that have occurred since 1993 with regard to the theme of *Computers as Cognitive Tools*.

NO MORE WALLS

In an attempt to clarify how theory influenced practice, Derry and Lajoie (1993) provided an analogy in an effort to categorize the theoretical positions that existed in the field of artificial intelligence and education at that time. The analogy described three imaginary camps: modelers, nonmodelers, and middle camp. The modelers represented the traditional intelligent tutoring system paradigm that maintains that students' thinking processes can be modeled, traced, and corrected in the context of problem solving using computers. The nonmodeler camp suggested that a computer could not be responsible for student modeling, either because adequate cognitive models cannot be developed or because better or more cost-effective alternatives exist. As an alternative they suggest that students can be stimulated to monitor and diagnose their own learning and problem-solving performance through the use of well-designed cognitive tools and assistance from peers or human tutors. The middle camp position intersects the modeling and nonmodeling perspective by providing a broader interpretation of student modeling that is less restrictive, allowing for multiple perspectives and encompassing a greater emphasis on the development of cognitive tools within computer-based learning environments that help learners in the context of problem solving.

Having said all this, it is apparent that this camp analogy may have been misconstrued. The purpose of the camp analogy was to encourage people to share stories around the campfire rather than to confine individuals to separate lodges. It is time to tear down the walls between camps and to refine our shared purpose. The issue never should have been, "To model or not to model," but "who" or "what" should do the modeling and coaching given particular learning situations. Bandura (1977) defined modeling in the following context: "Learning would be exceedingly laborious, not to mention hazardous, if people had to rely solely on the effects of their own actions to inform them what to do. Fortunately, most human behavior is learned observationally through modeling: From observing others one forms an idea of how new behaviors are performed, and on later occasions this coded information serves as a guide for action" (p. 22). Those in the model camp developed student models that allowed the computer to interpret learners' actions dynamically in the context of a problem-solving activity and to provide adaptive feedback based on the students' actions. In this use of the word *modeling*, expert models of human activity may be automatically generated for the learners when the computer determines that assistance is needed. Student models generate computer models of learning for learners to observe and guide their future actions. The nonmodelers believed that it was impossible for computer models to be extensive enough to provide the adaptive feedback required. Hence, the nonmodelers used technology as tools for learning and often required human beings to serve as modelers or facilitators who used computer tools to enhance student learning. Thus, the question should not have been whether to model but who or what does the modeling: computers or human beings? The intent was never to throw out the need for modeling but to refine its definition.

THEORY CHANGE, PARADIGM SHIFT, AND COMPUTERS

Changes in the availability and flexibility of technologies are allowing for greater creativity in the ways in which these technologies are used for education and training. But are these changes in educational use driven by learning and instructional theories, or do technological advances drive them? The chapter authors in the book demonstrate how learning theories can guide the design of computer-based learning environments that provide cognitive tools for learners.

The choice of learning paradigm can guide instruction and research about learning and, consequently, the design of technologies for supporting learning. Shulman (1986) suggested that in the social sciences, more than one paradigm can coexist and drive research, whereas Kuhn (1970) described how science was guided by a leading paradigm, outlining what happens when paradigms collide or what conditions lead to scientific revolutions. The last decade has revealed some shifts in what can be considered guiding paradigms for learning theory (Anderson, Reder, & Simon, 1996, 1998; Brown, 1994; Greeno, 1997, 1998; Mayer, 1997). Some might perceive this shift as evolutionary, where coexistence is not problematic, and others as revolutionary, where one paradigm must be superior. From an evolutionary perspective, Mayer (1997) describes learning theory evolving from three metaphors: response strengthening (responses that are rewarded will occur more regularly; those that are punished will deteriorate), information processing (knowledge is transmitted and acquired by humans' taking in information as input and applying mental operators to that information and producing information as output; Newell & Simon, 1972), and knowledge construction (learners make sense of information). Mayer's description is evolutionary in the sense that one metaphor seems to grow out of another rather than being in direct opposition to one another, with information processing serving as a bridge. Although constructivism is being touted as the most current learning metaphor, Mayer points out that its two predecessors still live in various forms. Greeno (1998), on the other hand, tends to collapse this bridge when he suggests that a constructivist model of situativity can subsume the best parts of the response strengthening and information processing paradigms. A situative perspective is one that focuses attention on how learning occurs within systems in which people interact with each other and with material, informational, and conceptual resources in their environments. Greeno's stance is more revolutionary in that it suggests the situativity model is somewhat superior to existing cognitive models.

There is some tension in the literature regarding which paradigm will guide future research on learning and instruction and, consequently, computer uses in education. Anderson, Reder, and Simon (1996, 1998) suggest that situated cognition makes many claims that have not been supported empirically or have already been supported under existing cognitive paradigms. One such claim supported by Greeno (1998) is that all learning involves socially organized activity. Anderson et al. (1996) state, "Presumably, the situated view would correspondingly not deny that there are individuals interacting in all situations, that these individuals have minds, that much of their individuality comes from the (socially and individually acquired) knowledge contained in those minds, and that they are not just cogs in a social wheel" (p. 20). From Anderson's perspective, progress in understanding the social aspects of learning can be made by analyzing the social situation into relations among a number of individuals and to study the mind of each individual and how it contributes to the interaction. From Greeno's (1998) position, new methods of interactivity and design experiments will provide evidence of situativity.

In summary, operational definitions of new terms and replicable methodologies need to be built along with new theoretical positions so that empirical evidence can be collected and validated (Anderson et al., 1998). According to Greeno (1998), these methodologies are now being developed. It is interesting to note that this struggle is occurring at the international level as well. According to Du Boulay (chap. 12, this volume), who reviewed issues arising from a EuroAIED conference, an agenda for operationalizing a methodology for research on situativity seems to be developing in that issues relating to both the individual construction of knowledge and knowledge building within a community were described. Furthermore, he states that a heavy emphasis on learning as process permeated this conference, where issues of affect, dialogue, context, knowledge organization and representation, and learning style were central themes. Each of these issues could be considered in the context of individual and group learning situations.

This book's chapter authors demonstrate some variability in their choice of guiding learning paradigms, so readers have an opportunity to examine how such paradigms are operationalized and validated.

TECHNOLOGIES FOR SUPPORTING KNOWLEDGE BUILDING IN DISTRIBUTED LEARNING CONTEXTS

Akhras and Self (chap. 1, this volume) ambitiously take on the challenge of building a model of situated learning within a computer-based learning environment. They have refined the definition of student modeling by taking into consideration the context of learning, defining learning situations, and types of interactions that can be used to monitor learning over extended periods of time in the context of computer-based learning situations. This new methodology expresses concisely the issue of constructivist learning theory by operationalizing it into computational terms. Consequently, some of the assumptions of situativity that Greeno (1998) described might be testable.

Whereas Akhras and Self reveal how context and situations can be monitored computationally, Derry, Gance, Gance, and Schlager (chap. 2, this volume) explore another aspect of situativity: the assessment of knowledge building within a technology-mediated work group. They explore a multiuser virtual environment for teacher professional development, called TAPPED-IN, that was designed for teachers to share ideas and resources at a distance. In order to test the TAPPED-IN platform as a vehicle for knowledge building and to build indexes that assess changes in knowledge in such an environment, Derry et al. had their own research group use the platform. The group was geographically dispersed, and their use of the tool would simulate how novice teachers would use the tool.

The purpose of the research by Derry et al. was to develop a theoretical framework for studying social knowledge construction in online communities and use it to test their conceptualization, with their research group interactions serving as data. They have developed knowledge construction indexes that can provide other researchers with templates for studying online discourse patterns in other contexts. They suggest that a frequency of apprenticeship index can gauge the health of the knowledge construction system. For instance, if apprenticeship is rare, then perhaps the tool is not serving its purpose, members may not be engaging in discourse or not learning from one another, or help is not available when needed. On the other hand, they suggest that the frequency of mentoring dialogue does not necessarily imply effective apprenticeship. It could instead reflect overdominance by leaders, ineffective mentorship, or overly difficult tasks for the group.

Derry et al. also created a knowledge-building index that examines clusters of concepts and changes in how the constructs are used over time. Growth in knowledge building could be documented by examining time-series changes in what and how many such constructs the community is using. Frederiksen and Donin (1998) have documented the use of log-linear techniques for documenting transitions in learning in the context of computer-based learning environments. These transitions may be documented in communities of practice as well.

TAPPED-IN provides an excellent platform for understanding how technologies serve as cognitive tools for mediating the knowledge construction activity. Derry et al. used this platform to operationalize and assess some of the concepts of situated learning and constructivism. This is a first step toward developing a methodology for scientifically testing new learning theories.

BRIDGING SITUATIVITY
AND INFORMATION PROCESSING MODELS:
THE RENOVATED MIDDLE CAMP

Inasmuch as Derry et al. describe new methodologies for analyzing online discussion groups from a knowledge-building perspective, Greer, McCalla, Cooke, Collins, Kumar, Bishop, and Vassileva (chap. 3, this volume) describe how knowledge building is facilitated in mediated online discussions through intelligent peer support systems. They designed the Intelligent IntraNet Peer Help-Desk facility, which consists of an intelligent set of intranet cognitive tools that support peer learning. Two projects are described in their chapter: the cooperative peer response (CPR) system and the peer help system (PHelpS), which together have been integrated into a suite of cognitive tools provided in the Intelligent IntraNet Help-Desk facility. CPR was designed for a university course and consists of World Wide Web (WWW)–based tools that facilitate cooperative learning, peer help, and expert help. PhelpS, designed for a correctional organization, provides a facility for locating a peer helper in the organization who is ready, willing, and able to provide help.

These cognitive tools are unique in that they support peer help within specific learning contexts. From a theoretical point of view, peer help fits well into a model of social constructivism, in that learning occurs in social settings where individuals share their understanding with others. However, peer support in naturally occurring settings is often a hit-or-miss situation, in that not all peers are qualified to answer an individual's questions. Greer et al. support peer help intelligently in that the basis of providing individual help is modeling both the learner and peers so that matches between partners can be made to facilitate appropriate assistance. This approach to student modeling is much closer to Anderson et al.'s (1998) perspective of learning in social contexts. Greer et al. point out that theories involving situativity have failed to develop elaborate analytic models of group learning (Van Lehn, Ohlsson, & Nason 1994; Anderson et al., 1998), but based on what is known, they attempt to build a student model of peer help.

Peer help can be considered beneficial to both the learner and the teacher. New social mores are emerging as we move to distributed learning environments, such as TAPPED-IN, or online conferencing utilities available through the Internet. At times individuals may have difficulty finding proper assistance; they may not know whom to ask for help, or who is knowledgeable, or if that person is available to provide assistance (Greer et al.). The IntraNet Help-Desk facility makes this matching possible and appropriate. Extending this facility to new domains will be an excellent test of the model. An interesting research avenue would be to link the IntraNet Help-Desk facility with TAPPED-IN to provide the benefit of intelligent peer matching with the new assessment indexes related to knowledge building that Derry et al. describe.

APPLYING THEORETICAL PERSPECTIVES TO USES OF THE WORLD WIDE WEB

One advantage of an intranet over the Internet is that it provides more confidentiality and privacy (Greer et al.). For example, students participating in an intranet course develop into a community of learners and, by communicating with their peers and teacher, realize a level of comfort in sharing their opinions that they may not share as freely if access were open to the world. However, there are times when classrooms need wide access to resource materials such as those provided on the WWW. Sugrue (chap. 5, this volume) claims that the WWW has developed to the point where it has the technical capabilities to implement any instructional strategy. She tests this assumption by examining uses of the WWW from several theoretical perspectives that support cognition: information processing, situated learning, collaborative learning, and student modeling. The appropriate use of technology is based on the domain and audience in question. In other words, different learning paradigms and philosophies may be appropriate for different types of cognitive tasks within the same broad field of study (Lajoie & Azevedo, chap. 9, this volume, describe this in the context of three computer-based learning environments). Sugrue considers these questions in the context of the WWW.

Sugrue provides a critical examination of how the WWW is used for instructional purposes and provides exemplars guided by different theoretical perspectives. For instance, she describes the cognitive benefits of instructionally oriented information resources on the WWW: course notes, assignment instructions, and grouped sets of links to Web sites that relate to a particular topic. The standardization of navigation features and the integration of information resources with other learning resources on a topic reduce the cognitive load on the student and free up mental capacity for processing the information rather than finding the information. Sugrue suggests that another benefit is that criss-crossing a set of information units in a variety of ways for a variety of purposes can result in the acquisition of flexible knowledge (Spiro, Feltovich, Jacobson, & Coulson, 1992).

Sugrue also explores the guided learning approaches available on the WWW that use a myriad of student modeling techniques. One form of student modeling is conducted through self-tests and quizzes, where students get immediate feedback on the correctness of their answers and additional information to explain why an answer was correct or incorrect. A second is intelligent tutoring systems on the Web, where task-specific information in the form of hints or suggestions for further study is given to students based on ongoing analysis of their actions. Sugrue points to the combined tracking and communication capabilities of the Web as a way to facilitate diversity in student modeling and uses of the models. The chapters by Derry et al. and Greer et al. illustrate this diversity in models of collaborative learning on the Web, with students, teachers, and other professionals from any location interacting. Feedback based on such modeling can come from humans, be it synchronous or asynchronous, as well as be generated by computer-tracking algorithms.

COGNITIVE TOOLS THAT FOSTER NEW FORMS OF ASSESSMENT

One tenet of constructivist learning theory is that learners should be immersed in situated, problem-based learning environments that replicate real-world activity structures. Jonassen and Carr (chap. 6, this volume) support constructivist learning paradigms but suggest that putting this paradigm into educational practice requires too big a shift for educators. Alternatively, they suggest that educators would more readily accept the use of multiple forms of knowledge representation in assessments and that computers can provide the tools for such representations. Jonassen (1996) describes such tools as mindtools or knowledge construction tools that learners learn *with*, not *from* (see Salomon's 1990 discussion on the effects *of* and *with* technology). Computer tools, unlike most other tools, can function as intellectual partners that share the cognitive burden of carrying out tasks (Salomon, Perkins, & Globerson, 1991). Jonassen and Carr define mindtools as computer software applications, such as databases, spreadsheets, semantic networking programs, microworlds, hypermedia authoring tools, and computer conferencing software, that enable learners to represent what they have learned and know using different representational formalisms. By using mindtools, learners engage in a variety of critical, creative, and complex thinking, such as evaluating, analyzing, connecting, elaborating, synthesizing, imagining, designing, problem solving, and decision making (Jonassen, 1996). Mindtools provide structural, logical, causal, systemic, or visual-spatial formalisms that scaffold different kinds of thinking and knowledge representation; that is, they manipulate the task (supplant the student's performance by performing some part of the task or by adjusting the sequence or difficulty of the task) (Jonassen, Peck, & Wilson, 1998). Their chapter describes how different classes of mindtools, semantic organization tools, dynamic modeling tools, information interpretation tools, knowledge construction tools, and conversation tools enable learners to represent what they know in different ways, thereby engaging them in a range of cognitive activities.

Chapter 7, by Erickson and Lehrer, falls into the mindtool category in that they describe how students use a hypermedia authoring tool to construct their knowledge. They examine the student as hypermedia author and how the student-author's conception of a hypermedia link and the function it serves during composition affects the use and design of links. Erickson and Lehrer examined students' conception of links and transitions in such knowledge over multiple design activities. They found that students developed a repertoire of the rhetorical functions of links (those that reflect a consideration of purpose, audience, and composition or text conventions) throughout the year, along with an increase in the use of elaborative and structural links. These transitions in student knowledge were described as evolving from decoration to communication. Such documentation of learning through the use of mindtools or cognitive tools demonstrates what Jonassen and Carr described as new forms of assessment opportunities where multiple representations are valued. Both the process of designing such hypermedia knowledge bases and the product—interconnected multimedia stacks—can be assessed with a goal of documenting emerging expertise (Glaser, Lesgold, & Lajoie, 1987).

Harper, Hedberg, Corderoy, and Wright (chap. 8, this volume) provide another example of designing cognitive tools to assist students in making the transition from novice to expert. The chapter describes a learning environment, Exploring the Nardoo, that provides a series of supportive cognitive tools that assist students in solving complex problems. High school students who use Exploring the Nardoo engage in long-term studies involving ecology that require problem solving, measuring, collating, elaborating, and communicating; they manage a set of multimedia resources and create their own meanings of the phenomena rather than one generated by their teacher or by the application designer. However, since students are novices, support is provided to enable them to work in a knowledge domain with which they are only partially familiar. Support is provided for the study of interactions between living organisms and the physical and chemical environment in which they operate. Students prepare multimedia reports, and cognitive tools are embedded within the multimedia tools that scaffold the problem solving and support the writing process. The embedded tools enable successful multimedia reporting and support the manipulation of complex ideas, which can be represented in different visual forms. These tools allow students to provide multiple forms of understanding through multiple multimedia representations such as text, video, and audio. Exploring the Nardoo demonstrates ways in which computer environments can be designed with cognitive tools that facilitate both learning and assessment. It presents an interesting platform

for examining processes such as information analysis, knowledge generation, and argumentation.

Computer-supported collaborative argumentation has been described
as a mindtool (Jonassen & Carr, this volume) that can scaffold formal
argumentation in order to help students reason more effectively. Informal
reasoning entails the analysis, evaluation, and formulation of arguments
(or problem solutions) based on reason (Toulmin, Rieke, & Janik, 1984).
The product of reasoning is an argument, and, analogously, the product of
a problem-solving activity is a solution that must be justified in the same
way as an argument: by providing supporting evidence or explanations
(Jonassen & Carr). Examples of computer support of collaborative argumentation are illustrated in this book (Derry et al., Greer et al., Harper et
al., and Lajoie & Azevedo).

Computer-supported collaborative argumentation is a goal of the Bio-
World environment that Lajoie and Azevedo describe. Bio-World is a system that supports scientific reasoning about disease. Through an
argumentation process, students form a diagnostic hypothesis and collect
evidence to confirm or disconfirm their current diagnosis. Bio-World
facilitates scientific thinking through argumentation tools made available
during problem solving (Lajoie et al., 1995). These tools are used to document the argumentation process by posting the student hypotheses along
with the evidence that collaborators agree supports their hypothesis claim.
Students revise their hypotheses and can organize, categorize, and rate the
evidence before making a final summary argument. As they construct
arguments to defend their hypotheses, Bio-World monitors their actions
and determines the kind of advice or hints to generate in response to student requests. By making arguments visible, students can begin to monitor
their own scientific thinking in the context of problem solving. This phase
allows time for reflection and communication among group members as to
what information was most important in the problem-solving process.
Students then compare their solutions with an expert argument as an alternative solution path that helps them reflect on their own problem-solving
process.

Another example of computers used as cognitive tools is when computers make students' plans, actions, and consequences of their actions visible to learners. Such tools externalize internal knowledge representations
(Jonassen, this volume). Such tools were designed in the context of a
computer-based learning environment that supports nurses' assessments
of patients in a surgical intensive care unit (Lajoie & Azevedo, this volume). A memory and metacognitive tool is provided by the "where am I"

button, which, when selected, presents a graphical representation of the learner's problem-solving process. The graph is created based on where that student is at a particular time. The representation is hierarchical in that the nurse's plans, and actions within each plan, are noted. These external representations remind nurses of their prior actions, thereby reducing repetition and the cognitive load of managing this high-information-flow environment. The tutor ensures that learners reflect on their plans and actions by forcing them to state explicitly whether they accomplished their goals within each plan. This helps them reflect on their actions in the context of their stated hypotheses. Furthermore, students can compare their problem-solving processes with those of an expert. The comparison process ensures that students assess their own plans and actions and helps them expand their repertoire of problem-solving strategies to include a model of expertise.

One of the legacies of empirical research using the information processing paradigm in studies of learning was the identification of domain-specific individual differences in mental representations, cognitive processing, and strategies (Mayer, 1997). Identifying such differences is crucial in the development of computer-based learning approaches that are based on the assumption that cognitive processes can be modeled, traced, and corrected in the context of problem solving (Anderson, Corbett, Koedinger, & Pelletier, 1995; Shute & Psotka, 1994). The RADtutor is a computer-based learning environment that supports the training of medical residents' interpretation of mammograms (Lajoie & Azevedo, this volume). A cognitive task analysis resulted in a cognitive model of mammogram interpretation that was used to design the tutoring system. Cognitive task analysis, although a rich and rewarding methodology, has often been considered a bottleneck in the development of tutoring systems, since it requires time and analysis of complex verbal protocols to identify the cognitive processes and strategies underlying individual differences in a specific domain.

Shute, Torreano, and Willis (chap. 11, this volume) provide insights into how one might automate the knowledge elicitation phase and reduce the burden of analysis. Similar to the Greer et al. research that builds an intelligent peer help desk facility based on previous computer tools that were empirically tested, Shute et al. describe a set of tools that can feed into the development of intelligent tutoring systems. DNA (Decompose, Network, Assess) extracts and organizes knowledge and skills from subject-matter experts. SMART (Student Modeling Approach for Responsive Tutoring; Shute, 1995) uses the resulting structured curriculum elements from DNA as the basis for assessment, cognitive diagnosis, and instruction. Shute et al. state that DNA relates to the "what" to teach, while SMART addresses the "when" and "how" to teach it.

Schwartz, Biswas, Bransford, Bhuva, Balac, and Brophy (chap. 10, this volume) link knowledge assessment and instruction through computer environments. Their investigations are based on a dynamic model of assessment that emphasizes students' preparedness for learning Bransford & Schwartz, in press). In other words, their assessments go beyond indicating what type of problem a student can or cannot solve by addressing whether a student is ready to learn and what format of instruction is most appropriate. This view of dynamic assessment includes providing opportunities for multiple assessment as well as self-assessments, which are tenets of authentic assessment (Lajoie, 1995), but goes beyond what a student knows in addressing what he can learn. An assessment of domain learnability, according to Schwartz et al., needs to address what students know, what misconceptions they have, and whether they can transfer what they have learned to new situations. Their assumption is that proper assessment and instructional resources can change the course of future learning. Assessing domain learnability has some parallels to what Glaser et al. (1987) described as assessing personal theories as an aspect of emerging proficiency.

In their chapter Schwartz et al. describe a computer tool, STAR.Legacy, that organizes assessment and instructional resources into an inquiry cycle. STAR stands for Software Technology for Action and Reflection. It is an authored, multimedia software shell that supports development and research on complex sequences of instruction that require students to act on and evaluate their understanding. It is intended to be flexible and readily adapted by other instructors and researchers. The chapter authors tested the benefits of STAR.Legacy in an introductory electricity course (DC.Legacy) to assess the learnability of the basic concepts of electrical circuits. In so doing they were able to identify which misconceptions or difficulties affect learning most strongly and which instructional resources were most helpful. This tool shows promise and generalizability to using computer tools to assess theories and misconceptions and their relationship to learning.

Assessing what students know is an important precursor to enabling future learning. Whereas Schwartz et al. examined ways of dynamically assessing student conceptions and misconceptions in order to improve instruction, White, Shimoda, and Frederiksen (chap. 4, this volume) explored theory change from the point of view of metacognition and collaborative knowledge construction in the context of scientific inquiry. ThinkerTools SCI-WISE was designed to support classroom research communities by providing instructional methods and materials to make inquiry processes and regulatory activities (like monitoring and reflecting) overt and explicit so that students can talk about, internalize, and improve them. White et al. have designed a system of pedagogical agents that interact to guide and counsel students as they engage in research and reflect on and revise their inquiry processes. These agents advise users concerning the development of inquiry goals and strategies, such as being inventive or collaborating effectively, but do not have enough expertise to carry out these tasks themselves without human partners. Inquiry activities are scaffolded by both human and computer agents. White et al. describe SCI-WISE as a mechanism to introduce students to a model of the mind as a community of agents who collaborate to facilitate inquiry learning, reflection, and self-improvement. This approach melds two paradigms: the information processing perspective that capitalizes on emphasizing the cognitive processes learners need to acquire, with the community of learners and constructivist paradigm, in that computer agents scaffold such skills, within specific communities of practice. Learners can modify the pedagogical agents by creating new advisers or revising old ones and conduct empirical research to determine which agents are the most useful by finding out which models produce the most helpful inquiry support environment. This type of inquiry about inquiry is carried out as students use their alternative versions of the inquiry support environment to design and conduct research projects in various domains.

IDENTIFYING OBSTACLES
TO INCORPORATING COGNITIVE
TOOLS MORE GLOBALLY

Although many advances have been made in the use of technology for educational purposes, the same problems that Chipman identified in the previous volume of *Computers as Cognitive Tools* remain today. Mandinach and Cline (chap. 13, this volume) discuss three issues that preclude the more widespread dissemination and use of computers as cognitive tools: a lack of adequate evaluation research designs, few or inappropriate measures of cognitive activity, and an abundance of financial and practical problems. Proper research designs and appropriate cognitive measures must be considered in all classroom research, and not just research on computers as cognitive tools. New methodologies must be provided with changing learning paradigms (Anderson et al., 1998; Greeno, 1998). Such methodologies may be complicated or eased by the use of technology. Many of this book's chapter authors address issues of integrating instruction and assessment, and along with this integration come new types of evaluation research and new measures of cognitive activity.

The third issue that Mandinach and Cline raise, financial and practical concerns for implementing such research in the classroom, is a difficult one to overcome. These authors present a thought-provoking discussion regarding curriculum change, the integration of technology into classrooms, and the need for teacher training along with this integration. They also point to the problems of putting research ideas into practice. In their own work on the use of computers for modeling and simulation in science and mathematics classes, Mandinach and Cline (1994) found that it took three to five years for teachers to integrate such activities into their curriculum in a way that they felt was effective. They caution that time to become proficient in using new materials and techniques can be reduced, but it will always be a substantial cost in any curriculum innovation project.

Mandinach and Cline also point to the positive examples of computers as cognitive tools in classrooms that have demonstrated significant changes in teaching and learning. They have found that the teacher role in these contexts, especially ones where constructivist learning paradigms are followed, is one of "guide on the side" and the student role becomes more of the "explorer." Bracewell, Breuleux, and Le Maistre (in press) have studied teacher change in such classrooms and state that teachers report a "release of agency" as they become more comfortable using computers as cognitive tools. Teachers note that distributing the expertise among students frees up their own time for monitoring and assessing both individual and group participation, and hence more time to support learners who have reached impasses. For example, instead of teachers' controlling the entire learning situation by presenting project topics, students choose their own goals. Furthermore, instead of looking to the teacher for all the answers, students can seek out other students who have such expertise.

In the final chapter of this book, Lesgold places the use of tools in education in a historic context and addresses the reasons for developing the theme of computers as cognitive tools. He sagely points out that tools are created for a purpose and often by those who see the need for innovation. Hence, there is a great need for cooperative efforts among teachers, educational researchers, and information scientists to build and revise tools that can be used with successful outcomes in classrooms.

Computers as Cognitive Tools, Second Edition: No More Walls: Theory Change, Paradigm Shifts, and Their Influence on the Uses of Computers for Instructional Purposes provides examples of state-of-the-art technology-based research in the field of education and training. These examples are theory driven and reflect the learning paradigms that are currently in use in cognitive science, ranging from information processing perspectives to situativity theories. An array of instructional and assessment approaches is described, along with new techniques for automating the design and assessment process. New considerations are offered as possibilities for examining learning in distributed situations. This book reconsiders the initial camp analogy posited in 1993 and presents a mechanism for breaking camp to find new summits.

REFERENCES

Anderson, J. R., Corbett, A., Koedinger, K., & Pelletier, R. (1995). Cognitive tutors: Lessons learned. *Journal of Learning Sciences, 4,* 167–207.

Anderson, J. R., Reder, L. M., & Simon, H.A. (1996). Situated learning and education. *Educational Researcher, 25 (4),* 5–11.

Anderson, J. R., Reder, L. M., & Simon, H. A. (1997) Rejoinder: Situative versus cognitive perspectives : Form versus substance. *Educational Researcher, 26 (1),* 18–21.

Anderson, J. R., Reder, L. M., & Simon, H. A. (1998). Radical constructivism and cognitive psychology. In D. Ravitch (Ed.), *Brookings papers on education policy* (pp. 227–278). Washington, DC: Brookings Institution Press.

Bandura, A. (1977). *Social learning theory.* Englewood Cliffs, NJ: Prentice Hall.

Bracewell, R. J., Breuleux, A., & Le Maistre, C. (in press). The role of the teacher in opening worlds of learning with technology. In B. M. Shore, M. W. Aulls, M. A. B. Delcourt, & F. G. Rejskind (Eds.), *Inquiry: Where ideas come from and where they lead.* Hillsdale, NJ: Lawrence Erlbaum Associates.

Bransford, J. D., & Schwartz, D. L. (in press). Rethinking transfer: A simple proposal with multiple implications. In A. Iran-Nejad & P. D. Pearson (Eds.), *Review of Research in Education* (vol. 24). Washington, DC: American Educational Research Association.

Brown, A. L. (1994). The advancement of learning. *Educational Researcher, 23*(8), 4–12.

Derry, S. J., & Lajoie, S. P. (1993). A middle camp for (un)intelligent computing. In S. P. Lajoie & S. J. Derry (Eds.), *Computers as cognitive tools* (pp.1–11). Hillsdale, NJ: Lawrence Erlbaum Associates.

Frederiksen, C., & Donin, J. (1998, October). *Cognitive assessment in coached learning environments*. Paper presented at the Conference on Measurement and Evaluation: Current and Future Research Directions for the New Millennium, Banff.

Glaser, R., Lesgold, A., & Lajoie, S. P. (1987). Toward a cognitive theory for the measurement of achievement. In R. Ronning, J. Glover, J. C. Conoley, & J. C. Witt (Eds.), *The influence of cognitive psychology on testing, Buros/Nebraska symposium on measurement* (vol. 3, pp. 41–85). Hillsdale, NJ: Lawrence Erlbaum Associates.

Greeno, J. (1989). A perspective on thinking. *American Psychologist, 44*, 134–141.

Greeno, J. G. (1996). Response: On claims that answer the wrong question. *Educational Researcher, 26(1)*, 5–17.

Greeno, J. (1998). The situativity of knowing, learning, and research. *American Psychologist, 53*(1), 5–26.

Jonassen, D. H. (1996). *Computers in the classroom: Mindtools for critical thinking*. Englewood Cliffs, NJ: Prentice Hall.

Jonassen, D. H. (1998). Designing constructivist learning environments. In C. M. Reigeluth (Ed.), *Instructional design theories and models* (2nd ed.). Hillsdale, NJ: Lawrence Erlbaum Associates.

Jonassen, D. H. (in press). *Mindtools for engaging critical thinking in the classroom* (2nd ed.). Englewood Cliffs, NJ: Prentice Hall.

Jonassen, D. H., Peck, K. L., & Wilson, B. G. (1998). *Learning WITH technology: A constructivist perspective*. Englewood Cliffs, NJ: Prentice Hall.

Koschmann, T. (1996). Paradigm shifts and instructional technology: An introduction. In T. Koschmann (Ed.), *CSCL: Theory and practice of an emerging paradigm* (pp. 1–23). Hillsdale, NJ: Lawrence Erlbaum Associates.

Kuhn, T. (1970). *The structure of scientific revolutions* (2nd ed.). Chicago: University of Chicago Press.

Lajoie, S. P. (1995). A framework for authentic assessment in mathematics. In T. A. Romberg (Ed.), *Reform in school mathematics and authentic assessment* (pp. 19–37). Albany: State University of New York Press.

Lajoie, S. P., Greer, J. E., Munsie, S. D., Wilkie, T. V., Guerrera. C., & Aleong, P. (1995). Establishing an argumentation environment to foster scientific reasoning with Bio-World. In D. Jonassen & G. McCalla (Eds.), *Proceedings of the International Conference on Computers in Education* (pp. 89–96). Charlottesville, VA: Association for the Advancement of Computing in Education.

Lesgold, A. (1993). Information technology and the future of education. In S. P. Lajoie & S. J. Derry (Eds.), *Computers as cognitive tools* (pp. 289–318). Hillsdale, NJ: Lawrence Erlbaum Associates.

Mandinach, E.B., & Cline, H.F. (1994). *Classroom dynamics: Implementing a technology-based learning environment.* Hillsdale, NJ: Lawrence Erlbaum Associates.

Mayer, R. E. (1997). Learners as information processors: Legacies and limitations of educational psychology's second metaphor. *Educational Psychologist, 31*(3/4), 151–161.

McFarland, T. D., & Parker, R. (1990). Intelligent computer assisted instruction. In T. D. McFarland & R. Parker (Eds.), *Expert systems in education and training* (pp. 177–227). Englewood Cliffs, NJ: Educational Technology Publications.

Newell, A., & Simon, H. (1972). *Human problem solving.* Englewood Cliffs, NJ: Prentice Hall.

Salomon, G. (1990). Cognitive effects with and of computer technology. *Communication Research, 17*, 26–44.

Salomon, G., Perkins, D. N., & Globerson, T. (1991). Partners in cognition: Extending human intelligence with intelligent technologies. *Educational Researcher, 20*, 10–16.

Shulman, L. S. (1986). Paradigms and research programs in the study of teaching: A contemporary perspective. In M. C. Wittrock (Ed.), *Handbook of research on teaching* (3rd ed., pp. 3–36). New York: Macmillan.

Shute, V. J., & Psotka, J. (1994). Intelligent tutoring systems: Past, present, and future. In D. Jonassen (Ed.), *Handbook of research on educational communications and technology* (pp. 570–600). New York: Scholastic Publications.

Spiro, R. J., Feltovich, P. J., Jacobson, M. J., & Coulson, R. L. (1992). Cognitive flexibility, constructivism, and hypertext: Random access instruction in ill-structured domain. In T. M. Duffy & D. H. Jonassen (Eds.), *Constructivism and the technology of instruction: A conversation* (pp. 57–75). Hillsdale, NJ: Lawrence Erlbaum Associates .

Toulmin, S., Rieke, R., & Janik, A. (1984). *An introduction to reasoning.* New York: Macmillan.

VanLehn, K., Ohlsson, S., & Nason, R. (1994). Applications of simulated students: An exploration. *Journal of Artificial Intelligence and Education, 5*, 135–175.

I

TECHNOLOGIES FOR SUPPORTING KNOWLEDGE BUILDING IN DISTRIBUTED LEARNING CONTEXTS

1

Modeling the Process, Not the Product, of Learning

Fabio N. Akhras and John A. Self
University of Leeds

The general definition of a model as something that an "observer" uses to understand the "object" modeled indicates that the notion of modeling permeates the computer-based learning system design activity. The disagreements have to do with who (systems, students, teachers, designers) does the modeling when, how, and about what. However, concerning the modeling carried out by a computer system, the "to model or not to model" question of Lajoie and Derry (1993) was interpreted entirely within the context of student modeling, which refers to techniques that "enable an instructional system to develop and update an understanding of the student and her performance on the system" (p. 2).

This chapter focuses on the nature of "the object" modeled by a computer-based learning system. So far, a "student model" has been regarded, naturally enough and almost by definition, as a "model of the student," that is, of what she believes, misunderstands, or wants, for example. It has been generally assumed (by student model designers) that it is beneficial to seek the maximum fidelity of the student model, while acknowledging the practical difficulties in achieving this. In other words, it has been assumed that the object modeled is the student—that there really is some objective knowledge about the student that we may seek to represent.

This approach applies objectivism to student modeling, the philosophy of knowledge that holds that the world may be completely and correctly structured in terms of entities, properties, and relations and that rational thought consists of the manipulation of abstract symbols viewed as representing reality (Lakoff, 1987). Duffy and Jonassen (1992) have considered the implications of objectivism for instructional design. Typically system designers begin by trying to specify the "objective" knowledge-to-be-learned as precisely as possible as computational representations and then interpret the student's knowledge with respect to such representations. The aim of the system might be to help learners acquire the entities, properties, and relations of this purportedly complete and correct representational structure.

In contrast, one of the basic assumptions of constructivist philosophies of knowledge is that knowledge cannot be objectively defined and statically represented. Instead, it is individually constructed from what learners do in their experiential worlds (Piaget & Garcia, 1991). Knowing, according to constructivism, is an adaptive process. By means of acting in a world, learners assimilate new concepts to their previously constructed cognitive structures or modify their cognitive structures to accommodate interpretations of the new experiences (von Glasersfeld, 1989).

It follows, according to this philosophy, that knowing and doing cannot be separated and that the activity and context of an experience become an integral part of the meaning of that experience (Bednar, Cunningham, Duffy, & Perry, 1992; Brown, Collins, & Duguid, 1989; Greeno, 1997). Moreover, further understanding may change the meaning of previously constructed knowledge about a domain, making it necessary that ideas be revisited many times so that they can be understood in the context of the other ideas that have been encountered in the meantime (Winn, 1993). Therefore, the focus is on the process by which knowledge is constructed rather than on a target domain knowledge to be acquired (Fosnot, 1996; Jonassen, 1992).

Constructivists would not represent target knowledge as some kind of fixed data structure and therefore could not represent the student's knowledge as some approximation to it. For a constructivist, a student model (as usually understood) directly contradicts a basic tenet of the philosophy, and as a result, many reasons are put forward as to why a student model is philosophically, computationally, and educationally undesirable.

It is possible, however, that these views require a different interpretation of student modeling rather than no student modeling at all. Recent discussions of the nature of learning and knowledge concern the properties that a process of learning should have to be conducive to learning. This then leads to suggestions that designers should design systems that enable such desirable properties to hold.

The original rationale for needing student models was that individual students are so different that their needs cannot be anticipated at design time. Similarly, the properties of a process of learning cannot be fixed at design time; indeed, it would be self-contradictory for a constructivist to claim that designers can know such properties in advance. The perceived properties of a process of learning depend on what the student already believes and what she does while interacting with the system. Therefore, systems may need to be able to adapt to try to ensure that desirable properties hold. To enable such adaptations, a system needs to model the properties of the interactions between system and student.

In this chapter we present a formalism for defining the properties of a sequence of learning events (in our case, interactions with a computer-based learning system, such as a simulation). Given a sequence of learning events, with certain properties holding, a possible following event would lead to other properties holding. To the extent that educationalists agree that certain properties are more desirable than others (in that they are considered more likely to lead to learning), so the system may adapt itself to ensure that events that lead to those desirable properties are more likely to occur. We illustrate the general approach by an application to a system to support the learning of software engineering concepts.

The main contribution of this chapter is to provide a methodology for making precise the concepts of contemporary theories of learning and knowledge, which emphasize the context of learning and the fact that learning is a process extended in time. This leads to the development of a different view of the nature of and need for modeling in computer-based learning systems.

THE NATURE OF LEARNING

Learning is a multifaceted process. Many of the facets that cognitive psychologists and machine learning researchers study are, in fact, quite compatible with conventional student modeling techniques such as overlays, bug catalogues, and model tracing. These tend to concentrate on relatively small-grain, incremental, narrowly focused learning processes and hence to relate to the kind of moment-to-moment decision making that typical student models are intended to support. In this chapter, however, we focus on views of learning that, according to those who put them forward (e.g., Clancey, 1993; Sack, Soloway, & Weingrad, 1992), are inimical to the student modeling enterprise as it is usually understood. It is not our purpose to argue which view of learning is "right"—no doubt, there is something of merit in all of them—but to consider how certain views of learning, which have led others to decry modeling efforts, can be interpreted to provide a different view of modeling. Our aim is to broaden the notion of modeling so that it is not seen as inherently contradictory to those views of learning.

The defining axiom of constructivism—that students learn by constructing their own knowledge and that previously constructed knowledge influences the way new experiences are interpreted—is one that most learning theorists, whether overtly constructivist or not, would accept. The distinguishing properties of constructivism lie instead in three corollaries that are not so readily accepted:

- Learning occurs within a context that is itself part of what is learned (Brown et al., 1989; Greeno, 1997; Resnick, 1987).
- Knowing and doing cannot be separated (Piaget & Garcia, 1991; von Glasersfeld, 1995).
- Learning is a process that is extended over time (von Glasersfeld, 1989, 1995; Vygotsky, 1978; Winn, 1993).

These three concerns—context, activity, and time extension—are not directly or satisfactorily addressed by current modeling methodologies. Moreover, they cannot be addressed in a piecemeal fashion. Clearly, if knowledge is inseparable from action, then we need to recognize that actions occur in a context and take place over time. We need to integrate the psychological with the contextual, physical, and temporal factors. This move toward integrated theories has been discussed by Vosniadou (1996), who argues that we need to improve our understanding of how cognitive processes interact with environmental variables, and by Resnick (1996), who is concerned with developing "situated rationalism," which joins two perspectives: one that focuses on learning as inherently social and another that emphasizes individual learning and cognitive development. The idea is to develop a theory that takes into consideration the social, cognitive, and physical dimensions of situations and how activity in one situation might prepare individuals to enter another.

Overall, the aim is to model the process of learning as one that happens over time, through interactions between cognitive structures and context and through activity. Before defining these terms clearly, we provide an outline of the argument in nontechnical terms.

SKETCH OF THE ARGUMENT

For ease of explanation, we confine ourselves to considering a single learner using a computer-based learning environment. (The methodology itself is not so confined, but it is outside the scope of this chapter to consider other contexts in detail.)

First, we need to describe the environmental contexts in which interactions occur. This requires describing the objects, relations, and properties of a situation. Then we need to consider the events that are possible in a situation—their preconditions and their effects. A series of events creates a sequence of situations that we call a "course of interaction." As an example, a course of interaction may be said to possess the property of "pig-headedness" if it shows the learner performing exactly the same action over and over, generating identical situations.

Of the many properties that may be defined, some may be considered "better" than others. That is, learning theorists may have argued, or perhaps provided experimental evidence, that a course of interaction with a particular property is more likely to lead to learning than a course of interaction without that property. In fact, this is precisely what most learning theories aim to provide: a set of guidelines for determining whether certain courses of interaction are more likely to lead to learning. They tend not to say what will actually be learned from such courses of interaction.

So far, we have in outline a purely descriptive account of learning interactions. On the assumption that students do not always follow an ideal course of interaction, we now seek to extend this to enable the system to adapt itself so that desirable courses of interaction occur.

After a particular course of interaction, we have passed through a sequence of situations $\{s_1, s_2, ..., s_m\}$ by means of a series of events $\{e_1, e_2, ..., e_{m-1}\}$ (see Fig. 1.1). In the situation s_m reached, a set of events $\{e_{m1}, e_{m2}, ..., e_{mn}\}$ are possible. If a particular event e_{mi} were to occur, then a new situation s_{mi} would be reached. The (potential) course of interaction, $\{s_1, s_2, ..., s_m, s_{mi}\}$, would possess a set of properties $\{p_1, p_2, ..., p_r\}$. We may say that the situation s_m affords each of these properties p_j through event e_{mi}.

Clearly some of the putative courses of interaction will possess more desirable properties than others. (These properties are what learning theorists try to identify. They generally do not tell us much about what a

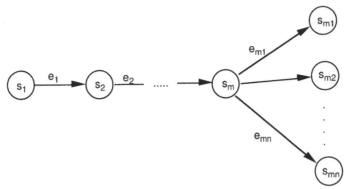

FIG. 1.1. *A course of interaction.*

learner will actually learn from an activity, but they do try to identify activities, or types of activity, that they consider beneficial for learning.) Therefore, the system could seek to adapt itself to ensure that an event occurred that led to the desired properties. For example, imagine that a learner has reached a situation where the next event has to be the selection of an item from a menu, and the system can determine that only one such item will lead to a particular property sought; the system could (temporarily) remove the other items from the menu. This would be a rather heavy-handed form of adaptation, amounting to direct guidance of the student. In general, there is a set of potential properties available, each of which is more or less desirable than others, and there needs to be some heuristic strategy for guiding the student toward events that, on balance, are more likely to lead the learner to encounter contexts that allow a continuing learning experience.

Before fleshing out the details, it is worth contrasting this approach to conventional student modeling. In the latter, it is usual to attempt to represent what the student has come to know (believe, misunderstand, etc.) after a course of interaction. Typically there is some measure of the goodness of this representation, often with respect to some target knowledge representation. Then the system will attempt to ensure that some event occurs that leads to improvements in (the representation of) the student. In our case, we have no explicit representation of the student's knowledge or beliefs. Instead we focus on the events that have occurred. We say that if a "good" course of interaction occurs, then the student will (according to those learning theorists who have identified this course of interaction as a "good" one) learn, but we do not attempt to represent precisely what has been learned. This seems closer to the spirit of constructivism in that the content of learning is intimately related to the activity of learning, and what is actually learned is a construction of the learner from the activities she has carried out. In our case, we have no target knowledge we are aiming for; we simply seek to ensure that the learner passes through courses of interaction considered conducive to learning.

DEFINING SITUATIONS AND INTERACTIONS

If an intelligent learning environment is to reason about a student's learning experiences in a series of situations, aspects of those situations need to be represented in the environment. The problem of formalizing context has recently become a focus of research in artificial intelligence (AI) (Akman & Surav, 1996; Barwise & Perry, 1983), and the approaches developed there may be adapted for our purposes. We define (or at least discuss) the primitives needed to represent situations and interactions, leading eventually to derived definitions of some of the properties of courses of interaction.

A *situation* is considered to be an instance of a *situation-type s* occurring at time *t*, where a situation-type is an abstract entity defining a context in which interaction can occur. The static properties of a situation-type may be defined using the predicates of conventional AI; in particular, we can represent the objects that occur in the situation-type, the properties of those objects, and the relations between objects. We may also represent the potential states of objects in the situation-type and possible transitions between them. In addition, situation-types may be placed in an abstract hierarchy. The following terms may be part of our representation:

    property(ingredient(lettuce),taste(light))
    state-type(ingredient(tomato),whole)
    tran-type(ingredient(tomato),whole,sliced)
    kind(sit-type(salad-making),sit-type(meal-making))

The dynamics of situations are represented by defining events—their preconditions and effects. An *event* is considered to be an instance of an *event-type* carried out by an agent, such as the learner, and to have preconditions and effects definable in the normal way—for example:

    event(learner, wash-ingredient)

pre(wash-ingredient, state (ingredient(x),unwashed))
effect(wash-ingredient, state (ingredient(x),washed))

A set of events defined for an agent in a situation-type describes the behavior defined for that agent in the situation-type. In the example, the behavior defined for the learner in the situation-type includes doing things like washing ingredients. Other agents may be defined in the same way in order to describe the behavior of other learners or artificial agents that interact in a type of situation.

An *interaction* may now be defined as the occurrence of an event by action of an agent in a situation, such as:

occurs (wash-ingredient, learner, salad-lab-a,9)

That is, at Time 9, the event "wash-ingredient" occurred by action of the learner in "salad-lab-a" (which might be the name of a computer simulation for preparing salads, which provides the operation "wash-ingredient").

In order to track the changes that occur through interactions, it is necessary to define those entities that hold or are "in" a situation:

in (state (ingredient (lettuce), washed), salad-lab-a,7)

and to define axioms of situation development (which is an instance of the frame problem in AI):

$\text{occurs}(e,a,s,t)$ & $\text{define}(\text{pre}(e,x),s)$ & $\text{define}(\text{effect}(e,y),s)$ & $\text{in}(x,s,t)$
   -> $\text{in}(y,s,t+1)$

A *course of interaction* is defined to be a sequence of situations and denoted by $\text{course}(s_1,t_1,..., s_n,t_n)$ where $t_2 > t_1$, and so forth.

So far, we have elaborated an approach to defining the properties of an environment and the changes that may occur within it (a more extensive and rigorous description of these properties is given in Akhras, 1997). Other approaches toward formalizing the design of learning environments focus on the properties of the learner (on what the learner believes and wants) and how they change during interaction. However, one of the implications of constructivist theories is that knowledge does not arise solely from the entities of the environment or from the learner but from the interaction between environment and learner considered as a unit. A fundamental consequence is that individual cognitions can be explained only in terms of their contributions to interactions (Greeno, 1997). Therefore, before we can proceed to develop a constructivist analysis of learning environments, we need to consider patterns of interaction that relate a learner's activity to situations.

In tackling this, we are trying to come to grips with the rather nebulous notion of constructivism that the meaning of an object is basically "what can be done with it" (Piaget & Garcia, 1991) and hence that knowledge lies in action rather than in cogitation. Work on computational models of interaction (Agre, 1995) is in its infancy but can at least be seen as focusing on the integration of models of properties of agents and environments, rather than on the more classical AI approach of reasoning to develop plans that an agent then executes to achieve goals.

We consider the three aspects that characterize a learning interaction: context, activity, and cognitive structures. In following the discussion about interaction and the inseparability of these three aspects, we focus on the relationships that develop between these aspects in a learning interaction rather than on their independent characteristics. We are aiming for a principled description of the interactions that occur between human learners and computational learning environments, so that (eventually) the latter may analyze the interactions to benefit the former. The concepts developed to relate these three aspects should all be defined in terms of the more primitive predicates already presented but provide a more meaningful, useful, and higher order set of descriptions.

According to constructivists, cognitive structures develop from acting in situations. Although we are not directly concerned with the product of learning (i.e., the cognitive structures developed), the way that prior knowledge influences the learner's interpretation of the content and dynamics of following situations and affects the course of interaction is part of our concern. Therefore, we must start defining some patterns of interaction that relate a learner's actions to the situations in which they happen. For example, if a learner initiates an event in situation $<s,t>$ and x is an effect of that event, then we may say that the learner "generates" the entity x through that event in that situation, or, more formally,

define(event(a,e),s) & occurs(e,a,s,t) & in(effect(e,x),$s,t+1$) <=>
generates(a,x,e,s,t)

Similarly, we may define terms representing that a learner "uses," "accesses," and so on an entity in a situation. The intention is that such intermediate-level predicates provide a more useful basis for defining the properties of courses of interaction, as we will in the next section.

We must also define terms relating a learner's cognitive state to situations, for, as constructivists say, the interpretations that learners make of situations are influenced by their prior knowledge. Two of the most basic properties that an entity of a situation may have for a learner are that the entity has been encountered before (is an "old" one) or has just been generated (is a "new" one). For example, an entity x in a situation $<s,t>$ may be said to be new to a learner if x has been neither used nor generated by the learner in a previous situation:

$$\text{in}(x,s,t) \ \& \ (\text{for all } i < t) \ \text{not}(\text{uses}(a,x,e,s,i)) \ \& \ \text{not}(\text{generates}(a,x,e,s,i-1)) <=> \\ \text{new}(a,x,s,t)$$

We also need higher order terms in order to be able to relate one situation to another. Learners need to explore multiple perspectives of a domain and to be able to connect, through experience, knowledge of different kinds. We need, for example, to represent that two situations share an entity:

$$\text{in}(x,s_1,t_1) \ \& \ \text{in}(x,s_2,t_2) <=> \text{share}(s_1,t_1,s_2,t_2,x)$$

A catalogue of such predicates may be defined relating the different kinds of entities and whether they co-occur, are additional to, or are missing from two situations (Akhras, 1997).

DEFINING PROPERTIES OF COURSES
OF INTERACTION

Most theories of learning, even behaviorist or cognitive ones, are about the process of learning rather than about what is learned. Shuell (1992), for example, says that "cognitive conceptions of learning stress that learning is an active, constructive, cumulative, self-regulated and goal-oriented process" (p. 23). In other words, discussions of the nature of learning tend to say much more about the properties of processes that may lead to learning than they do about the outcomes of those processes. Certainly constructivist theories focus much more on the conditions for learning because they are predisposed against a view of learning as producing specific outcomes.

A corollary of this emphasis on the process of learning is an increased focus on the time and context in which events occur. For that reason, the descriptions of patterns of interaction already set out include definitions of the contexts in which events occur, not simply the events alone. Similarly, to appreciate the significance of an event, it needs to be interpreted in the light of the history of interactions, which is preserved in our notion of a course of interaction.

In order to proceed, we must now scour the learning theory literature in an attempt to identify the properties that theorists say a learning process should possess. For example, a common view (as Shuell expressed) is that learning is cumulative; that is, nothing is learned in isolation but previous learning experiences influence and relate to new learning. Understanding involves the change of previously constructed conceptions in the light of new contexts. In general terms, then, we may say that a course of interaction has the (desirable) property of being cumulative if a learner uses an entity generated in a previous situation, or, more precisely,

$$\text{share}(s_1,t_1,s_2,t_2,x) \text{ \& (uses}(a,x,e_1,s_1,t_1) \text{ or generates}(a,x,e1,s_1,t_1 - 1)$$
$$\text{\& (uses}(a,x,e_2,s_2,t_2) \text{ or generates}(a,x,e_2,s_2,t_2-1)) \text{ \& } t_2 > t_1$$
$$\Rightarrow \text{cumulative(course}(s_1,t_1,s_2,t_2),a,x)$$

That is, if an entity x is shared by two situations and the learner a uses or generates the entity in both situations, then we say the course of interaction comprising those two situations is cumulative with respect to x for this learner. For example, suppose that the following patterns of interaction hold in the situations below:

share(salad-lab-a,8,salad-lab-a,11,ingredient(lettuce))
uses(learner,ingredient(lettuce), wash-ingredient,salad-lab-a,8)
uses(learner,ingredient(lettuce),add-ingredient-to-salad,salad-lab-a,11)

Then we may say that the course of interaction course(salad-lab-a,8,salad-lab-a,11) is cumulative for the learner with respect to the ingredient lettuce, that is,

cumulative (course(salad-lab-a,8,salad-lab-a,11),learner,ingredient(lettuce))

The basic idea that we are trying to capture is that in a productive learning process, an entity that is introduced should not be discarded or forgotten but should be built on; that is, the learner should accumulate a more refined notion of that entity. Clearly, if an entity is reused, this is more likely to occur.

The concept of cumulativeness is related to the contentious issue of transfer (Detterman & Sternberg, 1993): when knowledge learned in one situation is used later in another situation. The nonoccurrence of cumulativeness may be related to the problem of inert knowledge—the failure to use in one situation relevant knowledge learned before. In general, according to Greeno, Moore, and Smith (1993), the issue involves an understanding of "how learning to participate in an activity in one situation can influence (positively or negatively) one's ability to participate in another activity in a different situation" (p. 100).

Of course, one may object that this definition of *cumulative* does not capture the richness of the concept as discussed by learning theorists, and that is certainly so. However, it has the benefit of being precise and computationally useful, unlike the descriptions given by learning theorists, and there is the potential to add further precision if need be. Indeed, Akhras (1997) presents a score of variations on this definition of *cumulative*. However, our aims in this chapter are not to present a list of such definitions but to present the general methodology and show how it has the potential to give a formal, computational account of some of the process-related notions of constructivism.

Even with only a preliminary definition of the notion of *cumulative,* we may begin to see why the definition (and the constructivists' discussion of cumulativeness) may be inadequate. For example, if the entity x is, in fact, a misconception, then its cumulative reuse may not provide a productive learning process—but then constructivism does not have much to say about "misguided discovery learning." A constructivist approach to the problem of cumulative misconception would probably emphasize the need to combine cumulativeness with the notion of self-regulatedness in order to provide a productive learning process. We would also need to consider in detail whether a learner does, in fact, see the two occurrences of the entity x as being instances of the same entity, which in general involves a complicated process of comparing the similarities and differences between the two situations.

However, let us persevere in our search for useful properties of courses of interaction. The core idea of constructivism is, of course, that learning is "constructive" and thus that a learning process should have the property of being constructive. According to Glynn and Duit (1995), "Students learn science meaningfully when they activate their existing knowledge, relate it to educational experiences, and construct new knowledge in the form of conceptual models" (p. 4). In our terms, therefore, constructiveness refers to the property that a course of interaction has when knowledge constructed by the learner in a previous situation is elaborated and related to new knowledge in a later situation. One way of formalizing this is:

$$(\text{uses}(a,x_0,e_1,s_1,t_1) \text{ or generates}(a,x_0,e_1,s_1,t_1-1)) \& \text{uses}(a,x_0,e_2,s_2,t_2-1)$$
$$\& \text{ old}(a,x_0,s_2,t_2-1) \& \text{ generates}(a,x,e_2,s_2,t_2-1) \& \text{ new}(a,x,s_2,t_2) \& t_2 > t_1$$
$$\Rightarrow \text{constructive}(\text{course}(s_1,t_1,s_2,t_2),a,x)$$

or, less precisely, if an entity, which has been previously used or generated by a learner, is old for the learner when it is reused to generate a new entity, then we may say that the course of interaction comprising those two situations is constructive with respect to that entity for the learner. Such a simple definition may capture the essence of "constructiveness," but, as with cumulativeness, we may anticipate proceeding to define a series of elaborations of this definition, although we will refrain from doing so here.

The methodology should now be clear. Given a vocabulary for defining situations, events, courses of interaction, and so on (such as that presented in the previous section), search the literature on learning theory to identify properties that productive learning processes should have, reinterpret the natural language descriptions of those processes in terms of our formal notation, and then (as described in the next section) use such definitions to analyze and support interactions between learners and computer-based learning environments.

We will content ourselves with two further properties that are much discussed, but without precision, by constructivists. First, learning should, we are told, be self-regulated, that is, learners should monitor their own activities and regulate them by making decisions about what actions to take to attain their goals. A broad class of metacognitive activity has been considered under this heading (Boekaerts, 1997; Ertmer & Newby, 1996). For our purposes, we consider a course of interaction to have the property of being self-regulated if a learner's action performed in one situation is later considered by the learner by means of accessing information that constitutes the evaluation context for that action. In other words (or, rather, in other symbols):

$$\text{generates}(a,x,e_1,s_1,t_1) \& \text{ in}(\text{context}(e_1,c),s_2,t_2) \& \text{ accesses}(a,c,e_2,s_2,t_2)$$
$$\& t_2 > t_1 \Rightarrow \text{self-regulated}(\text{course}(s_1,t_1,s_2,t_2),a,x,e_1,c)$$

that is, if a learner generates an entity in a situation through an event and later accesses an entity that is an evaluation context for the event in another situation, then we may say that the course of interaction is self-regulated with respect to that entity and context for that learner. For example, suppose that the following context is defined in situation-type salad-lab-a for the event add-ingredient-to-salad:

context(add-ingredient-to-salad,book("Well balanced salads"))

In addition, suppose that the following entity of situation development and patterns of interaction hold:

generates(learner,part(salad,ingredient(lettuce)),add-ingredient-to-salad,
    salad-lab-a,26)
in(context(add-ingredient-to-salad,book("Well balanced salads")),
    salad-lab-a,28)
accesses(learner,book("Well balanced salads"),view-book, salad-lab-a,28)

Then we say that the course of interaction course(salad-lab-a,26,salad-lab-a,28) is self-regulated for the learner with respect to adding an ingredient lettuce to a salad, in the context provided by the book "Well balanced salads," that is:

self-regulated(course(salad-lab-a,26,salad-lab-a,28),learner, part(salad,
    ingredient(lettuce)),add-ingredient-to-salad,
    book ("Well balanced salads"))

Similarly, the process of learning should be reflective, that is, it should involve the "reconstruction or reorganization of experience which adds to the meaning of experience and which increases ability to direct the course of subsequent experience" (Dewey, 1933, p. 76). We may attempt to describe this in terms of a learner accessing some aspect of a previous event:

generates$(a,$part$(x,$occurs$(e_1,a,s_1,t_1)),e_1,s_1,t_1)$ & accesses(a,x,e_2,s_2,t_2)
    & $t_2 > t_1$ => reflective(course$(s_1,t_1,s_2,t_2),a,x)$

At this point, we have four properties—which we have called cumulativeness, constructiveness, self-regulatedness, and reflectiveness—defined for courses of interaction. The definitions may be given multiple variations and refinements, and we may, of course, seek further properties. However, this set of properties is enough for us to be able to discuss their use within learning environments.

DEFINING AFFORDANCES

Using this analytic apparatus, we may now take a course of interaction and determine what properties hold at the end of it. For example, referring to Fig. 1.1, we may determine, from the definitions of the properties, which of them hold in situation s_m. To the extent that those properties may be considered beneficial or detrimental to the learning process, we may consider that course of interaction to be a good or bad one from the point of view of the learning that may result.

When we have reached situation s_m only certain events may follow, that is, the preconditions of only some of the potential events actually hold in situation s_m. For each event e_{mi} that is possible, a new situation s_{mi} would be reached, as defined by the effects of that event, if it did actually happen. Each possible event provides a possible extended course of interaction, that is, the previous course $\{s_1, s_2, ..., s_m\}$ extended with the new possible situation s_{mi}. However, these possible events do not provide the same possibilities for learning, because the properties that hold for the different putative courses of interaction, $\{s_1, s_2, ..., s_m, s_{m1}\}$, $\{s_1, s_2, ..., s_m, s_{m2}\}$, and so on differ. Therefore, if a system can be provided with a means of determining the properties that may develop from the possibilities offered by a situation (and knows which properties are more beneficial than others), then the system may use this information to support its decision making concerning the situations that may be made available to a learner in the space of interaction at a particular time.

To formalize this idea, we have adopted the notion of affordance (Gibson, 1977). In general terms, we say that an entity is afforded by some situation-type if there is an event that may cause it to exist. We may, for example, specify that a particular pattern of interaction is afforded, as follows:

define(event(a,e),s) & define(effect(e,x),s) <=> affords(s,generates,a,x,e)

that is, a situation-type affords to a learner generating an entity through an event if that event is defined in that situation-type to have that effect.

Similarly, we may say that a property of a course of interaction is afforded in a situation-type if it affords the development of patterns of interaction that constitute that property—for example,

$(uses(a,x_0,e_1,s_1,t_1)$ or $generates(a,x_0,e_1,s_1,t_1))$
    & $affords(s,old,a,x_0,t)$ & $affords(s,uses,a,x_0,e)$
    & $affords(s,generates,a,x,e)$ & $affords(s,new,a,x,t)$ & $t > t_1$
        $=> affords(s,s_1,t_1,constructive,a,x)$

that is, if an entity is used or generated in a situation and a situation-type affords having that entity being an old entity for a learner and also affords having it used to generate a new entity, then we may say that the situation-type affords the development of a constructive course of interaction from that situation with respect to the new entity for that learner.

Clearly a large battery of definitions of various kinds of affordance may similarly be developed (Akhras, 1997). Given such a set of definitions, a system may determine the properties that may be developed by a continuing course of interaction, depending on the particular subsequent events that actually occur. Deciding which subsequent event is to be preferred, because it enables a course of interaction with properties most beneficial to the learner, is a complex matter, which might involve reasoning about various combinations of properties.

Our approach is to define a set of heuristic policies to express preferences regarding the putative properties, for example:

Prefer situation-types that afford
- first-time, rather than previously used, cumulations.
- constructions from more varied previous situation-types in the course of interaction.
- reflections that have less time spent on them in previous situations.
- . . .

This is, of course, a difficult problem but one that has not been considered at all by constructive learning theorists, who will happily put forward all kinds of desirable properties of learning processes, without considering how one may decide among them, if many are potentially available (the "one" being an individual learner or a system, although constructivists tend to consider that a system should not make such decisions).

INCENSE

This approach has been explored in the design of INCENSE, an intelligent learning environment in the domain of software engineering, where situa-

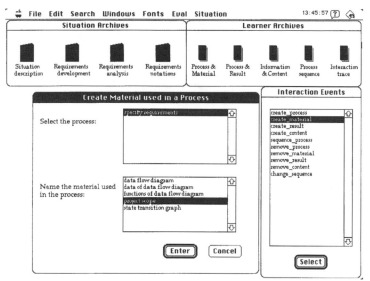

FIG. 1.2.   *The INCENSE interface.*

tions are ill defined and ill structured as they involve selecting appropriate techniques (from among many), getting the appropriate information (which may be ambiguous, inconsistent, incorrect, or incomplete), transforming this information in many ways, and so on. The setting (see Fig. 1.2) is a software engineering laboratory in which students may model a software engineering process (e.g., a software project planning process) so that it can be applied in some future software development process and apply a model of a software engineering process in a software development project. The students are provided with an archive of materials they may refer to and a menu of operations for working in this domain.

Let us imagine that a learner engages in the course of interaction indicated schematically in Fig. 1.3, where software engineering concepts available for the learner in the situation are represented by wiggly bubbles, processes that are part of the model created by the learner are represented by round bubbles, materials or results of processes are represented by rectangles, and the arrows indicate input and output of the learner's events. In the course of the interaction, the learner:

Creates a process(*specify requirements*).
Accesses archive on requirements analysis.
Creates a material (*project scope*).
Accesses the interaction trace.
Creates a result (*data flow diagram*).

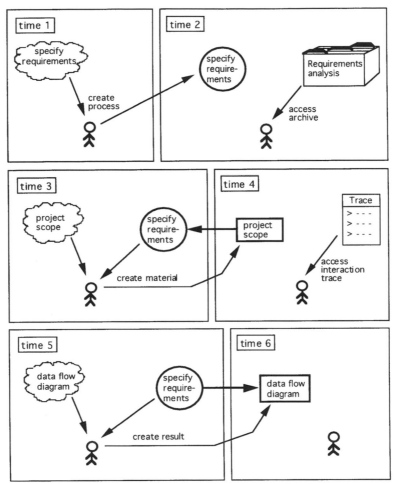

FIG. 1.3.   *A sequence of events in a situation for modeling the process
of requirements specification.*

The model that the learner creates represents that the software engineering
activity of specifying requirements uses a description of the project scope
as material and produces a data flow diagram as result. As a consequence
of this course of interaction, some of the properties determined by the system are:

cumulative wrto process(specify requirements)
constructive wrto relation(material(concept(project scope), process(specify
    requirements)))

    self-regulated wrto process(specify requirements) and context
        archive(requirements analysis)
    reflective wrto trace-modeling

Therefore, the sequence of the learner's actions shown in Fig. 1.3 trans-
lates into a learning process that exhibits these properties that denote particular ways in which interactions in a learning situation lead to
constructivist learning processes that are cumulative, constructive, self-
regulated, and reflective with respect to a set of software engineering
concepts.

Based on the properties and patterns of interaction developed so far,
and from the definitions of the situation-types and the various properties
(given in detail in Akhras, 1997), the system can determine that the following affordances (among many others) exist:

    cumulative wrto concept(specify requirements)
    constructive wrto relation(material(concept(x),process(y)))
    constructive wrto relation(before(process(x),process(y)))
    cumulative wrto concept(project scope)
    self-regulated wrto process(x) and context archive(requirements
        development)
    reflective wrto trace-modeling

For example, the fourth affordance in the preceding list indicates that in
one of the possible following situations, the property of cumulativeness
with respect to the notion of project scope would hold. On the basis of
these affordances and some criteria for selecting among desirable properties, the system may determine which of the putative following situations
is most beneficial to the learner in that they may lead to a continuing,
meaningful learning experience. Precisely how the system may adapt
itself to cause such a preferred course of interaction to occur is a matter of
instructional design. Our point is that we have provided an analytic apparatus for making such decisions.

REFLECTIONS AND CONCLUSIONS

Although INCENSE can be (and has been) used by students and is in
a domain deliberately chosen to avoid dismissal as a toy one, our aim is
not to impress with a detailed study of an implemented computer-based

learning system. The many hundreds of definitions (or variations of definitions) can be used to provide analyses of courses of interaction. But currently too many affordances are discovered, and we have no elegant way of prioritizing them or using them to determine forms of adaptation. Rather, our aim is to address the concern that cognitive modeling efforts have been regarded as irrelevant or misguided by many designers of interactive learning environments. In this section, we reflect more generally on the implications of the kind of approach we have advocated.

The tripartite division of intelligent tutoring systems (ITSs) discussed by Wenger (1987) and many others—that an ITS may be described in terms of the three components of a model of the domain knowledge, a model of the learner's knowledge, and a model of the teaching knowledge—is based on a view of the nature of knowledge, learning, and teaching. Attempts to provide such systems with decision-making capabilities naturally lead to attempts to develop computational formalisms attuned to such a view (Self, 1996). A different view of the nature of knowledge, learning, and teaching does not necessarily lead to the conclusion that there is no need to develop computational formalisms at all. It might mean that we need computational formalisms better attuned to the different view.

The architecture that emerges from our analysis is not one that is fundamentally opposed to the standard ITS architecture or any other. It is instead one that focuses on the different set of issues that arise from the different philosophy. In particular, it is clear that the attempt to develop intelligent systems to support learning is not inherently contradictory to a constructivist view of learning. In order to clarify how this is so, we may reconsider the traditional three ITS components.

Model of Domain Knowledge

An ITS designer tends to assume that knowledge can be described in terms of facts, principles, and so on, which can be represented symbolically and hierarchically and learned in an incremental fashion. Therefore, he invests his effort on developing complex representations of such knowledge. Constructivists emphasize that learners construct their own knowledge through interpreting their experiences in interactional contexts. Therefore, the designer of a constructively oriented learning environment focuses not on knowledge representations but on the nature of situations, contexts, and interactions. This leads to a consideration of the "content" of contexts and of the dynamics of the learning process.

However, a situation model may well contain representations of aspects of the domain of knowledge that a learner may access during interactions (e.g., INCENSE contains representations of the archive of software engineering materials). These representations may appear similar to the models of domain knowledge in ITSs, but their purpose may be very different. They are descriptions not of target knowledge but of resources that are available in a learning situation (and, of course, a nonconstructivist system designer may choose to regard them as descriptions of target knowledge). From this perspective, a model of domain knowledge may be seen as a subset of the broader notion of a situation model.

Model of the Learner's Knowledge

Typically the student model of an ITS is determined by analyzing the student's interactions with reference to the model of domain knowledge in order to determine gaps or errors that may form the basis for instructional interventions. If, however, as constructivists argue, the student's individual constructive process (leading to personal constructions perhaps unrelated to any target knowledge) is more important than the particular product of any learning process, then our model of the learner should focus more on the interactive process, extended in time, taking into account the learner's actions, the contexts in which they occurred, and the learner's cognitive structures at the time. Developing such an interaction process model enables us to consider the kinds of regularities of interaction sequences that lead to properties that benefit or hinder learning. However, these regularities are, as we have indicated, of a different kind from those previously considered in student modeling. For example, a review of student modeling methods for ITSs (Dillenbourg & Self, 1992) was organized on the basis of the kinds of knowledge involved, with the temporal dimension being considered only to the extent that it enabled some kind of statistical means of overcoming the problem of slips and of students' learning (if that may be considered a "problem").

As we have indicated, the learner's cognitive structures may form part of the descriptions of the time-extended interactive process, for the significance of interactive events may depend on individual cognitions. However, the aspects of cognitive structures to be considered are of a different nature and assume different roles, as they are taken in relation to the context and activity that constitute learning interactions, such as the patterns of learners' cognitive states in situations that we have defined. Thus, again, the notion of an interaction process model is, in a way, a superset of (rather than in opposition to) that of an ITS-style student model.

Model of Teaching Knowledge

ITS designers consider that their systems should, more or less deterministically, determine instructional plans by interpreting their student model with respect to a curriculum structure based on the model of domain knowledge. Constructivists would argue that the learning process is too unpredictable to be amenable to analysis by prespecified structures and that learning sequences emerge from interactions between the learner and the environment as influenced by the opportunities that become available. Therefore, according to the latter view, the pedagogical role of the system is not to determine instructional events but to provide profitable spaces for interaction to the learner based on some model of the affordances of potential situations.

In the previous section, the affordance model focused on the particular properties of courses of interaction afforded. However, if one had an objectivist view of knowledge, one could develop an affordance model in terms of the items of knowledge that may be learned through particular events (so, for example, an ITS event such as the presentation of remediational feedback might be considered to afford the learning of the item of knowledge remediated). So again we see the affordance model as broader than, not opposed to, the model of teaching as curriculum-based planning.

At the risk of oversimplifying, we present a tripartite model of the architecture of computer-based learning environments, which includes the standard ITS architecture as a subset (see Fig. 1.4). Like all other simple diagrams, it risks misleading by suggesting that the design and implementation of such systems are much, much harder than designing ITSs (which are hard enough) because the ITS architecture is shown as a small subset. In fact, the content of these components may be simpler to implement than those we strive for in ITSs. For example, the kind of student interaction process model we may need, based on properties of courses of interaction, may be simpler to construct than the high-fidelity cognitive models based on detailed considerations of knowledge structures we need in conventional ITSs.

Lajoie and Derry (1993) showed that their rhetorical "to model or not to model" dilemma was indeed illusory by presenting examples of different kinds of modeling activity carried out by different agents (students, teachers, designers, and systems), all of which may contribute to a com-

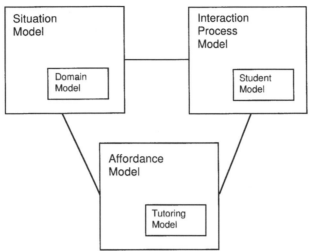

FIG. 1.4.   *An ILE architecture.*

puter-based learning activity. Within the context of system modeling, however, it was assumed that modeling involved building student models, as discussed by Wenger (1987), VanLehn (1988), and Greer and McCalla (1994), that is, representations related to objective knowledge representations. Although the modeling activities of the human agents (students, teachers, and designers) presented in Lajoie and Derry (1993) are compatible with constructivist philosophies, this view of system modeling as student modeling is not.

We have viewed the system modeling process in a broader perspective as an enterprise in developing precise, formal, and, in our case, computational (as we are engaged in designing computer systems) representations that we can use to understand and predict the modeled entity, which, in our case, is the process of learning, because that is what constructivism focuses on. We believe that system modeling can and should encompass objectivist, constructivist, and any other -ist philosophy, provided that the analysis is appropriately attuned to that philosophy.

ACKNOWLEDGMENTS

F.A. is grateful for the support of CNPq, the National Council of Scientific and Technological Development, Brazil. We are both very grateful to Susanne Lajoie for her careful review of this chapter.

The first-named author is now at the Institute of Mathematical Sciences and Computing, University of São Paulo, Brazil (akhras@icmc.sc.usp.br).

REFERENCES

Agre, P. E. (1995). Computational research on interaction and agency. *Artificial Intelligence, 72,* 1–52.

Akhras, F. N. (1997). *Reasoning about process in intelligent learning environments.* Unpublished doctoral dissertation, University of Leeds.

Akman, V., & Surav, M. (1996, Fall). Steps toward formalizing context. *Artificial Intelligence Magazine,* 55–72.

Barwise, J., & Perry, J. (1983). *Situations and attitudes.* Cambridge, MA: MIT Press.

Bednar, A. K., Cunningham, D., Duffy, T. M., & Perry, J. D. (1992). Theory into practice: How do we link? In T. M. Duffy & D. H. Jonassen (Eds.), *Constructivism and the technology of instruction: A conversation* (pp. 17–34). Hillsdale, NJ: Lawrence Erlbaum Associates.

Boekaerts, M. (1997). Self-regulated learning: A new concept embraced by researchers, policy makers, educators, teachers, and students. *Learning and Instruction, 7,* 161–186.

Brown, J. S., Collins, A., & Duguid, P. (1989). Situated cognition and the culture of learning. *Educational Researcher, 18*(1), 32–42.

Clancey, W. J. (1993). Guidon-Manage revisited: A socio-technical systems approach. *Journal of Artificial Intelligence in Education, 4,* 5–34.

Detterman, D. K., & Sternberg, R. J. (Eds.). (1993). *Transfer on trial: Intelligence, cognition, and instruction.* Norwood, NJ: Ablex.

Dewey, J. (1933). *How we think: A restatement of the relation of reflective thinking to the educative process.* Boston: Heath.

Dillenbourg, P., & Self, J. A. (1992). A framework for learning modeling. *Interactive Learning Environments, 2,* 111–137.

Duffy, T. M., & Jonassen, D. H. (1992). Constructivism: New implications for instructional technology. In T. M. Duffy & D. H. Jonassen (Eds.), *Constructivism and the technology of instruction* (pp. 1–16). Hillsdale, NJ: Lawrence Erlbaum Associates.

Ertmer, P. A., & Newby, T. J. (1996). The expert learner: Strategic, self-regulated, and reflective. *Instructional Science, 24,* 1–24.

Fosnot, C. T. (1996). Constructivism: A psychological theory of learning. In C. T. Fosnot (Ed.), *Constructivism: Theory, perspectives, and practice* (pp. 8–33). New York: Teachers College Press.

Gibson, J. J. (1977). The theory of affordances. In R. Shaw & J. Bransford (Eds.), *Perceiving, acting, and knowing* (pp. 67–82). Hillsdale, NJ: Lawrence Erlbaum Associates.

Glynn, S. M., & Duit, R. (1995). Learning science meaningfully: Constructing conceptual models. In S. M. Glynn & R. Duit (Eds.), *Learning science in the schools* (pp. 3–33). Hillsdale, NJ: Lawrence Erlbaum Associates.

Greeno, J. G. (1997). On claims that answer the wrong questions. *Educational Researcher, 26*(1), 5–17.

Greeno, J. G., Moore, J. L., & Smith, D. R. (1993). Transfer of situated learning. In D. K. Detterman & R. J. Sternberg (Eds.), *Transfer on trial: Intelligence, cognition, and instruction* (pp. 99–167). Norwood, NJ: Ablex.

Greer, J. E., & McCalla, G. I. (Eds.). (1994). *Student modeling: The key to individualised knowledge-based instruction.* Berlin: Springer.

Jonassen, D. H. (1992). Evaluating constructivistic learning. In T. M. Duffy & D. H. Jonassen (Eds.), *Constructivism and the technology of instruction: A conversation* (pp. 137–148). Hillsdale, NJ: Lawrence Erlbaum Associates.

Lajoie, S. P., & Derry, S. J. (Eds.). (1993). *Computers as cognitive tools.* Hillsdale, NJ: Lawrence Erlbaum Associates.

Lakoff, G. (1987). *Women, fire and dangerous things.* Chicago: University of Chicago Press.

Piaget, J., & Garcia, R. (1991). *Toward a logic of meanings.* Hillsdale, NJ: Lawrence Erlbaum Associates.

Resnick, L. B. (1987). Learning in school and out. *Educational Researcher, 16*(9), 13–20.

Resnick, L. B. (1996). Situated rationalism: The biological and cultural foundations for learning. *Prospects, 26*(1), 37–53.

Sack, W., Soloway, E., & Weingrad, P. (1992). Re: Writing Cartesian student models. *Journal of Artificial Intelligence in Education, 3,* 381–399.

Self, J. A. (1996). *Computational mathetics: Towards a science of learning systems design* (CBLU Tech. Rep. No. 96/23). Leeds: University of Leeds.

Shuell, T. J. (1992). Designing instructional computing systems for meaningful learning. In M. Jones & P. H. Winne (Eds.), *Adaptive learning environments* (pp. 19–54). Berlin: Springer-Verlag.

VanLehn, K. (1988). Student modeling. In M. Polson & J. Richardson (Eds.), *Foundations of intelligent tutoring systems* (pp. 55–78). Hillsdale, NJ: Lawrence Erlbaum Associates.

von Glasersfeld, E. (1989). Cognition, construction of knowledge, and teaching. *Synthese, 80,* 121–140.

von Glasersfeld, E. (1995). *Radical constructivism: A way of knowing and learning.* London: Falmer Press.

Vosniadou, S. (1996). Towards a revised cognitive psychology for new advances in learning and instruction. *Learning and Instruction, 6*(2), 95–109.

Vygotsky, L. S. (1978). *Mind in society.* Cambridge, MA: Harvard University Press.

Wenger, E. (1987). *Artificial intelligence and tutoring systems.* Los Altos: Morgan Kaufmann.

Winn, W. (1993). A constructivist critique of the assumptions of instructional design. In T. M. Duffy, J. Lowyck, & D. H. Jonassen (Eds.), *Designing environments for constructive learning* (pp. 189–212). Berlin: Springer-Verlag.

2

Toward Assessment of Knowledge-Building Practices in Technology-Mediated Work Group Interactions

Sharon J. Derry, Stephen Gance,
and Laura Lee Gance
University of Wisconsin-Madison

Mark Schlager
SRI-International, Palo Alto, California

The first volume of *Computers as Cognitive Tools* (Lajoie & Derry, 1993) focused on stand-alone instructional systems for classroom use. Today new models of education employ Internet technology to create forums for collaboration among new populations of lifelong learners. One such effort is the Teacher Professional Development Institute (referred to as TAPPED IN, or TI) at SRI International (Schlager & Schank, 1997; *http://www.tappedin.org/info/papers/cscl97/*), which is based on a multiuser virtual environment (MUVE). When users log into the TI environment on the Web, they are located virtually in an institute. The institute is based on a building metaphor with floors, wings, offices, meeting rooms, and other spaces that a physical institute would have. The virtual spaces of TI provide places where teachers and other educational professionals can "meet" and collaborate and where artifacts and tools can be created and stored.

The hope is that real-time collaboration and social interaction in TI will serve as mechanisms for learning new teaching strategies and practices. According to Schlager and Schank (1997):

The TAPPED IN concept is based on a vision of a shared virtual place where teachers with diverse interests, skills, and backgrounds can (a) meet and learn from one another at any time, (b) be exposed to a variety of education reform concepts and approaches, and (c) find high-quality resources and contribute those that they find useful. By sharing a single environment, organizations enable teachers to gain access to expertise, ideas, and resources that no single organization could provide by itself. (p. 2)

We are interested in how TI-type environments afford and constrain the social construction of new knowledge. Educators, researchers, and developers alike want to use technology to foster high-level discourse that supports growth of knowledge within professional communities, not just social chat. Theories of social knowledge construction, including situated cognition (Lave, 1991; Lave & Wenger, 1991a, 1991b), sociocultural (e.g., Vygotsky, 1978; Wertsch, 1991a, 1991b), and activity (e.g., Nardi; 1998; Roschelle, 1998) theories, claim that tools play important roles in shaping a community's thoughts and actions. Tools include intangible ones such as conceptual language, as well as tangible and technological ones such as communication systems and their features. Designing online environments that enhance knowledge construction is one concern of our research. Another is the development of methods for assessing online communities as knowledge-construction entities.

To help us better understand the tool we wanted to study, we began by using TI as the primary means of communication for our research team. Our group consisted of 12 members, including TI developers with considerable experience in online synchronous communication, and researchers who had not previously used TI or any similar system. Our group was dispersed geographically: on the West Coast of the United States, in the Midwest, and in Europe. Biweekly meetings occurred throughout most of our first year, and key members, including the authors of this chapter, attended most meetings. Through use and analysis of our own online conversational data, we came to a better understanding of how work can be influenced by the TI environment.

The project examined by this chapter had several purposes:

- To develop a theoretical framework for studying social knowledge construction in online communities.
- To pilot-test this conceptualization informally by using it to characterize our own TI working group.

- To outline a program of research and a practical set of metrics for studying and evaluating online professional communities as knowledge construction entities.

WHAT IS KNOWLEDGE CONSTRUCTION, AND HOW IS IT IDENTIFIED?

Protocol 1 is an example of project team dialogue during an online meeting of our research group. The issue addressed was how to identify when knowledge construction occurs. We began by addressing the simple question of whether this (or, more properly, the broader conversation of which this is a part) represented any worthwhile form of knowledge construction. If so, what characteristics of the computer environment hindered or supported it? We needed a psychological theory of knowledge construction to answer these questions, but there is no single definition or model of social knowledge construction.

We use four different theoretical frameworks as guides for our research: a situative-sociocultural perspective, sociocognitive theory, argumentation, and group information processing theory. Our aim is to show how the four frameworks together guide and enhance the study and evaluation of social knowledge construction in working online communities. Our work falls within recent trends to combine contextual and cognitive theories to produce integrated perspectives for conducting field-based research (e.g., Cobb & Yackel, 1996; Greeno, 1998).

A SITUATIVE FRAMEWORK

Our overarching theory of knowledge construction is based on what we call the situative perspective, following Greeno (1998), which we have conceptualized broadly to encompass key features of both socially situated cognition (e.g., Lave, 1991) and sociocultural theory (Wertsch, 1991a, 1991b). A characteristic of this view that distinguishes it from traditional cognitive approaches is its focus on whole complex systems of activity rather than the cognitive processes of individuals. The systems of interest in our research are long-term working groups, with various goals, that form within TI.

PROTOCOL 2.1.   Multiple Turns in Online Meeting, April 1, 1997

Line	Person	TI Command	Utterance Typed
1.	MM	SAY	lets defin social constr of knowledge as having certain features . . .
2.	MM	SAY	one might be documents that more than one person reads or edits
3.	MM	SAY	another might be dialogue of some type
4.	MM	SAY	join in: how would you define social construc of knowledge?
5.	MM	SAY	using the raw data we can mine for these features
6.	PM	SAY	An outcome that required input from two or more people
7.	MM	SAY	right so if we find that several ppl are dropping documents in a room, we can zoom in and look to see what they contain
8.	MM	SAY	or if someone creates a bboard that others post to, whould that be soc const of know?
9.	SF	SAY	(Others join in too: we'll drop the order for now) I think in a research group . . .
10.	MM	SAY	these raw data point to where the nuggets may be, but are not gold in themselves
11.	SF	SAY	such as this one, social construction of K would necessarily result in new . . .
12.	PM	SAY	The question I have is whether we would expect there to be a relationship between the weighted use of the categories and ways of identifying social construction of knowledge
13.	PM	EMOTE	likes MM's gold metaphor
14.	MM	WHISPER-PM	I don't thik quantity implis quality if that is what you are asking
15.	LF	EMOTE	waits for SF to finish her thought
16.	SF	SAY	theories, models, or ideas that are created out of multiple perspectives . . .
17.	SF	SAY	I was going to finish the sentence with the phrase :model or concept building.
18.	TM	SAY-PM	Patterns in use of certain categories can be pointers to goldmines, but

PROTOCOL 2.1.   *continued*

19.	TM	SAY-PM	you can answer your question by look-ing at the text that we just produced
20.	TM	SAY-PM	would you expect that we just defined for our group what social construction of k. means for us?
21.	SF	SAY	I'm not yet satisfied with our definition (or even that this is an important . . .
22.	SF	SAY	question for all of us. It seems we need to conceptualize our research better . . .
23.	SF	SAY	(or at least I need to) and an issue of importance is whether this tool helps or . . .
24.	SF	SAY	hinders that process. Also, what norms are essential to support it.
25.	PM	SAY-TM	It's a working definition, but your ques-tion makes me wonder if we also need to include agreement between different people

Groups as Apprenticeship Systems

The situative perspective views the working group as a form of commu-nity. Learning is viewed as a developmental trajectory that, for each indi-vidual, involves attaining membership, identity, and status within chosen communities of practice (Lave, 1991). According to Lave (1991), "Devel-oping an identity as a member of a community and becoming knowledge-ably skillful are part of the same process" (p. 65). Newcomers initially participate peripherally in the legitimate activities of an established com-munity. Theoretically, novices who are motivated and are assisted by more senior members will gradually master the practices of the group, including the tangible and conceptual tools of those practices.

As novices develop within contexts of their chosen communities, semi-otic mediation is involved in all aspects of their knowledge construction (John-Steiner & Mahn, 1996). Semiotic mediation occurs through the novice's appropriation and use of a community's tangible and psychological tools, where the term *tool* is broadly construed to include a community's language, conceptual understandings, symbol systems, customs, software, skills, and so on. Due to the interwoven "constraints and affordances"

(Greeno, 1998) they impose, the tools of a community help shape, or mediate, its members' thoughts, actions, and interactions.

Vygotsky described a mentoring-apprenticeship model of social interaction to account for novice members' internalization of a community's language and other cultural tools (John-Steiner & Mahn, 1996; Vygotsky, 1978). Briefly, established members serve as mentors who help set work-related tasks that ideally are above the level at which novices could perform alone. Mentors provide active support that enables novices to participate in high-level activity even early in their development. By helping novices engage in progressively more difficult tasks and by strategically fading support, mentors help novices gain full community membership. Theoretically, sustained communities of practice constantly renew themselves through new membership. Hence, a thriving community is expected to sustain some level of mentor-apprentice interaction.

From this perspective, it is possible to conceptualize a number of indexes for assessment of groups as knowledge construction systems. For example, a frequency-of-apprenticeship index might serve as one sign of a community's health. If apprenticeship is rare or nonexistent, this might indicate that the community is not regularly renewing with new members, that work is not challenging, that members are not learning from one another, or that help is not available when needed. If mentoring dialogue is very frequent or nearly continuous, this might imply overdominance by leaders, ineffective mentorship, or overly difficult group tasks.

We do not yet know in a quantitative sense what is too much or too little apprenticeship since we currently have no normative or evaluative data on apprenticeship practices within online communities. To our knowledge, no one has yet developed indexes or computational methods that will permit convenient quantification and measurement of online apprenticeship trends, much less used them to compare successful and unsuccessful communities. Toward this end, a method for automatically identifying patterns of mentor-apprentice interactions in discourse is one goal of our work. To illustrate how we are approaching this problem, an example of a typical apprenticeship-mentoring episode within our group is provided in Protocol 2.

In this segment, experienced technologists PM and MM mentor technology novice LF in the use of a TI tool, the drop command. A document named *freedom* is "dropped" by PM into a TI room so that all present in the virtual space can view it. PM's action "drop freedom" in line 1 causes LF to indicate to the group (using the "think-aloud" command) that she does not understand what drop freedom means. Both PM and MM then

PROTOCOL 2.2. *Multiple Turns Illustrating Knowledge Construction as Apprenticeship, Online Meeting, March 17, 1997*

Line	Person	TI Command	Utterance Typed
1.	PM	DROP	freedom [filename]
2.	LF	THINK	What does dropped mean?
3.	LF	THINK	PM and freedom?
4.	MM	SAY- LF	if I want to read freedom on my own, PM has to drop it in the room
5.	PM	SAY	I scanned in two notes and dropping them means others can pick them up
6.	LF	EMOTE	nods with thanks
7.	MM	SAY	when you type LOOK now you will see them under What is Here
8.	LF	SAY	This points to one of your suggestions, PM, about practicing more. . .
9.	MM	SAY	I can also use the web UI to view them and not have them, scroll away

explain the drop command to LF, who acknowledges understanding (lines 4–6). In lines 7 and 9, MM points out how the command can be useful in working group interactions.

This episode contains features that mark it as a mentor-apprenticeship interaction. First, it represents a just-in-time learning episode; the evidence for this is that the command is used and taught almost incidentally in the context of other work goals. Second, the episode illustrates a simple but typical apprenticeship discourse pattern, one that involves one apprentice and several mentors:

- Tool is used by experienced member in context of work.
- Question about tool is asked by novice.
- Response to novice's question is given by experienced member.
- Elaborations on response to novice are made by other experienced members.
- Acknowledgment of assistance is given by novice.

Third, TI commands reveal status differentiation and social norms associated with apprentice-mentoring episodes. For example, the technology novice apparently does not wish to interrupt the conversation directly to ask a question, but uses the "think command" to indicate as an aside that there is something about work the novice does not understand. Thus,

LF defers to experienced community members to decide whether other work will be interrupted for instructional purposes. In this case, the available user commands within TI (*http://www.tappedin.org/info/basic.html*) appeared to afford and encourage enactment of a status-differentiating social norm associated with mentor-apprentice interactions.

Many online communities, including both student and professional development communities, can appropriately be characterized as having important apprenticeship subsystems. For example, TI often brings members of a community who are versed in its technology together with inexperienced teachers who are potential new members, in hopes that newcomers will choose to belong as active participants. Although some formal training may be provided to initiates, experienced users offer a great deal of less formal assistance to new members, helping them acquire more in-depth knowledge and skill with community tools (Schlager, Fusco, & Schank, 1998; *http://www.tappedin.org/info/papers/ieee.html/*). Assessing the frequency and quality of such apprenticeships within communities is of great concern to system administrators, who oversee funding, design, management, and overall quality of online learning systems. Hence, computer-assisted methods for gathering evidence on a large scale would be welcomed by many, since many educational online communities are too large and complicated to be evaluated otherwise.[1] By identifying and studying online apprenticeship dialogues, we help to specify and quantify their characteristic features so that coding systems and computational methods can be devised to identify and quantify them for research and evaluative purposes.

Monitoring Boundary Constructs

A straightforward apprenticeship metaphor provides only a partial account of social knowledge construction in working communities. For example, Derry and DuRussel (Derry, DuRussel, & O'Donnell, 1998; DuRussel & Derry, 1996) observed an interdisciplinary research team in an early stage of its development. As its members struggled to understand one another and to integrate their viewpoints, status differentiation and other teaching-learning patterns that mark true apprenticeship did not clearly occur. It is likely that many groups within the TI environment similarly struggle to achieve integrated understandings and that metaphors

---

[1]There are many ethical issues surrounding the problem of monitoring online discourse. We acknowledge these and do not purport to have solved them, but we do not discuss ethical concerns in this chapter.

other than apprenticeship are needed to characterize other interactive forms of knowledge construction.

The situative perspective is associated with the metaphor of *boundary constructs,* an idea suggested by Hans Gadamer (Agar, 1986). In explaining Gadamer's view, Agar noted, every "tradition has a boundary—the limits of its point of view—called its horizon. Resolution occurs when the horizons of the different traditions have been 'fused'—changed or extended so that the breakdown disappears" (p. 21). (Derry et al., 1998; DuRussel & Derry, 1996) described various ways in which boundary constructs were used to help fuse different disciplinary traditions in the early stages of the interdisciplinary research team they observed. For example, members occasionally employed analogical or metaphorical reasoning to connect central concepts from different disciplines or sources (e.g., galaxies are like school systems). More often, members adopted terms (e.g., *experimental control*) that were common to multiple disciplines and had similar general meanings in all disciplines. However, because specific meanings for these terms were different for members from different disciplines, each boundary construct had to be negotiated and refined over time, within the context of the team's work.

An example from TI is our own group's evolving understanding of the boundary construct, social knowledge construction. In Protocol 1, one member described social knowledge construction as an outcome requiring input from two or more people, and another described it as developing new theories or models out of multiple perspectives. Still another member suggested that social knowledge construction in online discourse could be identified and to some extent characterized in terms of proposed TI data categories, codes that count or point to observable online behaviors, such as collaborative document editing. In a later meeting (on May 6, 1997), the concept of social knowledge construction began to build on the idea of joint product development, such that judgments of product value might be equated with judgments about quality of knowledge construction. Protocol 3, from a dialogue occurring two months later (on July 17), witnessed a return of this discussion topic. The idea of using machine- detectable behavior codes to identify knowledge-construction episodes within TI was once again addressed by the research group. But then the concept was elaborated to incorporate the ideas that social knowledge construction is associated with certain practices that foster it (which might be detected through automated codes) and involves the development of shared mental models (which might be studied using interview procedures).

To the extent that boundary constructs such as social knowledge construction become key ideas for conceptualizing group work over sustained periods of time, the study of their evolution may be an interesting and important key to understanding and assessing social knowledge construction that occurs within groups. Hence, we propose in our research to assess communities and teams as knowledge-building entities in part by identifying and tracing the history of what (if any) constructs emerge as important tools for work. As we envision it, developmental studies of boundary constructs would examine group discourse and tangible products for evidence of the following:

- Clusters of key terms indicating repeated use over time of major target constructs.
- Time-series changes in what and how much such constructs signify.
- Time-series changes in span of construct use, that is, whether increasing or decreasing numbers of community members embrace key constructs in their work.
- Importance, or centrality, of constructs to the community's discourse.

Our theoretical assumption can be summarized as follows: Communities developing many constructs that are adopted broadly within the community as central aspects of community work represent stronger knowledge-building systems compared to those that develop relatively few constructs that are used narrowly and infrequently. Hence, a normative composite index for comparing groups as knowledge-building entities should be derivable from scores representing the number of constructs developed within a community within a sampled range of time, weighted by judges' assessments of the quality or value of these constructs. This score could be combined with indexes derived from ratings that reflect the degree of evolutionary change measured for each construct and the span and frequency of each construct's use within the community. Although such analyses are currently labor intensive, we anticipate that evolving artificial intelligence techniques, such as latent semantic analysis (Foltz, 1996), may eventually help make computer-aided identification and examination of evolving constructs a more tractable problem for study and automatic online identification.

Discourse of Negotiation

In addition to examining the constructs that communities use and evolve, it is important to characterize a community's construct-evolving processes. Situated theorists characterize working groups as communities that negotiate (Greeno, 1998; Lave, 1991), through conversational and related communication activity, the knowledge required for conducting their work. Negotiation has been described generally (Greeno, 1998) as involving the conversational moves of presenting; giving responses that accept, question, or object to (we add elaborate on) presented ideas; and affirming or repairing interpretations to reach mutual understanding. Protocol 3 from our online research group highlights these categories with codes, illustrating in general how the processes of negotiating a complex construct can be characterized.

In turn 1 of Protocol 3, SF affirms (AFF) understanding PM's interpretation of SF's previously stated idea (that studies of knowledge construction in groups should address participants' mental models). SF then endeavors to repair (REP) PM's inaccurate understanding of her meaning by presenting (PRES) more detail (SF wants to collect data on participants' mental models). In turn 2, PM questions doubtfully (QUES/OBJ) what SF is saying (that she wants to collect online data on participants' mental models). (In turn 3, SF merely continues the unfinished thought of turn 1, and in turn 4, another participant, MM, asks for a definition of mental models [QUES].) In turn 5, SF ignores MM's query and directly addresses PM's doubt-question of turn 2, affirming (AFF) that SF understands his objection, then making a repair (REP) to PM's incorrect assumption that SF wants to collect mental model data on line. In turn 6, PM accepts (ACC) SF's suggestion, affirming (AFF) that he and SF both now understand there are two important types of data collection: online behavior codes and off-line data on mental models. In line 7, MM repeats his previously unanswered request for a definition of mental models, but this time MM frames his previously ignored question more precisely by asking for affirmation of a specific statement (QUES(aff)). In turn 8, SF finally turns to MM's question, and the negotiation continues.

There are several specific features that distinguish this negotiation from the apprenticeship discourse in Protocol 2. In the apprenticeship interaction, the conversation is motivated by use of a tool already adopted by an online community that is being used in the context of accomplishing a work goal and is being acquired as incidental learning by a novice member. In the apprenticeship of Protocol 2, there are several "teachers" and one learner, an expected imbalance resulting from dominance of a community knowledge base. There are also conversational status markers that differentiate between the learner and the teachers.

The negotiation episode in Protocol 3 also focuses on a tool, although an intangible one (a conceptual construct) applied in the context of ongoing work. In negotiation the tool and its use are not yet well defined or established. It is being resurrected from memory of past conversations and presented as a potential tool for work by one member (SF), who is adding to the idea and striving to be understood. There are equal-status "responders" trying to understand, question, and refine the idea and confirm that it is mutually understood. Compared to apprenticeship, negotiation is more argumentative and, in this case, more complex.

Like apprenticeship dialogue, negotiation is hypothesized to be an important form of knowledge-construction discourse in which productive, thriving communities continually engage. Hence, the development of quantitative methods for locating and assessing the frequency and quality of negotiation processes within online communities would be a valuable tool for a science that aims to understand and assess the knowledge-construction practices of online communities. The following goals are proposed for a line of inquiry focused toward this aim:

1. Find one or two online working groups that successfully employ target concepts of central importance to their work that they (the group members) believe have evolved through their work.
2. Trace back through available protocols to locate original boundary concepts that gave birth to target constructs.
3. Develop reduced protocols that represent the negotiation processes surrounding each concept's trajectory.
4. Code reduced protocols to permit algorithmic, machine-based identification of the patterns in negotiation activities associated with the observed evolutionary changes in target concepts.
5. Classify identified negotiation activities to create a taxonomy of practices underlying successful boundary construct evolution.
6. Apply codes and taxonomy to the assessment of social knowledge construction in other online communities.

Tools and Practices as Semiotic Mediators

As situative theorists, we are aware that semiotic mediators shape the knowledge-building discourses of negotiation and apprenticeship. And although we view technology design itself as an attempt to influence knowledge construction by imposing or suggesting certain mediating tools, we are aware that controlling knowledge construction through semiotic mediation is very difficult. In general, semiotic mediators comprise a

PROTOCOL 2.3. *Multiple Turns Illustrating the Return of Knowledge Construction as a Boundary Concept, Protocol Is Coded to Highlight Negotiation Processes, Online Meeting, July 17, 1997*

The protocol is coded to highlight negotiation processes:
AFF   **Affirms understanding**
REP   **Repairs a misunderstanding**
PRES   **Adds information from outside source**
ELAB   **Conceptually extends idea under discussion**
QUES   **Questions to clarify idea under discussion**
OBJ   **Objects to something understood**
ACC   **Accepts idea developed by discussion**

Code	Line	Person	TI Command	Utterancce Typed
AFF/ REP/ PRES	1.	SF	SAY-PM	Oh, I see what you are asking. Actually, I was thinking of coding systems for TI in general the KC [knowledge construction] codes. I looked back at earlier meeting transcript discussing MM's dc's [data categories]—meeting from way back. The discussion that ensued was about how to code for KC. We dropped that topic. I'm sort of returning to that idea.
QUES/ OBJ	2.	PM	SAY	How easy will it be to decide what mental models people are using from just that? [codes generated by system]
REP/ PRES (continue 1)	3.	SF	SAY-PM	Where KC stands for "knowledge construction" BTW. EM had some interesting ideas, and TM. The issue was how to identify KC in TI.
QUES	4.	MM	SAY	Can I get a definition of Mental Model straight?
AFF/ REP/ PRES	5.	SF	SAY-PM	Oh, OK. I am assuming we will look at TI data for indicators of KC practices (a simple one would be discussing a document, like we are doing now). But the mental models [that] people develop—that would be gleaned from interviewing people after meetings.

PROTOCOL 2.3. *continued*

AFF/ACC	6.	PM	SAY-SF	OK, that would be an important additional part.
QUES (aff) (cont. 4)	7.	MM	SAY	By Mental Model (MM) do you mean MM of the shared task?
REP/ QUES	8.	SF	SAY	Will you accept a non-specific, non-representational definition, such as "how members conceptualize the group task and the group (two parts)?"
ACC	9.	MM	SAY	Yes
REP/ PRES	10.	SF	SAY	Some lit I've read suggests the two parts are important for group members to align: Their perception of the group (including knowledge/ roles, etc. of members), and their perception of what the group is doing (perception being generally understood).
AFF/ PRES/ QUES	11.	AF	SAY	So for example - In the PD work shop I was haunting last week, much time was spent on the basic premises of the curriculum, views of science, etc. Those count as elements of the mental model to be shared, yes? (Dialogue omitted)
ELAB/ QUES	12.	MM	SAY-SF	So does KC lead to shared MM or vice versa? (Dialogue omitted)
ELAB/ QUES/ REP		AF	SAY	Aren't KC and MM mutually dependent? More KC can lead to better MM and vice versa.
QUES	13.	PM	EMOTE	wonders about what "shared" means
ELAB/ REP	14.	SF	SAY- MM	Well, I think there are different "practices," I called them KC practices because they are the kinds of things groups do when they are trying to develop/align their MM. . .
AFF	15.	PM	EMOTE	Agrees with AF

PROTOCOL 2.3. *continued*

AFF/ ELAB/ QUES	15.	MM	SAY-SF	and then once MMs are aligned the development of KC gets easier, no?
AFF/ ELAB	16.	EM	SAY	It sounds to me like creation of the metal model is a subset of knowledge contruction, if I'm understanding.

complex and dynamic interactive system of constraints and affordances for activity. These shapers of what people do and say include not only technological tools but also the procedures for using technological tools, work goals, the developing products of work including abstract constructs, and even the broader institutional contexts in which groups operate. Because systems of semiotic mediation are complex and contain many intertwined aspects that influence one another, it is difficult to pull such systems apart and focus on only one aspect, such as the communication technology itself.

Yet systems designers give status to those mediators of knowledge-construction activity that can be influenced by design. These include the designable tools themselves and, to some extent under the designer's control, the normative group practices that surround tool use. That practices and tools operate in semiotic relationship with one another makes it necessary for designers to understand how and why particular features of online technology might cause particular social norms to emerge within successful communities.

An illustrative example is provided by Protocol 4, where members are explicitly discussing what meeting practices might be adopted to minimize an "overlapping conversations" problem that is typical of text-based communication. An example of how confusing multiple conversational threads can occur within the TI environment was illustrated in Protocol 1. That interwoven conversational threads occur is a by-product of the TI design itself, which affords them. Hence, social knowledge construction in Protocol 4 represents an evolving culture of practice motivated by explicit discussion of social norms, which is motivated by the group's need to adapt to this particular online environment. (Multiple conversations might occur in face-to-face meetings too if there were not normative practices, as well as human information processing constraints, which usually prevent them.)

Not all norms that govern online work are negotiated explicitly. The broader cultural and institutional contexts within which smaller communities of practice develop and reside provide social norms (as well as other semiotic mediators) that may implicitly be appropriated and reproduced in specific group interactions. Protocol 5 illustrates the appropriation of social norms borrowed from the face-to-face interactions with which all participants were familiar. Protocol 5 can be viewed as an extension of a friendly face-to-face greeting that might occur when someone enters a room where a meeting is in progress. In addition to the participants' "waving" to acknowledge MM's arrival, MM makes sure to "whisper" to DF to get updated on what has been happening in order to avoid disturbing all the members of the group. Although there was no explicit requirement for the norms illustrated here, this group spontaneously appropriated these and other similar social norms almost from their beginning.

Another example of how normative tools and normative tool use interact to shape knowledge-construction negotiations was given in Protocol 3. This protocol shows how negotiation in the TI environment can move very quickly and overload human attentional capacity (despite its dependency on keyboard input), because many people can input responses simultaneously, and because the interface and real-time mode of online interaction encourage many short messages rather than fewer long ones. Thus, many responses to a presented idea can be addressed to a person or an audience in rapid succession, and each of these can generate multiple responses from various members, so that multiple conversational threads begin and become intertwined. In Protocol 3, SF manages what would otherwise be a confusing dialogue by selectively processing some responses but not others. In doing this, SF deals with overload by employing a politeness norm of dealing with questions and issues in the order they are received, completing one thread before moving to another. But SF does not follow another politeness norm of responding to every person who responds to SF. For example, SF negotiates an understanding with PM while ignoring a question by MM, and then finally moves to take up MM's (repeated) question, while ignoring several others. This illustrates how the structure of negotiation is constrained at one semiotic level, the technological-physical one, and reshaped within those constraints by another semiotic level, the social norm level.

If all knowledge-building communities flexibly adapt by developing normative practices that compensate for limits in their technical-physical environments, then tool design features do not exist in direct relationship to the processes and products of knowledge construction, since these are strongly mediated by the normative tool use practices that groups evolve. This viewpoint has important implications for how we may study the influence of tool design on social knowledge construction within online environments. Tool design features must be studied with respect to the normative group practices they tend to afford, which may directly influence knowledge construction, provided all other potential semiotic mediators are controlled. Thus, it would not be acceptable to vary features of tool design systematically and treat measures of knowledge construction as a dependent variable. However, it would make sense to investigate correlational or hypothesized relationships between categories of designed affordances and the presence and level of normative practices and discourse patterns they are designed to afford. It would also make sense to hypothesize relationships between specific normative tool use practices and various indexes of knowledge construction. For example, holding tool design constant across working groups, normative tool use could be varied systematically by imposing different instructions and training designed to influence practice on randomly assigned groups. The influence of these systematic variations in practice on indexes of knowledge construction could then be quantitatively measured. Or holding tool design constant, normative tool use could be allowed to vary naturally across different groups. Codes representing the different tool-based practices that evolve naturally might correlate with indexes representing specific discourse and knowledge-construction patterns. This would help us determine which naturally occurring online practices and forms of discourse are (or are not) associated with social construction of knowledge.

The Situative Perspective: Concluding Comment

As situative theorists, our goal is to characterize and evaluate knowledge construction within online communities by asking and answering such questions as the following:

- What levels and forms of apprenticeship occur within working groups?
- What and how many key constructs and related semiotic means do communities develop; what are their values, origins, and evolutionary stages; and how often are they used in work?
- What forms of negotiation characterize successful construction of important community constructs (research question), and are these found with sufficient frequency in online work groups and communities (evaluation question)?

PROTOCOL 2.4.   *Multiple Turns Illustrating an Explicit Discussion of Interaction Norms, Online Meeting, March 3, 1997*

Line	Person	TI Command	Utterance Typed
1.	SF	SAY	So I'm thinking that different rules of politeness. . .well I seem to be making my. . .
2.	PM	SAY-SF	SF that's why a free for all could get even more confusing
3.	SF	SAY	point. I can't say what I want cause the conversation gets all entangled.
4.	PM	SAY-SF	Do you want a means of slowing it down to finish your thought?
5.	MM	SAY- SF	what would be a good way for us to know you need to slow down
6.	SF	SAY	Well, I notice that in email collaboration, everyone sort of composes what they . . .
7.	EM	EMOTE	notes that if you chose to never let the talk get entangled, one tends to see two effects: 1. the people who type most slowly tend not to want to slow the meeting down by talking (depends on the person), 2. The rate of information exchange goes down significantly, to a degree approximating the number of people in the conversation.
8.	EM	SAY	Something for the analysis people to consider looking into. :)
9.	MM	EMOTE	waits for SF to finish
10.	SF	SAY	have to say. Here, everyone just jumps in and it doesn't always work out.
11.	PM	SAY	one can use the To command to follow a thread . . . are there other possibilities?
12.	EM	EMOTE	agrees the 'to' command is invaluable.
13.	MM	SAY	would a special alert that ppl could send out like the SIGN help?
14.	SF	SAY	Well, I'm not sure the rate of information flow is a good indicator of productivity. . .
15.	MM	EMOTE	sees. . .and waits

- What normative social practices involving tool use are associated with successful knowledge construction (research question), and are these found with sufficient frequency in online work groups and communities (evaluation question)?

PROTOCOL 2.5. *Multiple Turns Illustrating Norms Borrowed from Face-to-Face Interactions, Online Meeting, March 17, 1997*

Line	Person	TI Command	Utterance typed (or action indicated)
1.	MM		arrives from nowhere
2.	PM	EMOTE	waves to MM
3.	LF	EMOTE	waves to MM
4.	MM	EMOTE	waves and wipes his brow
5.	TM	EMOTE	waves
6.	PM	EMOTE	can see MM is a busy guy
7.	LF	THINK	It looks like he's been running.
8.	DF	EMOTE	waves at MM
9.	MM	WHISPER-DF	whats been going on
10.	DF	WHISPER- MM	they are talking about how to run meetings

Although the situative perspective is an interesting theory that points toward numerous ideas for understanding and assessing social knowledge construction, it is not an easy theory to emulate in practice. Moreover, it judges knowledge construction primarily in terms of the functioning of the group as a whole. But individuals alone may acquire valuable knowledge, even in communities that may be dysfunctional in situative terms. It is important to assess knowledge construction from an individual perspective as well, and for this we turn to sociocognitive theory.

SOCIOCOGNITIVE THEORIES OF KNOWLEDGE CONSTRUCTION

Compared to the situative perspective, which leads to functional analyses of interactivity within groups as wholes, sociocognitive theories are more concerned with mechanisms of individual mind change. Our version of sociocognitive theory is an information processing view that encompasses neo-Piagetian thinking and hierarchical schema theory as described in Derry (1996). From this perspective, newly constructed knowledge is always an evolved version of an individual's previously held schematic knowledge. Briefly, the initial conditions for knowledge construction occur when external events (e.g., a group discusses its task goal) cause an individual to activate (i.e., bring into attention or working memory) prior knowledge that serves as an interpretive schema for understanding the external events. When the information processed from an experience does not duplicate expectations based on the individual's active schema, the conditions for changing that individual's prior knowledge are in place. For example, through social interaction with a work group that is diverse in terms of members' prior knowledge, individuals will encounter mismatches between their conceptualizations of the task and those expressed by others, which sets up conditions for mutual mind change.

We assume that any part of a person's active knowledge is in a relatively stable state in that it is conceptually consistent with other salient beliefs activated within working memory. Encoding of incoming ideas that are inconsistent with one's active belief system is assumed to create a state of mental disequilibrium, or conceptual conflict. Conceptual conflict triggers regulatory mental activity that has as its goal the harmonization of new experience with active prior knowledge. If the conceptual conflict is minimal, then prior knowledge and current experience can be brought closer together by merely accepting and assimilating the new information, thereby updating active prior knowledge in a minor way. Elaborations or small repairs based on new information are made, and a small amount of knowledge construction takes place.

But if the conceptual conflict is major, the individual must equilibrate, and several strategies are possible. First, the individual may choose to reject or ignore incoming information, refusing to incorporate it. Second, the person might reconceptualize (perhaps distorting) the incoming information so that it fits better with her active beliefs. In neither of these cases does individual knowledge construction occur. However, if the individual constructs new explanatory linkages between her active prior knowledge and the incoming ideas, allowing both sets of ideas to coexist in equilibrium, knowledge construction occurs. Or if the individual accommodates her own active belief system, changing it to fit incoming information, knowledge construction occurs.[2] Of course, an individual might combine several such strategies for reducing conceptual conflict.

The discourse of conflict resolution, or negotiation in situative terms, can at least partially reveal what aspects of individual equilibration are taking place. As different viewpoints are expressed and debated during work, individuals may publicly weigh the new conceptions they hear or experience in terms of the conceptions they bring to the interaction them-

---

[2]More accurately, knowledge reconstruction takes place in the case of accommodation. In this chapter the phrase knowledge construction will be used broadly in reference to the creation of new knowledge through both elaboration and reconstructive accommodation.

selves. An example is illustrated by Protocol 6. In turn 3 of this protocol, MM has made available a description of the data on user activity that is automatically collected within TI. The sociocognitive analysis assumes that MM is implicitly presenting his view (i.e., his current schema) of data collection. In turns 9 and 10, PM is beginning to propose an extension to MM's categories, which suggests that PM does not see this data collection as adequate. In other words, PM's schema of useful data to gather differs from MM's, and so he initiates a process of negotiation that is eventually resolved around turn 175 (not shown).

The data in Protocol 6 provide evidence that conflicting mental models of data collection are being discussed, but in this portion of transcript, the disequilibrium seems not to be explicitly recognized. Only later in the meeting did the process of equilibration begin. Eventually PM comes to understand that the data collection facility operates at a lower level than what he needs when he says:

> The questions I have about building community and creating products don't seem to be easily answered by the categories of data TI can so elegantly gather.

And MM acknowledges that the data collected cannot answer certain questions:

> These raw data point to where the nuggets may be, but are not gold in them-selves. . . . But knowing how to code the discourse is independent of the data themselves . . . so in your case I would argue that we need to discuss data CODING. . . . Only human analysis of the transcripts will shed any light.

Such resolutions into shared understanding within discourse provide evidence within the sociocognitive framework that knowledge construction has occurred.

Within any working group, however, there are instances and forms of individual mental processing that are private to individuals and do not nec-essarily parallel what is revealed explicitly in discourse and other observ-able community behavior. From the previous exchange, for example, we cannot know in much detail whether PM and MM are truly aligned with respect to their views of PM's research questions or of how TI data should be coded for analysis. For this reason, studies of working groups as know-ledge-building communities should include examinations of individuals' private cognitive processing in addition to studies of their public discourse activity. Retrospective and online interviews and other verbal protocol techniques (Chi, 1997; Ericsson & Simon, 1984) provide methods for examining members' work-related knowledge and memories in greater detail than discourse analysis can afford. In this exploratory self-analysis of our TI group, we did not collect protocols that could be used to document and substantiate assumptions about individual mind change. However, many questions regarding the construction and reconstruction of individual perspectives could not be answered with our discourse data alone.

The Alignment Hypothesis

When people of diverse background knowledge are brought together in a working context, there is potential for the kinds of conceptual conflict that individual mind change requires. If work-related negotiations are productive, sociocognitive theory predicts that group members' task-related schemas should evolve into greater and deeper conceptual alignment with one another. Task-related schemas include members' mental representations of their goals and tasks and of the constructs and tools needed to perform tasks. In particular, research shows that alignment among members' mental models of their tasks and the group itself is related to successful group performance (Cannon-Bowers, Salas, & Converse, 1993; Orasanu & Salas, 1993). Conversely, misalignment among these mental models is related to performance failure (DuRussel & Derry, 1998).

The sociocognitive analysis thus leads us to conclude that a suitable way to study social knowledge construction in groups involves using protocol techniques to examine changes and alignments in individuals' task-related schemas. For example, one could draw a sample of members from each group studied, then employ knowledge-elicitation techniques grounded in verbal protocol approaches (Chi, 1997; Ericsson & Simon, 1984) to help construct formal representations of members' task-related schemas at selected times throughout the team's history. One type of schema that is especially important to examine is each individual's mental model of the group's tasks. If, from the sociocognitive perspective, the group is engaging in social knowledge construction, comparison judgments of these mental models over time should show two things: that intraindividual schemas are changing over time, and that interindividual schemas are gradually becoming more aligned. Quantified indexes of individual change and alignment might be developed to provide normative and comparative sociocognitive evidence of social knowledge construction across groups.

REASONED ARGUMENTATION
AS A NORMATIVE STANDARD
FOR INTERACTION

Following Abelson (1995), Halpern (1996), Kuhn (1991), and others, we propose that reasoned, evidential argument can and should play a role in the dialogues of negotiation that underlie social knowledge construction. For example, assume that group member A hears a well-reasoned evidential argument that A cannot refute and that supports a conclusion that is a new idea to A, and perhaps even contradictory to A's currently activated beliefs. If argumentation theory is the normative standard for negotiation and schema change, A should not distort or reject the argument and its conclusion because she disagrees with it, but should engage in constructive mental activity that will incorporate the argument and thus bring A's active beliefs into greater consistency with it. On the other hand, a purely emotional appeal that does not represent valid argumentation should have little or no influence on A's point of view. In sum, we propose a standard for successful knowledge building within groups that relies on reasoned argumentation as a means for explaining and resolving conceptual conflict. From the sociocognitive perspective, evidence of schema change and increasing alignment within groups can signify that knowledge construction has occurred. From the argumentation perspective, a higher quality of knowledge results if it is constructed in the context of valid argumentation.

In the view of Halpern (1996), valid argument must include at least one premise and one conclusion. Complex arguments contain multiple chains of interrelated premises and conclusions, such that the conclusions of sub-arguments become premises for higher-level arguments. Each premise contains a claim that can be a fact or an opinion. The conclusion is presented as justified based on the evidence in the premise or premises. Judgments or opinions that are given without such support are not arguments. In addition, arguments can include much more than premises and conclusions. They often contain assumptions, qualifiers, and acknowledgments of or attacks on counterarguments. Each of these components must be identified and considered in argument evaluation.

PROTOCOL 2.6. *Protocol 6. Multiple Turns Illustrating Knowledge
Construction in a Sociocognitive Framework, Online Meeting, April 1, 1997*

1.	SF	SAY	We're soliciting thoughts, ideas, concerns about data collection. MM?
2.	PF	LOOK BOARD	
3.	MM	SAY	I dropped the data categories not in here. I would like to see if anyone has comments or questions
4.	MM	SAY	I'll project it to you if you want
5.	MM	SAY	or you can READ it
6.	MM	SAY	it is called DC
			.
			.
			(various people read DC and make brief comments or pass)
			.
7.	MM	SAY-JM	Is what I envision for the Web database reports doable?
8.	JM	SAY-MM	Let me have another look . . . a sec.
9.	PM	SAY	I would be interested in being able to pull out bigger chunks. . .
10.	PM	SAY	. . . these categories are useful, but they are used in different ways, I think
11.	EM	EMOTE	was wondering if there will be a category of action called 'other' for commands not on your list. I'd expect people's use of 'other' commands to go up with experience, so it might be a useful measure of familiarity with the medium.
12.	JM	SAY-MM	should be doable. If I bump into anything major I'll let you know and find a way around it.
13.	MM	SAY-EM	we only log these so far. If we want other commands we need to inform R.
14.	EM	EMOTE	nods
15.	TM	EMOTE	misses think on the list
16.	MM	SAY	this is intended as a first pass scan to see if anything jumps out that deserves deeper exploration
17.	SF	SAY	Any thoughts from TM?
18.	TM	SAY	as for the data analysis, I would like to rely on bigger chunks from the verbal communication

PROTOCAL 2.6. *continued*

19.	MM	SAY	bigger chunks how?
20.	TM	SAY-MM	full passages from the group's communication, from different days
21.	MM	SAY	oh, that is the RECORDING method, right?
22.	TM	EMOTE	assumes that these tables record the use of the commands, not the contents ?
23.	JM	SAY	what do you mean by contents?
			.
			.
			(dialogue omitted)
.			
24.	PF	SAY-JM	by contents—e.g., WHAT people say or whisper. in these tables we're just recording HOW MANY TIMES they say/whisper, etc.

There are various discourse markers that can be used to help identify argument components in natural online discourse. For instance, words like *since*, *because*, *for*, or *whereas* often signal that a premise will follow. Conclusions are often indicated by conclusion indicators like *therefore*, *hence*, *so*, and *consequently*. However, in standard discourse, premises, assumptions, qualifiers, and even conclusions are often implied rather than explicitly stated, which can make argument structures difficult to detect automatically in online natural discourse.

An example of a simple argument observed in our TI self-study, containing a conclusion discourse marker and an implicit premise, is shown in line 11 of Protocol 6. This argument pertains to supporting a proposal to add an "other" category for coding user moves in TI. The first part of the second sentence, "I'd expect people's use of 'other' commands to go up with experience," contains a claim that is supported by an implied premise, the speaker's personal experience, marked by "I'd expect." The fact known to the group is that EM is an expert on system use, which implicitly strengthens the validity of this implied premise. The second half of the second sentence, "so it might be a useful measure of familiarity with the medium," is a second claim supported by the first and beginning with the discourse marker *so*. These claims and reasons constitute a short "rhetorical" (e.g., Kuhn, 1991) argument.

The simple rhetorical argument can be contrasted with more complicated forms of social, or dialogic, argumentation (Kuhn, 1991), which often involves multiple rhetorical arguments and counterarguments distributed over group members over time. Kuhn (1991) and others have pointed out that such reasoned argumentation is rare in natural groups. Our experience in TI tends to support that conclusion. Thus, applying reasoned argumentation as a normative standard for assessing language-based knowledge construction within online groups requires consideration that such processes may not obviously and spontaneously occur. Following Kuhn (1991), we hypothesize that dialogic argumentation probably requires group members to have special skills, cognitive and social, that might be acquired through training. But following Resnick, Salmon, Zeitz, Wathen, and Holowchak (1993), we are also mindful that group argumentation is complex and often subtle, requiring analytical methods that involve tracing and evaluating complex conversational chains. As Resnick et al. (1993) pointed out, their initial impressions of incoherence in group argumentation were based on attempts to apply textbook norms of elegantly structured arguments. Even in their relatively controlled laboratory environment, they discovered that components of arguments were present but difficult to find because many were implied and were widely distributed over participants and time.

Because we cannot observe the underlying reasoning of EM and no other speaker challenged or otherwise responded to EM's argument, we cannot determine from Protocol 6 whether this argument has precipitated any knowledge construction. However, if the suggested strategy (to interpret use of the *other* command as a measure of system familiarity) is adopted in subsequent work, we can reasonably assume a connection between this strategy and EM's rhetorical argument. An index representing a group's tendency to adopt or reject strategies for work on the basis of reasoned argument would be one feasible comparative measure for judging groups as knowledge construction entities on the basis of argumentation norms. Sophisticated forms of such indexes would take into consideration the importance or cost of the adopted or rejected strategy, its relation to the goals of the group, and the quality of the argument that supported it.

The problem of automatically identifying argumentation in natural, online discourse is very difficult. And even if arguments could be identified and matched to group strategies for the purpose of creating argument-strategy indexes, the arguments would have to be evaluated in order to produce meaningful measures. Argument strength can be evaluated (Halpern, 1996) by verifying that premises relate to the conclusion; multiple premises supporting a single argument are not inconsistent with one another; sources for premises are credible (e.g., experts); counterarguments have been considered; there are no missing or distorted claims; and relevant qualifiers and assumptions are understood and accepted.

At this time, automatic evaluation of unconstrained online discourse using natural language processing techniques is not currently a feasible solution for TI or other online communities. However, better argumentation skills could probably be trained, afforded, and evaluated within TI-like communities. The most immediate solution lies in constructing and tracking use of collaborative tools and command structures designed specifically to support argumentation. For instance, the University of Wisconsin Secondary Teacher Education Program will soon bring student work groups online within TI. It should be possible to develop commands and tools that would encourage group members to suggest and post strategies for work and other ideas, for argumentative consideration by their entire group. A strategy utterance from a student work group member might take the form: "*Suggestion* [command name]: The topic for our instructional design project should be . . . ." Alternatively, an argument schema could be implemented as a shared whiteboard or document template. Participants could use a normal discourse style in real time. In parallel to the discussion, they could "construct" an argument as a metacognitive activity (similar to how we write brainstorming ideas on a whiteboard as we discuss them) or as a reflective activity following the session using the log of the meeting.

In sum, specific tools, commands, and practices could be put in place to encourage users to present supporting arguments and counterarguments in synchronous or asynchronous communication. We envision tools that represent argument schemas with slots for conclusions, premises, qualifiers, counterarguments, and assumptions. If such tools were built and user groups were trained and encouraged by team leaders to adopt them in their normative practices during synchronous and asynchronous communication, argumentation within work groups and larger TI communities would be encouraged and scaffolded. Moreover, groups' argumentation practices could be quantified through the relatively easy tracking of online tool use, with more extensive and accurate tool use leading to higher quantifiers. To justify development of such tools, however, we first need to test assumptions that argument in general, and specific argument-tool practices within TI in particular, can boost the quality of social knowledge construction.

A GROUP INFORMATION PROCESSING
FRAMEWORK

From the group information processing framework perspective, social knowledge construction involves the sharing of information in the context of accomplishing group goals, a process that should also build the group's capacity for carrying out future work. Like the situative perspective, group information processing theory focuses on groups as units of analyses. As presented here, it differs from situative theory in being grounded in the literatures of social cognition and both traditional and distributed (e.g., Pea, 1993) cognitive information processing theory.

Social Dynamics of Distributed Cognition

Hinsz, Tindale, and Vollrath (1997) published an integrative review of small-group research based on the emerging view of groups as information processing systems. Group information processing was defined as "the degree to which information, ideas, or cognitive processes are shared, and are being shared, among group members and how this sharing of information affects both individual and group-level outcomes" (p. 43). The distinction between *shared*, which refers to homogeneity of knowledge distribution, and *sharing*, which refers to processing activity, is important. The sharing process affects not only the tangible products that groups develop, but also what knowledge resources come to be shared and distributed among the group. Available group knowledge may be distributed among different human memories or mechanical storage devices, or may even be represented in tools and artifacts that a group appropriates or creates. If the group is able to access and use information for work, then such information is part of that group's capacity regardless of where it resides. However, the degree of "sharedness," or the ratio of overlapping versus individually owned information, is an important characteristic of groups that influences information processing. Too much duplication of knowledge within a group may narrow capacity undesirably, although lack of sufficient overlapping knowledge is associated with communication difficulties. For example, in face-to-face group discussions, individuals tend to share ideas that are held in common with other members, while ideas representing a single, minority viewpoint are less likely to be expressed. Also, high-status individuals talk more, while low-status members listen. Hence, groupthink (Janis, 1982) tends to reflect, even exaggerate, the dominant viewpoint representing the social in-group.

These and many other findings can be found within a large social cognition literature that views group effectiveness as a function of how information is distributed among members, plus the extent to which that information is shared and combined during processing. This perspective has influenced research on computer-mediated communication (CMC) in natural environments. For example, Sproull and Kiesler (1991) compared face-to-face with electronic communication by looking for patterns of information sharing as a function of variables such as group homogeneity and individual status and belonging. Based on eight years of research on organizational communication, they reported that in face-to-face meetings, half of the members talked only 10% or 20% of the time, and one or a few people dominated. Managers dominated subordinates, and men dominated women. Vocal members often did not have more expertise on the topic. High-status people talked first, and as positions taken tended to confirm those of previous speakers, groups often reached consensus quickly.

Sproull and Kiesler (1991) also reported that status and background were less salient in online communications relative to face-to-face ones. Both synchronous and asynchronous CMC resulted in more balanced participation. In electronic discussions, high-status people did not dominate as much, and more ideas were generated simultaneously without ordering due to status. And since personal satisfaction with group work was related to personal contributions, working online increased member satisfaction with their group experience. Sproull and Kiesler concluded that CMC technologies "do not simply cross space and time; they also can cross hierarchical and departmental barriers, change standard operating procedures, and reshape organizational norms" (p. ix). Moreover, although online meetings were more democratic, groups displayed deeper conflict and tended not to reach consensus as quickly. Although consensus and cohesiveness may seem desirable, recall that sociocognitive theory predicts that cognitive conflict is the basis for social knowledge construction, and this may result in more fruitful collaboration over time.

The group information processing perspective suggests that one important goal of community design is to ensure broad sharing of knowledge across status, cultural, and professional boundaries. But although TI technology may theoretically be able to minimize the effects of status, gender, and other factors that influence sharing, it is not certain what sharing patterns and status relationships will form within different online work groups. Hence, designing methods for assessing and monitoring the social dynamics of collaboration in TI and similar environments is an important aspect of our research.

One approach is to develop coding systems for characterizing participants in terms of their group memberships, using these as a basis for collecting online data on the types of cross-talk in which they engage. For example, in the Secondary Teacher Education Program at the University of Wisconsin-Madison, online work groups comprise practicing teachers, university faculty from education and subject matter fields, and students in preservice programs. In monitoring this community, we will count cross-talk exchanges of different types (e.g., subject matter faculty to student and in-service teacher to education faculty). Our initial assumption is that healthy group interaction should be characterized by balanced cross-talk across membership categories, with imbalance indicating problems requiring intervention.

Information Processing:
Critical Stages Assessments

Knowledge sharing involves information processes such as attending, encoding, storing, transforming, and accessing information. The language of information processing helps identify ways in which tools or practices block or enhance stages of information processing.

The information processing concept of attention is used to help explain how the environment affected sharing within our TI group. In Protocol 7, SF, the facilitator, opens the agenda with a statement that spans turns 1, 5, 6, 8, and 11. It can be seen in turn 2 that EM is not attending. Instead, he is responding to what came before. Similarly, there are multiple turns where people are looking at or posting documents, greeting latecomers (JM), and dealing with a crashed machine. Only MM (MM1 and MM2 are the same person testing two different methods of logging on) and PM give any indication that they are attending to what SF has typed. Obviously the group will not process this agenda item. As can be seen in turn 28, the agenda item is restated, in a somewhat different form, and again in turn 32. At this point it seems the original statements by SF have been lost, replaced by a simplified form of the agenda item, now expressed in as few as five words. Only PM and MM have processed SF's suggestion for the group to read an article (a major information-sharing attempt).[3]

Recall that situative theory focuses on how external environments, including tools and practices, constrain and afford task performance. As

---

[3]However, one compensating feature of TI is that participants can and often do look back over meeting transcripts to recapture what they have missed.

situative and group information processing theorists, we look at what structural aspects of the environment shaped members' attentional processes in this episode. In fact, the distraction and subsequent confusion within the first few minutes shown in Protocol 7 are at least partly associated with the technology itself. JM in turn 10 complains about a time lag that may be making it difficult for him to follow the conversation, and MM indicates in turn 20 that one login has crashed. An example of indirect effects of technology is the lack of visual cues for SF about whether people are ready to begin the meeting, which raises a need for new meeting-initiation practices. Another example of an indirect effect, also arising from the lack of visual contact, is the exchange of greetings when JM enters late, at turn 9. In a face-to-face meeting, such a late intrusion would be a distraction, but it might have been handled with less disruption by an exchange of visual greetings. In this case the technology intersecting with normative practices (or, more accurately, lack of suitable normative practices) helps create attentional deficits within the group.

In other ways, technology constraints have been observed to enhance attentional processes associated with knowledge sharing. For example, in one of our self-studies, we compared discourse from a telephone conference call meeting of our group with discourse from a similar online meeting. Whereas speakers took long, involved turns during the conference call, these same speakers "spoke" in short, precise turns when constrained by the relatively narrow bandwidth of the TI system. In this comparison, the narrow bandwidth appeared to have a positive effect on group participation and attention. During the conference call, two participants engaged in a lengthy exchange pertaining to a theoretical topic about which they, but not others, were well informed. (We have often observed similar phenomena in face-to-face meetings of other groups.) The sheer volume of information in these exchanges appeared to create an information overload for other "participants" who did not share relevant background knowledge. Although online conversations can sometimes overload attention due to multiple conversational strings, TI and similar environments afford the breaking down of lengthy arguments into manageable chunks, which facilitates processing of complex messages by members with less relevant shared knowledge. Shorter utterances can also allow participants with less knowledge to interject comments or questions without appearing to interrupt the main speaker, enabling the speaker to address questions or clarify points of confusion before the conversation gets too far afield.

Group information processing theory also suggests useful ways of thinking about group productivity in terms of stages that involve transforming information from one form to another. Smith (1994) identified three classes of information produced by groups: tangible, intangible, and ephemeral. Tangible knowledge is divided into target products that represent completion of a group's task and instrumental products that merely support the group's work. Intangible information represents stored potential, some of which is shared by multiple individuals, while other information remains private (owned by one individual). Ephemeral products, such as unrecorded conversation or temporary board sketches, exist only briefly during group interactions. Smith (1994) proposed that productive groups are those that are able to transform knowledge from one state to another successfully. For example, working together in face-to-face situations typically involves integrating private and shared intangible knowledge by passing it through an ephemeral stage in which it is transformed into more widely distributed, shared, intangible knowledge, and ultimately into instrumental and final tangible products. A study of a natural working group by Derry, DuRussel, and O'Donnell (1998) illustrated how breakdowns in these stages of information transformation can waste time and resources within groups. For example, the group they observed created several instrumental documents that did not represent good translations of their conversations and were never built on to achieve final products. Hence there were breakdowns in the information processing phrases associated with the translation of ephemeral shared ideas into instrumental and goal products.

We believe that monitoring of information-transformation phases in online groups can produce diagnostic evidence concerning social knowledge construction. However, the information transformation stages for online work may differ from those in face-to-face situations, since more tangible information and less ephemeral knowledge is created. Hence, studies and codification of information-transformation phases within online groups are important to our broader research agenda.

Groups as Information Processors: Implications for Research and Assessment

The group information processing perspective suggests the following agenda for research and evaluation.

Theoretically, productive information sharing should lead to increased group capacity, signified by a gradual increase in available shared knowledge. Hence, a method and summary metric are needed for succinctly quantifying and characterizing the degree of diversity and knowledge overlap within groups. Such a metric could serve as an independent variable in studies of how knowledge distribution affects groups. Importantly, it would supply a basis for measuring time-related increases in shared distributed knowledge, which could serve as one form of evidence for social knowledge construction. We believe the route to this metric has been suggested in our discussion on measuring mental model alignment in the section on sociocognitive theory. In this respect, the predictions and assessment techniques for group information processing theory and sociocognitive theory overlap in a complementary way.

Theoretically, a goal for design of online communities should be to ensure broad sharing of information across status, cultural, and professional classes within the diverse groups that participate. Accordingly, there is a need for taxonomies and coding systems for identifying and enumerating cross- and within-class informational exchanges within online communities and groups. Metrics derived from these systems could be used to help locate and facilitate those groups with dysfunctional (such as in-group/out-group) communication patterns.

Information processing theory can guide study of how technological contexts and features both restrict and enhance group attention. Dialogue and tool use patterns could serve as machine-detectable diagnostic indicators of attentional roadblocks to information sharing. Such indicators might include regular late arrivals at meetings, frequent machine difficulties, repeated reminders of topic, and subconversations. However, because online communication may be revolutionizing how groups process information, it will also be necessary to identify patterns indicating practices that compensate for attentional deficits. For example, if occasional latecomers are able to review meeting transcripts before joining a conversation, this should be counted as a compensating use of tools. In general, groups exhibiting more attention-supporting practices and fewer attention-blocking ones should receive higher attention ratings.

The efficacy of group processes can be characterized in terms of whether information is being successfully transformed from one state to another. For example, it is likely that successfully-sharing, face-to-face groups produce substantial ephemeral information prior to product development, so absence of an ephemeral phase would be usefully diagnostic. However, we do not know what phases of information transformation are associated with successful performance in online work groups. Following Smith (1994), it may be possible to develop a system that will help identify sequences of information transformations that are normative for productive online work, as well as methods for automatically detecting their presence and absence online.

PROTOCOL 2.7. *Multiple Turns Illustrating Knowledge Construction Within the Information Processing Framework, Online Meeting, April 1, 1997*

1.	SF	SAY	OK. First real item. Let's talk about research, data collection. I have one . . .
2.	EM	THINK	I guess its an experiment worth finding out for sure, though. Ugh!
3.	TM	LOOK BOARD	
4.	MM	DROP	DC (file name)
5.	SF	SAY	suggestion for a group reading. The latest Psych Bull has a review called . . .
6.	SF	SAY	Groups as Information Processors. I suggest it as a basis for some discussion . . .
7.	PM	READ	freedom (file name)
8.	SF	SAY	You don't have to respond to this idea exactly in your turn. Just say whatever . . .
9.	JM	EMOTE	waves hi to all.
10.	JM	EMOTE	is suffering from bad lag.
11.	SF	SAY	you want to say.
12.	MM1	SAY	is it online anywhere?
13.	MM1	(makes command error)	
14.	SF	SAY	No, MM. APA doesn't allow that I don't think?
15.	PM	SAY	Did you want us merely to respond to the idea of Groups as Information Processors?
16.	PF	EMOTE	will update JM via whisper
17.	MM2	SAY	who is the author
18.	MM2	EMOTE	will do a web search
19.	PF	WHISPER- JM	we just set up some rules, SF will call on folks in the following order for comments as we go along. . .
20.	MM2	THINK	MM1 crashed as expected
21.	PF	SAY	PF, MM, LF, NF, PM, EM, TM, JM
22.	SF	SAY	The authors are Hinsz, Tindale, and Vollrath
23.	PF	THINK	oops sorry, i forgot to whisper
24.	PF	WHISPER-JM	you get it :)
25.	JM	EMOTE	nod
26.	PF	EMOTE	smiles

PROTOCOL 2.7. *continued*

27.	SF	SAY	Let's just go around and each person say whatever they would like to say on #1 [refers to item on whiteboard]
28.	SF	SAY	Ideas for research/data collection. PF?
29.	JM	LOOK	(looks at board item 1)
30.	PF	SAY	whoops sorry, i was updating JM so i have to read back
31.	PF	SAY	pass for now
32.	SF	SAY	We're soliciting thoughts, ideas, concerns about data collection. MM?

TOWARD A SYNTHESIS OF FRAMEWORKS

Figure 2.1 represents our synthesis of the four theories discussed in this chapter into a comprehensive framework for guiding research and assessment of online communities. As illustrated, members (M) of various groups and cultures enter the community as newcomers and can eventually become old-timers through their participation in community activity. Boundary constructs are ideas brought to the problem initially by members of diverse backgrounds, and are so named because they represent common concepts within overlapping boundaries of disciplinary knowledge. Through processes of argument, negotiation, conflict, and sharing of information, the boundary constructs evolve into more complex shared ideas, behavioral norms, and other intangible constructs that shape and are shaped by the community's work. Hence, the model illustrated in Fig. 2.1 is consistent with the sociocultural-situative viewpoint discussed previously. This view suggests that by monitoring communities for the presence of important evolving boundary constructs, one can assess whether social knowledge construction is taking place. It also suggests that both negotiation and apprenticeship should account for a large percentage of community interactions. Hence, measures reflecting the presence, frequency, and quality of such processes can be used to judge the efficacy of groups as knowledge construction entities.

In addition to representing a sociocultural-situative viewpoint, Fig. 2.1 is compatible with a sociocognitive perspective, so named because it views knowledge construction as an individual cognitive activity driven by social interaction. Knowledge construction is seen as involving changes and realignments among individuals' mental representations of

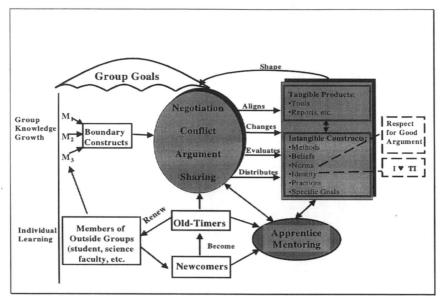

FIG. 2.1.

the community's constructs. As team members work together, their individual mental representations of the community's central constructs will become more compatible through negotiation and apprenticeship. A substantial degree of alignment is considered a necessary precondition for productive work, although some misalignment is desirable as a basis for cognitive growth. When people with different points of view work together, their interactions produce cognitive conflicts that lead to argument, which drives conceptual change. Hence, from the sociocognitive perspective, insurance that communities are operating as knowledge construction systems can be derived from evidence of conceptual and belief change within individuals, and from evidence that there is a trend toward increasing compatibility among members' task-related viewpoints.

Our model in Fig. 2.1 also assimilates a literature that views knowledge construction as both process and product of valid argumentation. This "critical thinking" (e.g., Halpern, 1996) view suggests that negotiation processes should be judged against established standards for argument form and content. It also suggests that the knowledge resulting from valid argument is superior to knowledge resulting from less logical processes. Hence, "respect for good argument" should be a prominent social norm within knowledge-building communities. Communities that base decisions on valid argument should receive high evaluations as knowledge-construction entities. However, recognizing that valid argument in conversation is both infrequent and difficult to detect, both training and tools are required to scaffold it within online environments. Online patterns of usage associated with such tools could be used to help measure and evaluate group knowledge construction.

Assessments of groups as knowledge construction entities must also consider the processes by which information is shared and, as a result, is transformed from one form (e.g., private, unshared knowledge) to another (e.g., shared ephemeral ideas) to another (e.g., a tangible group product). Successful sharing theoretically increases group knowledge and knowledge distribution; hence, measures showing progressively greater and deeper conceptual alignment among members are valid indicators from the information processing viewpoint (as they are from the sociocognitive one). Assessment designs based on group information processing theory can capitalize on the fact that a number of factors are known to shape group information processing. These include social factors, such as member status. Hence, a composite score indicating high cultural–professional diversity within groups (indicative of broad knowledge capacity) and high levels of sharing among all social categories is one potentially excellent normative index for comparing and judging groups as knowledge-construction systems. Other factors shaping group information processing include contexts that have an impact on important information processing phases. In this regard, we limited our discussion to two important phases of information processing: attention and information transformation. In comparatively evaluating the functioning of online communities, we propose incorporating an index derived from observable signs of group attentional deficits. We propose balancing this index by considering evidence that groups employ technological features and practices to compensate for attentional deficits. In addition, we propose evaluating groups by seeking evidence of gaps in the phases whereby information is successfully transformed from one phase to another. A prototype of an assessment strategy following this logic is given in Derry and DuRussel (1999).

The methodologies and assessment techniques that follow from the four theories discussed differ widely. The sociocultural-situative view leads to the examination of teams as units of analysis within the social contexts that constitute them. Observations of groups supply quantitative indexes of knowledge construction that can be used to compare teams and communities with one another. In contrast, the sociocognitive view leads to interviews and other verbal protocol techniques that allow researchers to look inside participants' heads to examine belief change. Measures of individual cognitive conflict and belief change derived from the sociocognitive viewpoint supply types of knowledge-construction indexes that are complementary to the sociocultural-situative ones. One premise of our work is that an integrated approach involving use of multiple perspectives and methodologies will allow a much fuller picture of knowledge construction than could be gained from only one view. For example, we have found that when TAPPED IN discourse does not follow good argument form, the apparent cause is sometimes attentional interference due to multiple conversational threads (as suggested by the group information processing viewpoint) and at other times politeness norms in conversation (as suggested by the sociocultural perspective). We continue to use our multiple-frameworks model as the basis for developing assessment indexes for our investigations within online communities.

REFERENCES

Abelson, R. P. (1995). *Statistics as principled argument*. Hillsdale, NJ: Lawrence Erlbaum Associates.

Agar, M. (1986). *Speaking of ethnography*. Thousand Oaks, CA: Sage.

Cannon-Bowers, J. A., Salas, E., & Converse, S. A. (1993). Shared mental models in expert team decision making. In N. J. Castellan, Jr. (Ed.), *Current issues in individual and group decision making*. Hillsdale, NJ: Lawrence Erlbaum Associates.

Chi, M. T. H. (1997). Quantifying qualitative analyses of verbal data: A practical guide. *Journal of Learning Sciences, 6*(3), 271–316.

Cobb, P., & Yackel, E. (1996). Constructivist, emergent, and sociocultural perspectives in the context of developmental research. *Educational Psychologist, 31*(3/4), 175–130.

Derry, S. J. (1996). Cognitive schema theory and the constructivist debate. *Educational Psychologist 31*, 163–175

Derry, S. J. DuRussel, L. A. (1999). Assessing knowledge construction in on-line learning communities (pp. 431–438). In S. P. Lajoie & M. Vivet (Eds.), *Artificial intelligence in education*. Amsterdam: IOS Press

Derry, S. J., DuRussel, L. A., & O'Donnell, A. M. (1998). Individual and distributed cognitions in interdisciplinary teamwork: A developing case study and emerging theory. *Educational Psychology Review, 10*(1), 25–56.

DuRussel, L. A., & Derry, S. J. (1996). Sociocultural approaches to analyzing cognitive development in interdisciplinary teams. *In Proceedings of the Eigh-*

teenth Annual Meeting of the Cognitive Science Society (pp. 529–533). Hillsdale, NJ: Lawrence Erlbaum Associates

DuRussel, L., & Derry, S. J. (1998). *Mental models in educational research teams.* Poster presented at the 1998 American Educational Research Association Conference, San Diego, CA

Ericsson, K. A., & Simon, H. A. (1984). *Protocol analysis: Verbal reports as data.* Cambridge, MA: MIT Press

Foltz, P. W. (1996). Latent semantic analysis for text-based research. *Behavior Research Methods, Instruments and Computers, 28*(2), 197–202.

Greeno, J. G. (1998). The situativity of knowing, learning, and research. *American Psychologist, 53*(1), 5–26.

Halpern, D. F. (1996). *Thought and knowledge* (3rd ed.). Hillsdale, NJ: Lawrence Erlbaum Associates.

Hinsz, V. B., Tindale, R. S., & Vollrath, D. A. (1997). The emerging conceptualization of groups as information processors. *Psychological Bulletin, 121,* 43–64.

Janis, I. (1982). *Groupthink* (2nd ed.). Boston: Houghton Mifflin.

John-Steiner, V., & Mahn, H. (1996). Sociocultural approaches to learning and development: A Vygotskian framework. *Educational Psychologist, 31*(3/4), 191–206.

Kuhn, Deanna (1991). *The skills of argument.* New York: Cambridge University Press.

Lajoie, S. P., & Derry, S. J. (Eds.). (1993). *Computers as cognitive tools.* Hillsdale, NJ: Lawrence Erlbaum Associates.

Lave, J. (1991). Situated learning in communities of practice. In L. B. Resnick, J. M. Levine, & S. D. Teasley (Eds.), *Perspectives on social shared cognition* (pp. 63–82). Washington, DC: American Psychological Association.

Lave, J., & Wenger, E. (1991). *Situated learning.* New York: Cambridge University Press.

Nardi, B. A. (1998). Activity theory and its use within human-computer interaction. *Journal of Learning Sciences, 7*(2), 257–262.

O'Donnell, A. M., Derry, S. J., & DuRussel, L. A. (1997, April). *Cognitive processes in interdisciplinary groups: Problems and possibilities.* NISE Research Monograph Number 5. University of Wisconsin-Madison, National Institute for Science Education.

Orasanu, J., & Salas, E. (1993). Team decision making in complex environments. In G. A. Klein, J. Orasanu, R. Calderwood, & C. E. Zsambok (Eds.), *Decision making in action: Models and methods.* Norwood, NJ: Ablex.

Pea, Roy (1993). Practices of distributed intelligence and designs for education. In G. Salomon (Ed.), *Distributed cognitions* (pp. 47–87). New York: Cambridge University Press.

Resnick, L. B., Salmon, M., Zeitz, C. M., Wathen, S. H., & Holowchak, M. (1993). Reasoning in conversation. *Cognition and Instruction, 11*(3&4), 347–364.

Roschelle, J. (1998). Activity theory: A foundation for designing learning technology. *Journal of Learning Sciences, 7*(2), 241–256.

Salomon, G. (Ed.). (1993). *Distributed cognitions.* New York: Cambridge University Press.

Schlager, M. S., & Schank, P. K. (1997, December). *TAPPED IN: A new online teacher community concept for the next generation of Internet technology.* Paper presented at CSCL '97, Second International Conference on Computer Support for Collaborative Learning, Toronto.

Smith, J. (1994). *Collective intelligence in computer-based collaborations.* Hillsdale, NJ: Lawrence Erlbaum Associates.

Sproull, L. & Kiesler, S. (1991). *Connections: new ways of working in the networked organization.* Cambridge, MA: MIT Press.

Vygotsky, L. S. (1978). *Mind in society.* Cambridge, MA: Harvard University Press.

Wenger, (1990). *Toward a theory of cultural transparency.* Unpublished doctoral dissertation, University of California-Irvine.

Wertsch, J. V. (1991a). *Voices of the mind: A sociocultural approach to mediated action.* Cambridge, MA: Harvard University Press.

Wertsch, J. V. (1991b). A sociocultural approach to socially shared cognition. In L. B. Resnick, J. M. Levine, & S. D. Teasley (Eds.), *Perspectives on socially shared cognition* (pp. 85–100). Washington, DC: American Psychological Association.

3

Integrating Cognitive Tools for Peer Help: The Intelligent Intranet Peer Help-Desk Project

Jim Greer, Gordon McCalla, John Cooke,
Jason Collins, Vive Kumar,
Andrew Bishop, and Julita Vassileva
University of Saskatchewan

This chapter presents an example of computers as cognitive tools that is somewhat different from those presented in the other chapters of this book. Instead of designing an artificial environment (based on a certain cognitive theory) supporting human learning, we created a tool that supports peer help, which happens naturally in any learning context.

Many authors have pointed out the advantages of peer help as a learning method (Pressley et al., 1992). First, it is deeply situated in a shared context and can therefore provide a stronger learning experience for the person who is asking for help. Second, it promotes processes of self-explanation (Chi, de Leeuw, Chiu, & La Vancher, 1994) and reflection in the helper, and in this way reciprocal learning takes place (Nichols, 1993). Third, it is cost effective, since it uses the learners themselves as a teaching resource. Fourth, it facilitates social interaction in a group of learners and helps to create knowledge-anchored personal relationships among them.

Peer help often happens naturally within cooperative groups of learners. When the group of learners is distributed, however, obstacles arise that interfere with this process. Learners who need help may not know whom to turn to, since they are not able to identify which member of the group is knowledgeable; in fact, they may not even know the other learners. If they did know a potential helper, they would not know (without asking) whether the helper was currently available, which could mean a loss of time and a loss of the immediate context in which the problem had arisen.

Peer help is further diminished in distributed learning environments, which are becoming increasingly popular, especially for organizations providing training courses for their employees on intranets. In distributed intranet learning environments, employees can take a course at their place of work, during their preferred time. In this way companies save a lot of money by not taking people away from their job, not needing to find replacement workers, and not hiring instructors or paying travel expenses. Slowly but steadily, universities are moving toward this model of education too, by providing access to Web-based course materials. But this model of instruction tends to isolate learners and threatens access to peer help.

Through the use of technology, the natural process of peer help in distributed learning environments can be facilitated in several ways:

- By providing an appropriate forum where people can ask subject-related questions and give answers and discuss problems of common interest either synchronously (like a chat facility) or asynchronously (like a newsgroup facility).
- By finding appropriate peer helpers who are knowledgeable and likely to be able to answer a learner's question.
- By providing a shared work space for helper and the person being helped, where they can share the context of the problem.
- By helping the helper better understand the problem of the person asking for help and suggesting a pedagogically appropriate way of helping. For example, sometimes it is pedagogically better not to give any help but to encourage the learner to solve the problem alone.

We have addressed the first two ways of supporting peer help by developing and integrating a set of cognitive tools. The first one, called the Cooperative Peer Response system, provides a suite of World Wide Web–based tools to facilitate cooperative learning, peer help, and expert help within a university course. The CPR discussion forum (the newsgroup facility) encourages peer help, while other knowledge-based components focus on system-generated help. CPR has been deployed in a number of university courses and has proved to be an effective learning support tool.

Another tool, the Peer Help System (PHelpS), contributes to the second way of supporting peer help. PHelpS provides a facility for locating somewhere on the network a peer helper who is ready, willing, and able to provide help, that is, someone who is likely to know the answer (or willing to help find the answer) to a particular help request. A PHelpS prototype has been deployed in a distributed workplace environment, and preliminary experiments suggest that it is an effective training and performance support tool (Collins et al., 1997; McCalla et al., 1997).

The advantage of using an intranet instead of the Internet is that access is restricted to students attending the course; they can communicate only with their peers and teachers. In this way students are protected from possibly disturbing comments made by occasional "visitors" who are not involved in the course. In an Intranet, it is easier to track down what students are doing and to collect information about the topics discussed. This information is used both for improving the peer help facility and as feedback to teachers to adapt the course accordingly. It also eliminates some concerns about the privacy of user information gathered during students' work with the system.

CPR and PHelpS, together with various related spin-off projects, have led to an attempt to integrate several cognitive tools into a new style of intelligent intranet peer help desk facility. Such a help desk draws together a variety of cognitive tools, particularly tools for peer help, into a comprehensive environment to support many styles of learning, like learning by exploring Web-based online materials, discussing, explaining (Webb, 1985), or by teaching (Palthepu, Greer, & McCalla, 1991). This chapter outlines the design of the Intelligent Intranet Help-Desk, focusing on the peer help tools (Collins et al., 1997; McCalla et al., 1997) that act as its structural skeleton.

RATIONALE FOR THE RESEARCH

Universities are experiencing large growths in student/teacher ratios and face the difficult problem of providing adequate help resources for their staff, faculty, and students. Help resources are needed at an institution-wide and a course-specific level due to the limited time that instructors have to provide help and answer questions. Computer technology offers several approaches to facilitating and providing the necessary personalized help resources that can be made available to a mass audience. By deploying intranets in universities, different kinds of resources (e.g., lecture notes, exercises, quizzes, syllabi) can be made available on request to any student. There are numerous positive examples of implementing online course materials and discussion groups at universities, for example, the Virtual-U Project (Virtual-U, 1997), WebCT (Goldberg, 1997), and Quorum (Canas, Ford, Hayes, Brennan, & Reichherzer, 1995). A review of other cognitive approaches on the WWW is presented in Surgue (chap. 5, this volume).

Merely providing access to appropriate material via a network does not solve the problem of providing help. The effects of learning with technology differ from those of learning from technology-based environments. One way to decrease the load of teachers is to provide conditions for students to help each other. Peer help has many pedagogical advantages. For example, it promotes the socializing of students in the context of work and increases their motivation by giving social recognition for their knowledge and helpfulness. Computer technology can be applied to support peer help. There are many computer-supported collaborative learning (CSCL) tools that facilitate communication among peers, for example, Odisseus (Wilkins), Leap (Mitchell, Keller, & Kedar-Cabelli, 1986), Sherlock (Katz & Lesgold, 1993), MemoLab (Dillenbourg, Mendelsohn, & Schneider, 1994), Integration Kid (Chan, 1991, 1993), and PeoplePower (Dilenbourg & Self, 1992). However, they rarely provide personalized help on demand. We propose to develop cognitive tools that support peer help in an individualized way and just in time.

WHAT HAS BEEN DONE?

Cooperative Peer Response Project

Created in the Computer Science Department at the University of Saskatchewan in 1996, the Cooperative Peer Response (CPR) system sought to meet some of the urgent help needs of students in the department. The system provides a discussion forum (a newsgroup-like facility) where students can post questions or comments; an interface to support rapid responses from peers, tutors, or instructors; an accounting system to recognize students who provide and use peer help; a facility for frequently asked questions (FAQ); tools to aid the moderator in constructing and organizing the FAQ; and a database of potential peer helpers. The system can be customized to a particular course, providing peer help and FAQ

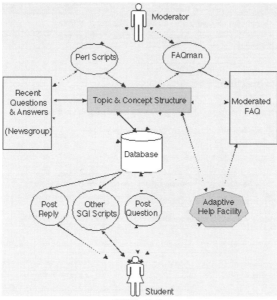

FIG. 3.1.

facilities via the Web. Figure 3.1 presents the complete CPR architecture (the grey components are currently under development).

At the core of the CPR system is a database that keeps tracks of interactions between the user and the system. It is used to create and to maintain Web pages, and keep a profile of each user. To keep the posted material relevant to the particular class, access to the system is restricted to registered users. Three sources of help information (modules) are available in CPR: a rapid response area, called Discussion Forum; an archived section called the Moderated FAQ; and a User Adapted help resource.

Discussion Forum. The presentation and function of the Discussion Forum are similar to a newsgroup, with the content provided by the users themselves. Links to the latest questions and their associated replies are stored on this one HTML page, which is used to organize and index the information found in each separate question file. The most recent questions are placed at the top of the page, and the most recent replies to a particular question are placed at the top of that particular list of replies. This threaded scheme is used in both the Discussion Forum index page (see Fig. 3.2) and the individual HTML page for each particular question and its replies (see Fig. 3.3).

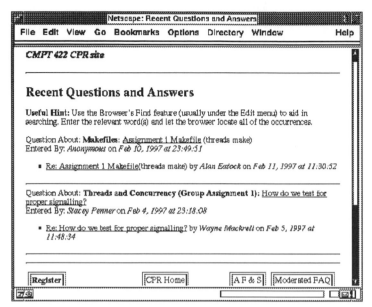

FIG. 3.2.

Each entry in the Discussion Forum consists of a class-specific category or topic; an author (who may be anonymous); subject and keywords (both optional); the posting time; and the text of the question, comment, or reply. If a student posts a question, a peer can post a reply immediately. Thus, help can be available to the user on demand. The class experts can be extremely useful in this medium, increasing the possibility that many good solutions will be proposed for the same problem. The discussion form is maintained by the moderator—an instructor or knowledge manager. A suite of tools supports the moderator to remove from or add entries to the Discussion Forum quickly. This makes it easier to correct erroneous postings. The role of the moderator is to install and maintain the CPR site (including managing user accounts and maintaining the web pages), answer any unanswered postings, and correct any erroneous items. In particular, he or she has to enter the categories that will be used to organize the postings.

Moderated FAQ. The Discussion Forum periodically needs to be pruned to remove outdated entries. Some of these entries might be discarded, but others should be entered into the Moderated FAQ, an archive,

FIG. 3.3.

for future use. The design of the Moderated FAQ pages is similar to a traditional FAQ, with a list of class topic categories, cross-postings of messages in relevant categories, and a table of contents to organize the postings.

A problem with traditional FAQs is maintaining the consistency of messages that have been posted under several topics or easily adding to or removing entries from one or more FAQ subtopics. CPR handles this by manipulating the structure of the FAQ pages through modification of the underlying database. This method also makes it easier to maintain consistency when the actual text of the FAQ entry has been modified. Only the moderated FAQ entry itself needs to be updated as the changes are reflected in all of the relevant class category pages.

The job of the moderator is made easier because the main task is to organize and maintain the archive by selecting the best peer questions and answers rather than to dream up questions and provide answers to all of the questions. Peers will answer the majority of the questions; only the really difficult ones need the moderator. The role of the moderated FAQ is to serve as a repository of reference material available to the class. The information can be expected to be accurate since it was edited by a knowledgeable individual before inclusion, usually after being proposed by classmates.

Evaluation.   The first version of CPR containing these two modules (without the adaptive help facility) has been in use in several computer science courses since the fall of 1996. Throughout each of these courses, different approaches to evaluating the use and user satisfaction with the system were taken. For each of three semesters, data were collected from observation of the system in use, questionnaires completed by the users, and Web server statistics. The students who used the system had high praise for it, but complained about the infrequency of participation of their peers in the discussion forum. The majority of the students thought that the system should be available in all of their courses.

One of the problems that students complained about was that their questions were sometimes unanswered. The time delay in obtaining a useful response was also a complaint. Response time was heavily dependent on who else was online at that time, as well as whether these other users were able and, if so, willing to respond. Sometimes when questions were answered, the responses were not what were required. Subsequent online communication was needed to refine these responses until a useful answer was obtained. These problems highlight the need for automatic help response and for integrating the system with a peer help system like PHelpS, which would find a peer helper with whom the student could communicate online and receive just-in-time help. For this reason CPR is being upgraded with an adaptive help facility.

Adaptive Help Facility.   In order to provide an automatic help facility, CPR must "understand" the student's question. Two of the things that are necessary are a concept map of the topics covered in the course and a keyword synonym dictionary for finding matches to user-entered keywords. A concept map underlying the course was included in CPR so that the threads and FAQs were indexed with respect to the concepts. Using the concept map as a guide, terms that can be used as keywords have to be identified. The system seeks these terms in the question that the student posts. In this way the thread or the FAQ offered to the student is selected by the system depending on the context provided by the question (by use of keywords retrieved from the help-request); in other words, adaptation to the help request takes place.

In order to customize the generated or retrieved answers to the particular student—to take into account in adaptation not only the current help request but also some student-specific information, like his history and knowledge—a student modeling facility had to be developed for CPR. This requires the system to diagnose the student's knowledge related to his current information needs from the history of his reading and posting in CPR and from evaluations of other students and the moderator about such postings. Students have the option to vote for a certain posting (both question and answer) when reading it if they find it especially good or bad. The moderator also has means to "reward" by praising particularly good questions and answers. This leads to updating the student model of the person who submitted the posting by increasing or decreasing the knowledge value of the related concepts. The student model is updated also by taking into account the general activity of the student in CPR: the number of postings he submitted and how many times he has provided answers and about which concepts. Some of the functionality of this adaptive help facility is being developed by Bishop (1998).

In summary, CPR provides a discussion forum for students to post their questions and receive answers from their peers, and a list of FAQs and questions with answers that the moderator considers important and useful. CPR is being upgraded to include an adaptive help facility, which allows the system to suggest to the student a list of FAQ items and discussion threads that may be relevant to the help request. Without generating help or explanation, CPR gives the student a list of pointers to resources where he may find the answer to his question. In this way human peer help is reused in the system.

Peer Help System

Another initiative for employing cognitive tools to enable peer help has focused on learning outside the university context. PHelpS supports workplace training.

In addition to extreme time constraints, workplace training often has very specific task-oriented goals. Workers need authentic learning activities that reflect the tasks for which they are being trained. Also, any environment to support on-the-job training should be consistent with the social environment of the workplace: the worker-to-worker peer interactions, workplace authority structures, and corporate management style.

PHelpS was developed in conjunction with the Correctional Services of Canada (CSC), Canada's prison system. At the heart of CSC activities is the Offender Management System (OMS), an information system that keeps track of information about the inmates in the prison system. Many different kinds of workers at different institutions and locations carry out a variety of tasks with OMS and have to learn to use it effectively. PHelpS supports the training needs of the CSC by helping workers as they carry out these real tasks on the job. The key feature of PHelpS is its ability to assist in locating an appropriate peer to help a worker who is having problems using the OMS.

Peer help within organizations is a valuable activity for a number of reasons: it is cost-effective; it supports decentralization of the organizational knowledge and thus preserves organizational memory; it builds a sense of collegiality within the organization; and it reinforces the knowledge of both the helpers and the persons being helped.

At the heart of PHelpS is a knowledge representation scheme that captures at many levels of detail the authentic tasks carried out at CSC (see Fig. 3.4). Such task hierarchies can become the basis for performance support on the job, structuring training activities in the training center, and structuring communication during peer help interactions. Task hierarchies provide a terse description of steps that must be carried out and the recommended sequence for achieving them. Some of these steps involve the completion of forms in OMS or consultation using information contained in OMS. Workers completing a task with the PHelpS can use the task hierarchy as a checklist to record the subtasks that have been achieved. Task steps can be opened to a finer grain size or left at a coarse grain size, depending on how much detail the worker needs to see in carrying out the task. The worker can check off the tasks undertaken (see the check marks in Fig. 3.4) as a reminder of where she is in undertaking a task. The task checklist is also hyperlinked to OMS, so clicking on a task step can take the user to the relevant OMS screen.

The most important feature of PHelpS is the help facility. When a step in the checklist is causing difficulty, the worker can request a peer helper, which will be selected automatically by the system by consulting the workers' user models. PHelpS consults a knowledge base to locate a set of potential peer helpers who are (a) knowledgeable about the problem area of the specific task; (b) are available to provide help in the time frame required; (c) have not been overburdened with other help requests in the recent past; and (d) have other characteristics critical to a successful peer help session—for example, they speak the same language as the worker (approximately one third of CSC workers speak French as a first language; the rest speak English as their first language). The help request and

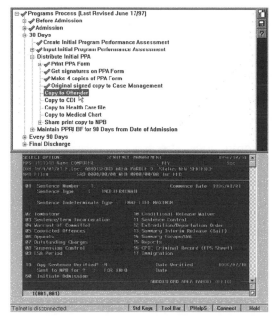

FIG. 3.4.

these criteria form the inputs to a constraint solver embedded in PHelpS, which produces a set of candidate helpers ranked according to their suitability on these criteria. The user selects a preferred helper from the candidate list.

The key to generating a reasonable candidate list intelligently involves maintaining knowledge profiles for every potential helper. The knowledge profiles are organized as overlays on the tasks that need to be achieved within the organization. Thus, for each user, a knowledge profile is constructed that contains a copy of the organization task hierarchies. Each task or subtask is associated with a variable, which can take one of two possible values: 1 (*can help*) or 0 (*can't help*). This knowledge profile, along with other information about each potential helper (language spoken, rank in CSC, current availability), together constitute the user model of each peer helper. (The process of creating and maintaining these user models is described in more detail in Collins et al., 1997.)

In summary, PHelpS incorporates artificial intelligence techniques in a variety of places: to assist with selecting peer helpers, to help maintain learner (and helper) models, and to help structure and mediate communication. (More details about PHelpS architecture and functionality as well as the interesting user modeling and privacy issues that arise can be found in McCalla et al., 1997, and Collins et al., 1997.)

The PHelpS approach can also be applied to support peer help in non-procedural domains. In this case, the task hierarchy should be replaced with another cognitive structure that can help in representing user knowledge and providing context for communication. For example, if PHelpS is going to support peer help in a university course, a topic-concept structure of the course can serve this purpose. That means that the user (the student) is going to communicate her help request via a topic-concept-based interface, where she has to pinpoint the topic or concept related to the request. The student model will contain an overlay over the topic-concept structure, where the student's knowledge on the individual topics or concepts will be recorded. In finding an appropriate partner, PHelpS will have to match the student model with the models of other students, to find peers who are knowledgeable on the topic or concept about which help was requested. In this way, the cognitive structure (task based), which was appropriate for a workplace situation and therefore was used as a basis for organizing the human-computer interaction and user modeling in PHelpS, will be mirrored in another cognitive structure (topic or concept based), which is more appropriate in the new domain of university teaching. This shows how flexible and widely applicable the PHelpS approach is.

WHAT HAD TO BE DONE?

The evaluation of CPR pointed clearly to the need for ensuring just-in-time (JIT) help for students. The reason is that some students are not prepared to wait long for answers to their questions or prefer not to reveal their request to a large audience. Whatever the motives might be, there are also a number of pedagogical advantages of JIT help given by a human peer learner. Usually JIT help is embedded into the system in which the users are performing their workplace tasks, and this makes JIT help highly authentic. JIT help provides training on demand, which happens in an appropriate context for acquiring the piece of knowledge that is of central importance according to socio-constructivism (Clancey, 1992). Therefore, the integration of CPR and PHelpS approaches follows logically as a next step toward comprehensive peer help support.

The Intelligent Intranet Help-Desk is an integration of CPR and PHelpS that provides individualized online multimodal peer help. In this integrated system, CPR acts as a medium for multiple users to communicate with one another in electronic and asynchronous ways and provides a

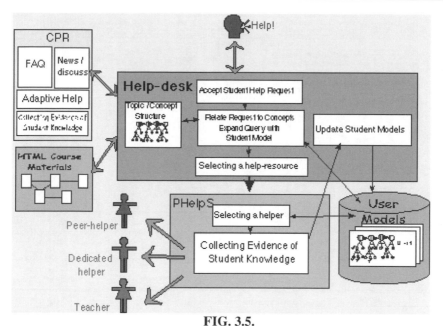

FIG. 3.5.

resource for adaptive help. The role of PHelpS is to select an appropriate human helper when necessary and to facilitate the subsequent direct communication between the peers.

The Help-Desk accepts and interprets help requests from students. Help requests can be made directly or while browsing through course materials or working with CPR. The Help-Desk locates an appropriate help resource (e.g., related FAQs, a discussion thread related to the help request, or Web pages addressing the concepts involved in the help request) or a knowledgeable peer helper (see Fig. 3.5).

Architecture

The main idea is to use a representation of the course topic and concept structure in order to map the content of help requests to the available help resources (FAQ items, discussion threads) and with the knowledge profiles of potential peer helpers. Therefore, the Help-Desk is a knowledge-based component. It contains a representation of the concepts and topics taught in the course. This representation is needed in order to "understand" the student's request and relate it to articles and relevant discussion threads in CPR and to the knowledge of her peers. We use a two-layered knowledge representation, similar to the one used in BIP (Woolf &

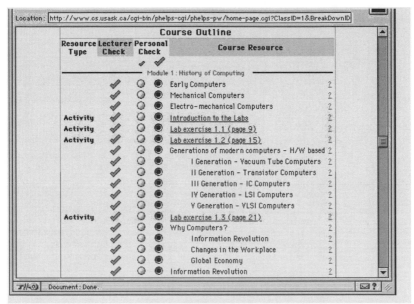

FIG. 3.6.

McDonald, 1984). The first, coarser topic level (see Fig. 3.6) represents the organization of the course and the activities taking place during it (lectures, chapters or subchapters, exercises, labs, assignments, tests).

On the second level, the deeper concepts addressed by the topics taught in the course are represented. Several topics can relate to one concept (e.g., several lectures, exercises, or assignments may relate to various aspects of recursion). Similarly, one topic may address several concepts (e.g., a lecture on Web searching might refer to concepts such as "browsing" of "search strategies"). A student who wants to ask a question selects a topic or a concept from the specially developed interface based on the topic or concept (in PHelpS manner), which is shown in Fig. 3.6. (Currently, there is no graphical distinction between topics and concepts in the interface in order not to overload the student cognitively.)

Student Modeling

We have adopted a pragmatic approach to student modeling, which is based on known techniques combined in a novel way to support the various functions the model has in supporting adaptation to the student and peer helper selection. We have been looking into the three major theories of learning and cognition in collaboration (Dillenbourg, Baker, Blaye, & O'Malley 1994): socio-constructivist (Doise, 1990; Piaget, 1928, 1932), socio-cultural (Vygotsky, 1978), and the shared cognition theory (Brown, Collins, & Duguid, 1988; Lave & Wenger, 1991) in order to find a theoretical background for developing our own student modeling approach. However, all of these theories have failed so far in developing elaborate analytic models of group learning (VanLehn, Ohlsson, & Nason, 1994). Therefore, it is difficult, if not impossible, to apply existing cognitive theories of group learning fully in the construction of intelligent learning or help environments. Nevertheless, we strongly believe that partial solutions should be sought.

In the Help-Desk we have applied two simple and well-known representation techniques for student modeling: a numeric overlay and a profile of several general parameters. The student models are stored in a database (see Fig. 3.5). Two types of evidence are used to update the student models: direct and indirect. The direct evidence comes from observed students' actions. During students' work with the Web-based materials, CPR, and PHelpS, the Help-Desk collects evidence about student knowledge and updates the individual student models. There are at least 10 sources of direct evidence about the student that can be used:

- The history of studied topics in the course.
- The assignment grades of students (providing direct evidence for concept knowledge).
- Explicit testing on topics.
- The student's self-assessment.
- The teacher's assessment.
- Voting in the newsgroup in CPR (about which answers are good).
- Posted questions and answers in CPR.
- Observation of CPR browsing (threads visited, participation).
- Observation of browsing in the Web-based course materials.
- Feedback by the peer helper about the student.
- Feedback by the student about the peer helper.

All of these sources of evidence are domain independent. However, the mechanism for collecting evidence has to be contextualized for a different domain with respect to the reliability of the source.

Every student model has two parts. The first part contains general information about the student, such as name, alias (for students who wish to have one for privacy reasons), and several parameters providing a general evaluation of the student. These include general helpfulness, general knowledgeability, overall willingness to help, and history data (e.g., how active he has been in general and how many times he has given help recently). These general parameters contribute to the calculation of the score for every student when a peer helper has to be selected by PHelpS.

The kernel of the student model is a numeric overlay over the concept-topic structure. This overlay model provides information about how much the student knows about each concept and topic. The Help-Desk uses it in order to "understand" the student's help request better, that is, to place it in the right context (of the current topic) and to expand it eventually with related concepts, which are considered not known by the student (according to the student model).

The indirect evidence for updating the student models is gathered from the observed evidence about knowledge of certain concepts and topics and propagating it to related concepts and topics. In order to make this clear, we explain the concept-topic structure in more detail (see Fig. 3.7). The topic structure includes prerequisite links (what should be taught before what) and temporal links (which topic was actually taught before which). Each topic can be broken down into subtopics to decompose the structure further. In this way the topic structure is an AND/OR graph representing an aggregation hierarchy (McCalla et al., 1982) ordered according to prerequisite links and temporal links. Each of the topics may be connected to multiple concepts in the concept structure. Concepts represent the teaching goals—the elements of knowledge that the student has to develop as a result of taking the course. Concepts can be related to other concepts through various semantic links, including abstraction and aggregation (which may use AND/OR clustering semantics), causal links, analogy links, and prerequisite links.

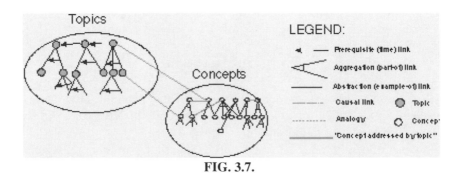

FIG. 3.7.

Why do we need a two-layered knowledge representation? The topic structure provides a natural way to represent the position of a student in a course. However, it is not fine-grained enough to represent the differences in knowledge or understanding among peers who are taking the same course. All it can state is the historical fact that the students have attended a certain lecture or have done a certain assignment. A finer distinction is needed in order to find capable peer helpers, which reflects the knowledge of students and their ability or understanding. This distinction can be found only at the concept level, since every topic, subtopic, assignment, and test is related to a (set of) concept(s). Another advantage of maintaining a concept level is the possibility of taking into account the various semantic links among concepts and propagating knowledge values in user profiles through the concept network. In this way the system will not only know what the student has been taught, but by observing knowledge about one concept (e.g., good performance on a test), the system is also able to deduce that the student is likely to have knowledge on a related concept. In this way the knowledge value on one concept can be propagated to related concepts. As a result, a help request addressing a given concept may be directed to a helper who has not demonstrated knowledge exactly on this concept, but is expected to have it because of having successfully mastered a closely related concept.

Knowledge propagation can happen among concepts or among topics and also between the two levels (from topics to concepts). Following the prerequisite links at the topic level, the system can conclude that if a student is currently working on topic B, which has topic A as a prerequisite, the student has some knowledge of A (see Fig. 3.8). Following temporal links, the system can conclude that if a student is currently working on topic C, which was preceded by B, the student should have some knowledge of B.

Following the topic-concept links, the system can conclude that if a student has learned topic A with related concepts 1, 2, and 3, she has some

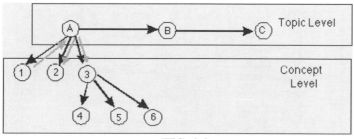

FIG. 3.8.

knowledge of these concepts. Propagation in the opposite direction is also possible. For example, if there was strong evidence that the student knows concept 1, which is related to topic A, which is related to two other concepts, 2 and 3, the system can conclude that the student has learned topic A and is also knowledgeable about concepts 2 and 3.

Following the semantic links among concepts, one can also make some conclusions about general knowledge levels. For example, if the student knows concept 3, which is an abstraction of 4, 5, and 6, the system can conclude that the student knows at least one of the examples 4, 5, or 6.

The propagation techniques have been developed ad hoc for the particular concept structure of the course. We intend to overlay Bayesian belief networks (Jameson, 1996) on these concept structures in the future. The updating and propagation of knowledge values through the topic and concept level of all student models take place all the time, even while the student is not online. In this way the models are always kept up to date, and when a help request is posed or a peer helper is required, the system can react quickly.

The student models are inspectable by both students and teachers (Paiva, Self, & Hartley, 1995). The interface (see Fig. 3.6) visualizes the knowledge values of each topic and concept from the individual student model. The student can change these values by clicking on the radio but-

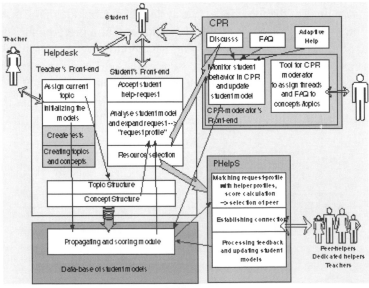

FIG. 3.9.

ton of the concept. In this way the unavoidable imprecision and errors that can happen in diagnosis (i.e., in the interpretation of direct evidence and propagation) can be corrected by a human.

Help-Desk Functionality

The scheme of the Help-Desk's functionality is shown in Fig. 3.9. The student's request for help, expanded with related concepts and topics that he is believed not to know (according to the student model), is passed further to CPR in order to recommend a thread or posting in the FAQ, which corresponds to the concepts related to the query. If no such resource is available in CPR or if the student has chosen explicitly to request a human helper, the expanded request is passed on to PHelpS to find an appropriate peer helper.

PHclpS finds a peer (student) who is currently online and is knowledgeable about the concepts related to the help request. PHelpS then contacts this student. If the student agrees to help, a synchronous or asynchronous connection is established, so that the helper can answer the question or explore some follow-up questions with the student needing help. If such a dialogue is established and carried through to conclusion, then the Help-Desk presents an evaluation form to both the student who asked for help and the helper so that both can provide feedback on the quality of help and the level of knowleddge of each other. This feedback is used to update the models of the helper and the student requesting help.

DISCUSSION

The Intelligent Intranet Peer Help-Desk can be considered an integration of tools for peer help. Some of them (CPR) provide electronic help, and some (PHelpS) provide human help. In both cases it is peer help, since the help originates from students themselves. In the case of CPR, students are the authors of postings that provide answers to student questions. In the case of PHelpS, student peers are directly contacted to provide help on request. It has been shown that those who benefit most in peer collaboration are those who provide the most elaborate explanations (Dansereau, 1988; Webb, 1985). That means that helping peers through explanation should contribute to the helpers' learning. Explaining and elaboration are found to be catalysts for effective collaborative learning process (Chi, Bassok, Lewis, Reinman, & Glaser, 1989). It has also been shown that peer help is most successful when there are small differences in the cognitive levels of the partners (Kuhn, 1972). Dufree, Lesser, and Corkill (1989) showed that nonoverlapping misconceptions in peers lead to better performance in collaboration. Therefore, the selection of a peer helper must take into account the knowledge of the students. By providing an environment supporting peer help, we create the basis for peer explanation and therefore, collaboration. The Help-Desk is a cognitive tool because it creates cognitively determined conditions for peer help and collaboration to happen by selecting an appropriate help resource (electronic or human), which is based on modeling student knowledge and on a cognitive (conceptual) model of the subject material. The user modeling technique employed (numeric overlay modeling with propagation and updating) is standard and is not a research contribution by itself. Our approach has to be seen as an application of simple but efficient user modeling techniques for supporting the provision of peer help in a distributed learning environment. This support takes place at two levels: the selection of appropriate electronic material relevant to the help request and the selection of a knowledgeable human peer who is likely to help.

One important issue in the Help-Desk is the motivation of students to give help to strangers when this is not explicitly rewarded. In a university environment, there exists a reward system (the grades) that can be employed in increasing students' motivation to act as peer helpers. This can be done by appropriately integrating the Help-Desk in the existing curriculum. Apart from such pragmatic benefits of using the Help-Desk as a helper, there might also be more intrinsic sources of motivation. Numerous studies (Bandura, 1986; Schlenker, 1985; Shamir, 1991) suggest that people are not only pragmatic, but also expressive of feelings, values, and self-identities. If technical expertise is important in self-identity, experts who help strangers on a computer network gain such personal benefits as an increase in self-esteem, self-respect, respect from others, and feelings of commitment. Slavin (1990) pointed out that providing help increases the social status of the helper.

We can summarize the main characteristics of our Intelligent Intranet Peer Help-Desk in the following way:

- It is not an artificial learning environment or agent.
- It supports the existing process of work and studies in a distributed learning situation.
- It relies on and coordinates electronic and human help.

- It places a "human in the loop" to whom the cognitively difficult tasks (generation of help and diagnosis) can be delegated naturally.

COMPARISON WITH OTHER WORK

There have been numerous approaches in the field of artificial intelligence and education aimed at providing peer help for the learner. Most of them, however, try to create an artificial peer: an intelligent component or agent who collaborates with the learner, an approach that was originally proposed by Self in 1986. Examples of such artificial peers are Gilmore and Self's (1988) or Dillenbourg and Self's (1992) artificial co-learners, Chan and Baskin's (1990) learning companions, and Aimeur and Frasson's (1996) "troublemaker." All of these systems are focused on collaborative problem solving (and consequently have a very restricted domain of application). They generate help and utterances themselves (using their knowledge bases) and decide when to interfere (using their pedagogical strategies). In this sense they are classic intelligent tutoring systems.

Our approach to providing peer help differs significantly from these classic approaches. First, our domain is not restricted to specific problem solving since the sources of evidence on which the updating of the student models is based are domain independent. The subject domain of the Help-Desk can be as wide as needed; the only requirement is the existence of some kind of domain structuring (into topics, concepts, tasks, or skills) to which help requests can be indexed. Second, there is minimal automatic generation of computer-based help, so the system can perform with a less extensive knowledge base and less sophisticated reasoning mechanisms. All the help entries are generated by the students themselves, by means of posting questions and answers to the discussion forums in CPR and by providing direct help using PHelpS. Third, the system does not interfere with the help dialogue and does not make pedagogical decisions. It is activated only by an explicit request from the student. In this way the Intelligent Intranet Peer Help-Desk involves human intellect at all points that are currently considered the Achilles' heels of artificial intelligence–based learning environments: the diagnosis of a student's knowledge, pedagogical decision making, and generating the instructional content.

The Intelligent Intranet Peer Help-Desk can be compared with other student model–based approaches for selecting an appropriate human helper. Hoppe's (1995) COSOFT project is the first ambitious project to address several issues related to the use of student modeling in order to parameterize human-human collaboration. These issues include the composition of a learning group from a known set of students, and especially the selection of a peer helper, the identification of problems to be dealt with in a collaborative session, or the selection of tasks that are adequate for a given learning group. Hoppe's approach has been primarily targeted at exploring possible improvements to group student modeling to support human collaboration. It focuses on a limited domain since it employs more sophisticated diagnosis, representation, and matching. In addition, it is intended to support only human-human collaboration, but not to be integrated with an automatic advice or help utility. Our Help-Desk uses the same student models for both selection of human partners and providing electronic help. Unlike COSOFT, the student modeling approach employed in our Help-Desk relies on human feedback in addition to computer diagnosis. This makes it easily transferable to a different domain. The modification of PHelpS (a task-based help system supposed to help in procedural domain) to a concept- and topic-based help system took about four weeks of work for one programmer. We expect that changing to a different topic-concept structure for a different domain will take even less time.

PROSPECTS FOR FUTURE WORK

There are two main trends for future development of the Intelligent Intranet Peer Help-Desk that we want to investigate: extending the support of the system from peer help to full peer collaboration and increasing the intelligence of this support. More specifically, we plan to pursue the following directions:

- *Ensuring common work spaces for helper and the person being helped in PHelpS.* By ensuring a shared clipboard, whiteboard, and Internet phone and providing the possibility for sharing applications, the context in which the student's problem has arisen will be more readily shared between the student and the peer helper. This will make the communication between all participants easier. Also the system will be able to track individual interactions for later analysis. This capability will provide the possibility of improving and deepening the diagnosis for student modeling, provided, of course, that an appropriate diagnostic component for the subject matter is found or created. This will narrow the domain but should increase the quality of the Help-Desk support.

- *Incorporating pedagogical competence in the system.*   Currently the Help-Desk does not make any explicit pedagogical decisions. For example, the decision as to whether to suggest electronic help (via CPR) or human help (via PHelpS) is implicitly encoded in the algorithm of the Help-Desk: a peer helper is sought only when there is no available electronic resource or when the student has requested a human helper. This decision can be made explicit and managed by some pedagogical rules— for example, if the student has not been active in CPR, to suggest that she post a question to CPR before calling a human helper .

- *Providing pedagogical support for helpers.*   Based on the student model, the system can provide pedagogical support for the helper (Kumar, 1998). As a simple example, it can suggest what kind of communication channel would be more suited to the student (e.g., shared whiteboard, or Internet phone, or just a chat environment) based on the type of communication channel that has been most successful with this student. It can also suggest a level of explanation based on how many times the student has asked for help (people who constantly ask for help could be given very general help in order to force them to try to solve the problem themselves). If the student model contains some deeper subject-dependent knowledge, instructional planning techniques could be used to provide the peer with a particular plan to explain the problem to the student needing help. Also, given a strong and reliable diagnostic component, the system will be able to suggest to the helper where the student's problem lies, taking into account the student model (of her knowledge or misconceptions) (Kumar, 1997).

- *Integrating collaboration tools with the Intelligent Intranet Peer Help-Desk.*   In addition to CPR and PHelpS, collaborative tools such as Microsoft NetMeeting could be integrated with the Help-Desk to support collaborative activity and teamwork. On the basis of the student models, the collaboration component could select not only one peer helper, but several partners to form a team for solving the problem or answering a help request. Also, given a catalogue of assignments, this component could create teams of students and select appropriate assignments for them. The selection of partners for a team could be based on principles of complementarily or competitiveness of skills proposed by Hoppe (1995) and implemented by Mühlenbrock, Tewissen, and Hoppe (1997) and Ikeda, Go, and Mizoguchi (1997).

- *Decomposing the architecture into smaller intelligent components* (plugins, or agents).   This system readily lends itself to an agent architecture (Nwana, 1996; Vassileva, 1998), where the components can pursue their own goals. For example, there could be an agent associated with every student who filters help requests from the agents of other students. Each personal agent would be equipped with pedagogical knowledge and knowledge about the student (a detailed student model). Based on this knowledge and the student's goal or request, the personal agents would search for appropriate other agents that can fulfill the student goal. This can be another personal agent (of a student who is willing to help), several other personal agents (of students who wish to collaborate), or an application agent. Application agents represent specific applications, like online courses, or CPR, or subcomponents of it. For example, the Discussion Forum could be represented by an agent offering a space to post questions and answers, or the FAQ could be represented by an agent that offers answers to certain questions. The agents can communicate via a broker or could be completely decentralized. The matching of requests and offers would happen through negotiation among the agents.

We are pursuing a simultaneous development of the Help-Desk in breadth (employing computer-supported collaborative work tools to facilitate sharing workspaces and applications and rebuilding the system in a highly flexible and modular way) and in depth (using artificial intelligence techniques to amplify the abilities of the Help-Desk in diagnosis, pedagogy, and collaboration support). We believe this broad and interesting research perspective should result in the construction of flexible, usable, robust, and sophisticated tools to support human learning that are characterized by their ability to react to individual differences among learners.

ACKNOWLEDGMENTS

This research was carried out under the auspices of the Canadian Tele-learning Network of Centres of Excellence, project 6.2.4.

REFERENCES

Aimeur, E., & Frasson, C. (1996). Analysing a new learning strategy according to different knowledge levels. *Computer and Education, An International Journal, 27*(2), 115–127.
Bandura, A. (1986). *Social foundations of thought and action: A social cognitive theory.* Englewood Cliffs, NJ: Prentice-Hall.

Bishop, A. (1998). *System-generated help responses for the cooperative peer response system.* Unpublished master's. thesis, Department of Computer Science, University of Saskatchewan.

Brown, J. S., Collins, A., & Duguid, P. (1988). *Situated cognition and the culture of learning* (Tech. Rep.). Institute for Research on Learning.

Canas, A., Ford, K., Hayes P., Brennan, J., & Reichherzer, T. (1995). Knowledge construction and sharing in quorum. In J. Greer (Ed.), *Artificial intelligence and education, Proceedings AIED'97* (pp. 218–225). Charlottesville, VA: Association for Advancement of Computers in Education.

Chan, T. W. (1991). Integration-Kid: A learning companion system. In J. Mylopoulos & R. Reiter (Eds.), *Proceedings of the 12th International Conference on AI* (Vol. 2, pp. 1094–1099). San Mateo, CA: Morgan Kaufmann.

Chan, T. W (1993). A tutorial on social learning systems. In T. Chan & J. A. Self (Eds.), *Emerging computer technologies in education* (pp. 71–96). Charlottesville, VA: Association for Advancement of Computers in Education.

Chan, T. W., & Baskin A. (1990). Learning companion systems. In C. Frasson & G. Gauthier (Eds.), *Intelligent tutoring systems: On the crossroads of AI and education* (pp. 6–33). Norwood, NJ: Ablex.

Chi, M. T., Bassok, M., Lewis, M., Reinman, P., & Glaser, R. (1989). Self-explanations: How students study and use examples in learning to solve problems. *Cognitive Science, 13,* 259–294.

Chi, M. T. H., de Leeuw, N., Chiu, M. H., & La Vancher, C. (1994). Eliciting self-explanations improves understanding. *Cognitive Science, 18,* 439–477.

Clancey, W. (1992). In defence of cognitive apprenticeship. *Journal of AI and Education, 3,* 139–168.

Collins, J., Greer, J., Kumar, V., McCalla, G., Meagher P., & Tkach, R. (1997). Inspectable user models for just in time workplace training. In A. Jameson, C. Paris, & C. Tasso (Eds.), *User modeling: Proceedings of the UM97 Conference* (pp. 327–337). New York: Springer.

Dansereau, D. (1988). *Learning and study strategies: Issues in assessment, instruction and evaluation.* New York: Academic Press.

Dillenbourg, P., Baker, M., Blaye, A., & O'Malley C. (1994). The evolution of research on collaborative learning. [Online]. Available: *http://tecfa.unige. ch/tecfa-research/lhm/ESF-Chap5.text.*

Dillenbourg, P., Mendelsohn , P., & Schneider, D. (1994). The distribution of pedagogical roles in a multi-agent learning environment. In R. Lewis & P. Mendelsohn (Eds.), *Lessons from learning* (pp. 199–216). Amsterdam: North-Holland.

Dillenbourg, P., & Self, J. (1992). A computational approach to socially distributed cognition. *European Journal of Psychology of Education, 7*(4), 353–372.

Doise, W. (1990). The development of individual competencies through social interaction. In H. Foot, M. Morgan, & R. Shute (Eds.) *Children helping children* (pp. 43–64). New York: Wiley.

Dufree, E. H., Lesser, V. R., & Corkill, D. D. (1989). *Cooperative distributed problem solving*. Reading, MA: Addison-Wesley.

Gilmore, D. & Self, J. (1988). The application of machine learning to intelligent tutoring systems. In J. Self (Ed.), *Artificial intelligence and human learning: Intelligent computer assisted instruction* (pp.179–196). New York: Chapman & Hall.

Goldberg, M. (1997). *WebCT—Word Wide Web Course Tools*. [Online]. Available: *http://www.webct.com*

Hoppe, H.-U. (1995). The use of multiple student modeling to parameterise group learning. In J. Greer (Ed.), *Artificial intelligence and education, Proceedings of AIED'95* (pp. 234–241). Charlottesville, VA: Association for Advancement of Computers in Education.

Ikeda, M., Go, S., & Mizoguchi, R. (1997). Opportunistic group formation. In B. duBoulay & R. Mizoguchi (Eds.), *Artificial intelligence and education, Proceedings of AIED'97* (pp. 167–174).Amsterdam: IOS Press.

Jameson, A. (1996). Numerical uncertainty management in user and student modeling. *User Modeling and User Adapted Interaction, 5,* 193–251.

Katz, S., & Lesgold, A. (1993). The role of the tutor in computer-based collaborative learning situations. In S. Lajoie & S. Derry (Eds.), *Computers as cognitive tools*. Hillsdale, NJ: Lawrence Erlbaum Associates.

Kuhn, D. (1972). Mechanisms of change in the development of cognitive structures. *Child Development, 43,* 833–844.

Kumar, V. (1997, December). *CSCL environment for distributed collaboration*. Paper presented at the Doctoral Consortium of the Conference of Computer Supported Collaborative Learning CSCL'97, Toronto.

Kumar, V. (1998). *Helping the helper in knowledge-supported, collaborative, distributed network of peers*. Unpublished doctoral dissertation proposal, Department of Computer Science, University of Saskatchewan.

Lave, J., & Wenger, E. (Eds.). (1991). *Situated learning: Legitimate peripheral participation*. New York: Cambridge University Press.

McCalla, G. I., Peachey, D. R., & Ward, B. (1982). An architecture for the design of large scale intelligent teaching systems. *Proceedings of the Fourth National Conference of CSCSI*. Saskatoon, Saskatchewan.

McCalla, G., et al. (1997). A peer help system for workplace training. In B. duBoulay & R. Mizoguchi (Eds.), *Artificial intelligence and education, Proceedings of AIED'97* (pp. 183–191). Amsterdam: IOS Press.

Mitchell, T., Keller, R., & Kedar-Cabelli, S. (1986). Explanation-based generalization: A unifying view. *Machine Learning, 1,* 47–80.

Mühlenbrock, M., Tewissen, F., & Hoppe H. U. (1997). A framework system for intelligent support in open distributed learning environments. In B. duBoulay & R. Mizoguchi (Eds.), *Artificial intelligence and education, Proceedings of AIED'97* (pp. 191–198). Amsterdam: IOS Press.

Nichols, D. (1993). Intelligent student systems: Learning by teaching. In P. Brna, S. Ohlsson, & H. Pain (Eds.), *Artificial intelligence and education: Proceedings of AIED'93* (p. 576). Charlottesville, VA: Association for Advancement of Computers in Education.

Nwana, H. (1996). Software agents: An overview. *Knowledge Engineering Review, 11,* 1–40.

Paiva, A., Self, J., & Hartley, R. (1995). Externalizing learner models. In J. Greer (Ed.), *Artificial intelligence in education: Proceedings of AI-ED 95* (pp. 509–516). Charlottesville, VA: AACE.

Palthepu, S., Greer, J., & McCalla, G. (1991). Learning by teaching. In *Proceedings of the International Conference on Learning Sciences* (pp. 357–363). Chicago: Northwestern University.

Piaget, J. (1928). *Judgement and reasoning in the child.* New York: Harcourt Brace.

Piaget, J. (1932). *The moral judgement of the child.* London: Routledge and Kegan Paul.

Pressley, M., et al. (1992). Encouraging mindful use of prior knowledge: Attempting to construct explanatory answers to facilitate learning. *Educational Psychologist, 27,* 91–109.

Schlenker, B. (1985). Identity and self-identification. In B. Schlenker (Ed.), *The self and social life.* New York: McGraw-Hill.

Shamir, B. (1991). Meaning, self and motivation in organizations. *Organization Studies, 12,* 405–424.

Self, J. (1986). The application of machine learning to student modeling. *Instructional Science, 14,* 327–388.

Slavin, R. E. (1990). *Cooperative learning: Theory, research and practice.* Englewood Cliffs, NJ: Prentice-Hall.

VanLehn, K., Ohlsson, S., & Nason, R. (1994). Applications of simulated students: An exploration. *Journal of Artificial Intelligence and Education, 5,* 135–175.

Vassileva, J. (1998). Goal-based autonomous social agents: Supporting adaptation and teaching in a distributed environment. In *Proceedings of ITS'98* (pp. 494–503). Berlin: Springer Verlag.

Virtual-U. (1997). Simon Fraser University. *Virtual-U Research Project* [Online]. Accessed November 10, 1999.

Vygotsky, L. (1978). *Mind in society: The development of higher psychological processes.* Cambridge, MA: Harvard University Press.

Webb, N. (1985). *Learning to cooperate, cooperating to learn.* New York: Plenum Publishing.

Wilkins, D. (1988). Apprenticeship learning techniques for knowledge-based systems, Stan-cs–88–142, Stanford University.

Woolf, B., & McDonald, D. (1984). Building a computer tutor: Design issues. *IEEE Computer, 17,* 61–73.

4

Facilitating Students' Inquiry Learning and Metacognitive Development Through Modifiable Software Advisers

Barbara Y. White and Todd A. Shimoda
University of California at Berkeley

John R. Frederiksen
Educational Testing Service, Oakland, California

In this chapter, we argue that young students need to develop conscious, explicit theories of their own and each other's cognitive and social processes. Such awareness can enable them to engage in reflective conversations about the nature, purpose, and utility of these processes and thereby come to understand them better, use them more effectively, and improve them. In particular, we discuss the importance of facilitating young students' development of widely applicable theories about collaborative inquiry and reflective learning. Enabling them to construct such theories should lead to improvements in their learning and reflection skills as well as to their metacognitive development in general.

Software could play a central role in such theory-building processes. Our hypothesis is that complex performances, such as collaborative inquiry and reflective learning, can best be understood as the product of a social system of interacting agents, each with expertise in accomplishing particular high-level goals. We have embedded this view of performance in a computer environment called the Thinker Tools SCI-WISE system. SCI-WISE houses a community of software agents, such as a Planner, an Inventor, and a Collaborator. The agents give strategic advice and guide users as they undertake research projects and as they reflect on and revise their inquiry processes. SCI-WISE also enables users to modify the advisory system so that it expresses their own theories of how to engage in inquiry and how best to coach and scaffold the process.

Our goal is for young students to work with SCI-WISE to develop explicit theories of the social and cognitive processes needed for collaborative inquiry and reflective learning. To facilitate this, we are creating curricular activities in which middle school students engage in inquiry about their own inquiry processes, thereby making inquiry and metacognition themselves into objects that they investigate. In these activities, students develop hypotheses about how best to support inquiry and use SCI-WISE as a modeling tool to represent their ideas. They then carry out research to evaluate their hypotheses by following the advice given by their SCI-WISE models. For example, they use their version of SCI-WISE to guide them as they do a physics project and, as they do this, they also evaluate the helpfulness of their SCI-WISE system. While the students undertake this research, we investigate whether this form of inquiry about inquiry does indeed foster their sociocognitive and metacognitive development.

METACOGNITION AND LEARNING THROUGH INQUIRY

Some of the most intriguing and important work in the field of cognition and instruction focuses on students' understanding of and theorizing about their own cognitive processes. Brown (1987) pointed out that discussion about the importance of what we presently refer to as "metacognition" and "theory of mind"[1] goes back at least as far as Plato. In the past century, Dewey, Piaget, Vygotsky, and other influential thinkers have argued that knowledge and control of one's own cognitive system play a key role in cognitive development. For example, Piaget (1976) held that being aware of and reflecting on one's cognition is an important capability that is one of the defining characteristics of the most advanced stages of cognitive development. Further, Vygotsky (1978) claimed that children progress from relying on others, such as teachers, to help regulate their cognition to

---

[1]Developmental psychologists frequently use the term *theory of mind* to refer to children's knowledge of other people's beliefs and intentions (Astington, Harris, & Olson, 1988; Feldman, 1992). Here we focus on their knowledge of their own as well as others' social, cognitive, and metacognitive processes, particularly those related to problem solving, learning, reflection, and learning to learn.

being able to regulate it themselves, having internalized the regulation and control skills that others have modeled.

Recent research adds additional theoretical and empirical support to arguments regarding the important role that metacognition plays in students' academic performance and cognitive development (Baird, Fensham, Gunstone, & White, 1991; Bassock, Chi, Glaser, Lewis, & Reimann, 1989; Glaser & Schauble, 1990; Schoenfeld, 1987). Our own work, for example, indicates that enabling students to develop metacognitive expertise plays a major role in facilitating inquiry learning, particularly for academically disadvantaged students (Frederiksen & White, 1998). In addition, certain types of social interactions and activities, such as collaborative work and peer tutoring, have been shown to facilitate learning and development (Brown & Palincsar, 1989; Driver, Asika, Leach, Mortimer, & Scott, 1994; Okada & Simon, 1997; Slavin, 1995), as have social structures introduced to create classroom communities that embody social constructivist approaches to learning (Bielaczyc & Collins, 1999; Brown & Campione, 1996; Palincsar & Brown, 1989). Such findings support the view that social processes as well as cognitive processes play a major role in students' academic performance and cognitive development (Damon, 1990; Vygotsky 1978; Wertsch, 1991). We conjecture that enabling students to develop explicit theories about social processes, like collaboration, as well as cognitive processes can further enhance their learning and development.

These considerations lead us to a broad view of metacognition that encompasses (a) knowledge about knowledge, including knowledge of the form and content of cognitive and social expertise and when and why such expertise is useful; (b) regulatory skills, including skills needed to employ sociocognitive expertise, such as planning and monitoring skills; and (c) developmental expertise, including the ability to reflect on sociocognitive and metacognitive knowledge and its use in order to modify and improve both of these.

Given its importance, how can we enable young students to develop such metalevel expertise? We think one promising approach is to start by helping students learn about the nature and processes of scientific inquiry. It has long been argued that there may be correspondences between children's learning and cognitive development in the classroom and scientists' theory creation and revision processes in the scientific community (Dewey, 1910; Piaget, 1976; Vygotsky, 1978). For example, Piaget (1976) used the metaphor of "child as scientist" and argued that being able to consciously invent, test, and modify theories as well as talk about them with others is a characteristic of the most advanced stage of cognitive development, which he termed *formal operations*. Further, a post-Piagetian paradigm is emerging, sometimes termed the *theory theory*, which holds that there are similarities between how young children develop theories and how theories evolve in science (Brewer & Samarapunghavan, 1991; Nersessian, 1991) and, furthermore, that such theory formation and inquiry processes are central to children's learning (Dewey, 1938; Gopnik, 1996; Karmiloff-Smith & Inhelder, 1974–1975; White, 1993). To develop these critical inquiry skills, some educational researchers have taken the approach of transforming classrooms into learning communities in which young students engage in scientific research (Brown & Campione, 1996; Scardamalia & Bereiter, 1994). We conjecture that taking the additional step of having students create and test explicit theories about their inquiry processes, making inquiry itself a topic of research, will further enhance the development of students' learning skills as well as foster their metacognitive development in general.

In our prior work (White, 1993; White & Frederiksen, 1998), we attempted to create classroom research communities and worked on facilitating students' awareness of their own inquiry processes. We also focused on developing students' ability to monitor and reflect on these processes so that they can improve their ability to learn through inquiry. This involved creating instructional methods and materials to make inquiry processes and regulatory activities, like monitoring and reflecting, overt and explicit so that students can talk about, internalize, and improve them. In this approach, learning about inquiry is used not only to aid the learning of science and other school subjects, but also to help students develop theories about their own learning and self-regulation processes and thereby learn how to learn. Furthermore, actively building and modifying theories about such processes helps students become aware that these processes can be learned and improved. This approach can thus be used to combat the view that academic ability is innate and enables students to develop the metacognitive expertise needed to control their own learning and development.

GOALS FOR THE DESIGN
AND USE OF SCI-WISE

Our recent work focuses on creating a computer environment to reify and support key aspects of metacognition related to learning through inquiry.

This environment, called the ThinkerTools SCI-WISE system, advises users as they design and carry out research projects. It also enables them to modify the support system so that it expresses their own theories of how to do inquiry and how best to coach and scaffold the process. We are experimenting with the pedagogical uses of this software in urban middle school classrooms, with students aged 11 to 14.

SCI-WISE[2] represents a new genre of software that allows users to express their metacognitive ideas and sociocognitive practices as they undertake complex tasks. Such tasks include engaging in scientific inquiry by formulating research questions, generating hypotheses, designing investigations, analyzing evidence, and constructing theories. Such tasks also include higher order activities like reflecting on and modifying one's inquiry processes for the purpose of learning how to learn through inquiry. SCI-WISE provides scaffolding and coaching to students as they undertake these various activities, while also providing a composing environment that enables students to represent their own ideas about how best to model and support inquiry.

The problem in designing such a system is determining a good method for representing ideas about how to carry out inquiry tasks, how to scaffold them, and how to talk about them. The system has to make explicit the purpose of the various tasks, strategies for carrying them out, and ways of monitoring and improving performance on them. Our hypothesis is that this complex set of cognitive and social activities can be made most understandable by representing them as a system of interacting agents who each have particular areas of expertise. These agents, such as the Inventor and Collaborator, have goals that they pursue (such as inquiry goals and pedagogical goals), beliefs that they form (such as beliefs about the users and the context), advice that they can give (such as strategic advice and monitoring advice), and ways of communicating these goals, beliefs, and advice to other agents and users. This system of agents, working together, guides and counsels students as they engage in research and as they reflect on and revise their inquiry processes. Agents advise users concerning the development of goals and strategies, such as being inventive or collaborating effectively, but do not have enough expertise to carry out these tasks themselves without human partners. Thus the complexity

---

[2]SCI-WISE is an acronym with alternative meanings that relate to different functions that the system can serve, such as (1) Scaffolding Collaborative Investigations Within an Inquiry Support Environment (the emphasis is on supporting inquiry) and (2) Social and Cognitive Intelligences Working Interactively at Scientific Enquiry (the emphasis is on presenting a theory of expertise).

of the goals, strategies, and monitoring behavior employed in doing inquiry emerges from interactions among human and computer agents.

Working with SCI-WISE introduces students to a model in which a research culture is portrayed as a community of agents engaging in collaborative inquiry and critical reflection, with members contributing their own particular expertise. This also potentially provides students with a way to view their own minds as a diverse community of expert advisers who work together to facilitate problem solving, learning, reflection, and self-improvement. Such a modular, agent-based view of the mind is related to Minsky's (1985) "Society of Mind" and Wertsch's (1991) "Voices of the Mind" theories of cognition (although SCI-WISE advisers have a higher level of agency than either Minsky or Wertsch advocated). Development of such theories of individual minds and of research cultures should, we conjecture, facilitate students' collaborative inquiry as well as their learning how to learn through inquiry.

SCI-WISE allows students to modify these agent-based theories about cognitive and social processes needed for inquiry and to conduct research on how best to model and support the inquiry process. They can modify SCI-WISE by creating new advisers or revising old ones, as well as by changing their pedagogy, such as modifying how much and what type of advice users get. In this way, students can create alternative versions of the system that house, for example, different sets of advisers with different forms of expertise. They can then conduct educational research to determine which versions of the system are most helpful and thereby test their conjectures regarding the characteristics of the most effective inquiry support environment. This type of inquiry about inquiry is carried out as students use their alternative versions of SCI-WISE to do research projects in various domains (such as physics and biology). This process of constructing competing theories of cognitive and social processes that support inquiry and then investigating their utility should help students develop, reflect on, revise, and internalize their theories and thereby develop increasingly powerful inquiry learning skills along with metacognitive expertise.

The instructional question is, How do we introduce students to such a novel form for expressing and experimenting with metacognitive ideas and sociocognitive practices? The idea is to provide a "seed system" that will acquaint them with what a SCI-WISE system can be like, what it can do, and how it can be changed. We are also creating curricula in which students modify and experiment with the inquiry support environment, using the seed system as a starting point, with the aim of creating versions that better support their own and others' inquiry learning.

In creating SCI-WISE, we are thus developing and enabling young students to develop a theory of metacognitive expertise related to learning through inquiry. The expertise for the seed system is being generated by our research group as it attempts to characterize and reflect on its collaborative inquiry processes. As part of this process, we are working with graduate students to create a version of SCI-WISE that will be useful for young students as well as a version that will be useful to graduate students as they undertake their own research projects. Our middle school curricula, in which students design alternative versions of the inquiry support system, ask young students to engage in a similar process. We are thus creating a genre of software and accompanying curricula that encourage the invention, exploration, and revision of sociocognitive practices and metacognitive expertise.

Our ambition is to develop a pedagogical approach, centered around this software environment, that enables young students to engage in such explorations and theory development in a way that is interesting and meaningful to them. As part of this process, they are introduced to a language and process for discussing and modeling metacognition. We conjecture that the language about metacognition will be meaningful to students if they can use it to talk about how they engage in and support inquiry. Further, the modeling process will be interesting to students if they can employ it to create helpful artifacts, such as their own customized inquiry support system, which they will continue to use and share with others. Introducing students to these discourse and design processes should enable them to develop and revise their metacognitive expertise. An important objective is for them to acquire transferable skills for collaborative inquiry, so that they can apply their inquiry skills to any context they choose. Furthermore, we want them to develop an ability to reflect on their cognitive and social processes with the goal of improving them, so that they get better and better at learning through inquiry. Finally, we want to introduce them to understandable and useful models of how minds and communities work, which should facilitate the building of an effective research community within their classroom.

Our approach therefore embodies both a constructivist (von Glasersfeld, 1995) and a constructionist (Harel & Papert, 1990; Kafai & Resnick, 1996) approach to education in that students create and revise theories by designing artifacts, namely intelligent advisers and their embodiment in an inquiry support environment. In this chapter, we provide an overview of our preliminary work regarding the creation and use of such sociocognitive tools—tools that are aimed at enabling students to develop metacognitive knowledge and skills as they create explicit theories of how best to model and support inquiry.

THE SCI-WISE SYSTEM ARCHITECTURE

Our design decisions about the architecture and capabilities of our seed system are important because they constrain the ways in which students will think about their own and the system's cognitive and social behavior as they carry out tasks. We are attempting to create a system that is as simple, transparent, and easy to understand as possible. The design process is informed by research on metacognition, scientific inquiry, and social constructivism (Brown, 1987; Carey & Smith, 1995; Collins & Ferguson, 1993; Dunbar, 1995; Flavell, 1979; Palincsar, 1998; Salomon & Perkins, 1998; Scardamalia & Bereiter, 1991) as well as by research on the design of computer-based cognitive tools (Collins & Brown, 1988; de Jong & Rip, 1997; Derry, 1992; Dillenbourg, 1992; Kearsley, 1993; Lajoie, 1993; Schauble, Raghavan, & Glaser, 1993; Self, 1992). Although the existing system is limited to supporting work on tasks related to scientific inquiry, its architecture as well as the generic nature of its expertise will enable users to modify it so that it can support work on other tasks.

The programming platform being used to create a prototype of the seed system is Macromedia Director 6 and its Lingo code. Although it is not as sophisticated a language as C++ or LISP, it nonetheless allows an object-oriented, agent-based style of programming, and it can handle message passing and data tracking. More important, it provides multimedia authoring tools that allow for relatively quick interface design and prototyping. This is enabling us to conduct pilot studies with young students to see how they react to and benefit from a seed system that has some of the properties we envision. These results will enable us to improve the architecture and capabilities of subsequent versions of the system. In the next generation of SCI-WISE, which is currently under development, we are using other languages, reasoning engines, communication protocols, and interfaces, such as Java, JESS (Java Expert System Shell), KQML (Knowledge Query and Manipulation Language), and Web browsers like Internet Explorer.

To illustrate how the system works, we use examples from the prototype (see also Shimada, White, & Frederiksen, 1999). We also discuss some capabilities we envision that go beyond those that are currently implemented.

Task Contexts

Within SCI-WISE is a set of task contexts in which users work. We are creating four task contexts within our seed system, which correspond to authentic activities that scientists engage in as they do research: designing and carrying out a research project, preparing project presentations, evaluating research reports, and modifying the inquiry support system. In keeping with the idea that there are correspondences between scientists' inquiry processes and children's learning processes, these four tasks also correspond to important cognitive and metacognitive activities that children should engage in so that they learn how to learn: engaging in inquiry, explaining their inquiry to others, reflecting on their inquiry processes, and revising them so that the next time they engage in inquiry, they can draw on improved cognitive and social processes for assistance.

Task Documents. Associated with each task context is a task document in which users do their work for that task. For example, there is a project journal, a project report, and a project evaluation, as well as a system modification journal (in which users record a history of their system modifications and the reasons for them). These documents are organized around a possible sequence of subtasks (or subgoals) for that task. For example, the project journal is organized around the inquiry cycle that we employ in our ThinkerTools curriculum (shown in Fig. 4.1).

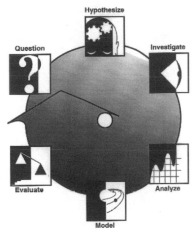

FIG. 4.1. *The Inquiry Cycle provides one possible structure for guiding students' research. It unpacks the inquiry task into a particular sequence of subgoals to be pursued.*

Task Advisers. In addition to task documents, each task context has a set of advisers associated with it, including a head adviser and a set of task specialists. There is a head adviser for each task context: the Inquirer for doing research projects, the Presenter for creating presentations, the Assessor for evaluating projects, and the Modifier for making changes to the SCI-WISE system. The head adviser gives advice regarding how to manage its associated task, suggests possible goal structures for that task, and puts together an appropriate team of advisers. For example, our version of the Inquirer follows the inquiry cycle shown in Fig. 4.1. It suggests pursuing a sequence of subgoals, and each such subgoal has a task specialist associated with it: the Questioner, Hypothesizer, Investigator, Analyzer, Modeler, and Evaluator. Figure 4.2 shows users consulting the Questioner, who advises them about how to come up with a research question. Users can modify the team of advisers available to assist with a task by simply turning some off or creating new ones.

General-Purpose Resources

In order for advisers and users to function within the various task contexts, SCI-WISE incorporates several general-purpose resources, which

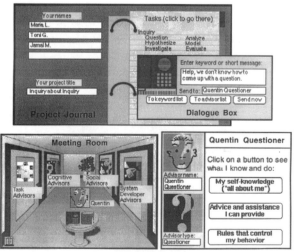

FIG. 4.2. *Students using SCI-WISE work in the context of various task documents, such as the Project Journal which serves to organize the task and house their work. Advisors can be called upon for help and can be accessed in a variety of ways. For example, they can be found in the Meeting Room, can be accessed via the Dialogue Box, or can simply pop up when appropriate. In the above figure, students have used the Dialogue Box to call upon Quentin Questioner for help in coming up with a research question.*

can serve users and advisers no matter what task they are engaged in. These include memory systems for keeping track of what has happened; communication systems for communicating between advisers, users, and artifacts; and a set of general-purpose advisers who can provide advice in almost any task context.

Memory Systems. Memory systems are useful to both users and advisers. For example, they can be accessed by advisers to determine which aspects of the task the users have already completed, what the context is, and so forth. They can also be accessed by students to help them recall and reflect on the processes they have gone through as they tried to accomplish a particular task.

Memory systems can include various types of work histories, like the project checklist, which makes the proposed goal structure for a task explicit and which students use to show what subgoals they have and have not accomplished. They can also include memories for things like user dispositions, which could contain information about which types of advice a group of users prefers. These memory systems can be displayed or hidden according to the needs or preferences of the users.

Communication Systems. Various communication systems allow adviser-to-adviser communication, adviser-to-user communication, and user-to-adviser communication. They can also allow advisers and users to get information from artifacts such as the project checklist. Three examples of interfaces that enable users to access and communicate with advisers are the meeting room, project journal, and dialogue box, all of which are shown in Fig. 4.2. Students can go directly to an adviser for advice through the meeting room, which provides access to all of the advisers. They can also access advisers through task documents, such as the project journal, which provide access to advisers for that task. And, finally, students can use the dialogue box to send a message directly to any adviser. The adviser then checks the words in the message against its lexicon of key words. If a match is found, the adviser responds accordingly, taking into account the current context.

General-Purpose Advisers. In addition to general-purpose memory and communication systems, SCI-WISE makes available general-purpose advisers, who can provide advice during any task or subtask. This set of advisers includes both cognitive and social advisers, whose purpose is to enable users to develop and employ widely applicable cognitive and social skills.[3] The cognitive advisers in our seed system include the Inventor, Planner, Representer, and Reasoner. The social advisers include the Communicator, Collaborator, Debator, and Mediator. These general-purpose advisers can pop up or be called on whenever they might be useful. For example, "being inventive" is often a useful goal to pursue at the beginning of each step in the inquiry cycle, and so the Inventor may pop up under such circumstances if it believes it can offer pertinent advice.

General-purpose advisers have various types of expertise that are metacognitive in nature. For example, they can describe their goals along with the characteristics of performance that effectively accomplish those goals. They also make available evaluation rubrics that ask users to evaluate their performance against those characteristics. For instance, the Inventor's goal is to help users generate multiple possibilities that fit the constraints of a given situation. It can provide characterizations of what it means to be inventive, as in, "You show originality and creativity in your work," and it encourages users to evaluate whether they have been inventive. It then asks them to think of ways in which they could be more inventive. In addition, general-purpose advisers can suggest heuristics for achieving their goals and can indicate when these heuristics might be useful, as well as provide examples that illustrate their use. For example, the Inventor suggests heuristics such as, "Turn your mind loose" and "Think of ideas and explore them." It can also inform users that such ways of being inventive are often useful at the beginning of each step in the inquiry cycle and can provide specific examples to illustrate the process.

The introduction and use of these general-purpose advisers within SCI-WISE embody a key component of our theory of metacognitive expertise and its development. These advisers serve two important functions. First, they provide an initial, workable set of metacognitive categories that are useful in learning to talk about and develop theories of the characteristics

---

[3]These advisers are based on the reflective assessment criteria and process developed for our ThinkerTools Inquiry Curriculum (White & Frederiksen, 1998), which helped students understand characteristics of good inquiry processes, including cognitive processes such as "being inventive" and "being systematic" and social processes such as "communicating well" and "collaborating effectively." For each such criterion, we gave students a functional characterization of what it means to be inventive, collaborate effectively, and so on. We then asked students to evaluate their own and each other's inquiry using this set of criteria. The purpose was to help students learn how to reflect on and improve their inquiry processes so that their future inquiry would have these characteristics. Exposing students to this type of metacognitive expertise and engaging them in this reflective process proved highly effective in helping students to understand the purpose and functionality of inquiry as well as in improving their inquiry skills. In SCI-WISE, these reflective-assessment criteria have been cast as general-purpose advisers.

of successful cognitive and social processes (Frederiksen & White, 1997; White & Frederiksen, 1998). Second, they provide a model of metacognitive expertise and of how such expertise can be employed when engaging in complex tasks like doing a research project.

System Development Tools and Advisers

SCI-WISE also makes available system development tools and advisers that aid students as they try to modify the system itself. These advisers can be called on when the users' goal is to revise the inquiry support system so that the next time they engage in inquiry, they will get better advice. Users work with the head system development adviser, called the Modifier, to create alternative versions of the system that embody their own theories about the nature of inquiry and the best means of supporting it.

The Modifier's goal is to help users talk about, reflect on, and revise inquiry support advisers, including possibly itself. It advises users as they make various types of changes to advisers,[4] including minor revisions (like rewording their advice), adding or deleting components of expertise (like adding a heuristic or strategy), and creating a new adviser (like adding a step to the inquiry cycle or adding a new general-purpose adviser).

New advisers can be constructed for each class of advisers (task, general purpose, and system development) through the use of adviser shells, which inherit the structure and capabilities of advisers in that class. Systems that are inherited include the adviser's memory system, its communication system, and its reasoning system. Users work with the Modifier to create alternative versions of an adviser so that they can experiment to find out which version users find most effective, or like best, and so forth. For this reason, advisers can be given proper names, like Quentin Questioner and Quincy Questioner, so that users can distinguish the various incarnations of an adviser. To help users create, modify, and test advisers effectively may require that the system eventually include other types of advisers, such as a Mind Modeler and a Community Creator, who could

---

[4]Currently, advisers are the only components of the system that are modifiable by users. Future generations of SCI-WISE may enable users to change other components, such as giving them tools to create new types of task documents or communication interfaces. However, we are starting with tools for modifying an adviser's knowledge and behavior, because we believe that the creation and modification of such pedagogical agents afford the most powerful vehicle for fostering the development of metacognitive expertise.

provide information about task advisers and general-purpose advisers and how they can work together to help users perform a task.

The Modifier can also work with users to alter when an adviser should give advice and what kind of advice it should give. How this can be done will become apparent later in this chapter (see "Rules for Controlling Behavior" and "How Advisers Decide What to Do"). Enabling users to make this type of revision in a manner that actually improves the inquiry support system may require that the Modifier call on a pedagogy adviser who has information about theories of learning and coaching. For instance, the Pedagogue could present users with pedagogical principles like, "Give less and less advice each time so that users learn how to do the task without help," or, "Only give advice when users say they want it; otherwise they may get annoyed at being told what to do all the time." In this way, the Modifier could help users make changes to the inquiry support system that alter the amount and type of advice users have access to. For example, students could experiment with how much assistance the advisers provide to users, such as whether the advisers recommend subgoals to be pursued at each step in the inquiry cycle or instead require users to generate the subgoals for themselves. In this way, students could modify the system to represent their own theories of inquiry learning and how best to support it. Furthermore, making such revisions should help them to realize that there are alternative theories of learning and that their own learning processes can be modified to embody different theories.

Working With Advisers

We have seen that there are three broad classes of advisers within the SCI-WISE system: task advisers, who are specialized to help students achieve the subgoals associated with a given task; general-purpose advisers, who help in understanding and developing general cognitive and social skills needed for a wide range of tasks; and system development advisers, who help students construct alternatives to the seed system. This taxonomy of advisers is outlined in Fig. 4.3. These classes of advisers are not the only ones that we could have created, but they satisfy our model of reflective, goal-driven inquiry (White & Frederiksen, 1998). Each plays a role in helping students to develop a theory of how inquiry can be modeled and supported, and an understanding of how this theory can be refined through modification and experimentation with the inquiry support system.

We now provide an illustration of what it is like to interact with each of these three classes of advisers. What follows is a hypothetical example of students getting advice as they work in the task context of designing and

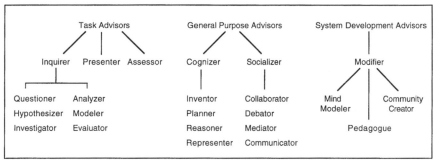

FIG. 4.3. *The SCI-WISE advisors are organized in a hierarchical taxonomy, which consists of the Advisor Class (top level), the Head Advisors (middle level), and the Specialists (bottom level).*

carrying out a research project. The students are working in their project journal, which is organized around the inquiry cycle. They are just about to start work on their hypotheses and go to the hypothesize section of their journal. At the top left of Fig. 4.4, the appropriate inquiry task adviser, Helena Hypothesizer, pops up to offer advice. She says, "Hi, I'm Helena Hypothesizer. I predict I can help you. Here are some things I can do for you: (1) I can describe the characteristics of good hypotheses; (2) I can suggest strategies for creating hypotheses and advisers who can assist; and (3) I can help you evaluate your hypotheses to see if they need revision." The students click on "suggest strategies," and Helena then says, "A good strategy to start with is to think of lots of ideas and then narrow them down to the good ones. For help in coming up with ideas, the Inventor might be worth checking out."

The Hypothesizer has recommended that the students consult one of the general-purpose advisers: the Inventor. The students decide to take her advice and click on the Inventor icon. As shown at the middle left of Fig. 4.4, Ingrid Inventor pops up and offers two strategies: "Fast and Loose" and "Control Freaks." The students click on "Fast and Loose," and Ingrid then says, "Good choice! Fast and loose is my favorite. Relax and turn your mind loose. Think of as many ideas as you can in five minutes. The ideas can be crazy or serious, it doesn't matter."

Now suppose that the students go to their project journal and write, "We still can't come up with any ideas, so we think Ingrid gives lousy advice." And they respond to Ingrid's prompts to evaluate both their own performance and hers by giving low ratings. This causes Ingrid to say, "Please reflect on why you didn't find me very helpful. Improve my advice so that next time I will be more useful to you." The students then decide to come up with a better strategy and want to give it to Ingrid.

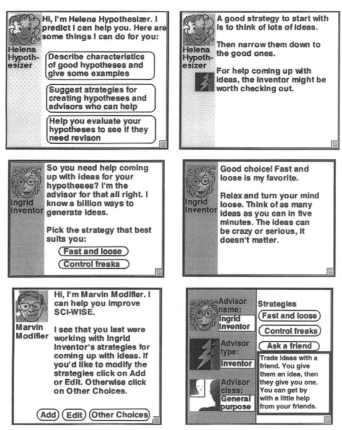

FIG. 4.4. *This sequence of illustrations (read from left to right) shows what it is like to interact with the three classes of SCI-WISE advisors. At the top, students start their research by consulting a Task Advisor. In the middle, they get advice from one of the General Purpose Advisors. At the bottom, they work with a System Development Advisor, called the Modifier, to try to improve the General Purpose Advisor.*

In order to give their proposed new strategy to Ingrid, the students need the help of one of the system development advisers, so they go to the meeting room to find Marvin Modifier, because that is who they need to work with to give Ingrid a new strategy. They click on Marvin, who pops up and says (shown at the bottom left of Fig. 4.4), "I see that you last were working with Ingrid Inventor's strategies for coming up with ideas. If you'd like to modify the strategies, click on Add or Edit. Otherwise click on Other Choices." The students click on Add, and the template for Ingrid pops up with a new, unmarked button on which they can enter the name of their new strategy. They type, "Ask a Friend," and then they click on that button so that they can enter their strategy. A text box pops up in which they type (shown at the bottom right of Fig. 4.4), "Trade ideas with a friend. You give them an idea, then they give you one. You can get by with a little help from your friends." In this way, the students have given Ingrid Inventor a new piece of strategic advice, which will now be available to all users of their inquiry support system whenever they consult Ingrid.

The preceding example illustrates how students can work with inquiry task and general-purpose advisers as they carry out an inquiry project. It also illustrates how they can use system development advisors and tools to modify such advisers.

What Advisers Know

What follows is a synopsis of the types of information and expertise that can be provided by the advisers in our seed system. To start with, they have self-knowledge. For example, they can inform users about what they know and when they might be useful. They also have advice and assistance to give, which includes knowledge about inquiry processes and products. For example, they can advise users about process goals, like generating hypotheses, as well as provide strategies for achieving those goals and referrals to other advisers who can help. And they can provide information about the characteristics of good inquiry products, like hypotheses and experimental designs, and can give critiqued examples of good and bad inquiry products. Finally, advisers also have adviser behavior rules, which they employ as they try to decide what to do in any given context. Users can modify all of these types of adviser expertise.

Self-Knowledge. SCI-WISE's advisers have self-knowledge, which they can articulate when giving advice. By self-knowledge we mean information an adviser has and can provide about its expertise. This information is put into its knowledge base by its creator. An adviser's self-knowledge includes answers to questions such as the following:

- What expertise do I have?
- Why is my expertise important?
- What are my goals?
- When might I be useful?
- How do I get information?
- How do I decide what to do?

- How do I monitor my performance?
- How do I improve myself?

Each adviser can thus provide characterizations of what it knows, when and why it is useful, how it decides what to do, and how it monitors and improves its performance. For example, the Assessor can say, "Hi, I'm the Assessor and I want to help you evaluate your work so that you can improve it. You might find me particularly helpful at the end of each task you undertake." These characterizations of things such as an adviser's expertise, its utility, and its functionality are linked to the actual advice and assistance that it can give, to its adviser behavior rules, or to its reasoning mechanisms (as appropriate) so that users can go from one to the other. Our conjecture is that these capabilities will help users to develop metacognitive expertise regarding the adviser's purpose and functionality. They might also help users understand why it is useful to have such self-knowledge and thereby motivate them to develop this type of metalevel knowledge regarding their own expertise.

Advice and Assistance.   All advisers have a knowledge base that houses their advice and assistance. This expertise is categorized in ways designed to help users find the advice they need, as well as to help the advisers select which piece of advice to give. The following illustrates one of the categorization schemes embedded in the inquiry task advisers of our seed system:

Process knowledge
- Task goals, subgoals, and their purposes
- Strategies for achieving goals
- Referrals to advisers who can help
- Assessment criteria for evaluating processes

Product knowledge
- Characteristics of products
- Critiqued examples of good and bad products
- Assessment criteria for evaluating products

With their advice categorized in this way, inquiry task advisers can support the inquiry process. For example, they can talk about goals that need to be pursued in order to accomplish a particular task, such as "come up with alternative hypotheses," as well as about the purpose of achieving those goals within the overall inquiry process. They can recommend strategies for achieving goals, such as "try being inventive," and can suggest asking general-purpose advisers, like the Inventor, for help. In addition, they can provide prompts to scaffold the process, such as, "What hypotheses do you have about possible answers to your research question? And explain the reasoning behind each of your hypotheses." Finally, they can work with other task and system development advisers, like the Assessor and Modifier, to help students evaluate and refine their inquiry process.

With regard to inquiry products, like hypotheses and models, inquiry task advisers can describe possible characteristics of inquiry products and can give critiqued examples of good and bad products, such as good and bad hypotheses. They can also advise users as to how to evaluate inquiry products, such as how to critique their experimental designs in order to determine if they need revision.

By providing these types of advice and scaffolding, advisers introduce a model of how to talk about and employ theories about inquiry processes. For instance, they talk in terms of developing goals and strategies for achieving those goals, and they discuss the need to monitor performance to see if the goals have been reached. This advice is in a form that is transferable and adaptable to a wide variety of situations. For instance, the Inventor provides generally applicable suggestions for how to be inventive, as well as how to determine whether one's inquiry process and products are indeed inventive. Interacting with a system that offers such generic advice concerning how to form goals, develop strategies, and monitor behavior should help users to develop and refine widely applicable forms of metacognitive expertise.

Advisers also enable users to pay attention to the concerns of others and appreciate the role they play in the functioning of a scientific community. For instance, the Investigator might suggest that the users consider what type of model they are trying to create when planning their investigations. It can also recommend that they call on the Modeler, who may have expertise about such considerations. In this way, students should learn about the expertise of the various advisers, as well as the relationships among them, which may help students in building their own communities.

Rules for Controlling Behavior. Advisers also have knowledge that enables them to decide when to pop up, which piece of advice to give, and when to keep silent. In the prototype version of SCI-WISE, this knowledge is encoded as a collection of condition-action rules such as those shown in

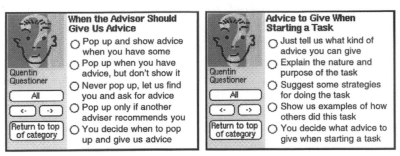

FIG. 4.5. *Advisors have rules that control their behavior. The box on the left shows a set of rules for determining how much advice to give, and the one on the right shows a set for determining which type of advice to provide. Student designers can select one rule from each such set of alternative rules. In this way, they can easily modify how an advisor behaves and can create versions of SCI-WISE with widely varying properties, such as one in which the advisors are in control versus one in which the users are in control.*

Fig. 4.5. Student designers[5] of new versions of SCI-WISE can select which rules each adviser should follow from sets of alternative rules that relate to how the adviser should behave in different contexts. Figure 4.5 presents examples of such alternative rules. The rule set on the left determines how much advice the adviser should give, and the one on the right determines which type of advice it should give. Student designers select one rule from each such set of alternative rules. In this way, they can easily modify how an adviser or class of advisers behaves. (These rules can be set globally for all advisers, for all advisers in a class, or locally for individual advisers.)

In future generations of SCI-WISE, we plan to provide a tool to enable student designers to compose these rules from sets of conditions and actions rather than simply having them select from premade alternatives. This tool will enable student designers to conjoin both conditions and actions as well as to type in an explanation for why their rule should be followed. In this way, they could create more complex rules of the form, "If a and if b, then do x and then y, because c." One example of such a rule is, "If the users have limited experience and if they are at the beginning of a task, then explain the nature and purpose of the task and then suggest some strategies for doing the task, because they need to understand why a task is important before they try to do it." With this tool, student designers will have the ability to

---

[5]In this chapter, our focus is on characterizing SCI-WISE as a metacognitive tool that enables young students to embody and test their theories of the cognitive and social processes needed for inquiry and how best to support them. Thus we use the term *student designers* even though designers can be anyone, including researchers and teachers.

create and justify rules, and the advisers will have the capability to explain to users both how and why it selected a particular piece of advice.

How Advisers Work

SCI-WISE's advisers are agents with certain reasoning capabilities that enable them to interpret information they acquire, decide on goals to adopt, and take actions in pursuit of their goals (Franklin & Graesser, 1997; Russell & Norvig, 1995). These capabilities are present only in limited forms in the prototype.

Advisory agents have a wide variety of goals that they can pursue, including:

- Help students learn about the adviser's expertise.
- Help students understand the nature of the task being undertaken.
- Help students get the task done.
- Help students develop widely applicable cognitive and social skills.
- Help students learn how to assess, reflect on, and improve their inquiry processes.

Such goals are found in each agent's self-knowledge and are linked to the advice and assistance that the agent can give. To enable advisers to decide which of its goals would be productive to pursue at a given time as well as what actions to take, the advisers have three subsystems. These subsystems enable them to acquire and interpret information, to decide what to do, and to monitor and improve their performance.

Ways of Acquiring and Interpreting Information. An adviser has various means of getting information with help from the communication and memory systems. For example, it can get information from other advisers, from task documents and user histories, and from communicating with the users directly. In order to decide what goals to pursue and what actions to take, advisers use this information to form beliefs about the current conditions. These beliefs are formed through a process of inference and abstraction that transforms information into forms and categories useful for making advisory decisions. The categories of beliefs, along with examples of such beliefs, are illustrated for the Hypothesizer:

Task context and status
- These users are working on the hypothesize subtask.
- They are in the middle of the task and have just entered two hypotheses.

Prior interactions with the agent
- They always ignore my advice to evaluate their work to see if it needs revision.
- They give me a low performance rating whenever I ask them to evaluate their work.

User's history and characteristics
- These users have done five projects already and have never modified the system.
- They recently gave themselves a low rating on "being reflective."

User's goals and desires
- These users say that their goal is to get the task done.
- They say that they want me to help them.

Agent's own goals and priorities
- My highest priority is to help users learn how to assess, reflect on, and improve their inquiry processes.

This set of beliefs is then used, as described below, to determine the adviser's goals as well as to select appropriate actions aimed at achieving those goals.

Mechanisms for Deciding What to Do. Agents need to have a mechanism for deciding what to do. To accomplish this, we employ a simple, forward-reasoning inference engine. In the SCI-WISE prototype, this decision making is done using condition-action rules. These take as inputs the beliefs that the agent currently holds, which form the conditions that determine which rules get activated. This decision-making process is done in stages. The agent first uses its beliefs about the current conditions to form a set of conjectures about which goals it should pursue. It then goes on to decide which of these goals to pursue and what actions to take in pursuit of those goals, such as which piece of advice to give and what form the advice should be in. Associated with each step in this decision process is a rule or set of rules that were specified by the student designers when they selected or created the rules that control adviser behavior. These rules enable the adviser to answer questions related to deciding how it should behave in the present context. These questions include: Am I relevant, should I give advice, and what advice should I give?

As a simple example, we illustrate the decision-making process of Helena Hypothesizer in the context of working with novice users. Imagine that she has formed the beliefs that the users are working on their first research project and that they have just advanced to the hypothesize step of the inquiry cycle. Her belief that the users are in the hypothesize step causes her adviser behavior rules to conjecture that she has relevant advice to give. Since Helena's creators also selected the rule, "If you have relevant advice, pop up and show the advice," this leads to the conjecture that she should give advice. Imagine that Helena's creators also gave her the rule that "if the task status is 'haven't started' and if the users have 'no prior experience,' then the goal should be to inform the users about the nature and purpose of the task." Since her beliefs also match this rule's conditions, Helena forms another conjecture: that her goal should be to "inform the users about the nature and purpose of the task." Since all of her conjectures about which goals she should pursue are compatible, she decides to adopt the goal of giving advice that will inform the users about the nature and purpose of the task. She then accesses and gives the appropriate advice (the advice that is linked to this goal in her "advice and assistance" knowledge base).

The decision-making process is not always as simple and straightforward as in the preceding example. It is possible for an adviser to have a set of beliefs and behavior rules that lead to conflicts about which goals the adviser should pursue. In fact, the set of beliefs illustrated for the Hypothesizer in the preceding section is highly likely to produce such a conflict. In that example, the users said they wanted help and that their goal was to get the task done; yet the Hypothesizer's priority was to get them to reflect on their work, which was reinforced by the fact that they had rarely done this in the past. As such problems occur, they are articulated by the adviser, who asks the users for assistance. For example, in cases of such goal-setting conflicts, it asks users to determine which of the proposed conflicting goals should have priority. (Alternatively, one could enable student designers to select from a set of conflict-resolution rules, such as "Always adopt the goal that has the highest priority for the adviser" versus "Always accede to the desires of the users.") Such articulation of cognitive conflicts and user involvement in the decision making process might lead students to be more able to think of their own cognitive processes in terms of setting goals, developing strategies, and monitoring progress. In this way, limitations of the system can be used as opportunities for discussions about metacognition.

Methods for Monitoring and Improving Performance. Advisers work with students to monitor and reflect on both the advisers' and the students' performance. They help users monitor whether they have achieved their goals and, if they have not, can give advice concerning how to proceed or can refer them to other advisers who can help. Advisers also need to do this for their own behaviors. That is, they should adopt the goal of improving their own performance. To accomplish this, they need to monitor whether they have achieved their own goals and, if not, modify their knowledge and behavior accordingly.

In the prototype, this monitoring and improvement is done by asking the users for assistance. The Hypothesizer, for example, can ask if its advice was helpful. If the users give its performance a low rating, the Hypothesizer says, "I'm sorry my advice didn't help you to achieve your goal of creating hypotheses. Here are the different types of advice I can offer you. Why don't you select some advice that you think might be more helpful to you." At the end of a task, users are also encouraged to modify advisers to make them more effective. For instance, the Hypothesizer can ask, "Please reflect on why you didn't find me very helpful. Improve my advice and my behavior rules so that next time I will be more useful to you." As part of this reflective process, students might decide, for instance, that the Hypothesizer's feature of constantly asking them to evaluate their performance is no longer useful and has become downright annoying. They could then work with the Modifier to alter the Hypothesizer's behavior rules so that it no longer prompts for such evaluations. Subsequently they could experiment with this new version of the Hypothesizer to see if it improves their performance. In this way, students can be introduced to reflective processes, and they can develop and test theories concerning their utility.

Our conjecture is that encouraging students to monitor advisers' usefulness and to improve them when necessary will serve a role in enabling students to monitor, reflect on, and improve their own performance. In future generations of SCI-WISE, we plan to experiment with giving advisers learning capabilities that will enable them to improve their own knowledge and performance. Thus, ultimately advisers will include additional expertise in self regulation and self improvement. In this way, they can provide more sophisticated models of these important metacognitive processes and may better enable students to learn how to learn.

How the Community of Advisers Behaves

Can students create a community of advisers who work together so that their advice appears coordinated and coherent to users, or will the behavior of their SCI-WISE systems be disjointed and confusing? Coordination is facilitated by the communications system. For instance, advisers can get information from the inquiry environment, from other advisers, and from users so that they are informed about the context. Given such information, how do advisers coordinate (or not coordinate) their behavior?

Coordination of advisers' behaviors is related to how advisers get activated. Within SCI-WISE, advisers can get activated in a variety of different ways. For example, users can seek out an adviser either because they know it is relevant or because their perusal of its self-knowledge (its information about what it knows and when it might be useful) indicates that it should be helpful in the present context. An adviser can also be called on when another adviser indicates that it might be useful. This happens either because the presently active adviser has the knowledge that the other adviser is relevant in the present context or because the other adviser sends a message informing the presently active adviser of its relevance. In addition, advisers can decide to pop up themselves because they know they are relevant based on the task context or something the users did, such as give themselves a low rating in their area of expertise, which might be, say, "inventiveness" or "collaboration."

Student designers have control over whether advisers have to be sought out, or recommended by other advisers, or can just pop up whenever they want. This is done by selecting alternative options in the adviser behavior rules, particularly those that govern when the agent should intervene (see Fig. 4.5). Choosing different options produces systems with different characteristics, ranging from total user control to total system control of sequentially presented advice. It can also produce hybrid systems such as one in which multiple advisers pop up and users control which ones they consult, or one in which different advisers behave in different ways, such as some popping up and some having to be invoked. Alternative versions of SCI-WISE can thus have very different emergent properties, depending on the choices that its student designers and users made. This capability to make modifications easily that produce widely varying system behaviors provides a vehicle for students to engage in research on the design of the system itself. For instance, they could engage in educational research regarding how best to support the inquiry process with sequential or parallel advice, or with user or system control.

Summary of SCI-WISE Architecture

SCI-WISE provides an environment in which students create a variety of artifacts in the form of task documents, such as the project journal and project report. Each task document has a set of task advisers associated with it. The system also makes available general-purpose advisers, such as the Inventor and the Collaborator, and communication and memory systems that are intended to be useful across a wide range of contexts. The expertise and behavior of the different types of advisers are easily modifiable by student designers using system development tools and advisers. This control over what advisers know and how they behave enables students to engage in educational research regarding how best to model and support the processes of collaborative inquiry and reflective learning.

USING SCI-WISE TO FOSTER METACOGNITIVE DEVELOPMENT

SCI-WISE integrates cognitive and social aspects of cognition within a social framework that takes the form of a community of advisers working together to guide and support reflective inquiry. To support the pedagogical value of SCI-WISE as a tool for fostering students' metacognitive development, we argue that metacognitive processes are most easily understood and observed in such a multiagent social system. After all, in a social context, one is concerned about what others are doing and why. Social systems provide a natural context for focusing on goals and motives, as well as for monitoring and reflecting on others' behavior and expertise. SCI-WISE models these types of metacognitive concerns as its advisers interact with one another and with users. It also allows students to create and represent this type of expertise as they work to improve the advisers.

In order to provide a richer social system that better illustrates the need for and use of metacognitive expertise, SCI-WISE could be augmented in various ways. For example, in the version of the system we have described, adviser-to-adviser interactions are limited to exchanging beliefs about the current context, deciding which adviser should pop up, and little else. One can imagine augmenting advisers' capabilities so that they can engage in a richer array of social behaviors. For example, the rules that control adviser behavior could include sets of alternative rules for governing social interactions, such as "Talk whenever you want" versus "Let other advisers talk" versus "Yield only to the head adviser." Student designers could then examine these explicit representations of social principles and make decisions about which rules each adviser should follow. Furthermore, advisers could be augmented so that they formulate a richer set of beliefs about others and engage in more types of interactions. For instance, one can imagine advisers forming beliefs about who it is that they agree and disagree with, and this could trigger collaboration or debate among advisers. One could then envision agents arguing publicly with one another about who has the most relevant advice to give in the present context. Further, one can imagine social advisers, such as the Mediator, being consulted by users to help resolve such disputes among the advisers. Through such augmentations, the social behavior of SCI-WISE could be enhanced, thereby making its metacognitive behavior more prevalent, necessary, and explicit.

Pedagogical Approaches to Fostering Metacognitive Development

Our primary approach to supporting students' metacognitive development is to reify metalevel expertise within a social system of advisory agents, namely SCI-WISE, and then to enable students to interact with this system in ways that foster the internalization of its expertise. How then can we enable students to internalize the expertise? That is, how can we enable individuals to appropriate external, social entities (the advisers) as internal, cognitive processes (Vygotsky, 1978)? As we have described, the metalevel processes are embodied within a system of agents who talk about their capabilities and concerns and are cued as functional units within a variety of application contexts. In this way, they are capable of having modularity and transferability. Our claim is that an agent's metalevel expertise can be internalized by students and then consciously invoked if, through a process of reflected abstraction (Piaget, 1976), it has been identified, explicitly labeled, and interacted with as a functional unit. By internalizing expertise as a system of such functional units in the form of advisers, they become accessible to reflected abstraction and conscious control, enabling students to "put on different hats" and "invoke different voices" when needed as they solve problems or engage in inquiry learning.[6]

---

[6]Suggesting that students need to internalize SCI-WISE in its entirety is an extreme position to take (cf., White & Frederiksen, 1990). Important questions that we plan to address in future research are how much of SCI-WISE is appropriated by students, in what forms do they internalize its expertise, and how much and what forms are needed to facilitate their sociocognitive and metacognitive development.

We are working with our collaborating teacher-researchers to develop a variety of pedagogical activities designed to foster the development of such metacognitive expertise. Students engage in these activities as they work with the inquiry support system to conduct research across a number of domains throughout the school year. The activities include having students put together advisory teams, act out the roles of the different advisers, and engage in inquiry about inquiry. Undertaking these activities should also serve to facilitate the functioning of the classroom as a research community. An important objective is to help teachers cultivate a community in which students engage in inquiry and thereby develop expertise that enables them to learn through inquiry in any domain that they choose.

Creating Teams of Advisers.   In this activity, students are encouraged to think about the roles and utilities of the different advisers. Students are asked to put together a team of advisers that will guide them in a research project or inquiry task that they are about to undertake. They start by discussing and trying to decide which advisers they think will be needed. They then work with SCI-WISE to create an advisory team designed to suit the needs of their task. For instance, students could decide that they want to engage in some exploratory research and that the inquiry cycle shown in Fig. 4.1 is not well suited to their goals. So they modify the head adviser for this task, namely the Inquirer, so that it has a more appropriate goal structure, such as investigate, analyze, and hypothesize. They then put together an advisory team headed by the Inquirer that includes the Investigator, Analyzer, and Hypothesizer as well as some of the general-purpose advisers. In this way, students are encouraged to think about the structure of tasks as well as the expertise of the different advisers.

Playing Roles: Research Groups as Communities of Advisers.   Creating a classroom research community in which sociocognitive processes are represented as areas of expertise associated with particular individuals, such as an inventor and a planner, should enable students to recognize, talk about, and take on the role of those experts in carrying out inquiry within the classroom. We developed a pedagogical activity in which students play such roles in a process we term *social enactment*. In this activity, research groups work with SCI-WISE to design and carry out a research project. Individual students within the group work in partnership with and take on the roles of one of its cognitive and one of its social advisers. So, for example, one student is the Planner and Collaborator, another is the Inventor and Communicator, and so on. Students switch roles from time to time so that each gets an opportunity to be in charge of the different components of cognitive and social expertise that are needed when carrying out a complex task like scientific inquiry. As the group does its project, the student who is embodying a particular adviser works with that adviser to see what it would do, act out its behavior, and modify it when the group thinks its behavior needs improvement.

This activity enables students to apply the cognitive and social processes embedded within SCI-WISE to the actual functioning of their research group. In this way, they can investigate the utility of the advisers for enhancing their group's functioning. Playing the different roles may also serve to help students internalize the expertise of the different advisers (Vygotsky, 1978). Pedagogical activities of this type use SCI-WISE as a tool for supporting collaborative inquiry among the students themselves and may help teachers to transform their classrooms into more effective learning communities.

Engaging in Inquiry About Inquiry. To further students' awareness of sociocognitive and metacognitive processes related to collaborative inquiry and reflective learning, we are also developing activities in which students engage in inquiry about inquiry. That is, they create and experiment with explicit theories of processes needed to support inquiry learning. Students embed their various theories in alternative versions of SCI-WISE and then investigate the effectiveness of these alternative inquiry support environments to assess the utility of their theories. In these activities, students collaborate as they work to improve SCI-WISE by developing and refining the expertise of its advisers. The advisers, in turn, collaborate with the students as they engage in these processes of reflection and improvement. Such pedagogical activities, in which students become both members of and developers of this multiagent social system, should be particularly effective in fostering metacognitive development.

The Vision and Its Obstacles

Our hope is that by modifying the system to test their own theories of collaborative inquiry and reflective learning, by working with the system to conduct research on a wide variety of topics, and by enacting the roles of the different advisers within their research groups, students will internalize the advisers' expertise and be able to generalize the use of their expertise to different contexts. Furthermore, we hope that they may come to view both their minds and their research groups as a community of advisers who collaborate as they engage in inquiry and reflection. Nevertheless, nightmarish scenarios are possible. For instance, it is relatively easy to create versions of SCI-WISE that many would find annoying and confusing—annoying in that the system provides too much advice and structure and confusing in that there are too many agents who are indistinguishable from one another. In fact, in developing our seed system, we keep heading toward this nightmarish scenario by creating complex systems whose behavior is potentially mysterious. So how can we possibly expect young students to create versions of the system that successfully model and support collaborative inquiry and reflective learning and, by so doing, enable them to develop powerful metacognitive expertise as well as productive theories of mind and community?

Students as Educational Researchers

To achieve these challenging goals, we build on the idea of engaging students in inquiry about inquiry. We are experimenting with having students become cognitive scientists and educational researchers who address many of the same research questions that we investigate in our own work. One such question is, What makes a good adviser? In other words, what characteristics does an adviser need to possess to be effective? For example:

- Would giving advisers distinct personalities make them more appealing to users, or would all that unnecessary chatter just be annoying?
- Do advisers need to be "metacognitively articulate" and talk about their goals and strategies, or is it better if they just tell users what to do?
- Does it help if advisers make their expertise available for inspection and modification by users, or will that just waste users' time and degrade the advisers?
- Is an adviser's expertise more useful if it is generic and applies to many contexts, or does it need to be context specific to be useful?

Students could also investigate aspects of system design that relate to long standing issues in the field of computers and education. For example:

- Is it more important to provide a system's users with autonomy and freedom or with guidance and support?
- Should the system adapt to individual differences, or is it better to treat all students the same?

- Should one worry more about developing a system that keeps students motivated or that makes sure they learn?
- Which seed system provides the best starting point for pedagogical purposes: one that is complex and rich or one that is simple and more easily understood?
- Does the modeling of social processes like collaboration play a useful role in students' social and cognitive development (such as enabling them to develop collaboration skills and metacognitive expertise)?

We are putting together a collection of such research questions that meet two important criteria: they are interesting to young students, and they are productive in terms of fostering students' metacognitive development. In our pilot work, we have found that issues that relate to control and to social factors can be highly motivating for middle school students. For example, one control issue is that of autonomy versus guidance. More specifically, how do you give users control while also providing sufficient guidance? Investigating alternative positions with respect to this question involves making design decisions, such as these:

- Do users have to ask for advice, or is it given automatically?
- Are users required to follow the advice, or can they ignore it?
- Are users stuck with a given version of the system, or can they modify it?

To enable students to engage in investigating such questions, we are creating curricula to accompany the SCI-WISE software that are aimed at facilitating this type of inquiry about inquiry. In these curricula, students conduct educational research on issues like autonomy versus guidance. The collaborating teachers are overlaying this inquiry about inquiry onto their regular science curriculum, which includes group work and inquiry activities in domains such as physics, ecology, and nutrition. So, for example, their students are conducting research on the best strategies for collaboration as they do their ThinkerTools physics projects.

Engaging young students in such inquiry about inquiry is effective for a variety of reasons. First, the topics addressed, like collaboration and autonomy, can be highly motivating—more so for many middle school students than, say, Newton's laws of motion. Furthermore, such inquiry can enable young students to do "publishable" research on, for instance, their findings regarding alternative collaboration strategies. Also, this research is potentially useful to themselves, their teachers, and future students. It can enable a teacher to work with students to develop, for isntance, a set of collaboration strategies that she can recommend to her classes in the future. Finally, it can enable students to develop metacognitive expertise related to collaborative inquiry, reflection, and learning how to learn.

After conducting such research, students could publish their research reports along with their inquiry support systems (or particularly interesting and effective components of them) on the World Wide Web. For instance, as part of their research, a class might create a set of advisers that are useful for a particular task, such as reflective assessment or system modification. In this way, classrooms around the world could share and build on one another's work. A similar process could occur with professional researchers. For example, the graduate students in our research group are working with us to create versions of SCI-WISE that are useful to themselves and their peers as they do their master's and doctoral research projects. Such software can thus provide widely applicable tools for fostering the development and dissemination of expert practices as well as computer-based models of how best to develop and support those practices.

CONCLUSION

In this chapter, we have argued that the types of sociocognitive modeling tools found in SCI-WISE are needed in order to make metacognition itself an object of thought and investigation. Furthermore, we have argued that, to be effective, such tools need to be embedded in curricula that engage students in inquiry about their own inquiry learning processes. In this way, students can develop theories about their own skills, such as collaboration and reflection, which should enable them to develop and refine widely useful cognitive and social skills. The architecture and capabilities of SCI-WISE will undoubtedly evolve as we gain experience with students' ideas regarding how best to model and support sociocognitive processes. In addition, there is the intriguing possibility that the students' own research on inquiry learning and metacognitive expertise could make significant contributions to educational research. With the support of a system such as SCI-WISE for reifying and testing their theories, students and their teachers could collaborate with educational researchers to address some of the difficult issues related to the nature of lifelong learning skills and the design of effective learning environments.

ACKNOWLEDGMENTS

This research was supported by the U.S. Department of Education's Office of Educational Research and Improvement, the James S. McDonnell Foundation, and the Educational Testing Service. This chapter contains material from White, Shimoda, and Frederiksen (1999) that is reprinted here with permission from its original publisher. We gratefully acknowledge numerous conversations with the ThinkerTools Research Group, whose members have contributed to this research. We thank Allan Collins for many stimulating discussions that have influenced this work. Finally, we thank Suzanne LaJoie, John Self, Christopher Schneider, and two anonymous reviewers for their constructive comments on an earlier version of this chapter.

REFERENCES

Astington, J., Harris, P., & Olson, D. (Eds.). (1988). *Developing theories of mind.* Cambridge: Cambridge University Press.

Baird, J., Fensham, P., Gunstone, R., & White, R. (1991). The importance of reflection in improving science teaching and learning. *Journal of Research in Science Teaching, 28*(2), 163–182.

Bielaczyc, K., & Collins, A. (1999). Learning communities in classrooms: A reconceptualization of educational practice. In C. M. Reigeluth (Ed.), *Instructional design theories and models* (pp. 269–292). Mahwah, NJ: Lawrence Erlbaum Associates.

Brewer, W. F., & Samarapungavan, A. (1991). Children's theories vs. scientific theories: Differences in reasoning or differences in knowledge? In R. R. Hoffman & D. S. Palermo (Eds.), *Cognition and the symbolic processes: Applied and ecological perspectives* (pp. 209–232). Hillsdale, NJ: Lawrence Erlbaum Associates.

Brown, A. (1987). Metacognition, executive control, self-regulation, and other more mysterious mechanisms. In F. E. Weinert & R. H. Kluwe (Eds.), *Metacognition, motivation, and understanding* (pp. 60–108). Hillsdale, NJ: Lawrence Erlbaum Associates.

Brown, A., & Campione, J. (1996). Psychological theory and the design of innovative learning environments: On procedures, principles, and systems. In L. Schauble & R. Glaser (Eds.), *Innovations in learning: New environments for education* (pp. 289–325). Hillsdale, NJ: Lawrence Erlbaum Associates.

Brown, A., & Palincsar, A. (1989). Guided, cooperative learning and individual knowledge acquisition. In L. Resnick (Ed.), *Knowing, learning, and instruction* (pp. 393–451). Hillsdale, NJ: Lawrence Erlbaum Associates.

Carey, S., & Smith, C. (1995). On understanding the nature of scientific knowledge. In D. N. Perkins, J. L. Schwartz, M. M. West, & M. S. Wiske (Eds.), *Software goes to school: Teaching for understanding with new technologies* (pp. 39–55). New York, NY: Oxford University Press.

Chi, M., Bassock, M., Lewis, M., Reimann, P., & Glaser, R. (1989). Self-explanations: How students study and use examples in learning to solve problems. *Cognitive Science, 13,* 145–182.

Collins, A., & Brown, J. S. (1988). The computer as a tool for learning through reflection. In H. Mandl & A. Lesgold (Eds.), *Learning issues for intelligent tutoring systems* (pp. 1–18). New York: Springer-Verlag.

Collins, A., & Ferguson, W. (1993). Epistemic forms and epistemic games: Structures and strategies to guide inquiry. *Educational Psychologist, 28,* 25–42.

Damon, W. (1990). Social relations and children's thinking skills. In D. Kuhn (Ed.), *Developmental perspectives on teaching and learning thinking skills* (pp. 95–107). Basel, Switzerland: Karger.

de Jong, H., & Rip, A. (1997). The computer revolution in science: Steps towards the realization of computer-supported discovery environments. *Artificial Intelligence, 91*(2), 225–256.

Derry, S. J. (1992). Metacognitive models of learning and instructional systems design. In M. Jones & P. H. Winne (Eds.), *Adaptive learning environments* (pp. 257–286). Berlin: Springer-Verlag.

Dewey, J. (1910). *How we think.* Boston: Heath.

Dewey, J. (1938). The pattern of inquiry. In *Logic: The theory of inquiry* (pp. 101–119). New York: Henry Holt.

Dillenbourg, P. (1992). The computer as a constructorium: Tools for observing one's own learning. In R. Moyse & M. Elsom-Cook (Eds.), *Knowledge negotiation* (pp. 185–198). London: Academic Press.

Driver, R., Asika, H., Leach, J., Mortimer, E., & Scott, P. (1994). Constructing scientific knowledge in the classroom. *Educational Researcher, 23*(7), 5–12.

Dunbar, K. (1995). How scientists really reason: Scientific reasoning in real-world laboratories. In R. Sternberg & J. Davidson (Eds.), *The nature of insight* (pp. 365–395). Cambridge, MA: MIT Press.

Feldman, C. (1992). The new theory of mind. *Human Development, 35,* 107–117.

Flavell, J. (1979). Metacognition and cognitive monitoring: A new area of cognitive-developmental inquiry. *American Psychologist, 34,* 906–911.

Franklin, S., & Graesser, A. (1997). Is it an agent, or just a program? A taxonomy for autonomous agents. In J. P. Müller, M. J. Wooldridge, & N. R. Jennings

(Eds.), *Intelligent agents III: Agent theories, architectures, and languages* (pp. 141–155). Berlin: Springer-Verlag.

Frederiksen, J. R., & White, B. Y. (1997). Cognitive facilitation: A method for promoting reflective collaboration. In *Proceedings of the Second International Conference on Computer Support for Collaborative Learning*. Toronto: University of Toronto Press.

Gopnik, A. (1996). The post-Piaget era. *Psychological Science, 7*(4), 221–225.

Harel, I., & Papert, S. (1990). Software design as a learning environment. *Interactive Learning Environments, 1*, 1–32.

Kafai, Y. B., & Resnick, M. (Eds.). (1996). *Constructionism in practice: Designing, thinking, and learning in a digital world*. Hillsdale, NJ: Lawrence Erlbaum Associates.

Karmiloff-Smith, A., & Inhelder, B. (1974–1975). If you want to get ahead, get a theory. *Cognition, 3*, 195–212.

Kearsley, G. (1993). Intelligent agents and instructional systems: Implications of a new paradigm. *Artificial Intelligence in Education, 4*(4), 295–304.

Lajoie, S. (1993). Computer environments as cognitive tools for enhancing learning. In S. P. Lajoie & S. J. Derry (Eds.), *Computers as cognitive tools* (pp. 261–288). Hillsdale, NJ: Lawrence Erlbaum Associates.

Minsky, M. (1985). *The society of mind*. New York: Simon & Schuster.

Nersessian, N. (1991). Conceptual change in science and in science education. In M. Matthews (Ed.), *History, philosophy and science teaching: Selected readings*. Toronto: OISE Press, Teachers College Press.

Okada, T., & Simon, H. (1997). Collaborative discovery in a scientific domain. *Cognitive Science, 21*, 109–146.

Palincsar, A. (1998). Social constructivist perspectives on teaching and learning. *Annual Review of Psychology, 49*, 345–375.

Palincsar, A., & Brown, A. (1989). Classroom dialogues to promote self-regulated comprehension. *Advances in Research on Teaching, 1*, 35–71.

Piaget, J. (1976). *The grasp of consciousness: Action and concept in the young child*. Cambridge, MA: Harvard University Press.

Russell, S., & Norvig, P. (1995). Intelligent agents. In *Artificial intelligence: A modern approach* (pp. 31–52). Upper Saddle River, NJ: Prentice-Hall.

Salomon, G., & Perkins, D. (1998). Individual and social aspects of learning. *Review of Research in Education, 23*, 1–24.

Scardamalia, M., & Bereiter, C. (1991). Higher levels of agency for children in knowledge building: A challenge for the design of new knowledge media. *Journal of the Learning Sciences, 1*(1), 37–68.

Scardamalia, M., & Bereiter, C. (1994). Computer support for knowledge-building communities. *Journal of the Learning Sciences, 3*(3), 265–283.

Schauble, L., & Glaser, R. (1990). Scientific thinking in children and adults. In D. Kuhn (Eds.), *Developmental perspectives on teaching and learning thinking skills* (pp. 9–27). Basel: Karger.

Schauble, L., Raghavan, K., & Glaser, R. (1993). The discovery and reflection notation: A graphical trace for supporting self-regulation in computer-based laboratories. In S. P. Lajoie & S. J. Derry (Eds.), *Computers as cognitive tools* (pp. 319–337). Hillsdale, NJ: Lawrence Erlbaum Associates.

Schoenfeld, A. H. (1987). What's all the fuss about metacognition? In A. H. Schoenfeld (Ed.), *Cognitive science and mathematics education* (pp. 189–215). Hillsdale, NJ: Lawrence Erlbaum Associates.

Self, J. (1992). Computational viewpoints. In R. Moyse & M. Elsom-Cook (Eds.), *Knowledge negotiation* (pp. 21–40). London: Academic Press.

Shimoda, T., White, B., & Frederiksen, J. (1999). Acquiring and transferring intellectual skills with modifiable software agents in a virtual inquiry support environment. In *Proceedings of the 32nd Annual Hawaii International Conference on System Sciences*. Los Alamitos, CA: IEEE Computer Society.

Slavin, R. (1995). *Cooperative learning: Theory, research, and practice* (2nd ed.). Needham Heights, MA: Allyn and Bacon.

von Glasersfeld, E. (1995). *Radical constructivism: A way of knowing and learning*. London: Falmer Press.

Vygotsky, L. (1978). *Mind in society: The development of higher psychological processes*. (M. Cole, V. John-Steiner, S. Scribner, & E. Souberman, Eds. and Trans.). Cambridge: Cambridge University Press.

Wertsch, J. (1991). *Voices of the mind*. Cambridge, MA: Harvard University Press.

White, B. (1993). ThinkerTools: Causal models, conceptual change, and science education. *Cognition and Instruction, 10*(1), 1–100.

White, B., & Frederiksen, J. (1998). Inquiry, modeling, and metacognition: Making science accessible to all students. *Cognition and Instruction, 16*(1), 3–117.

White, B., & Frederiksen, J. (1990). Causal model progressions as a foundation for intelligent learning environments. *Artificial Intelligence, 24*, 99–157.

White, B., Shimoda, T., & Frederiksen, J. (1999). Enabling students to construct theories of collaborative inquiry and reflective learning: Computer support for metacognitive development. *International Journal of Artificial Intelligence in Education, 10*(2), 151–182.

5

Cognitive Approaches to Web-Based Instruction

Brenda Sugrue
University of Iowa

The World Wide Web has the technical capabilities to implement any instructional strategy. Its most obvious instructional use is as a limitless online library of hyperlinked information that students can access from any computer with an Internet connection and browsing software. Another obvious use is for collaborative learning, using asynchronous communication tools such as e-mail and bulletin boards, or synchronous tools such as chat rooms and video-conferencing. It is becoming increasingly easy to deliver online assessment and multimedia resources and to access online databases for data entry and retrieval. Finally, with the advent of integrated online authoring systems such as WebCT (Web Course Tools) (Goldberg, 1997; *http://homebrew1.cs.ubc.ca/webct/*), which permit the management and tracking of student use, the Web has become a universal metaenvironment for learning.

Any of the programs described in the *Computers as Cognitive Tools* books could be adapted for Web-based delivery. Indeed, many successful non-Web systems, such as Interactive Multi-Media Exercises (IMMEX; Stevens, McCoy, & Kwak, 1991; *http://www.immex.ucla.edu/*) and Computer Supported Intentional Learning Environments (CSILE; Scardamalia

& Bereiter, 1994; *http://csile.oise.utoronto.ca/*), are going "online," making their tools and resources accessible via the Web. The same issues and debates that surround the design of non-Web computer-based instruction apply to Web-based instruction. The three camps introduced in the first *Computers as Cognitive Tools* book are represented on the Web. There are full-blown intelligent tutors constantly modeling the current state of learners' knowledge based on learners' responses to questions and tasks presented in the browser. There are sites that act as jumping-off points from which students can explore subsets of information on the Web to construct unique and personally meaningful cognitive structures with little or no system control. And there are middle-ground applications that attempt to balance learner freedom and system control, perhaps providing feedback to students as data for self-reflection, but not dictating what they should do next.

What makes the computer (or the Web) a cognitive tool is itself open to interpretation. Lajoie (1993) used the term *cognitive tool* to refer to any tool that can support aspects of learners' cognitive processes, for example, taking over some of the more mundane elements of a task to free the learner's cognitive space for higher order thinking, or allowing learners to generate and test hypotheses in the context of problem solving. Salomon, Perkins, and Globerson (1991) viewed the computer as a potential "partner in cognition," either extending the cognitive capabilities of the user temporarily or increasing the cognitive capabilities of the user permanently by leaving behind a cognitive residue in the mind of the user.

Jonassen and Reeves (1996) took perhaps the broadest view of the term, using it to refer to any tools "that enhance the cognitive powers of human beings during thinking, problem solving, and learning" (p. 693). They included in the category tools such as databases, spreadsheets, expert systems, multimedia and hypermedia construction software, computer-based conferencing, collaborative knowledge construction environments, computer programming languages, and microworlds. Some uses of these tools render them more cognitively powerful than other uses. For example, having a student create a hypermedia program to represent a body of information may be a more powerful cognitive experience, and result in deeper understanding of the domain, than having a student search an existing hyperstructure of the information.

In this chapter, the term *cognitive* is interpreted as a variable attribute of any Web-based instructional application or learning environment. The extent to which a tool is performing a cognitive function in the learning process depends on the extent to which it embodies instructional strategies that have been shown (in other instructional contexts) to have specific and powerful cognitive effects. Four aspects of any learning environment organize this chapter and consider the extent to which instructional resources on the Web incorporate, or might incorporate, cognitively powerful instructional strategies. The four instructional elements are information organization and access, authentic activities, collaborative learning, and student modeling. These elements provide support for four cognitive processes involved in learning: acquisition of declarative knowledge (Anderson, 1993); connecting knowledge to situational conditions that trigger application and proceduralization of knowledge (Anderson, Reder, & Simon 1996); refining and constructing shared understandings of knowledge (Lave & Wenger, 1991); and the metacognitive monitoring of knowledge acquisition to ensure accuracy and efficiency (Flavell, 1979). These four issues also reflect popular trends in cognitive approaches to instruction and can be linked to particular capabilities of the Web, such as hypermedia, multimedia, communication, and recording.

The hypermedia capabilities of the computer, and of the Web in particular, have been hailed as having potentially powerful cognitive effects (Erickson & Lehrer, this volume; Jonassen, 1989; Rouet, Levonen, Dillon, & Spiro, 1996). For example, it has been hypothesized that learning is facilitated if information is organized in a manner that reflects the organization of knowledge in human memory, that is, in a linked network of nodes. However, hypertext capabilities alone do not make the Web a cognitive tool. To qualify as a cognitive approach to instruction, strategies for supporting the cognitive processing of the information have to be embedded in either the structure of the hypertext or the activities that constrain and focus students' exploration of information on the Web.

A second criterion that can be used to determine whether the Web is used as a cognitive tool is the extent to which it provides opportunities for situated learning. Most current cognitive models of instruction adhere to the principle of situated learning: that knowledge acquired while doing authentic activities is more transferable than knowledge acquired during more abstract or abstracted activities (Brown, Collins, & Duguid, 1989; Greeno, Smith, & Moore, 1992). Authentic activities are the hallmark of instructional approaches such as cognitive apprenticeship (Collins, Brown, & Newman, 1989), anchored instruction (Cognition and Technology Group at Vanderbilt, 1992), and problem-based learning (Barrows, 1986).

Instructional approaches that emphasize authentic activities usually involve collaborative learning as well. The theory behind collaborative learning is that the social construction of knowledge leads to deeper processing and understanding than learning alone (Slavin, 1990). The communication capabilities of the Web make it easier than ever before to support collaborative learning environments. However, as with the hypermedia capability, mere access to communication tools on the Web does not guarantee desirable cognitive effects. The use of those tools has to be structured or linked to situated learning activities to support development of appropriate cognitive processes and knowledge. An example of a structured collaborative environment is found in the Web version of CSILE; students use a bulletin board to create a database in which they construct and extend their knowledge about particular domains, categorizing their contributions as one of five "thinking types."

The fourth instructional component considered as an indicator of cognitive approaches to instruction on the Web is student modeling. The modeling versus nonmodeling debate was explored in the first *Computers as Cognitive Tools* book (Lajoie & Derry, 1993). Student modeling has been most closely associated with the kind of system control and guidance of learning activities that characterize intelligent tutoring systems. However, Derry and Lajoie (1993) pointed out that student modeling does not have to be accompanied by system control. Student modeling can be embedded in computer programs that also support self-direction, self-monitoring, or social construction of knowledge. There are fully fledged intelligent tutoring systems on the Web (e.g., ELM-ART; Brusilovsky, Schwarz, & Weber, 1997; *http://cogpsy.uni-trier.de:8000/TLServ-e.html*). However, the combined tracking and communication capabilities of the Web facilitate a great variety of student modeling and uses of the models.

This chapter describes uses of the Web that reflect these four aspects of cognitive approaches to instruction: information organization and access, authentic activities, collaborative learning, and student modeling. My conclusion is that at a minimum, to function as a cognitive tool for learning, the Web should support exploration of constrained knowledge spaces to complete online or offline authentic activities. To ensure accurate and shared acquisition of knowledge, this approach can be combined with opportunities for collaboration with peers and experts and for individualized monitoring and feedback.

INFORMATION ORGANIZATION AND ACCESS

A number of assumptions about the cognitive effects of learning from hypermedia have become popular. Tergan (1997) summarized those assumptions and provided a convincing argument that empirical evidence does not support them. Specifically, it is now clear that information presented to students in nonlinear networks of nodes and links does not result in "better" processing and representation of that information in memory. In addition, merely providing information in hypermedia structure does not lead students to regulate their own paths through that information and construct well-integrated, personally meaningful knowledge structures in their minds. The benefits of hypermedia are evident only when combined with other instructional strategies, such as well-defined goals and tasks, modeling, and scaffolding (Jacobson, Maouri, Mishra, & Kolar, 1996; Jonassen, 1992). In the absence of these instructional strategies, only students with high self-regulatory skills or high prior knowledge of the domain or a propensity for exploration tend to profit from the kinds of exploratory environments that are associated with hypermedia (Jacobson et al., 1996; Lee & Lehman, 1993).

The hypermedia capabilities of the Web can support a variety of approaches to providing information to learners. Learners can get information from at least four kinds of sources on the Web:

- Non-instructional sources that provide multipurpose searchable databases of information on specific topics, for example, museum sites, government sites, online databases, and expert systems.
- Instructionally oriented information resources that have been created or compiled for specific topics or audiences, for example, course notes, assignment instructions, or grouped sets of links to Web sites that relate to a particular topic.
- Student-controlled embedded help systems that can be accessed during performance of a task or activity.
- System-controlled feedback (immediate or delayed) that is provided based on analysis of a student's performance on some task or activity.

Non-Instructional Information Sources

The hypermedia capabilities of the Web make it possible to access any information source that is linked to the Web and follow a series of links to related information. For example, museum sites, government sites, corporate sites, newspapers, and radio stations can all be accessed by students in their searches for information related to topics they are studying. Search engines can be used to find sites that might have relevant information. Some of these sites incorporate link structures and navigation support that make it easier for students to find information. For example, the Smithsonian museum sites include clickable image maps of the museums (*http://www.nasm.edu/NASMDOCS/MUSEUM.html*); the White House site has forms to search text and image databases (*http://library.whitehouse.gov/Search/Query-Photo.html*).

In addition to sites that consist of pages of hyperlinked information, online expert systems are being developed for the Web. An expert system contains the procedural knowledge (if-then rules) that one or more experts use to make decisions in a particular domain. A user is asked questions about the current state of a situation or problem, and the system returns the decision that the expert would make in that case. The sites *http://www. emsl.pnl.gov:2080/proj/neuron/ai/demos.html* and *http://www.exsysinfo. com/Wren/menu.html* contain links to demonstrations of how these systems work on the Web. In some cases, the user progresses through a series of screens, each requiring the selection of a response to one question, and at the end the system responds with a conclusion. In other cases, the user makes selections for multiple parameters on one screen while the conclusion is presented dynamically in a window on the same screen.

Jonassen and Reeves (1996) make the point that expert systems become cognitive tools only if the user is involved in the creation of the knowledge base, engaging in cognitive task analysis. Cognitive task analysis can involve a variety of techniques for extracting the decision rules and supporting declarative knowledge from experts (see Shute, this volume). However, an expert system can also have a cognitive effect if the user can view the if-then rules underlying the system or the reasoning that the system has used to arrived at a particular conclusion. Some of the current online expert systems do display their rules or reasoning, or both, for particular cases.

Instructional Information Sources

Many commercial Web sites are deliberately constructed to be instructional resources for teachers, students, or the general public. One instructional site for the general public, The Ability Utility (*http://learn2.com/*), has step-by-step instructions for common tasks, such as ironing a shirt and changing the oil in a car. The content of these how-to pages is cognitively supportive because it clearly lays out the conditions and actions for each step in a procedure, uses graphics and simple animations to demonstrate steps, and contains definitions and examples of concepts that are mentioned in the steps.

Some commercial sites include resources to help teachers integrate the information at the site with other resources. For example, the Discovery Channel's Web site has complete lesson plans, which include the learning goals targeted, study questions, activities, and links to other Web sites that relate to the topics of particular television programs (*http://school.discovery. com/spring98/programs/ultimateguide-snakes/index.html*). Clips from the television programs can be previewed at the site, the broadcast schedule can be checked, and videos can be ordered. Noncommercial sites developed for instructional purposes also contain many resources that teachers and students can integrate into classroom activities. For example, the Knowledge Integration Environment (KIE; Linn, 1996; *http://www.kie.berkeley.edu/*) provides an interface through which students access a selected set of Web sites that are relevant to a scientific issue they are debating. The Science Learning Network (*http://www.sln.org/*) has compiled sets of links to resources related to specific scientific topics.

Passport to Knowledge, a government-sponsored program involving the National Aeronautics and Space Administration (NASA) and the National Science Foundation, offers electronic field trips to places like Antarctica and the Amazon basin rain forest (*http://passport.ivv. nasa.gov/*). These field trips allow learners to acquire information in realistic contexts. They also allow learners to interact live online with experts in scientific fields. These experts tell stories that give students anchors to which they can link scientific knowledge. The experts also act as role models for the students. The NASA site has activities that students can do offline to apply knowledge they gained during electronic field trips.

A site can combine instructional resources for many audiences. For example, the University of Iowa's Virtual Hospital guides patients' and doctors' searches for online information on specific medical problems (*http://indy.radiology.uiowa.edu/Patients/Patients.html*). It also contains all of the information on particular cases ("virtual patients") from graphic and text descriptions of symptoms, to test results, diagnoses, and treatment recommendations (*http://www.vh.org/Providers/Simulations/VirtualPeds Patients/ Case03/Case03.html*; see Fig. 5.1). These cases are used for continuing medical education and have online practice and real tests associated with them. The Virtual Hospital comes close to being an online electronic performance support system (EPSS). An EPSS provides access to information, resources, and tools needed to perform a job (Kirkley & Duffy, 1997). The line between performance support tools and information sources such as expert systems is fuzzy. An expert system can be part of an EPSS. Generally an EPSS is designed to provide support for on-the-job learning

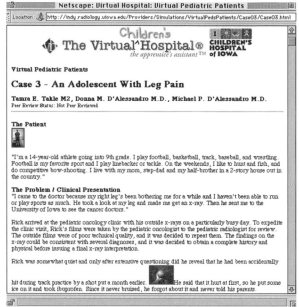

FIG. 5.1.   *Case-based information in the Virtual Hospital ®.*

and performance, with the performer's need for support diminishing over time. (Examples of browser-based EPSSs can be found at the Web site *http://www.tgx.com/enhance/dddemos.htm.*)

Many instructional sites have been created by instructors themselves. Some of these contain pages of links to sites that are relevant to a particular topic, or they embed links to relevant sites within instructor-generated information on a page. Both of these techniques structure the learner's exploration of the Web. Within Web sites for particular courses, information relating to particular topics or assignments can be organized in hierarchical structures. WebCT has a built-in tool for creating these kinds of hierarchical structures of information. Another example from an Introduction to Principles of Sociology course at the University of Iowa uses the same organization for the information related to course assignments (see Fig. 5.2). In addition, with the WebCT system, pages of information can be linked to audio or video clips, as well as to other built-in tools, such as bulletin boards, a student note pad, self-tests, and quizzes. The standardization of navigation features and the integration of information resources with other learning resources on a topic reduce the cognitive load on the student and free up mental capacity for processing the information rather than finding the information.

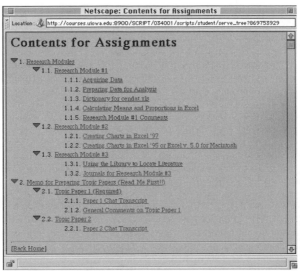

FIG. 5.2. *Hierachically structured information.*

Spiro maintains that environments in which the learner can criss-cross a set of information units (e.g., cases or examples), in a variety of ways, for a variety of purposes or from different conceptual perspectives, result in the acquisition of flexible knowledge (Spiro, Feltovich, Jacobson, & Coulson, 1992). This is called cognitive flexibility theory, and hypertext or hypermedia facilitate its implementation. To be implemented, this approach requires multiple structuring of the same set of information nodes, or a set of goals that require the learner to interact with the same network of information in different ways. Jonassen et al. (1997) describe some Web-based cognitive flexibility hypertext environments that allow students to approach and develop solutions for cases using multiple themes and perspectives (e.g., *http://www.ems.psu.edu/Wolf*). A single case can be viewed from multiple perspectives, or multiple cases can be crisscrossed from one perspective or theme by following the appropriate links. This approach to structuring networks of information on the Web has the added cognitive support of a context or task to focus the learner's exploration.

User-Controlled Embedded Help

Just as non-Web computer-based instructional programs incorporate context sensitive help systems (Derry & Hawkes, 1993), the Web can also be used as the interface to online help systems. Embedded help can be student or system controlled. If it is system controlled, then it is categorized as feedback (and will be discussed in the next section). Most computer software includes user-controlled embedded help; if a help button is clicked during performance of a particular function of the software, a help window pops up with the specific instructions for completing that function.

A student-controlled online help system can be embedded in a program with specific instructional goals. For example, in the Speech Writing Assistant, which was developed for a course at the University of Northern Colorado (*http://etip.unco.edu/SPCO100/spco100.htm*), students work through the steps in writing a speech and at any time can click on four help buttons that provide different types of help: What now? How do I do that? Why? and Show me an example (see Fig. 5.3). These help options are similar to those embedded in Schank's goal-based scenario programs (Schank & Jona, 1991; Schank & Kass, 1996).

Brusilovsky et al. (1997) described a Web-based system called ELM-ART that incorporates help buttons that take the learner to pages with prerequisite knowledge for the content on the page where the student requests the help (*http://cogpsy.uni-trier.de:8000/TLServ-e.html*). Students can also request help as they complete online exercises. The ELM-ART system includes system-controlled help, based on maintenance of a student model. Another example of a learning environment that includes user-

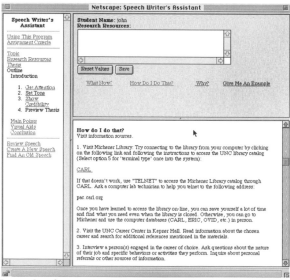

FIG. 5.3. *Example of an authentic activity with user-controlled embedded help.*

controlled embedded help is IMMEX, a system for problem-based learn-ing and assessment developed at UCLA (Stevens, McCoy, & Kwak, 1991; *http://www.immex.ucla.edu/*). IMMEX allows students to access different types of information sources in order to solve a problem.

An online application that provides embedded help provides a higher level of cognitive support than nonembedded information for at least three reasons. First, the fact that the information is embedded implies that the learner is engaged in some activity and is acquiring information in the context of its use. Therefore, the learner is more likely to proceduralize the knowledge. Second, a learner is exposed only to essential information, reducing the risk of cognitive overload from too much information. Third, as with expert systems, embedded help systems require extensive cogni-tive task analysis during their design so that the knowledge and thought processes of experts are used to structure the task and link appropriate help scripts to elements of task performance. Thus, the cognitive validity of both the task and the procedural knowledge acquired is increased.

System-Generated Feedback

Feedback given to a learner during performance is information that the system has determined the learner needs at a particular point in the instructional program in order to acquire accurate knowledge. Feedback implies that a model of the student's emerging knowledge is being main-tained. However, the extent of the student model can vary. The system might keep track of only the accuracy of the most recent response, for example, the response to an item on a self-test, giving feedback that explains why the selected response was correct or incorrect. The system might keep track of the total number of items answered correctly on a quiz without tracking which items the student misses, feedback being limited to an overall score. At the other extreme, the system might record the entire sequence of actions that the student took to solve a complex prob-lem. These data might be used to identify patterns that indicate particular knowledge gaps and misconceptions, with the feedback highlighting information that might fill those gaps.

Currently on the Web, there are many examples of self-tests and quizzes where students get immediate feedback on the correctness of their answers and additional information to explain why an answer was correct or incor-rect (e.g., see *http://omie.med.jhmi.edu/LectureLinks/index.html* and *http://www.kumc.edu/instruction/medicine/pathology/ ed/exams/ exam850.html*). There are also examples of intelligent tutoring systems on the Web where task-specific information in the form of hints or suggestions for further study is given to students based on ongoing analysis of student actions (e.g., *http://cogpsy.uni-trier.de:8000/TLServ-e.html*).

There is an expectation that information received as help or feedback during computer-based instruction must be immediate. The communication capabilities of the Web make it possible to have a human involved in the feedback loop. There are sites on the Web where students can submit work and receive feedback later by e-mail or as direct edits to their work. For example, at the Logal site (*http://www.logal.net/*), students can record answers, ideas, and questions as they work through online materials and activities. The students can save their work in files on a server or on their own computers, and their teachers can access those files, add comments to them, and return them to the students' online folders. Similarly, within the WebCT system, students can upload their documents to a student presentation area. The instructor can download those documents, edit them, and upload the edited documents so that the student can access them. In the quiz module of the WebCT system, the instructor can enter specific feedback on student responses (see Fig. 5.4); students receive this feedback when they access the "graded" quiz.

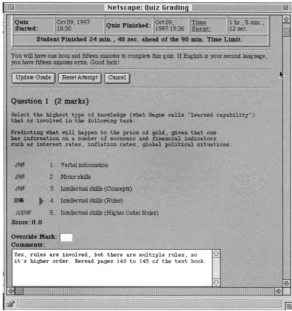

FIG. 5.4.   *Information as feedback.*

Summary

The hypermedia capabilities of the Web make it possible to provide a variety of types of informational resources that can support the internal cognitive processes involved in the acquisition of declarative and procedural knowledge. One of the basic principles of learning is that the greater the investment of mental effort during acquisition, the more transferable and usable the knowledge is (Salomon, 1984; Schmidt & Bjork, 1992). Therefore, any system that encourages learners to invest mental effort to find and integrate information could be regarded as a cognitive approach. However, simply linking information sources into the Web does not constitute a cognitive approach to instruction. Other instructional activities (either online or offline) have to be created to guide students' use of non-instructional information that exists on the Web. Sites that integrate information with other instructional resources or that structure information so that it reflects expert knowledge provide more support for knowledge acquisition.

One can embed information within activities so that students can access specific information they need at any point during task completion. In this case, the learner has to invest less mental effort to get the appropriate information, but the information is acquired in the context of use which is another powerful cognitive approach. To some (Anderson, Corbett, Koedinger, & Pelletier, 1995), the most cognitively powerful instructional systems are those that monitor student performance and prescribe appropriate information based on analysis of that performance. The Web supports traditional intelligent tutoring systems as well as systems where informational feedback is generated by a human.

AUTHENTIC ACTIVITIES

Situated learning advocates (Greeno et al., 1992) believe that knowledge is more transferable if it is acquired in contexts similar to those in which it is likely to be used. Authentic activities provide an environment for situated learning. Authentic activities are designed to induce the kind of cognitive processes engaged in by experts in a domain and to lead novices to confront and complete gaps in their knowledge. Authentic activities are the basis of instructional approaches such as cognitive apprenticeship (Collins et al., 1989), anchored instruction (Cognition and Technology Group at Vanderbilt, 1992), and problem-based learning (Barrows, 1986).

Authentic activities can function as learning activities and as opportunities for dynamic assessment. Dynamic assessment, which occurs while students are in the process of solving a problem or completing some task (Lajoie & Lesgold, 1992), provides diagnostic information on the current cognitive abilities, weaknesses, and potential for improvement of students in a particular domain. That information is used to provide "just-in-time" assistance in the form of hints or other scaffolding to help individual students incrementally increase their proficiency. In some cases, the level of assistance that a student requires to complete a problem successfully becomes the index of proficiency (Campione & Brown, 1990).

Authentic activities do not have to be as realistic as one might think in order to serve as dynamic assessments and generate useful diagnostic information. Royer, Cisero, and Carlo (1993) point out the difference between assessments or activities that have task authenticity and those that have process authenticity. They define tasks that have processing authenticity as tasks that measure (or provide opportunity to develop) critical component skills of the larger authentic task—skills that if absent would "prevent the acceptable performance of the authentic task" (p. 238). Anderson, Reder, and Simon (1996) also advocated less emphasis on the surface authenticity or "real-world trappings" (p. 9) of the problems presented to students. Anderson suggested that the critical aspect of a task is that it engage learners in cognitive processes that will transfer to a wide variety of future tasks.

There are many examples of instructional programs on the Web that incorporate authentic activities and therefore support situated learning. These activities usually involve students' working on realistic cases or problems. The Web can also be used for activities that might appear less contextually authentic but have cognitive processing authenticity. In addition to contextually and cognitively authentic tasks, the Web is an ideal environment for construction activities, in the spirit of Papert's (1993) notion of constructionism, which is similar to the more popular term *constructivism*. Papert suggests that the kind of knowledge construction that students do in their heads is best supported by the provision of opportunities for the construction of public artifacts. Construction activities in the context of the Web involve students' building their own web pages or products that will themselves reside on the Web. The cognitive processing that learners have to go through to find, organize, and integrate information into a presentation for others increases retention and transfer (Kafai, 1995; Lehrer, 1993).

There are what might be regarded as three distinct types of authentic activities on the Web: contextually authentic activities, cognitively authentic activities, and construction activities.

Contextually Authentic Activities

Many computer-based learning environments that were developed for problem-based learning are being adapted for Web delivery. For example, the IMMEX system developed at UCLA has been transferred to the Web. Students work on realistic cases and problems by accessing information to make the decisions involved in solving the problem. In a problem-based Web course at Simon Frasier University (Teles & Collings, 1997), students complete assignments in a virtual lab environment using software for circuit analysis, circuit simulation, and circuit prototyping. They can conduct virtual lab experiments, as well as collaborate and share information with others.

The problem-based learning environments developed by researchers at the Georgia Institute of Technology (Guzdial et al., 1996) have adapted their CaMILE system to the Web-based Web-SMILE environment (*http://www.cc.gatech.edu/gvu/people/Faculty/mark.guzdial/WStour/tour. html*). In Web-SMILE, students work collaboratively on real problems using bulletin boards and a shared whiteboard that classifies the activities into the four original components of problem-based learning (Barrows, 1986): sharing already known facts about the problem, proposing ideas for solutions, listing information that needs to be found (learning issues), and creating action plans.

Another example of using the Web to support authentic activity comes from an online course on sociology principles at the University of Iowa. Students are given all of the instructions to download real data from the Census Bureau Web site, and they are asked to do some analysis of the data using Excel software. Students enter the results of their analysis in a form on another web page (see Fig. 5.5).

Cognitively Authentic Activities

The Web can be used for a wide variety of cognitively authentic assessments. I designed activities that elicit the cognitive processes used by experts in a field for a course on performance analysis. Many of the activities consisted of a scenario followed by a series of multiple-choice or

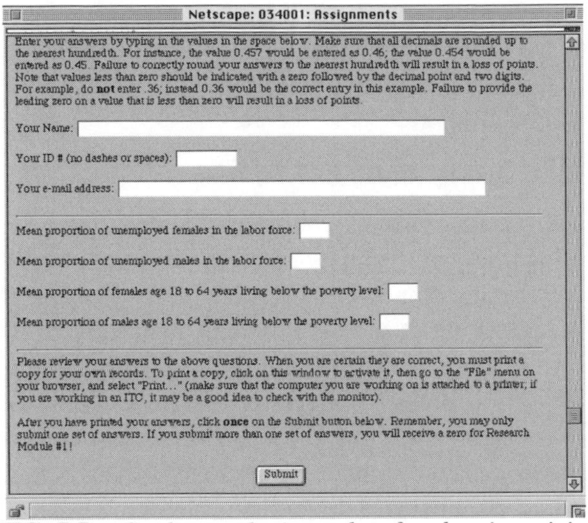

FIG. 5.5. *Students submit results of authentic activity.*

matching questions that asked students to make decisions that experts would make (see Fig. 5.6). Then students would be asked to type a paragraph explaining their selections. Students were instructed to use aspects of the scenario and references to instructional theory and research in their explanations.

Many instructional Web sites incorporate self-assessment activities that require learners to think like experts. For example, Johns Hopkins School of Medicine has a set of self-assessments based on an online database of full-color histology images. Students can choose the parameters of the self-test, get hints, and see the correct answers. After each question, the student indicates whether her own answer was correct or incorrect. (*http://omie.med.jhmi.edu/LectureLinks/HistologyLinks.html*). A score is computed based on the student's self-assessment.

Cognitively authentic multimedia assessments are also possible on the Web; for example, instead of presenting a text-based case or scenario or a graphic image, one could present a short video clip or audio segment that students would analyze or interpret to make a diagnosis, decision, or recommendation for action.

Construction Activities

Having students create their own web pages or products that can be accessed on the Web is another cognitive approach to using the Web as a

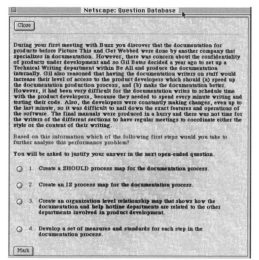

FIG. 5.6.   *Example of a cognitively authentic task.*

learning environment. The cognitive effects would be similar to those reported by Lehrer (1993). The learner must create and externalize a knowledge structure of a domain. Lehrer found that students who designed their own hypermedia programs were able to remember and elaborate on the content one year later, whereas students in a control group could not. When students become designers of information resources, they are forced to integrate and process information deeply (Jonassen & Reeves, 1996). As they learn to use links within their hypermedia documents, they become more conscious of the audience for their compositions and of their power to structure multiple pathways through information for an audience (Erickson & Lehrer, this volume).

Solis (1997) described a project called Galileo's Web (*http://riceinfo.rice.edu/armadillo/Rice/Galileo/*), where "students had access to a variety of learning activities to motivate them and engage them in a constructive process" (p. 394). The Web-based activities were combined with more traditional activities such as visits from experts in the field and consultation of other media such as books and movies. One of the activities presented students with the goal or problem of designing a home for Galileo, with the restrictions of a number of rules. Students used html and vmrl editing software to construct their blueprints as actual architects would do. The blueprints were posted to the Web for others to view.

Sites such as the Discovery Channel and NASA have student showcase areas where students' work can be submitted and displayed (e.g.,

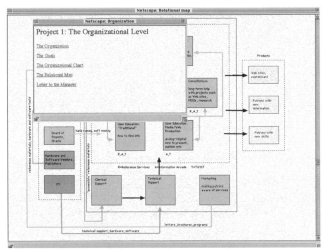

FIG. 5.7. *Sample student presentation area.*

http://school.discovery.com/showcase/parismiddleschool/index.html).
Oliver (1997) described many other Web sites where student-constructed
products and pages are accessible. The site ThinkQuest (*http://io.
advanced.org/thinkquest/create/*) is completely devoted to helping students develop their own instructional homepages that others can access.

The WebCT development and delivery environment has a student presentation area where students can upload files and create links to the files
so that anyone can view their work, which can include graphics, video,
and sound (see Fig. 5.7). Another integrated system for creating Web-
based instruction, Web Course in a Box (*http://www.madduck.com*), has
built-in forms to help students create their own homepages.

Summary

Three cognitive approaches to support situated learning exist on the Web:

- Contextually authentic activities that require students to think and act like
  experts in order to solve realistic problems.
- Cognitively authentic activities that allow the practice of cognitive
  processes that are critical to developing expertise in a domain.
- Construction activities that require analysis, integration, and organization
  of information in order to communicate it to others in a variety of products
  such as multimedia reports or Web sites.

COLLABORATIVE LEARNING

The potential of the Web for supporting collaborative learning is unprecedented. Learning communities can now involve students, teachers, and other professionals from any location. Scientists can work on collaborative projects with teachers and students in classrooms without ever leaving their labs. Students can collaborate with students in other schools and other countries as they develop ideas, skills, and products. Students in a class can collaborate outside class without having to meet in person. The theory behind collaborative learning is that the social construction of knowledge leads to deeper processing and understanding than does learning alone (Slavin, 1990).

The bulletin board and the chat room have become the backbone of many Web-based learning environments. Sophisticated Web-based collaborative learning environments incorporate not only real-time, text-based conversation, but also audio- and videoconferencing, and shared work spaces, where multiple users can collaboratively work on the same document or application. These multimedia shared work spaces are facilitated by software such as Microsoft's Netmeeting (*http://www. microsoft.com/netmeeting/*), Intel's Proshare (*http://www.intel.com/proshare/ conferencing/index.htm*), and CU-SeeMe (*http://cu-seeme.cornell.edu/*). Multiuser object-oriented (MOO) text-based virtual reality environments now have a Web-based equivalent, WOOs (Web object oriented), which provide browser-based access to virtual rooms for a variety of collaborative text-based and multimedia learning activities (e.g., *http:// lingua.utdallas.edu:7000/11*).

With so many online communication tools, the challenge is to use the tools to facilitate deep and effortful cognitive processing for all of those involved in the collaboration. The rest of this section describes some examples of online collaborative environments that appear to do this by either structuring the collaborative activity or linking the collaboration to situated learning activities.

The Knowledge Forum, the Web version of CSILE (*http://kf.oise. utoronto.ca/webcsile/demo.html*), uses a bulletin board system to facilitate the collaborative production and use of dynamic knowledge bases. Students post items that are categorized as five "thinking types": Problem, My Theory, Need for Understanding, Plan, and New Learning. A teacher monitors the forum and coaches students toward discovery of expert knowledge.

The WebSMILE environment already described as an example of an environment that had students engage in authentic problem-based learning activities is similar to the Knowledge Forum, in that it has students collaboratively contribute facts, ideas, and learning issues to a collaborative white board. Most Web-based environments that incorporate authentic or construction activities also involve collaboration among students to solve problems or generate Web-based products.

The WebCT system includes a number of tools to support collaborative learning: chat rooms, a bulletin board that can have multiple public and private forums, and a student presentation area where text, graphic, and multimedia files can be jointly constructed and viewed. Bulletin boards can be linked to specific pages of content, and messages posted can include attachments that are text and nontext documents. The instructor can give feedback by downloading a document, editing it, and uploading the corrected version so that individual students or students in a small group can view the feedback.

AT&T has a site where teachers and students can form and work in cross-classroom learning circles on theme-based projects (*http://www.att. com/education/lcguide/toc.html*). Teachers and students use online instructions, checklists, and other tools to progress through a sequence of six phases for any learning circle: getting ready, opening the circle, planning projects, exchanging student work, publication, and closing the learning circle.

A Global Schoolhouse project called "Scientist on Tap" has scientists at facilities such as the Jet Propulsion Labs in California and Carnegie Mellon University engage in live discussions with students using the CU-SeeMe software (*http://www.gsn.org/teach/articles/sot.html*). NASA's online program Sharing NASA allows students to work on projects with each other and interact with experts in online chat rooms and through e-mail (*http://quest.arc.nasa.gov/interactive/*).

The nonprofit company GlobaLearn Inc. has a Web site that allows students to participate (vicariously) in live expeditions all over the world (*http://www.globalearn.org*). At each stopping point on the expedition, the team is hosted by a local school child who becomes part of the online community, sharing information about life in the other country. Video and photographs of the expedition are transmitted by satellite to the server daily and can be viewed on the Web. The site includes databases compiled by the explorers to which students can add their own data and make dynamic comparisons between aspects of life in different countries.

The Science Learning Network (*http://www.sln.org/schools/index. html*) provides a cyberplace where schools can collaborate on scientific topics (e.g., *http://www.sci.mus.mn.us/sln/monarchs/*). Students communicate through a message board, contribute data from scientific experiments and observations, and follow reports from live expeditions around the world.

The Discovery Channel provides opportunities for the development of virtual learning communities to work on topics introduced in Discovery Channel television programs (*http://school.discovery.com*). There are online archives of student showcases. The Discovery Channel site provides complete sets of instructional resources to support online and offline learning related to specific national academic standards and benchmarks (e.g., *http://school.discovery.com/spring98/programs/ thebigwet/index.html*).

The Web is not only a venue for collaborative learning among students or between teachers and students. It is also becoming a vehicle to facilitate collaborative professional development for teachers, as described by Derry , Gance, Gance, and Schlager (this volume). Derry et al. discuss the difficult issue of how to monitor and assess the quality of the knowledge that is built by virtual learning communities.

STUDENT MODELING

The concept of student modeling comes from intelligent tutoring systems, in which a student's actions are recorded and analyzed to create a model of the student's level of mastery of specific knowledge units in a curriculum. In addition, students' motivational states can be modeled, based on perception and preference data gathered during a set of learning activities. For example, students can rate their perceived difficulty of tasks or topics, and from that the teacher can infer how much effort a student is likely to invest, based on the theory that students with very low and very high perceived difficulty will not invest appropriate effort (Clark, 1999).

Information maintained in a model of a student's knowledge and motivation can be used to adapt many aspects of the instructional environment for individual students. Alternatively, the student model can be reported to students as information that individual students or groups of students can use to direct their own future learning activities. Without system intervention based on the model, the model is acting as an external support for the metacognitive skill of monitoring.

Just like any other computer environment, student performance and motivation can be monitored on the Web. Information access, task performance, and interactions during collaborative learning events can all be tracked. The information gathered can be interpreted and used in a variety of ways. There are complete intelligent tutoring systems on the Web (e.g., ELM-ART; Brusilovsky et al., 1997; *http://cogpsy.uni-trier.de:8000/ TLServ-e.html/*). ELM-ART is an extremely sophisticated adaptive environment for learning LISP programming. It combines elements of learner control with continuous updating of a student model on which system-generated guidance is based.

Each lesson in ELM-ART has a test of prior knowledge for which a complete diagnosis and suggestion for what to do next is returned. Each lesson covers a set of content units and includes exercises that are used to update the learner model for the lesson. At any time during a lesson, the learner can view the learner model, which has four columns. The first column lists the knowledge units to be mastered in the lesson. The second gives the system's suggestion for whether the student is ready to work on each unit in the lesson. The third shows the percentage mastery of each unit based on performance on the exercises. The fourth, titled "User Modification," allows the learner to override the system's diagnosis and indicate that, for example, he already knows that knowledge unit. Mastery of higher order units and user modifications are inherited to knowledge units that are considered prerequisites for the higher-level units.

In addition to being able to override parts of the student model, students can set global preferences for the course; for example, they can choose to have access to a chat room or to have the completion status of units in a lesson displayed. Students can also choose to attempt a lesson that the system does not think they are ready for. ELM-ART is an example of the most comprehensive self-contained learning environment on the Web. In addition to the dynamic student modeling feature, it incorporates on-demand help, system-generated help, information and related activities that are monitored, an online note pad where students can take and store notes, a chat room where students can have live discussions, a feature to e-mail questions to a human tutor, and a window where LISP programs can be written and evaluated as if in a real-time programming environment.

Many Web development systems have built-in assessment and survey functions that can be used to generate student models. The construction and use of these models depend to varying degrees on input from a human instructor. For example, the student management and quiz modules of WebCT work together to generate and report data that can be interpreted

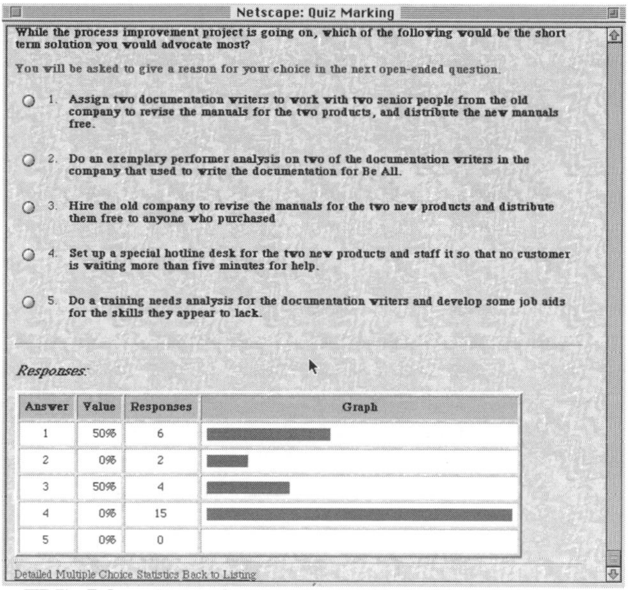

FIG. 5.8. *Data display for multiple-choice question.*

by a human instructor. Some types of student activities are automatically scored and reported to students and instructors in useful ways. For example, an instructor can examine the performance of individual students and groups of students on sets of items and look for patterns that indicate misconceptions (see Fig. 5.8). An instructor can view all student responses to an open-ended question and look for patterns in those too (see Fig. 5.9). Feedback can be preset to occur automatically based on performance on automatically scored items or can be entered during the process of reviewing open-ended responses (see Fig. 5.10). One can select individuals or groups of students whose performance fits a particular profile and automatically send an e-mail message to all of them.

Systems like WebCT also track other aspects of student use of online course materials, for example, how many messages a student contributes and reads in a discussion forum and which pages of content the student has accessed. The text of online chats is recorded and could be analyzed for evidence of individual understanding. The problem is no longer capturing data during the learning process but how to distill and use the various data sources to determine what students know and do not know.

An example of a Web-based system that distills learning process data into a form that facilitates interpretation comes from the IMMEX system for developing and delivering problem-based learning environments. The

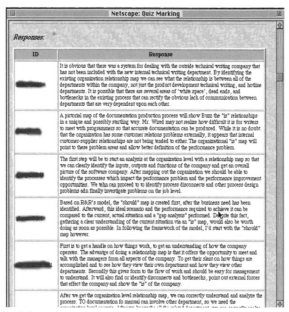

FIG. 5.9. *Aggregated responses to open-ended questions.*

Netscape: Quiz Grading

Quiz Started: Mar 12, 1998 13:11	Quiz Finished: Mar 12, 1998 15:14	Time Spent: 2 hrs., 2 min., 44 sec.

Student Finished 27 min., 16 sec. ahead of the 150 min. Time Limit.

This quiz contains a total of 9 items, two matching, two multiple choice, and five open ended. All questions except the first two are related to the same case. You have 90 minutes to complete the exam. Non-native speakers can have an extra 20 minutes. Be sure to save each answer as you go and click the finish button when you have completed all questions.

[Update Grade] [Reset Attempt] [Cancel]

Question 1 (3 marks)

Match each of the following six activities to the performance level it is helping to analyze.

creating a relationship map	--> organization level	Correct
identifying environmental barriers and enhancers	--> job/performer level	Correct
determining the competencies of exemplary performers	--> job/performer level	Correct
developing role/responsibility matrices for jobs within a functional unit	--> job/performer level	**Incorrect** Correct Answer: process level
identifying critical dimensions of output measures	--> job/performer level	**Incorrect** Correct Answer: process level
operationalizing organizational goals	--> organization level	Correct

Score: 2.0

Override Mark: [ ]

Comments:

```
You seem to be mixing up the process and job/performer
levels of analysis.
```

FIG. 5.10. *Automatic and instructor-entered feedback.*

menu items that a student accesses during solution of a problem are tracked along with the sequence of items accessed and time spent in each one. This information is compiled into a network diagram and displayed visually. A human instructor can view the display for an individual of for groups of students and diagnose weaknesses in the problem solving. The strategies of experts can be overlaid on the student strategies to see how close the students' thinking is coming to experts' thinking.

To gather motivation-related data, one can use built-in survey functions in a system like WebCT (see Fig. 5.11) or create forms that gather data and save them directly to a database such as FileMaker Pro for offline analysis and report generation. Reports can be made available on the Web (see Fig. 5.12). Students' maladaptive perceptions can be singled out and sent e-mail to probe or adjust their affective states.

CONCLUSION

The theme of computers as cognitive tools has been interpreted in many ways, although all interpretations adhere to an underlying premise that the

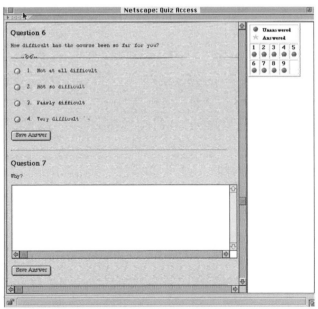

FIG. 5.11.   *Example of questions in online survey.*

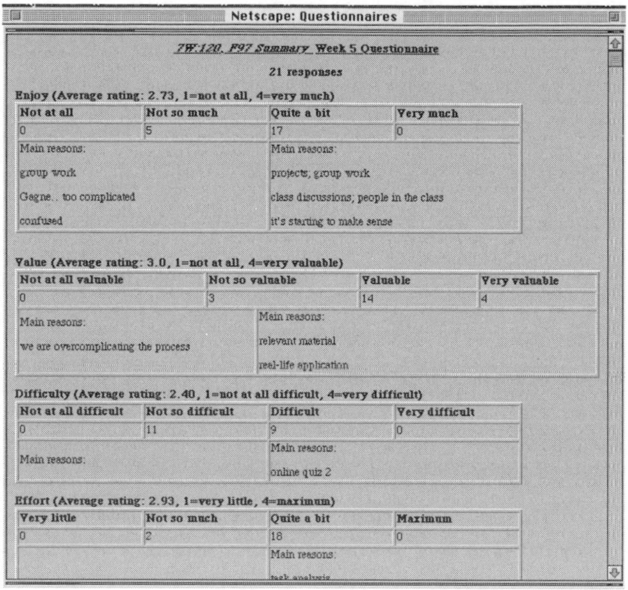

FIG. 5.12. *Group report of survey responses.*

computer can extend, either temporarily or permanently, the cognitive capabilities of users (Jonassen & Reeves, 1996; Lajoie, 1993; Salomon et al., 1991). This echoes Gagne's (1965) definition of instructional events as external support for internal cognitive processes. The Web can provide a variety of types and amounts of support for acquisition of declarative and procedural knowledge. It can also facilitate opportunities for collaboration without barriers of time or distance; communities of learners can be made up of people anywhere in the world. Finally, the Web permits monitoring of the learning process in a variety of ways, for example, by tracking and organizing records of learners' actions for interpretation by human instructors or by feeding data on performance back to the learner. Even the kind of full-blown student modeling found in intelligent tutoring systems is possible on the Web. The examples described in this chapter are just a small sample of what currently exists.

The challenge is to design learning environments that integrate the separate capabilities of the Web and balance the mix of guidance and freedom that each learner needs and can handle. To function as a cognitive tool for learning, the Web should, at a minimum, support exploration of constrained knowledge spaces to complete online or offline authentic activities. To ensure accurate, efficient, and shared acquisition of knowledge, this activity-based approach should be combined with opportunities for collaboration with peers and experts and opportunities for individualized monitoring and feedback related to both performance and perceptions.

REFERENCES

Anderson, J. R. (1993). *Rules of the mind.* Hillsdale, NJ: Lawrence Erlbaum Associates.

Anderson, J. R., Corbett, A. T., Koedinger, K. R., & Pelletier, R. (1995). Cognitive tutors: Lessons learned. *Journal of the Learning Sciences, 4*(2), 167–207.

Anderson, J. R., Reder, L. M., & Simon, H. A. (1996). Situated learning and education. *Educational Researcher, 25*(4), 5–11.

Barrows, H. S. (1986). A taxonomy of problem-based learning methods. *Medical Education, 20,* 481–486.

Brown, J. S., Collins, A., & Duguid, P. (1989). Situated cognition and the culture of learning. *Educational Research, 18*(1), 32–42.

Brusilovsky, P., Schwarz, E., & Weber, G. (1997). Electronic textbooks on the World Wide Web: From static hypertext to interactivity and adaptivity. In B. H. Khan (Ed.), *Web-based instruction* (pp. 255–262). Englewood Cliffs, NJ: Educational Technology.

Campione, J. C., & Brown, A. L. (1990). Guiding learning and transfer: Implications for approaches to assessment. In N. Frederiksen, R. Glaser, A. Lesgold, & M. Shafto (Eds.), *Diagnostic monitoring of skill and knowledge acquisition* (pp. 141–172). Hillsdale, NJ: Lawrence Erlbaum Associates.

Clark, R. E. (1999). The CANE model of motivation to learn and to work: A two-stage process of goal commitment and effort. In J. Lowyck (Ed.), *Trends in Corporate Training. Belgium: University of Leuven.*

Collins, A., Brown, J. S., & Newman, S. E. (1989). Cognitive apprenticeship: Teaching the crafts of reading, writing, and mathematics. In L. B. Resnick (Ed.), *Knowing, learning, and instruction: Essays in honor of Robert Glaser* (pp. 453–494). Hillsdale, NJ: Lawrence Erlbaum Associates.

Cognition and Technology Group at Vanderbilt. (1992). Technology and the design of generative learning environments. In T. M. Duffy & D. H. Jonassen (Eds.), *Constructivism and the technology of instruction: A conversation* (pp. 77–89). Hillsdale, NJ: Lawrence Erlbaum Associates.

Derry, S. J., & Hawkes, L. W. (1993). Local cognitive modeling of problem-solving behavior: An application of fuzzy theory. In S. P. Lajoie & S. J. Derry

(Eds.), *Computers as cognitive tools* (pp. 107–140). Hillsdale, NJ: Lawrence Erlbaum Associates

Derry S. J., & Lajoie, S. P. (1993). A middle camp for (un)intelligent instructional computing: An introduction. In S. P. Lajoie & S. J. Derry (Eds.), *Computers as cognitive tools* (pp. 1–11). Hillsdale, NJ: Lawrence Erlbaum Associates.

Flavell, J. H. (1979). Metacognition and cognitive monitoring: A new area of cognitive developmental inquiry. *American Psychologist, 34*, 906–911.

Gagne, R. M. (1965). *The conditions of learning*. New York: Holt, Rinehart & Winston.

Goldberg, M. W. (1997). Using a Web-based course authoring tool to develop sophisticated web-based courses. In B. H. Khan (Ed.), *Web-based instruction* (pp. 307–312). Englewood Cliffs, NJ: Educational Technology.

Greeno, J. G., Smith, D. R., & Moore, J. L. (1992). Transfer of situated learning. In D. Detterman & R. J. Sternberg (Eds.), *Transfer on trial: Intelligence, cognition, and instruction* (pp. 99–167). Norwood, NJ: Ablex.

Guzdial, M., Kolodner, J. L., Hmelo, C., Narayanan, H., Carlson, D., Rappin, N., Hubscher, R., Turns, J., & Newstetter, W. (1996). Computer support for learning through complex problem-solving. *Communications of the ACM, 39*(4), 43–45

Jacobson, M. J., Maouri, C., Mishra, P., & Kolar, C. (1996). Learning with hypertext learning environments: Theory, design, and research. *Journal of Educational Multimedia and Hypermedia, 5*(3/4), 239–281.

Jonassen, D. H. (1989). *Hypertext/hypermedia*. Englewood Cliffs, NJ: Educational Technology.

Jonassen, D. H. (1992). Designing hypertext for learning. In E. Scanlon & T. O'Shea (Eds.), *New directions in educational technology* (pp. 123–130). Berlin, Germany: Springer-Verlag.

Jonnasen, D. H., Dyer, D., Peters, K., Robinson, T., Harvey, D., King, M., & Loughner, P. (1997). Cognitive flexibility hypertexts on the Web: Engaging learners in meaning making. In B. H. Khan (Ed.), *Web-based instruction* (pp. 119–133). Englewood Cliffs, NJ: Educational Technology.

Jonassen D. H., & Reeves, T. C. (1996). Learning with technology: Using computers as cognitive tools. In D. H. Jonassen (Ed.), *Handbook of research for educational communications and technology* (pp. 693–719). New York: Macmillan.

Kafai, Y. B. (1995). *Minds in play: Computer game design as a context for children's learning*. Hillsdale, NJ: Lawrence Erlbaum Associates.

Kirkley, J. R., & Duffy, T. M. (1997). Designing a Web-based electronic performance support system (EPSS): A case study of Literacy Online. In B. H. Khan (Ed.), *Web-based instruction* (pp. 139–148). Englewood Cliffs, NJ: Educational Technology.

Lajoie, S. P. (1993). Computer environments as cognitive tools for enhancing learning. In S. P. Lajoie & S. J. Derry (Eds.), *Computers as cognitive tools* (pp. 261–288). Hillsdale, NJ: Lawrence Erlbaum Associates.

Lajoie, S. P., & Derry, S. J. (Eds.). (1993). *Computers as cognitive tools.* Hillsdale, NJ: Lawrence Erlbaum Associates.

Lajoie, S. P., & Lesgold, A. (1992). Dynamic assessment of proficiency for solving procedural knowledge tasks. *Educational Psychologist, 27*(3), 365–384.

Lave, J., & Wenger, E. (1991). *Situated learning: Legitimate peripheral participation.* Cambridge: Cambridge University Press.

Lee, Y. B., & Lehman, J. D. (1993). Instructional cuing in hypermedia: A study of active and passive learners. *Journal of Educational Multimedia and Hypermedia, 2*(1), 25–37.

Lehrer, R. (1993). Authors of knowledge: Patterns of hypermedia design. In S. P. Lajoie & S. J. Derry (Eds.), *Computers as cognitive tools* (pp. 197–227). Hillsdale, NJ: Lawrence Erlbaum Associates.

Linn, M. C. (1996). Key to the information highway. *Communications of the ACM, 39*(4), 34–35.

Oliver, K. (1997). Getting online with K–12 Internet projects. *Tech Trends, 42*(6),33–40.

Papert, S. (1993). *The children's machine: Rethinking school in the age of the computer.* New York: Basic Books.

Rouet, J. F., Levonen, J. J., Dillon, A., & Spiro, R. J. (1996). *Hypertext and cognition.* Hillsdale, NJ: Lawrence Erlbaum Associates.

Royer, J. M., Cisero, C. A., & Carlo, M. S. (1993). Techniques and procedures for assessing cognitive skills. *Review of Educational Research, 63*(2), 201–243.

Salomon, G. (1984). Television is "easy" and print is "tough": The differential investment of mental effort in learning as a function of perceptions and attributions. *Journal of Educational Psychology, 76*(4), 647–658.

Salomon, G., Perkins, D., & Globerson, T. (1991). Partners in cognition: Extending human intelligence with intelligent technologies. *Educational Researcher, 20*(3), 2–9.

Scardamalia, M., & Bereiter, C. (1994). Computer support for knowledge-building communities. *Journal of the Learning Sciences, 3*(3), 219–225.

Schank, R. C., & Jona, M. Y. (1991). Empowering the student: New perspectives on the design of teaching systems. *Journal of the Learning Sciences, 1*(1), 7–35.

Schank R. C., & Kass, A. (1996). A goal-based scenario for high school students. *Communications of the ACM, 39*(4), 28–29.

Schmidt, R. A., & Bjork, R. A. (1992). New conceptualizations of practice: Common principles in three paradigms suggest new concepts for training. *Psychological Science, 3*(4), 207–217.

Slavin, R. E. (1990). *Cooperative learning: Theory, research, and practice.* Engelwood Cliffs, NJ: Prentice-Hall.

Solis, C. R. (1997). Virtual worlds as constructivist learning tools in a middle school education environment. In B. H. Khan (Ed.), *Web-based instruction* (pp. 393–398). Englewood Cliffs, NJ: Educational Technology.

Spiro, R. J., Feltovich, P. J., Jacobson, M. J., & Coulson, R. L. (1992). Cognitive flexibility, constructivism, and hypertext: Random access instruction in ill-structured domain. In T. M. Duffy & D. H. Jonassen (Eds.), *Constructivism and the technology of instruction: A conversation* (pp. 57–75). Hillsdale, NJ: Lawrence Erlbaum Associates.

Stevens, R. H., McCoy, J. M., & Kwak, A. R. (1991). Solving the problem of how medical students solve problems. *M.D. Computing, 8*(1), 13–20.

Teles, L., & Collings, T. (1997). Virtual experiments and group tasks in a Web-based collaborative course in introductory electronics. In B. H. Khan (Ed.), *Web-based instruction* (pp. 399–402). Englewood Cliffs, NJ: Educational Technology.

Tergan, S. O. (1997). Misleading theoretical assumptions in hypertext/hypermedia research. *Journal of Educational Multimedia and Hypermedia, 6*(3/4), 257–283.

II

COGNITIVE TOOLS
THAT FOSTER NEW FORMS
OF REPRESENTATION

6

Mindtools: Affording Multiple Knowledge Representations for Learning

David H. Jonassen
University of Missouri

Chad S. Carr
Northern Illinois University

PROBLEM: OVERRELIANCE ON
SINGLE-KNOWLEDGE REPRESENTATIONS

Numerous reports decry the deficiencies in thinking skills of students at all educational levels. An important cause of these deficiencies (among many others), we argue, is the overreliance of educators at all levels on a singular form of knowledge representation for assessment. Representing what learners know in only a single way engages a limited set of cognitive skills. Engaging students in instructional activities and assessments that employ a single formalism for representing their knowledge necessarily constrains their understanding of whatever they are studying. For example, in a physics class at Harvard, students who were competently solving physics problems that were represented mathematically (known as plug-and-chug) failed a test of conceptual understanding of the problems and their underlying principles (Panitz, 1998). Students had memorized and could apply the equations and problem-solving procedures without understanding the physics concepts they were representing mathematically.

In another example, we recently analyzed examinations administered in core courses in a university business curriculum (e.g., management, marketing, finance) and found that 65% of the questions (all were multiple choice) in the course examinations assessed recall, memorization, or knowledge of what students were taught in lectures or read from the text; 25% were at the concept level; and 10% assessed higher order thinking (such as rule, principle, inference, and implication). Based on a series of examinations like these, business faculty are willing to certify (by virtue of a bachelor's degree) that graduates are competent to conduct business. Graduates' business competence, however, relies on their ability to recognize instances of the concepts that they memorized for those examinations in the real world and to know how to apply them in real-world practice, which requires understanding that was never examined or practiced in the large lecture courses. Business graduates, like most other students in all levels of education, have deficient understanding of content because they were required to represent what they know in only one way (e.g., worksheets in K–12 classes, textbook problems in the sciences, definitional essays in the social sciences, and multiple-choice guessing everywhere), which engaged only a single set of cognitive skills.

SOLUTION: MULTIPLE REPRESENTATIONS OF KNOWLEDGE

There are numerous solutions to the overreliance on single formalisms for knowledge representation. Contemporary theories of learning recommend that students who are constructive learners should be immersed in situated, problem-based learning environments that replicate real-world activity structures (Greeno, 1989; Jonassen & Rohrer-Murphy, 1999). That solution, unfortunately, probably requires more of a paradigm shift in educational practice than most institutions are ready to accommodate. A more likely solution involves the use of multiple forms of knowledge representation in assessments. Every educator knows that learning is assessment driven. So an effective way to scaffold different kinds of learning is through alternative assessments (Lehrer, 1993). Because learners are motivated to exert intellectual effort to fulfill course task requirements, another solution to problems associated with over-reliance on single-knowledge representation formalisms is to require learners to represent what they are learning in different ways using active learning strategies. Computer technologies can facilitate that solution.

An effective method (though not the only method) for supporting the representation of learner knowledge through multiple formalisms is to use computers as mindtools (Jonassen, 1996, 2000) to represent their knowledge. Mindtools are knowledge construction tools that learners learn *with*, not *from*. In this way, learners function as interpreters, organizers, and designers of their personal knowledge. Each mindtool uses a different formalism for representing learners' knowledge that engage a different set of critical cognitive skills.

MINDTOOLS AS COGNITIVE TOOLS

By using computers as mindtools, we use technologies as knowledge construction tools that support, guide, and extend the thinking processes of their users (Derry, 1990). Mindtools provide structural, logical, causal, systemic, or visuospatial formalisms that scaffold different kinds of thinking and knowledge representation; that is, they manipulate the task (supplant the students' performance by performing some part of the task or by adjusting the nature or difficulty of the task). Using computers as mindtools enables learners to think in ways that they otherwise would not and could not.

Mindtools are computer software applications, like databases, spreadsheets, semantic networking programs, expert systems, systems modeling tools, microworlds, hypermedia authoring tools, and computer conferencing, that enable learners to represent what they have learned and know using different representational formalisms. With some proficiency in using software applications, learners decide how to organize and represent their knowledge, rather than replicating or regurgitating teachers' interpretations. Using mindtools to represent what they know necessarily engages learners in a variety of critical, creative, and complex thinking, such as evaluating, analyzing, connecting, elaborating, synthesizing, imagining, designing, problem solving, and decision making (Jonassen, 1996). When using computers as mindtools, learners reflect on what they know and use those reflections to construct knowledge bases. They are teaching the computer, just as artificial intelligence researchers do when they build intelligent tutors.

An underlying issue of this book and its first volume was the role of expert and student modeling in artificially intelligent tutoring systems. Derry and LaJoie (1993) argued that "the appropriate role for a computer system is not that of a teacher/expert, but rather, that of a mind-extending cognitive tool rather than a teaching agent." We agree, and suggest that the purpose of mindtools is student modeling—by the student, not by the knowledge engineer for encoding in the system. We claim that the individuals who learn the most from intelligent tutors are the ones who build them, not the students who use them. So why not allow the learners to assume responsibility for knowledge modeling, using mindtools to construct knowledge bases and functioning as knowledge engineers, just as artificial intelligence (AI) researchers do? Mindtools represent a form of guerrilla AI, with students wrestling intellectual authority and control of the technology from the experts. If knowledge engineering activities engage constructive learning that is dormant in reproductive learning activities, why not allow learners to engage in them?

The remainder of the chapter describes how different classes of mindtools—semantic organization tools, dynamic modeling tools, information interpretation tools, knowledge construction tools, and conversation tools—enable learners to represent what they know in different ways, thereby engaging a range of cognitive activities.

SEMANTIC ORGANIZATION TOOLS

Semantic organization tools enable learners to analyze and organize what they know (Quillian, 1968; Rumelhart, 1980). Two of the most commonly used semantic organization tools are databases and semantic networking (concept mapping) tools.

Databases as Mindtools

Database management systems are computerized filing systems designed to accelerate the storage and retrieval of information. Information is broken down into files that consist of matrices of records and fields. The records are instances, and the fields describe their characteristics. Databases use boolean logic (using AND, OR, and NOT functions) to access relevant information from databases. The capabilities of high-speed sorting and searching to answer queries about information in the database make them essential for applications such as directories and catalogues.

Databases may also be used as tools for interpreting, analyzing, and organizing subject content by learners. Students who construct databases using a concept development strategy and an interpretation of data strategy must select information to collect and organize it into meaningful cat-

cell type	location	function	shape	tissue systems	specialization	related cell
Astocyte	CNS	Supply Nutrients	Radiating	Nervous	Half of Neural Tissue	Neurons, Capillaries
Basal	Stratum Basale	Produce New Cells	Cube, Columnar	Epithelial	Mitotic	Epithelial Cells
Basophils	Blood Plasma	Bind Imm. E	Lobed Nuclei	Connective, Immune	Basic, Possible Mast	Neutrophil, Eosinophil
Cardiac Muscle	Heart	Pump Blood	Branched	Muscle	Intercalated discs	Endomysium
Chondroblast	Cartilage	Produce Matrix	Round	Connective		
Eosinophil	Blood Plasma	Protozoans, Allergy	Two Lobes	Connective, Immune	Acid, Phagocytos (Prote	Basophil, Neutrophil
Ependymal	Line CNS	Form Cerebralspinal Fluid	Cube	Nervous	Cilia	
Erythrocytes	Blood Plasma	Transport O2, Remove CO2	Disc	Connective	Transport	Hemocytoblast, Proeryt
Fibroblast	Connective Tissue	Fiber Production	Flat, Branched	Connective	Mitotic	
Goblet	Columnar Epithelial	Secretion	Columnar	Epithelial	Mucus	Columnar
Keratinocytes	Stratum Basal	Strengthen other Cells	Round	Epithelial		Melanocytes
Melanocytes	Stratum Basale	U.V. Protection	Branched	Epithelial	Produce Melanin	Keratinocytes
Microglia	CNS	Protect	Ovoid	Nervous	Macrophage	Neurons, Astrocytes?
Motor Neuron	CNS(Cell Body)	Impulse Away from CNS	Long, Thin	Nervous	Multipolar, Neuromuscul	Sensory Neuron, Neurog
Neutrophil	Blood Plasma	Inflammation, Bacteria	Lobed Nuclei	Connective, Immune	Phagocytos, Neutral	Basophils, Eosinophil
Oligodendrocyte	CNS	Insulate	Long	Nervous	Produce Myaline Sheath	Neurons
Osteoblast	Bone	Produce Organic Matrix	Spider	Connective	Bone Salts	Osteoclasts
Osteoclast	Bone	Bone Restoration	Ruffled Boarder	Connective	Destroy Bone	Osteoblasts
Pseudostratified	Gland Ducts, Respir	Secretion	Varies	Epithelial	Cilia	Goblet

FIG. 6.1.

egories (Rooze, 1988–1989). Student-constructed databases have been used to support history instruction (Knight & Timmons, 1986) and lessons on seashells (Goldberg, 1992) and as an inquiry tool to aid higher-level thinking in a fourth-grade Native American studies course (Pon, 1984). Constructing database queries is a form of hypothesis testing (Katzeff, 1987). The database shown in Fig. 6.1 was developed by learners studying cells and their functions in a biology course. Although the intellectual benefits of building knowledge databases are obvious, more formal research on the efficacy of these activities is needed.

There are three basic activities in developing and using knowledge databases, each of which engages a different combination of cognitive processes. The simplest application is filling in an existing database by searching for information that fits into the data structure. For instance, in the database in Fig. 6.1, students could consult their textbooks to locate information about cell types, locations, shape, specialization, and tissue systems to include in the database. Constructing their own knowledge databases about cells would represent a more complex activity, in which students would develop the data structure (identify the fields), locate relevant information, and insert it in appropriate fields and records. Finally, in order to apply their databases, students would search and sort the database to answer queries about the content or to identify interrelationships and inferences from the content, such as, "Do different-shaped cells have specific functions?" Students can create such queries to test their own understanding of the database or provide meaningful higher order activities for their peers.

Designing a database requires the learner to identify a content domain, sense an information need, and develop a data structure for accommodating the information to be included. Building databases involves analyzing, synthesizing, and evaluating information (Watson & Strudler, 1988–1989). Database construction is an analytic process that engages important critical thinking skills such as evaluating, organizing, and connecting information; a few creative skills such as analogical reasoning and planning; and several complex thinking skills such as designing a product, problem solving, and decision making (Jonassen, 1996). Building knowledge databases enables learners to represent their knowledge of topics they are studying as organized tables of interrelated concepts using heterarchical knowledge structures and as queries for identifying specific subsets of information.

Semantic Networking as Mindtools

Semantic networking tools provide visual screen tools for producing concept maps. Concept mapping is a visual study strategy that requires learners to construct visual maps of concepts connected to each other by lines (links) (see Fig. 6.2). Programs such as SemNet, Learning Tool, Inspiration, Mind Mapper, MindMan, Axon Idea Processor, VisiMap, and Activity Map enable learners to identify important concepts, graphically

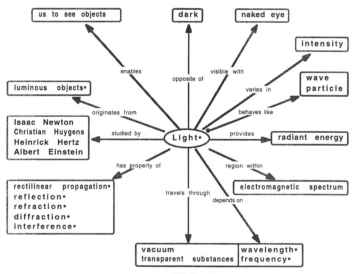

FIG. 6.2.

interrelate those concepts in multidimensional networks, and label the relationships between those concepts.

Semantic networks are spatial representations of the constructs and their interrelationships that are stored in memory, that is, structural knowledge (Jonassen, Beissner, & Yacci, 1993). Structural knowledge is the knowledge of how concepts within a domain are interrelated. "It enables learners to form the connections that they need to describe and use scripts and complex schemas" (Winn & Snyder, 1996, p.128). In semantic network theory (Quillian, 1968) schemas (concepts or nodes) are arranged in networks of interrelated ideas known as semantic networks. Semantic networking programs provide tools for visualizing these networks.

Semantic networking has been related to formal reasoning in chemistry (Schreiber & Abegg, 1991) and biology (Briscoe & LeMaster, 1991; Mikulecky, 1988). Creating semantic nets helps learners to organize what they are learning by constantly using new propositions to elaborate and refine concepts that they already know. Semantic networking improves content learning (Lahtinen, Lonka, & Lindbloom, 1997; Roth & Roychoudhury, 1993) and student attitudes toward learning (Horton, McConney, Gallo, & Woods, 1993), and it enhances content knowledge because it facilitates learners' using the skill of searching for patterns and relationship (Slack & Stewart, 1990).

Semantic networking also facilitates problem-solving performance, which is dependent on well integrated domain knowledge. Students with semantic networking experience were more successful in solving biological problems than were those who did not (Okebukola, 1992). They approached each problem by sketching a map of the elements of the problem, enabling them to know where to begin in solving them (Okebukola, 1993). Robertson (1990) found that the extent to which the learner's cognitive structures contained relevant structural knowledge was a stronger predictor of how well learners would solve transfer problems in physics than either their aptitude or performance on a set of similar problems. There is little doubt that facilitating the integration of knowledge structures facilitates most forms of learning.

Constructing computer-based concept maps engages learners in (a) reorganization of knowledge through the explicit description of concepts and their interrelationships; (b) deep processing of knowledge, which promotes better remembering, retrieval, and the ability to apply knowledge in new situations; (c) relating new concepts to existing concepts and ideas, which improves understanding (Davis, 1990); and (d) spatial learning through the spatial representation of concepts within an area of study

(Fisher et al., 1990). Semantic networks may be used to represent the learner's structural knowledge (Jonassen et al., 1993) or for assessing cognitive structure (Jonassen, 1987). By comparing semantic networks created at different points in time, they are theoretically powerful and psychometrically sound tools for assessing conceptual changes in learners (Markham, Mintzes, & Gail, 1994). Semantic networking programs are being used increasingly to reflect the process of knowledge construction.

Important thinking skills that are engaged in by semantic networking include critical thinking skills such as evaluating, analyzing, and connecting information; some creative thinking skills such as expanding, extending, concretizing, analogizing, and visualizing ideas; and complex thinking skills, especially planning a product (Jonassen, 1996).

Constructing a semantic net engages many cognitive skills similar to building knowledge databases; semantic nets enable learners to represent their knowledge of what they are constructing as multidimensional concept maps. This spatial representation makes them extremely popular with students of all ages.

DYNAMIC MODELING TOOLS

Semantic organization tools help learners to represent the semantic relationships among ideas, but the nature of the connections that they describe are static. An important characteristic of complex systems is the dynamic nature of the relationships among its components. They are causal, inferential, probabilistic, and even stochastic. Dynamic modeling tools help learners to describe those dynamic relationships among ideas mathematically as well as semantically. Dynamic modeling tools include spreadsheets, expert systems, systems modeling tools, and microworlds.

Spreadsheets as Mindtools

Spreadsheets are computerized, numerical record-keeping systems that were designed to replace paper-based, ledger accounting systems. Essentially a spreadsheet is a matrix of empty cells with columns identified by letters and rows identified by numbers. Each cell is a placeholder for values, formulas relating values in other cells, or functions that mathematically or logically manipulate values in other cells. Functions are small, programmed sequences that may, for instance, match values in cells with other cells, look up a variable in a table of values, or create an index of values to be compared with other cells.

Spreadsheets were originally developed and are most commonly used to support business decision-making and accounting operations. They are especially useful for answering "what if?" questions—for instance, what if interest rates increased by 1%? Changes made in one cell automatically recalculate all of the affected values in other cells.

Spreadsheets also may be used as mindtools for amplifying mental functioning. In the same way that they have qualitatively changed the accounting process, spreadsheets can change the educational process when working with quantitative information. Spreadsheets model the mathematical logic that is implied by calculations and so are useful for learning to solve algebra problems, for instance. Using spreadsheets helps students move from thinking in local cause-and-effect relations to general rule using in terms of the unknown and the mathematical relationships expressed in the problem (Sutherland & Rojano, 1994). Making the underlying mathematical reasoning obvious to learners by allowing them to manipulate them improves their understanding of the interrelationships and procedures. Spreadsheets are flexible mindtools for representing, reflecting on, and speculating with quantitative information. They promote more open-ended investigations, problem-oriented activities, and active learning by students (Beare, 1992).

Building spreadsheets requires the learner to use abstract reasoning. Spreadsheets are rule-using tools that require that users become rule makers (Vockell & van Deusen, 1989). They support problem-solving activities, such as decision analysis. Perhaps more important, spreadsheets enable learners to consider implications of conditions or options and speculate and hypothesize about outcomes. Spreadsheets are being used increasingly to model or simulate complex phenomena such as auditory encoding on the basilar membrane (Bremner & Denhem, 1992); visual information processing in the retina, lateral geniculate nucleus, and visual cortex (Halff, 1987); and neural networks. This form of dynamic systems modeling is the most powerful application of spreadsheets.

Important thinking skills that are engaged by modeling and speculating with spreadsheets include analyzing skills such as recognizing patterns, classifying, identifying assumptions, and finding sequences; connecting skills such as comparing and contrasting, logical thinking, deductive reasoning, and identifying causal relationships; a few creative thinking skills; and several complex thinking skills, especially in the design and problem-solving categories. Building and speculating with spreadsheets enable learners to represent their knowledge of topics they are studying as mathematical patterns and complex mathematical models of phenomena.

Expert Systems as Mindtools

Production rule expert systems have evolved from research in the field of artificial intelligence. An expert system is a computer program that simulates the way human experts solve problems using a production rule (if-then) formalism. They have traditionally been used to model expert knowledge in order to provide decision support and model the expert's knowledge in intelligent tutoring systems (see Shute & Ross, this volume). For example, expert systems have been developed to provide decision support for geologists in deciding where to drill for oil, bankers for evaluating loan applications, computer sales technicians for configuring computer systems, and employees for deciding among an array of company benefits alternatives. Problems whose solutions require decision making are good candidates for expert system development.

Before the availability of these tools, we claimed that the people who learned the most from instructional materials were the knowledge engineers who designed them. Jonassen, Wilson, Wang, and Grabinger (1993) reported this discovery while developing expert system advisers that were designed to supplant the thinking required by instructional designers. The process of articulating their knowledge about the domain of instructional design forced them to reflect on their knowledge in a new and meaningful way. The development of expert systems provides an intellectual environment that demands the refinement of domain knowledge, supports problem solving, and monitors the acquisition of knowledge (Trollip, Lippert, Starfield, & Smith, 1992). Building the knowledge base requires the learner to articulate causal knowledge or procedural knowledge in the form of rules. The rules shown in Fig. 6.3 were generated by students in a meteorology class who were building expert systems to predict weather phenomena.

Expert system shells (high-level programs for creating, executing, and analyzing expert system rule bases) are being used increasingly as mindtools. Nursing students who developed medical expert systems realized enhanced reasoning skills and acquired a deeper understanding of the subject domain (Lai, 1989). Physics students who used an expert system shell to predict projectile motion developed more refined, domain-specific

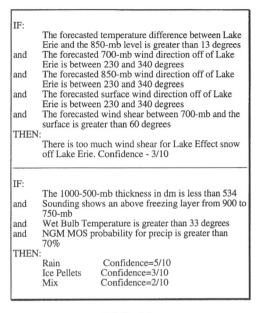

FIG. 6.3.

knowledge due to greater degrees of elaboration during encoding and the greater quantity of material processed in an explicit, coherent context, and therefore in greater semantic depth (Lippert & Finley, 1988).

Building expert system rule bases engages learners in analytical reasoning, elaboration strategies such as synthesis, and metacognition (Lippert, 1987). The part of the expert system that makes expert systems a cognitive tool is the knowledge base. Building knowledge bases by articulating causal knowledge requires more complex, formal reasoning than nearly any other mindtool. Identifying the causal relationships and procedural knowledge underlying a knowledge domain necessarily engages designers in higher order thinking.

Building expert system rule bases engages learners in forward-chaining and backward-chaining types of causal reasoning. Rule bases are the most common representation of procedural knowledge. Important thinking skills that are engaged by building expert system rule bases include critical thinking skills, such as including evaluating, analyzing, and connecting information in causal chains, and several complex thinking skills such as designing (imagining, formulating, inventing, assessing, and revising) a product, problem solving, and decision making (generating alternatives, assessing consequences, and evaluating choices; Jonassen, 1996). Building expert system rule bases enables learners to represent their knowledge as patterns of causality.

Systems Modeling as Mindtools

Complex learning requires students to solve complex and ill-structured problems as well as simple problems. Complex learning requires that students develop mental representations of the phenomena they are studying. A number of tools for developing these mental representations are emerging. Stella, Extend, Model It and PowerSim, for instance, are powerful and flexible tools for building simulations of dynamic systems and processes (systems with interactive and interdependent components). They use a simple set of building block icons to construct a map of a process.

The Stella model in Fig. 6.4 was developed by an English teacher in conjunction with his 10th-grade students to describe how the boys' loss of hope drives the increasing power of the Beast in William Golding's novel, *The Lord of the Flies*. The model of Beast power represents the factors that contributed to the strength of the Beast in the book, including fear and resistance. Each component can be opened up, so that its values may be stated as constants or variables. Variables can be stated as equations containing numerical relationships among any of the variables connected to it. The resulting model can be run, changing the values of faith building, fear, and memory of home experienced by the boys while assessing the effects on their belief about being rescued and the strength of the Beast within them.

Stella has been used frequently in high schools and colleges for simulating a wide range of conceptual understanding, including Hamlet's motivation for avenging the death of his father (Hopkins, 1992) and the motion of a spring-powered toy car in a physics class (Niedderer, Schecker, & Bethge, 1991). Using Stella and other dynamic modeling tools, such as Model-It from the Highly Interactive Computing Group at the University of Michigan, to model and simulate dynamic, complex processes provides the most complete intellectual activity in which students can engage (Spitulnik et al., 1995).

Systems modeling tools allow learners to design and run elaborate models in only a fraction of the time that is usually required to use a programming language. Important thinking skills that are engaged by systems modeling include virtually all of the critical thinking skills; a number of creative thinking skills, such as elaborating, synthesizing (analogical

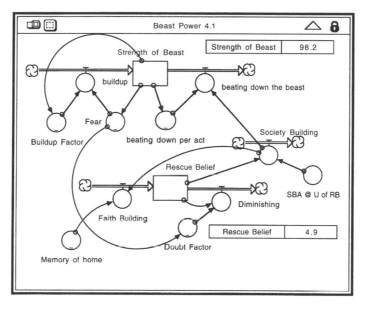

FIG. 6.4.

thinking, hypothesizing, planning), and imaging skills such as speculating and visualizing; and nearly every complex thinking skill. Building system models enables learners to represent their knowledge as complex semantic and quantitative simulations of reality. Moreover, these tools enable learners to test and revise their models

Microworlds as Mindtools

"A computer microworld is an environment that allows the learner to explore and manipulate a rule-governed universe, subject to specific assumptions and constraints, that serves as an analogical representation of some aspects of the natural world" (Pea, 1984). Microworlds are composed of objects, relationships among objects, and operations that transform the objects and their relationships (Thompson, 1985). At the core of a microworld is a knowledge domain to be investigated by interaction with the software. As learners interact with the microworld, they manipulate objects (or variables) in order to reach a goal state. For example, in CHANCE, a simulation-oriented computer microworld that runs using Object Logo, the goal state is that of accurately predicting the probability of an occurrence given a certain set of conditions (Jiang, 1994). The student predicts the number of times a coin will land heads up out of 10 tosses, 100 tosses, and so on. Other goal states are much more complex, such as conducting psychological research (Colle & Randall, 1996).

Seymour Papert (1980) coined the term *microworld* for describing exploratory learning environments. He created a computer microworld that used Logo turtles to teach principles of Newtonian physics. For example, two turtles would behave opposite each other to demonstrate Newton's law of action and reaction. In order to elucidate the relationships between objects in a microworld, other complex interactions and random factors present in the real environment are often sequestered. Consequently, some microworlds oversimplify relations to the extent that they often produce false representations of reality. Every microworld, according to Papert, is schematic; it talks about a fairyland in which things are so simplified that almost every statement about them would be literally false if asserted in the real world. The suggestive and predictive powers of microworlds as learning environments have led to their increasing popularity in education.

Microworlds are exploratory learning environments or discovery spaces in which learners can navigate, manipulate, or create objects and test their effects on one another. They contain constrained simulations of real-world phenomena that allow learners to control those phenomena and construct deeper knowledge of the phenomena they are manipulating. They provide the exploratory functionality (the observation and manipulation tools and testing objects) needed to explore phenomena in those parts of the world. Video-based adventure games are microworlds that require players to master each environment before moving to more complex environments. They are compelling to youngsters, who spend hours transfixed by these adventure worlds. Microworlds are perhaps the ultimate example of active learning environments, because users can exercise so much control over the environment.

Many microworlds are being produced and made available from educational research projects, especially in math and science. In mathematics, the Geometric Supposer and Algebraic Supposer are standard tools for testing conjectures in geometry and algebra by constructing and manipulating geometric and algebraic objects in order to explore the relationships within and between these objects (Yerulshamy & Schwartz, 1986). The emphasis in most microworlds is the generation and testing of hypotheses. They provide a test bed for testing students' predictions about geometric and algebraic proofs.

The SimCalc project teaches middle and high school students calculus concepts through MathWorlds, a microworld consisting of animated worlds and dynamic graphs in which actors move according to graphs. By exploring the movement of the actors in the simulations and seeing the graphs of their activity, students begin to understand important ideas in calculus. In the MathWorlds activity illustrated in Fig. 6.5, students match two motions. In the process, they learn how velocity and position graphs relate. Students must match the motion of the green and red graphs. To do this, they can change either graph and iteratively run the simulation to assess their hypothesis. Students may also use MathWorld's link to enter their own bodily motion. For example, a student can walk across the classroom, and the motions would be entered into MathWorld through sensing equipment. MathWorld would plot the motion, enabling the students to explore the properties of their own motion.

Most microworlds provide an outside view of a simulated organism. Albers, Brand, and Cellerier (1991) took microworlds one step further by developing a microworld that "takes the exploratory idea of the MIT group, but adds various *inside* views of the animal that constitute the subjective phenomenological view." According to Albers et al. (1991),

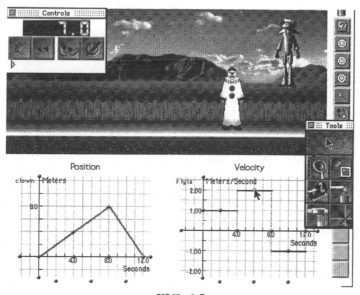

FIG. 6.5.

The microworld (and microorganism) editor [they] have developed allows
for the construction of a range of different organisms interacting in various
sensorimotor ways in the pursuit of various goals with different objects,
object configurations, and other organisms in space. Programming a graded
sequence of cognitive organisms that "live" in such a universe allows for
very simple and transparent realizations of behavioral schemes like scripts,
regulators, servomechanisms, hill climbers, and various forms of condition-
ing, etc. . . . One can move from "organisms" with minimal learning and
representation to more "realistic" systems realized in a variety of programming styles with a variety of representation, problem-solving and memory-
organization schemes, and introduce organism-organism interaction at any
level. We thus see the learner's framework and focus as being from the very
start no different from that of a researcher's, or in other words, research as
a natural form of learning.

Microworlds provide an environment that encourages active participation
and exploration. Interactions with virtual subjects in microworlds necessarily involve gamelike scenarios that are intrinsically motivating
(Driskell & Dwyer, 1984; Goble, Colle, & Holland, 1988; Lepper, 1985).
The dynamic nature of microworlds encourages the production of sensory
pluralities. This production can be regarded as a fundamental operation of
intelligence on which the construction of numerical concepts, composite
units, number sequences, and more general quantitative reasoning is
based (Steffe, 1991). It has been shown that children as young as 2 years
old have mastered sorting tasks in computer microworlds (Brinkley,
1988). In corporate applications, research has revealed that microworlds
can create meaningful, lifelike roles and reward intelligent, rational, and
well-planned, executive-type decisions (Keys, Fulmer, & Stumpf, 1996).
    The critical, creative, and complex thinking skills that are engaged by
microworlds vary with the simulation. They probably engage more critical and creative thinking skills such as recognizing patterns, inferring
inductively, hypothesizing, predicting, speculating, and visualizing than
many other mindtools (Jonassen, 1996, 2000). Using microworlds is sel-
dom a constructionist activity (allowing the learner to construct artifacts,
rather than study something that already exists; Papert, 1990), so they do
not enable learners to represent their knowledge as overtly as other mindtools do. Yet they are unquestionably one of the best tools for engaging
learners in constructing and testing internal mental models. If those internal models were manifested in systems models using systems modeling
tools, the combination of microworlds and systems modeling tools would
represent the most complete reification of mental models that exists.

VISUALIZATION TOOLS

Humans are complex organisms who possess well-balanced sensorimotor systems with counterbalanced receptor and motor effector systems, which enable them to sense perceptual data and act on them using complex motor systems. Humans also have reasonably keen aural perception, allowing them to hear a large range of sounds. Those sounds can be replicated or at least responded to orally by humans by forcing air through the diaphragm, palate, and lips to create an infinite variety of sounds. However, our most sophisticated sensory system, vision, where the largest amount and variety of data are received, has no counterpoising effector system. We can receive visual input but have no output mechanism for visually representing ideas, except in mental images and dreams. Unfortunately, these visions are not easily shared. Therefore, humans need visual prostheses for helping them to represent ideas visually (see Harper, this volume).

Some might think that draw and paint packages represent powerful visualization tools. To some degree, they do, because they provide sophisticated tools that enable us to draw and paint objects electronically. However, in order to represent our mental images using these programs, we have to translate those images into a series of motor operations. Although it is not yet possible to dump our mental images directly from our brains into a computer, a new and growing class of visualization tools is mediating this process by providing tools that allow us to reason visually. These tools help us to interpret and represent visual ideas and to automate some of the manual processes for creating images. Unlike the generalized representational capabilities of most mindtools, visualization tools tend to be very task and domain specific. That is, there are no general-purpose visualization tools. Rather, these tools closely mimic the ways that different images must be interpreted in order to make sense of the ideas. We next describe two different kinds of visualization tools that learners use to make sense of ideas.

Visualization Tools as Mindtools

Snir (1995) argued that computers can make a unique contribution to the clarification and correction of commonly held misconceptions of phenomena. For example, a computer can be used to form a representation for the phenomenon in which all the relational and mathematical wave equations are embedded within the program code and reflected on the screen with graphics and other visuals. This ability makes the computer an efficient tool for penetrating some of the processes that create obstacles to facilitate scientific understanding of waves. By using computer graphics, one can shift attention back and forth from the local to the global properties of the phenomenon and train the mind to integrate the two aspects into one coherent picture (Snir, 1995).

Numerous visualization tools provide reasoning-congruent representations that enable learners to reason about objects that behave and interact (Merrill, Reiser, Bekkalaar, & Hamid, 1992). Examples include programs such as Mathematica and MathLab, which are used to represent mathematical relationships visually in problems so that learners can see the effects of any problem manipulation. The graphical proof tree representation in the Geometry Tutor (Anderson, Boyle, & Yost, 1986) visualizes a causal decision-making path.

Another kind of visualization tool is provided by the Collaborative Visualization (CoVis), which provides scientific visualization software to students to help them observe climatological patterns. For example, the Weather Visualizer provides user-customizable weather maps, both visible and infrared, from the GOES-7 weather satellite. A point-and-click palette allows students to select the variables and different representations they want drawn on their customized map—for example, pressure gradients, temperatures, and isobars to represent weather conditions. The student can save these maps in a notebook as part of ongoing research, using them for representing weather events and making weather predictions.

Another excellent example of visualization tools is the growing number of tools for visualizing chemical compounds. Understanding chemical bonding is difficult, because the complex atomic interactions are not visible and are therefore abstractions. Static graphics of these bonds found in textbooks may help learners to form mental images, but those mental images are not manipulable and cannot be conveyed to others. Tools such as MacSpartan enable students to view, rotate, and measure molecules using different views (see Fig. 6.6) and also to modify or construct new molecules. These visualization tools make the abstract real for students, helping them to understand chemical concepts that are difficult to convey in static displays (Crouch, Holden, & Samet, 1996).

The use of visualization tools to facilitate learning outcomes is new and as yet uninvestigated. Using visualization tools probably engages learners in the use of more creative thinking skills than most other mindtools, especially synthesizing and imaging skills such as predicting, speculating, visualizing, and intuition. Using visualization tools also enables learners to represent their knowledge visually so they are appealing.

FIG. 6.6.

KNOWLEDGE CONSTRUCTION TOOLS

Papert (1990) coined the term *constructionism* to describe the process of knowledge construction associated with constructing artifacts. The belief is clear: When learners function as designers of objects, they learn more about those objects than they do from studying about them. A variety of desktop publishing and multimedia tools for producing hypermedia and World Wide Web sites enables students to become knowledge construction engineers. In this chapter, we focus only on hypermedia construction as mindtools.

Hypermedia Construction as Mindtool

Hypermedia consists of information nodes, which may be pages of text, graphics, sound bites, video clips, or any other chunk of information (see Erickson & Lehrer, this volume). In many hypermedia systems, users can modify nodes. The links in hypermedia transport the user through the information space to other nodes as selected, enabling the user to navigate through the knowledge base. The node structure and the link structure form a network of ideas in the knowledge base, the interrelated and interconnected group or system of ideas.

Hypermedia systems have traditionally been used as information retrieval systems through which learners browse; learners may construct their own hypermedia knowledge bases that reflect their own understanding of ideas. Jonassen (1996) described a number of hypermedia construction projects in which students created information kiosks, instructional materials for their peers, and structured knowledge bases that reflected their own interests. Research showed that students worked harder, were more interested and involved, and collaborated and planned than students who merely studied content (Carver, Lehrer, Connell, & Erickson, 1992). Students who built hypermedia knowledge bases organized knowledge about a subject in a more expert-like fashion, represented multiple linkages between related ideas, and organized concepts into meaningful clusters (Spoehr, 1993), all of which supported more complex arguments than in written essays. The results of research on hypermedia design are clear: When learners become designers, they engage readily and willingly in higher order thinking.

We recently participated in a study with seventh-grade students in which we examined the rhetorical constructions, cognitive strategies, and social negotiations that students use when constructing their own hypermedia documents (Jonassen, Myers, & McKillop, 1996; McKillop, 1996). We used ethnography, grounded theory, and phenomenology (including questionnaires, student learning logs, interviews, document analysis, videotaping, and observation as data sources) to study the process of composing hypermedia: the composing process, construction of hyperpathways, use of media, utilization of potentials and constraints of the technology, and the social construction of the knowledge presented.

The students wrote and shared poetry, illustrated their poems, wrote scripts, scanned images, recorded and digitized sound, created movies, and planned and executed spaces in a node-link "web view" (see Fig. 6.7). Most of the linking that these students did was implicit in the narrative structures that their projects were presented in, and they planned almost no other linking. Students' contributions were affected by their interactions with the technology, the groups, and the goal of publishing a hypermedia document. "Publishing" their work made them more conscious of how it was presented, and so they exploited multimedia formats to extend their ideas. They were very concerned about the appeal of their presentations and felt empowered to observe others' work critically.

Like other cognitive tools, multimedia and hypermedia construction is based on the idea of knowledge as design, which refocuses the educational process away from one of knowledge as information and the teacher

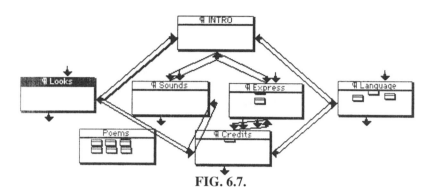

FIG. 6.7.

as transmitter of that knowledge to one of teachers and students as collaborators in the knowledge construction process (Perkins, 1986). Designing multimedia presentations is a complex process that engages many skills in learners and can be applied to virtually any content domain. Carver et al. (1992) list some of the major thinking skills that learners need to use as designers: project management skills, research skills, organization and representation skills, presentation skills, and reflection skills. These skills are engaged when learners determine the problem and research organization, pose thoughtful questions, search for information, analyze and interpret information, organize information segment and sequence information, represent information (in text pictures, movies, and audio), map their design onto the presentation, attract and maintain the audience's interest, evaluate their program, and revise the design (McKillop, 1996).

Constructing hypermedia programs engages more creating and thinking skills such as elaborating (expanding, modifying, extending, and concretizing), imaging (fluency, visualizing and intuition), and complex designing and planning skills than most other mindtools (Jonassen, 1996). Building hypermedia knowledge bases enables learners to represent what they know as interconnected and interrelated multimedia stories. These representations make hypermedia construction probably the most compelling mindtool for most learners.

SOCIALLY SHARED COGNITIVE TOOLS

According to traditional mentalistic conceptions, learning is an individual, interpretive process requiring learners to process percepts, relate them to prior knowledge, and encode them into memory for later use. Knowledge is personally constructed. "But directly experienced events are only part of the basis for that construction. People also build their knowledge structures on the basis of what they are told by others. Our daily lives are filled with instances in which we influence each other's constructive processes by providing information, pointing things out to one another, asking questions, and arguing with and elaborating on each other's ideas" (Resnick, 1991, p. 2). Social constructivist beliefs see learning more as conversation, relying on knowledge negotiation as an essential part of knowledge construction. Rather than internal and individual, cognition is socially shared.

Computer Conferencing as Mindtool

Two kinds of computer-based tools can be used to foster socially shared cognition through conversations: live (synchronous) conversations and reflective (asynchronous) conversations in computer conferences. Synchronous conversation environments, such as multi-user dungeons (MUDs) and MUDs–object or united (MOOs), MOOs and MUDs, function as networked, text-based virtual environments for immersing learners in conversation. Early fears about addiction and loss of personal identity have been replaced by the importance of sociality and a preference for strong interpersonal interactions over large social gatherings in MUDs (Schiano, 1997). Asynchronous conversations, including electronic mail, listservs, bulletin boards, and computer conferences, are typically less immersive, relying more on reflective conversation than immersion. Both kinds of conversation environments stress the creation of a community of learners and, of course, the encouragement of reading and writing.

Interpersonal exchanges may include keypals, global classrooms, electronic appearances, electronic mentoring, and impersonations (Harris, 1995). They may also focus on collaborative construction of databases, electronic publishing, electronic field trips, and pooled data analysis. Environments that foster learning communities that share common goals and collaborate to accomplish them exemplify sociocognitive tools.

Computer-Supported Collaborative
Argumentation as Mindtool

Perhaps the best use of conversation tools to support social negotiation is computer-supported collaborative argumentation (CSCA). This instructional practice can help promote the development of argumentative reasoning skills required to negotiate effectively. Voss (1991) characterized informal argumentation as "reasoning performed in non-deductive situations that are essentially everyday situations of life and work, including the academic and professional disciplines." This implies that informal argumentation is not bound by rules of logic, but involves inference making, justification, and explanation. However, argumentation is the central intellectual ability involved in solving problems (Cerbin, 1988), especially in collaborative or group settings. So CSCA may be used to scaffold formal argumentation in order to help students to reason more effectively.

Collaborative informal reasoning entails the analysis, evaluation and formulation of arguments (or problem solutions) based on reasons (Toulmin, Rieke, & Janik, 1984). At the heart of informal reasoning is the claim-support relationship. Informal arguments are based on claims that are supported by some kind of evidence. One makes an assertion and then builds a case for it by bringing to bear relevant and sound support, and by explaining the weaknesses of opposing claims (Cerbin, 1988). Thus, the product of reasoning is an argument. Analogously, the product of a problem-solving activity is a solution that must be justified in the same way as an argument, by providing supporting evidence or explanations. Solutions are justified by either descriptive explanations or warrants (i.e., supported claims, operationally defined as claims linked to evidence within the problem-based learning case resources). The identification of the warrant is crucial for better critical thinking, because so much of our thinking, reasoning, and persuading is done with implied warrants. Only by understanding the role of the warrant in an argument and by being able to identify which warrants work in a particular situation can a student progress to choosing intelligently the reasons, or justifications, for an argument or a solution (Leeman, 1987). CSCA supports students' ability to seek warrants as supporting evidence for claims. Bell and Linn (1997) suggested that conjecturing (with warrants, as opposed to descriptions) enables students to generate more cogent problem solutions in science.

A number of online communication environments have been designed to support students' argumentation skills, such as the Collaboratory Notebook (O'Neill & Gomez, 1994; CaMile, Guzdial, Turns, Rappin, & Carlson, 1995), and Bio-World (Lajoie et al., 1995). Since these environments do not explicitly connect evidence to assertions by warrants, we have created and are beginning to evaluate a Web-based environment that scaffolds argumentation by mapping a formal argument structure on the conference. Arguments evolve in four levels. At the argument level, instructors pose problems, issues, or dilemmas. Using a concept mapping interface where every communication is represented as a labeled node, any student may attach a claim to any argument. The claim is opened and classified as a fact, policy, solutions, opinion, proposal, or something else. Each claim may be supported by any learner with evidence in the form of facts, statistics, observations, testimony, common knowledge, and so forth. Finally, on the justification level, warrants such as beliefs, theories, laws, formulas, or rules are added to each node on the evidence level. This environment is intended as a generic argumentation structure that can support myriad issues. This environment may be modified to support alternative forms of discourse, such as concept elaboration, decision making, comparison-contrast, and illustration. A research program around this environment is planned.

There is little research on CSCA, but we speculate that it engages critical thinking skills such as evaluating information (e.g., assessing information, prioritizing, recognizing fallacies, and verifying), creative skills such as elaborating (especially expanding and modifying), and complex skills such as decision making (identifying issues-generating alternatives, and assessing the consequences). Socially negotiating through computer conferences enables learners to represent their personal knowledge text in asynchronous conferences and as visual objects and avatars in newer object-oriented conferencing environments.

RATIONALES FOR USING
TECHNOLOGY AS MINDTOOLS

Why do mindtools work? Why should we use them in classrooms?

Knowledge Construction, Not Reproduction

Mindtools represent a constructivist use of technology. Constructivism is concerned with the process of how we construct knowledge. How we do that depends on what we already know, which depends on the kinds of experiences that we have had, how we have organized those experiences into knowledge structures, and what we believe about what we know.

Constructivist approaches to learning strive to create environments where learners actively participate in the environment in ways that are intended to help them construct their own knowledge rather than having the teacher interpret the world and ensure that students understand the world as they have told them. In constructivist environments like mindtools, learners are actively engaged in interpreting the external world and reflecting on their interpretations. Mindtools function as formalisms for guiding learners in the organization and representation of what they know.

Learners as Designers

The people who learn the most from designing instructional materials are the designers, not the learners for whom the materials are intended. The process of articulating what they know and are studying in order to represent it to others forces learners to engage in much more cognition than merely studying the materials. The homily, "The quickest way to learn about something is to have to teach it," explains the effectiveness of mindtools, because learners are teaching the computer. Mindtools often require learners to think harder about what they are studying. While they are thinking harder, they are also thinking more meaningfully as they construct their own realities by designing their own knowledge bases.

Learning With Technology

Traditionally, technologies have been used to deliver instructional messages in preprogrammed lessons that constrain student thinking. When technologies are used to deliver instructional lessons, students learn *from* the technology. Rather than using computer technologies to lead learners through prescribed interactions, learners should use technologies to represent and express what they know—to learn *with* the technology. Learning with computers refers to the learner's entering an intellectual partnership with the computer, where the computer amplifies the student's thinking. This partnership is now more "intelligent" than the student alone (Pea, 1985). Learning with mindtools depends "on the mindful engagement of learners in the tasks afforded by these tools and that there is the possibility of qualitatively upgrading the performance of the joint system of learner plus technology" (Salomon, Perkins, & Globerson, 1991). When students learn with computers instead of being controlled by them, they enhance the capabilities of the computer, and the computer enhances their thinking.

Distributing Cognitive Processing

Computer tools, unlike most other tools, can function as intellectual partners that share the cognitive burden of carrying out tasks (Salomon,

1993). When learners use computers as partners, they off-load some of the unproductive memorizing tasks to the computer, allowing the learner to think more productively. Our goal should be to allocate to the learners the cognitive processing that they perform best while requiring the technology to perform the processing that it does best. Rather than using the limited capabilities of the computer to present information and judge learner input (neither of which computers do well) while asking learners to memorize information and later recall it (which computers do with far greater speed and accuracy than humans can), we should assign cognitive responsibility to the part of the learning system that does it the best. Learners should be responsible for recognizing, judging, and organizing patterns of information, while the computer system should perform calculations and store and retrieve information. Using computers as mindtools engages learners in meaningful rather than reproductive processing.

Cost and Effort Beneficial

Mindtools are personal knowledge construction tools that can be applied to any subject matter domain. For the most part, mindtools software is readily available and affordable. Many computers come bundled with the software described in this chapter. Most other applications are in the public domain or available for less than $100. Mindtools are also reasonably easy to learn. The level of skill needed to use them often requires limited study. Most can be mastered within a couple of hours. Because they can be used to construct knowledge in nearly any course, the investment of mental effort is minimal.

CONCLUSION

The following underlying principles warrant the use of computers as mindtools (Jonassen & Reeves, 1996):

- Mindtools can be applied only within constructivist epistemology.
- Mindtools empower learners to design their own representations of knowledge rather than absorbing knowledge representations that others preconceive.
- Mindtools can be used to support the deep reflective thinking that is necessary for meaningful learning.

- As a form of cognitive technology, mindtools have two kinds of important cognitive effects: those that are *with* the technology in terms of intellectual partnerships and those that are *of* the technology in terms of cognitive residue that remains after the mindtools are used.
- Mindtools enable mindful, challenging learning rather than the effortless learning promised but rarely realized by other instructional innovations.
- The ownership of the tasks or problems to which mindtools are applied should be the learners', with only guidance, and not directions, from teachers. Experience has shown that student knowledge bases often look the same because of overly directive teachers.
- Ideally, tasks or problems for the application of mindtools should be situated in realistic contexts with results that are personally meaningful for learners.
- Mindtools do not contain preconceived intelligence in the sense that intelligent tutoring systems are claimed to possess, but they do enable intellectual partnerships in the form of distributed cognitive processing.

REFERENCES

Albers, G. B., Heiner, G., & Cellerier, G. (1991) A microworld for genetic artificial intelligence. In R. W. L. Masoud Yazdani (Ed.), *Artficial intelligence and education* (Vol. 7). Norwood, NJ: Ablex.

Anderson, J. R., Boyle, C. F., & Yost, G. (1986). The geometry tutor. *Journal of Mathematical Behavior, 5*, 5–19.

Beare, R. (1992). Software tools in science classrooms. *Journal of Computer Assisted Learning, 8*, 221–230.

Bell, M. C, & Linn, P. (1997, March). *Scientific arguments as learning artifacts: Designing for learning on the Web*. Paper presented at the American Educational Research Association, Chicago.

Bremner, F. J., & Denhem, D. L. (1992). Lotus 1-2-3 simulation of frequency encoding on the basilar membrane. *Behavior, Research Methods, Instruments, and Computers, 25*, 208–211.

Brinkley, V. M. (1988). Effects of microworld training experience on sorting tasks by young children. *Journal of Educational Technology Systems, 16*(4), 349-364.

Briscoe, C., & LeMaster, S. U. (1991). Meaningful learning in college biology through concept mapping. *American Biology Teacher, 53*(4), 214–219.

Carver, S. M., Lehrer, R., Connell, T., & Ericksen, J. (1992). Learning by hyper-media design: Issues of assessment and implementation. *Educational Psychologist, 27*(3), 385–404.

Cerbin, B. (1988, April 24–27). *The nature and development of informal reasoning skills in college students.* Paper presented at the National Institute on Issues in Teaching and Learning, Chicago.

Crouch, R. D., Holden, M. S., & Samet, C. (1996). CAChe Molecular modeling: A visualization tool early in the undergraduate chemistry curriculum. *Journal of Chemical Education, 73*(10), 916–917.

Davis, N. T. (1990). Using concept mapping to assist prospective elementary teachers in making meaning. *Journal of Science Teacher Education, 1*(4), 66–69.

Derry, S. J., & LaJoie, S. P. (1993). A middle camp for (un)intelligent instructional computing: An introduction. In S. P. LaJoie & S. J. Derry (Eds.), *Computers as cognitive tools* (pp. 1–14). Hillsdale, NJ: Lawrence Erlbaum Associates.

Driskell, J. E., & Dwyer, D. J. (1984). Microcomputer videogame based training. *Educational Technology, 24,* 11–16.

Edelson, D. C., Pea, R. D., & Gomez, L. (1996). Constructivism in the collaboratory. In B. G. Wilson (Ed.), *Constructivist learning environments: Case studies in instructional design* (pp. 151–164). Englewood Cliffs, NJ: Educational Technology Publications.

Fischer, K. M., Faletti, J., Patterson, H., Thornton, R., Lipson, J., & Spring, C. (1990). Computer assisted concept mapping. *Journal of College Science Teaching, 19*(6), 347–352.

Goble, L. N., Colle, H. A., & Holland, V. M. (1988). Development and evaluation of a computerized hand-held instructional prototype (CHIP). In *Proceedings of the Sixth Conference on Interactive Instructional Delivery* (pp. 859–864). Warrenton, VA: Society for Applied Learning Technology.

Goldberg, K. P. (1992, April). Database programs and the study of sea shells. *Computing Teacher*, pp. 32–34.

Greeno, J. (1989). A perspective on thinking. *American Psychologist, 44,* 134–141.

Halff, L. A. (1987). A spreadsheet simulation of the early stages of visual processing. *Behavior, Research Methods, Instruments, and Computers, 19,* 117–122.

Harris, J. (1995, February). Organizing and facilitating telecollaborative projects.*Computing Teacher, 22*(5), 66–69. Available: *http://www.ed.uiuc.edu/Mining/February95-TCT.html.*

Hopkins, P. L. (1992). Simulating *Hamlet* in the classroom. *Systems Dynamics Review, 8*(1), 91–98.

Horton, P. B., McConney, A. A., Gallo, M., & Woods, A. L. (1993). An investigation of the effectiveness of concept mapping as an instructional tool. *Science Education, 77*(1), 95–111.

Jiang, Z. (1994). A computer microworld to introduce students to probability. *Journal of Computers in Mathematics and Science Teaching, 13*(2), 197–222.

Jonassen, D. H. (1987). Verifying a method for assessing cognitive structure using pattern notes. *Journal of Research and Development in Education, 20*(3), 1–14.

Jonassen, D. H. (1996). *Computers in the classroom: Mindtools for critical thinking.* Columbus, OH: Merrill/Prentice-Hall.

Jonassen, D. H. (1999). Designing constructivist learning environments. In C. M. Reigeluth (Ed.), *Instructional design theories and models* (2nd ed.). Hillsdale, NJ: Lawrence Erlbaum Associates.

Jonassen, D. H. (2000). *Computers as mindtools in schools: Engaging critical thinking* (2nd ed.). Columbus, OH: Prentice-Hall.

Jonassen, D. H., Beissner, K., & Yacci, M. A. (1993). *Structural knowledge: Techniques for representing, assessing, and acquiring structural knowledge.* Hillsdale, NJ: Lawrence Erlbaum Associates.

Jonassen, D. H., Myers, J. M., & McKillop, A. M. (1996). From constructivism to constructionism: Learning *with* hypermedia/multimedia rather than *from* it. In B. G. Wilson (Ed.), *Constructivist learning environments: Case studies in instructional design* (pp. 9–106). Englewood Cliffs, NJ: Educational Technology Publications.

Jonassen, D. H., & Reeves, T. C. (1996). Learning with technology: Using computers as cognitive tools. In D. H. Jonassen (Ed.), *Handbook of research for educational communications and technology* (pp. 693–719). New York: Macmillan.

Jonassen, D. H., & Rohrer-Murphy, L. (1999). Activity theory as framework for designing constructivist learning environments. *Educational Technology: Research and Development.*

Katzeff, C. (1987). *Strategies for testing hypotheses in database query writing* (Rep. No. 669). Stockholm: Department of Psychology, University of Stockholm.

Keys, J. B. F., Robert, M., & Stumpt, S. A. (1996). Microworlds and simuworlds: Practice fields for the learning organization. *Organizational Dynamics*, 24(4), 36-49.

Lahtinen, V., Lonka, K., & Lindbloom, S. (1997). Spontaneous study strategies and the quality of knowledge construction. *British Journal of Educational Psychology, 67*, 13–24.

Lajoie, S. P., Greer, J. E., Munsie, S. D., Wilkie, T. V., Guerrara, C., & Aleong, P. (1995). Establishing an argumentation environment to foster scientific reasoning with Bio-World. In D. Jonassen & G. McCalla (Eds.), *Proceedings of the International Conference on Computers in Education* (pp. 89–96). Charlottesville, VA: Association for the Advancement of Computing in Education.

Leeman, R. W. (1987). *Taking perspectives: Teaching critical thinking in the argumentation course.* Paper presented at the Speech Communication Association, Boston.

Lehrer, R. (1993). Authors of knowledge: Patterns of hypermedia design. In S. P. LaJoie & S. J. Derry (Eds.), *Computers as cognitive tools.* Hillsdale, NJ: Lawrence Erlbaum Associates.

Markham, K. M., Mintzes, J. J., & Jones, M. G. (1994). The concept map as a research and evaluation tool; Further evidence of validity. *Journal of Research in Science Teaching, 31*, 91–101.

McKillop, A. M. (1996). Unpublished doctoral dissertation, Pennsylvania State University.

Mikulecky, L. (1988). *Development of interactive programs to help students transfer basic skills to college level science and behavioral sciences courses.* Bloomington, IN: Indiana University. (ERIC Document Reproduction Service No. ED 318 469)

Niedderer, H., Schecker, K., & Bethge, T. (1991). The role of computer-aided modeling in learning physics. *Journal of Computer-Assisted Learning, 7*(2), 84–95.

O'Neill, D. K., & Gomez, L. M. (1992). The collaboratory notebook: A distributed knowledge building environment for project learning. *Proceedings of ED MEDIA, 94.* Vancouver B.C., Canada.

Panitz, B. (1998). The 15-minute lecture. *Prism, 7*(6), 17.

Papert, S. (1990). Introduction to I. Harel (Ed.), *Constructionist learning.* Boston: MIT Laboratory.

Pea, R. (1984). *Integrating human and computer intelligence* (Tech. Rep. No. 32). New York: Bank Street College of Education.

Perkins, D. N. (1986). *Knowledge as design.* Hillsdale, NJ: Lawrence Erlbaum Associates.

Pon, K. (1984). Databasing in the elementary (and secondary) classroom. *Computing Teacher, 12*(3), 28–30.

Quillian, M. R. (1968). Semantic memory. In M. Minsky (Ed.), *Semantic information processing* (pp. 43–67). Cambridge, MA: MIT Press.

Resnick, L. B. (1991). Shared cognition: Thinking as social practice. In L. B. Resnick, J. M. Levine, & S. D. Teasley (Eds.), *Perspectives on socially shared cognition* (pp. 1–20). Washington, DC: American Psychological Association

Robertson, W. C. (1990). Detection of cognitive structure with protocol data: Predicting performance on physics transfer problems. *Cognitive Science, 14*, 253–280.

Rooze, G. E. (1988-89). Developing thinking using databases: What's really involved? *Michigan Social Studies Journal, 3*(1), 25–26.

Roth, W. M., & Roychoudhury, A. (1993). The concept map as a collaborative tool for collaborative construction of knowledge: A microanalysis of high school physics students. *Journal of Research in Science Teaching, 30*, 503–534.

Rumelhart, D. E. (1980). Schemata: The building blocks of cognition. In R. J. Spiro, B. C. Bruce, & W. F. Brewer (Eds.), *Theoretical issues in reading comprehension: Perspectives from cognitive psychology, linguistics, artificial intelligence, and education.* Hillsdale, NJ: Lawrence Erlbaum Associates.

Salomon, G., Perkins, D. N., & Globerson, T. (1991). Partners in cognition: Extending human intelligence with intelligent technologies. *Educational Researcher, 20*(3), 2–9.

Schiano, D. J. (1997). Convergent methodologies in cyber-space: A case study. *Behavior, Research Methods, Instruments, and Computers, 29*(2), 270–273.

Schreiber, D. A., & Abegg, G. L. (1991, April). *Scoring student-generated concept maps in introductory college chemistry.* Paper presented at the Annual Meeting of the National Association for Research in Science Teaching, Lake Geneva, WI. (ERIC Document Reproduction Service No. ED 347 055)

Spitulnik, J., Studer, S, Finkel., Gustafson, E., Laczko, J., & Soloway, E. (1995). The RiverMUD design rationale: Scaffolding for scientific inquiry through modeling, discourse, and decision making in community based issues. In T. Koschman (Ed.), *Proceedings of Computer Support for Collaborative Learning.* Hillsdale, NJ: Lawrence Erlbaum Associates.

Spoehr, K. T. (1993, April). *Profiles of hypermedia authors: How students learn by doing.* Paper presented at the annual meeting of the American Educational Research Association, Atlanta, GA.

Steffe, L. P. (1991). Operations that generate quantity. *Learning and Individual Differences, 3*, 61–82.

Sutherland, R., & Rojano, T. (1993). A spreadsheet approach to solving algebra problems. *Journal of Mathematical Behavior, 12*, 353–383.

Thompson, P.W. (1985, September). A Piagetian approach to transformation geometry via microworlds. *Mathematics Teacher*, pp. 465–471.

Toulmin, S., Rieke, R., & Janik, A. (1984). *An introduction to reasoning.* New York: Macmillan.

Trollip, S., Lippert, R., Starfield, A., & Smith, K. A. (1992). Building knowledge bases: An environment for making cognitive connections. In P. Kommers, D. H. Jonassen, & T. Mayes (Eds.), *Cognitive tools for learning*. Heidelberg: Springer-Verlag.

Winn, W., & Snyder, D. (1996). Cognitive perspectives in psychology. In D. H. Jonassen (Ed.), *Handbook of research for educational communications and technology* (pp. 112–143). New York: Macmillan.

Yerulshamy, M., & Schwartz, J. (1986). The geometric supposer: Promoting thinking and learning. *Mathematics Teacher, 79*, 418–422.

7

What's in a Link? Student Conceptions of the Rhetoric of Association in Hypermedia Composition

Julie Erickson and Richard Lehrer
University of Wisconsin–Madison

Restructuring classrooms by placing student design at the center of teaching and learning affords students opportunities to acquire complex skills and to participate in communities that incubate a critical stance toward knowledge (Erickson & Lehrer, 1998; Lehrer, 1993; Perkins, 1986). In our work, we collaborate with teachers to restructure classrooms so that students design hypermedia documents (electronic writing that combines multiple forms of media) that peers use to learn about topics in social studies (e.g., the impact of the industrial revolution on government). The goal of restructuring the learning environment in this way is for students to acquire research and communication skills typically featured in language arts and social studies curricula (e.g., finding information, interviewing a person) and to orchestrate these skills in the pursuit of inquiry about a topic (Carver, Lehrer, Erickson, & Connell, 1992). In the process of designing tutorial documents in hypermedia, students develop and integrate new ideas about domain content and about themselves as authors of knowledge (Lehrer, 1993; Lehrer, Erickson, & Connell, 1994; Liu, 1998; Liu & Rutledge, 1997).

The notion of association, ideas about links (i.e., a means to associate one informational node with another) and the functions they serve in composition, may profoundly affect the nature of students' hypermedia design. On the one hand, students can employ links simply to tell about a topic, a process that Scardamalia and Bereiter (1987) suggested involves minimal restructuring of the content. On the other hand, students can employ links to provoke reader interest and comprehension, a process of transforming content that is likely to lead to greater learning (Scardamalia & Bereiter, 1987). It is this transformation process, in which authors successfully coordinate aspects of both the content and the rhetorical problem, that indicates emerging proficiency in the domain (Flower, 1994, 1996; Lehrer, 1993; Slatin, 1991).[1]

Unfortunately, using links to tell or to transform content is not simply a matter of author choice. Authoring a hypermedia document, like authoring any other text, involves juggling or negotiating a large number of constraints, like thinking of what to say, translating ideas to text, and dealing with rhetorical goals regarding audience and purpose (Flower & Hayes, 1980). Novice writers often reduce this large cognitive load by operating solely with the content problem space, using a simpler knowledge-telling strategy (Scardamalia & Bereiter, 1987) in which attention is fully occupied by finding "the next thing to say."[2] This "think-say" process often results in "this, and then this, and then . . ." In hypermedia composition, the knowledge-telling strategy is reflected by employing links simply to move from one screen to another ("next, and next . . .").

To transform instead of tell, hypermedia composers, like other writers everywhere, must develop means to coordinate content and rhetoric. This coordination requires knowledge of rhetorical devices (such as types of purposes, audiences, and text conventions) and the conditions of their application. Thus, hypermedia authors must expand their repertoire of potential functions of links well beyond simple association, and they must also develop a rhetorical sense of how best to employ these expanded functions in the service of communication with readers.

---

[1] According to Flower and Hayes (1980), the rhetorical problem includes an author's purpose in writing, sense of the audience, and projected selves or imagined roles. Slatin (1991) discussed this more specifically in terms of hypermedia composition, specifying that the problem of identifying links and nodes depends on an author's understanding of both the ways in which material is related and the sense of whom the readers are and what the readers are to do with the information.

[2] Once a unit of text has been produced, it serves as an additional source of topic and genre identifier (cueing retrieval of additional content).

Because electronic links in hypermedia permit different reading pathways, an author needs to assist the reader to control the unfolding of
understanding (Landow & Delany, 1991). Both the static (e.g., a button)
and dynamic aspects (e.g., visual effects) of links can indicate aspects of
structure and navigation. For instance, an author may create a button to
signal potential traversal from a main menu (say, Events in the Civil War)
to a particular card or topic area (Battle of Gettysburg), where a reader
may then browse among related subtopics (General Lee, General Meade,
or Pickett's Charge). In addition to moving the reader from one card to
another, an author can develop links in ways that orient readers toward a
particular conceptual understanding. For instance, an author could create
an iconic button (a cannon) and/or name (battles) to define a link that
communicates a type of relation among ideas (a class of events—battles).
Consequently, the common association among ideas is signaled to readers: The link signals relationships of a particular type, such as battles
(Lehrer, 1993; Lehrer et al., 1994). In addition, Slatin (1991) argued that
visual effects like wipes and dissolves, if used consistently and meaningfully with particular nodes, can function as a kind of subliminal aid to prediction, helping the reader to perceive the hyperdocument as coherent.
Thus, just as in a book, hypermedia requires stylistic and rhetorical
devices (e.g., how does a link give readers enough information about
where links will take them or how to return to an area?) to orient readers
as to structure, navigation, and relationships among domain content
(Landow, 1991).

Previous research on student hypermedia composition suggests that
instruction plays a major role in the development of rhetorical functions of
links—those that reflect a consideration of purpose, audience, and composition or text conventions. For example, in several studies, students
changed the structure of their compositions and the types of links contained within their compositions toward that more appropriate of the tutorial purpose and peer audience (e.g., created more explanatory links)
following a revision period in which an audience tried to learn from their
documents (Lehrer, 1993; Lehrer et al., 1994). In another classroom study,
frequent peer critique sessions helped to make the evolving standards for
hypermedia design visible to students (Erickson & Lehrer, 1998). Students initially thought that "good" links were those that helped readers
move from card to card (in a linear string or continuum of cards). But after
two years, students' standards about good links came to include the goal
of making relationships among topics visible to readers; the document
was now considered an integrated structure and not merely a string of

screens, suggesting an integration of content with consideration of audience and purpose (rhetorical notions).

These previous studies suggest that instructional context plays a fundamental role in students' conceptions of association in hypermedia composing. Moreover, student notions of association may evolve with time and experience. Consequently, we explored students' changing conceptions of links in classes where we collaborated with teachers to structure a learning environment so that students learned about social studies and language arts by designing hypermedia documents (Wilhelm, Friedemann, & Erickson, 1998). The design of the learning environment was informed by our previously developed framework for characterizing the research and communication skills required for composing tutorial hypermedia documents (Carver et al., 1992; Lehrer, 1993).

Our conjectures about student authors' notions of rhetorical functions of links were similarly informed by our previous work, and we observed significant variation in the rhetorical purposes of links in these studies. Early in the design process, students often employed links simply to move from one screen to another, a functional use that fit well with knowledge-telling strategies for composition (Scardamalia & Bereiter, 1987). Links involved in simple knowledge telling signal to the reader only "and next." In contrast, developing links that signal a particular kind of semantic relationship or indicate the structure of a document, a practice that we observed only after repeated design experiences in previous studies, requires anticipation of audience and is more consistent with knowledge transformation. Yet these endpoints, knowledge telling on the one hand and knowledge transformation on the other, left unexplored the space of possible states, and potential trajectories within these states, of a rhetoric of links. Hence the object of this study was to investigate the nature of this rhetorical space of links. Accordingly, the study reported in this chapter examined student authors' ideas about links as they composed several hypermedia documents during a school year.

THE STUDY

The study explored seventh-graders' conceptions of links as they composed multiple hypermedia documents throughout the school year. Ten students were selected as participants in an effort to discover in some detail the evolution of student beliefs about links (what are they? what is their purpose? how are they used in design?). Semistructured interviews, hypermedia compositions, and other student data were collected five times during the school year in order to understand how conceptions of links evolved as students became more skilled in composing in hypermedia. The study was set in a larger context of two teachers' attempts to restructure classroom learning toward constructivist process-oriented practices that assist students with knowledge transformation (Erickson, 1997).

Instructional Setting

Two teachers (one in reading and one in social studies) initiated a series of student-designed hypermedia projects throughout the year to promote students' critical thinking skills and their understanding of the reading and social studies domains. They had consulting help from both of us to initiate the hypermedia projects in their classrooms, with instruction focused on helping students acquire research and communication skills, like posing questions, searching for information, and analyzing data (e.g., Lehrer, 1993; Lehrer et al., 1994). The teachers had worked with the hypermedia-based curriculum for two years, focusing on the skills that students learned through design and developing new types of assessment tools (portfolios, new rubrics) to measure these skills. Throughout the year with the hypermedia and other projects, the teachers encouraged student autonomy and attempted to create a classroom community of learners (Brown & Campione, 1994, 1996).

Students designed three hypermedia documents about social studies topics during the year. In order to complete the documents, students found information, created new information, analyzed and organized information, presented to others, and reflected about a topic and its connection to that of others (for the complete list of cognitive skills, see Appendix A). As students worked through each hypermedia project, they needed to think about how best to communicate their topic to others. Should they represent information through text or graphs or pictures? How should they structure their document so that others might read it?

To foster these cognitive skills, for each design project students were required to receive feedback from other classmates and from one adult in order to revise their compositions. Also, at the beginning of each design project, students and teachers together constructed an assessment rubric so that everyone knew what standards of design were needed for a good hypermedia document (Erickson & Lehrer, 1998). In addition, teachers presented student examples to the class for critique throughout the course of each project; they provided examples from past student hypermedia projects as well as examples from in-progress student work.

Hypermedia Projects. The three hypermedia projects that students designed were sequenced to increase in scope and complexity over time (Collins, Brown, & Newman, 1989). The school year began in the fall with students designing a small hypermedia document in order to learn to use the hypermedia programming tools (Hypercard™). Students created a document about themselves called a personality profile to share with others so the class could get to know one another. The teachers had developed a scaffolded hypermedia stack (blank screens of information that were linked into a particular structure) so that students needed only to fill in information and pictures. The document also contained help buttons that students could click for more information about what to do next. Students also needed to create some novel cards and links. An example of a screen from this scaffolded stack is shown in Fig. 7.1, in which a student has completed the screen with text and a drawing to portray his ideas. Note that the two buttons with icons on the screen were designed by the teachers, whereas the link marked with text only (bottom right corner: "to family") is a student link that reports the destination (a card about the student's family).

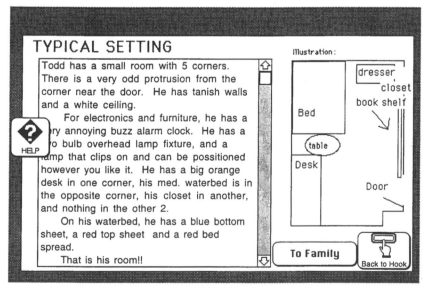

FIG. 7.1.

The second hypermedia project was three weeks long and followed completion of a psychology unit in the social studies class. Students were asked to choose a topic from the unit (such as Freud or Pavlov's theories, dreams, right versus left brain functions), break it down into components, and organize and design a hypermedia document so that peers could learn about the topic.

The final project involved working in collaborative design teams over three months to create a hypermedia composition about a culture of the world. Students chose topics, specified a purpose (e.g., travel guide for foreign exchange student), asked questions, researched information, interviewed a person from the culture, and organized and designed the hypermedia document. Then they presented their documents to one another, evaluated each of the designs, and provided feedback to one another for revision. In addition, peers helped to evaluate student compositions for final grades (teachers averaged five students' evaluations to obtain a grade) based on an assessment rubric that the class created together.

Students worked on these projects during one or both of their reading and social studies classes anywhere from 2 to 5 days per week. The students had access to a computer lab with approximately 28 Macintosh computers, 1 scanner, and 2 printers. Teachers provided instruction on hypermedia programming during the initial personality profile project and more advanced programming before and throughout the psychology project.

It is important to note that each of the projects increased in scope and complexity over time: the teachers' instruction expanded the number of cognitive skills that students were asked to integrate and coordinate over time (Collins et al., 1989, 1996). The first stack was scaffolded so that students needed only to fill in information and create one or two novel cards and links; this was the first time they learned computer tools and the overall design process (the cognitive skills in Appendix 7). The second document was an entire individual stack, where students went through the design process; yet the "research" did not have to include original information, in that the topic chosen could come from class notes from the previous social studies unit. By the final project (a much longer period of time), students not only completed an individual document, but were asked to coordinate the research with group members, so that individual documents could be joined into one large stack about the culture (via a menu screen) at the conclusion of the project (after students had revised their individual documents). Although each project required students to create an individual hypermedia document, by the end of year, students also had to research all information (including interviews with someone from the culture and letters to foreign embassies) and collaborate with others. Thus, over the school year, students extended and refined the inquiry skills with each project in terms of the number of cognitive skills they were asked to coordinate and the sophistication of those skills.

Participants

The study took place in a large, rural middle school in the Midwest. Five classes of seventh-grade students ($N = 125$), 20% of whom were classified as learning disabled students and mainstreamed, rotated through two subject areas (reading and social studies) each day for 45 minutes each. Participants of this study were 10 seventh-grade students taken from the five seventh-grade classes. Students were selected by the teachers to represent a range of ability and effort levels (including one student classified as learning disabled) and to represent two students from each of the five classes. The two teachers planned curriculum together and did several collaborative projects throughout the school year but taught their classes individually.

Procedure

Several sources of data were gathered in order to study student conceptions of links. Student interviews about links and their functions in hypermedia composition were the primary source of data and were triangulated with student documents and teacher reports. The students' hypermedia compositions were collected at each of the interview dates (other artifacts such as classroom notes and plans for screen designs were also collected at the interview dates). In addition, sources of teacher data were gathered to elaborate on issues that had arisen during the student interviews. Teachers were asked to keep journals, paying particular attention to their own instruction and to student ideas about links and hypermedia composing. We also interviewed teachers periodically about instruction, their own beliefs about links, and whether the target students' notions about association were representative of the rest of the students in the classes. The student compositions and teacher reports were mainly used to triangulate the student notions of association from the interviews.[3]

During the semi-structured interviews, students were asked about the nature of links, the purpose of links, whether there were different types

---

[3]Because students' evolving conceptions of links are the focus of this chapter, we place less emphasis on many aspects of teacher instruction such as the ongoing deliberations by the two teachers about how to improve the instruction for hypermedia projects and their ideas about student learning, some issues that were described in the teacher journals and cited elsewhere (Erickson, 1997).

of links, and strategies for various design issues, such as the appearance and role of buttons. In addition to general questions, students also were asked about links in the context of their particular compositions (how they used and designed links, relationships among particular screens, and so forth).

The 10 student participants were interviewed five times during the school year. The first two interviews took place after students completed separate compositions (personality profile and psychology documents), and the rest took place in one extended composition over several months (culture document: planning, completion, revision). Recall that students' hypermedia documents (and artifacts such as planned screen designs) were also collected at each of these interview dates.

We sampled most heavily from analyses of student interviews because students' attempts to articulate their beliefs and rationales provided the most transparent window to their thinking. Moreover, these episodes allowed us to probe the robustness of ideas, so that this hour or two of reflective articulation also provided opportunities for observing how stable ideas and beliefs were and when student thinking would become circular or break down.

Analysis

Student interviews were coded and analyzed for ideas about links and their functions in hypermedia composition across time. We then triangulated these with evidence from student hypermedia documents and teacher data (interviews and journals).

Coding and Analyzing Transcripts.   Audiotape transcripts of the student interviews were coded using verbal analysis (Chi, 1997). Segmentation of transcripts during coding was based on ideas about links. Link functions noted in previous studies guided initial coding (e.g., go to, use link to mark destination in the document). Codes were then refined and revised on the basis of the transcript data. For example, initially all student ideas about links as movements were coded as "go to." Later, it became apparent that students were making a subtle distinction between a local move (between two cards only) and a general notion of moving through the document (navigation). The codes were refined to distinguish between single, local moves in student ideas about links and references to navigation (a system of moves or abstracted movements anywhere in a document). Thus, the system of coding the audiotaped transcripts was an interactive top–down and bottom–up process (Chi, 1997).

After all transcripts were coded, the frequencies of various link functions at different points in time were obtained to examine patterns and transitions in students' conceptions of links (see Appendix 7 for the coding scheme and definitions of each code). Percentages were examined to compare student ideas about link functions for an individual over time as well as across students over time. One third of the student interview transcripts were randomly selected to determine interrater reliability of codes. A trained rater recorded presence or absence of each of the codes for a given student transcript. Percentage exact agreement was 85.

Hypermedia Documents.   Hypermedia compositions were analyzed after the student interviews had been coded to determine if student self-reports about link functions were indicative of their practice. Compositions were examined for evidence of the various codes (e.g., specified destination, navigational landmark, annotation). A coding scheme similar to the one used for student transcripts was used to record the various ways of instantiating each code. For example, we examined exactly how students "specified the destination" (text versus icons versus transition effects), and whether the icon choice could be understood by most readers, to obtain a more accurate report of how students used links in their compositions. Frequencies of link functions were calculated. In addition, several representative hypermedia screens were selected to serve as examples of the types of links and screen design that were common throughout different projects.

Teacher Interviews and Journals.   Teacher journals and audiotape transcripts of the teacher interviews were examined to understand the nature of instruction throughout each project and to determine if student conceptions of links coincided with teachers' perceptions. In particular, we focused on instruction about links during each project and on teacher reports of classroom standards for links (what makes a good one and how to design one). These teacher reports served as a comparison to student reports and indicated whether the target students' notions about association were representative of the rest of the students in the classes.

RESULTS

The data were gathered over a school year to permit the investigation of the evolution of students' conceptions of links as they composed multiple hypermedia documents. The evolution in student ideas is reported overall in summary sections, but the case of one student is used to detail this evolution more fully. The student, whom we refer to as Amy, was selected for presentation because she clearly articulated the evolution in ideas representative of the pattern of development found in the study (and followed the general pattern of development, though at a higher level than many other students).

In general, students' use of links during the school year (across three hypermedia documents) changed from links that tell ("next and next") to links that transform (indicate structure, navigation, relationships to reader). Students began with the idea of links as a local move between two cards, a fast, efficient alternative to moving with the arrow keys on a keyboard. All students reported that links functioned as a move (Go to) and specified the destination of the move (Go to Hobbies Card). These functions were consistently reported throughout the school year. However, students' ideas about link functions evolved throughout the year to include a multiplicity of rhetorical devices designed to enhance communication with the reader; by the end of the year, the predominant view was that links organized a document and oriented readers toward a particular understanding of the topic. The number of link functions increased throughout the year to include a variety of purposes: assisting with navigation (efficiently moving about the stack), elaborating movement (signal main menu, media type, annotation), organizing the document (organization/structure), communicating a topic to the reader (communication tool), and communicating a particular understanding of the topic to the reader (highlighting particular semantic relationships). The multiple purposes of links that students reported at the end of the year and the variety of link types used in the documents demonstrated that students were attending to the rhetorical aspects of the composition problem.

OVERVIEW OF KEY TRANSITIONS
IN STUDENTS' IDEAS

Table 7.1 reports a summary of some of the major developments in student ideas about link functions across the year. The table includes a variety of elaborative (i.e., signals both the destination and some additional information) and structural functions that the students reported during the year and specifies the percentages of students reporting a particular link function at a given interview period. Recall that the first two interviews

TABLE 7.1 *Major Transitions in Student Notions of Link Functions Across*

Percentages of Students Reporting Link Functions During Interviews

Link Functions	Example	T1	T2	T3	T4	T5
• Navigation	"You want the reader to be able to move around easily in your stack."	38	67	80	80	100
Elaborative information						
• Navigational landmark	"It shows you're going to the main menu."	25	78	100	100	100
• Transition in media	"The little cartoon icon means 'animation.'"	0	22	10	40	50
• Annotation	"You can add a pop-up field or animation."	0	11	50	70	70
• Signal local relationship	"Those two cards have similar topics."	63	44	40	20	10
Structure						
• Signal global relationships to reader	"They show the similarities and differences to help the reader understand it."	13	56	60	80	90
• Clusters, threads of traversal	"I have a Definition and Example, Definition and Example—those all like go together."	0	33	40	60	90
• Syntax	"You have to be conservative in the number of buttons you make, so that a reader can spot it and know it right away."	0	0	10	50	80

were separate compositions (personality profile, $N = 8$, and psychology document, $N = 9$), whereas Interviews 3 through 5 took place in one extended composition over several months (culture document, $N = 10$).[4] In the table, *navigation* refers to a system of moves within a hypermedia document. *Annotation* refers to the creation of an additional layer of information for the reader that elaborates an idea or otherwise assists reader comprehension, such as a pop-up text or animation. Two of the link functions report similarities among ideas and are mutually exclusive functions: A local similarity is a commonality between two cards only; global relationships indicate relationships among topic content as a whole. Clusters and threads of traversal indicate relationships among three or more links, and a syntax refers to the development of a consistent and limited number of link types to communicate a system of meanings to the reader (i.e., a library of meanings).

Inspection of Table 7.1 suggests greater student concern for the tutorial purpose of the hypermedia composition over time and thus greater awareness of the rhetorical functions of links (i.e., those that reflect a consideration of purpose, audience, and composition and text conventions). For example, the percentages of students reporting the use of links as navigational landmarks (e.g., a main menu) and as tools for establishing document-wide (global) relationships increased throughout the year, indicating that students were reflecting about how to orient readers toward major navigational landmarks and relationships among ideas. Table 7.1 indicates student development of a repertoire of link functions throughout the year; the percentages of elaborative and structural functions of links increased throughout the year across the five interviews. Emphasis on local relationships between cards decreased as emphasis on document-wide relationships increased.

Link functions related to navigation (moving around the stack) and navigational landmarks (e.g., Go to Main Menu) developed early and continued to increase throughout the year. These student conceptions about the navigational functions of links preceded recognition of the potential of links as tools for expressing semantic relationships. Development of the semantic roles of links unfolded gradually; ideas about a syntax of links (i.e., a limited number of consistent types) developed only after students reported other structural functions of links (global relationships and clusters of ideas) and elaborative functions (annotation). This indicates

---

[4]Two students dropped out of the study (one student after the first interview, and another after the second interview) and were replaced by the teachers with students from the same class period of similar gender, ability, and effort levels.

that students needed the technical means of hypermedia conventions (how to annotate) and attention to organization (how to cluster related material) to develop notions of a syntax of link types. Examination of student documents confirmed the same trends displayed in Table 7.1, although students were often able to report the various functions of links before they were able to implement the functions of links in their documents.

Initial Hypermedia Composition: Personality Profile (Interview 1)

After composing the Personality Profile document and creating a few novel cards and links, all students reported the function of move (Go to) and specified destination (Go to X Card), as demonstrated by Amy during her interview:

> Interviewer: What's it [a link] good for?
> Amy: So that you can, instead of going through all the cards, just go straight to that card . . . You use them when you want to get from place to place without going through the arrow keys.
> It could say, like, "to Surroundings card" and then go to your Surroundings card.

Students elaborated the function of "move": links were fast and direct, and an alternate way to move to a desired card in the document (links were easier than moving with the arrow keys on a keyboard, a default provided by Hypercard™).

Most students believed that link notations (the buttons) should be marked with text (however in a few cases, the student marked the origin card instead of the destination card reducing the function to an unspecified "Go To"). Figure 7.2 illustrates one of Amy's cards about her typical setting (her bedroom). Note that her link (in the upper right corner) marks, with text, where the reader will move. Whereas text was used to mark the destination, icons were for decorative (not communicative) purposes:

> Interviewer: What does the icon do for a link?
> Amy: It looks kind of neat.

Text was used to communicate the destination of the link and icons were used to make it "look good."

Many students (63%) reported that a link between two cards demonstrated that these cards showed a common topic (e.g., "like if two things

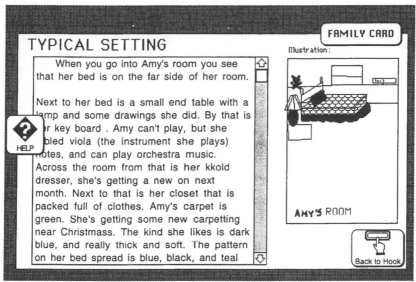

FIG. 7.2.

have something to do with each other"). However, this usually applied to a singular local relationship (between two cards only). There was little consideration of document-wide organization, little attention to structuring the document using links, or even awareness of the overall tutorial purpose of the document (to communicate to an audience). Students did not appear to consider the rhetorical problem space; most students used links for "moving to the card you want because it's faster that way" ("next, and next . . .").

Analysis of student documents confirmed these self-reports. Students used links, marked with text, to specify a local connection to another card in the document (e.g., my hobbies, my family) as opposed to links that might indicate structural relationships in the personality profile (such as recreation, family life, personal values) or other link types. In addition, several documents contained malfunctioning links—for example, a button that was not linked or that moved to the wrong card.

Second Hypermedia Composition: Psychology Stack (Interview 2)

Following completion of the psychology document, students began to report various elaborative functions of links. Most reported that links could designate a navigational landmark, and 90% of students' stacks contained a link to specify the main menu card within the document (a navigational landmark). Figure 7.3 shows Amy's main menu card. A few students also used links to signal a transition in media type (e.g., "to pictures of X"). For example, another card in Amy's parapsychology stack contained a link marked "About Pic" to specify a transition to a card solely containing pictures. Analysis of compositions, however, indicated that many students did not signal these elaborative functions of links consistently. For instance, the text and icons that many students used to signal the main menu card were not always consistent throughout the document and therefore would confuse a reader (although a few, like Amy, had consistent links). Several buttons that looked different represented the same location so that many students employed icons in the documents as "decoration" as opposed to a meaningful representation of the main menu.

Icons now served a dual purpose of "flash" (e.g., cool!) and alternate representation of the destination (e.g., a school building to represent the "school" card), suggesting a move toward the more meaningful consideration of hypermedia conventions (i.e., that icons can help to signal the destination as well as text)—for example:

Interviewer: What do icons do for links?
Amy: It kind of shows you what the word is . . . Like if it was, like, Telepathy, I'd put a telephone on it . . . because it's like connecting to people's minds . . . The picture kind of explains the title.
Interviewer: Do you think that they [icons] are necessary?
Amy: You don't need them. They're . . . they just look better; they're more for show.

Three students distinguished the dynamic notation of links (visual effects) as well as the static (button) portion of a link. These students used the movement of a link, transition effects, to add to graphic design, believing that it made a document more visually appealing; it "looked neat," one student said.

Moreover, many students were beginning to attend to various structural functions of links. A majority of students mentioned that links could show similarities among ideas so that the reader could understand the topic information (global relationships), although only one student deployed them for these purposes in the documents. (Perhaps this was due to the large number of constraints that must be juggled during composition.) One common way to organize the composition was the "link everything to

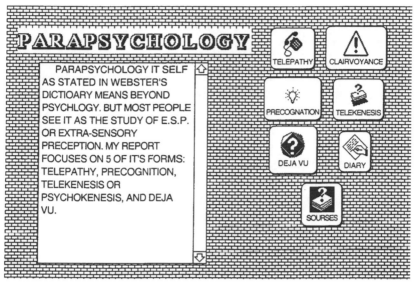

FIG. 7.3.

everything else" strategy, in which students would allow the reader to go to any card from any card within the stack. Students reported that multiple paths of access afforded greater reader interest and control: "You don't want them to get bored, you know" and "It's more fun if you have choices; then you're not forcing them to go where *you* want and they can go anywhere *they* want to." Teacher data (interviews, instructional materials) indicated that reader choice was emphasized during instruction, although teachers did not anticipate that students would instantiate this notion in such a pervasive way.

Third Hypermedia Composition: Culture Stack (Interviews 3–5)

Students worked in collaborative design teams to conduct research on a topic, but each student composed a hypermedia composition on some aspect of a culture. Teachers reported that because the psychology stacks varied so widely in terms of structure and organization, with some documents containing a clear structure and others lacking any coherent structure, their instruction targeted the organization of information. Specifically, instruction focused on various means for organizing information hierarchically (e.g., topics, subtopics). Teachers modeled several organization tools, . . . including outlines, webs, and pyramids) and how to translate those organizations to one's links in a hypermedia composition, which made it easier for teachers to monitor student progress (if documents contained similar hierarchical structures and had a clear structure).[5]

Students talked more about elaborative functions (navigational landmark, annotation), and these self-reports were indicative of practice. All students planned and created a main menu card and submenus for their stack, and documents contained links to mark the main menu card and subtopic menus, as well as marking the general destination of a card. In addition, more students recognized the annotative potential of links ("layering"): Links could "give you more information" by moving the reader to a screen that explained further and provided more detailed information than on the current screen. After completing the document, 70% of students reported the annotative function of links by creating media (animation, pop-up text fields, sound) to elaborate ideas.

An increased number of students reported structural and organizational functions of links. In practice, students were organizing their compositions into predominantly hierarchical structures of relationships (topic, subtopics, details). For example, Amy was a member of a group researching France and had decided to design her document about the fashion industry (and economy). She described the organization of her document in hierarchical relationships and the function of the links within that organization:

> Amy: I think the main menu is like at the top of a pyramid. And then it goes
> down to the subtopics. And underneath that you've got, like in the buying
> clothes [a subtopic], you've got sub-subtopics. And details. . . .
> Interviewer: What makes a good link?
> Amy: A good button has a good icon on it that helps describe like what
> you're going to go to next. And, um, the effect that you use, like corre-
> sponds. Like maybe everything that you're going into, like uses dissolve
> [a transition effect] for like all the details [level of information, such as a
> subtopic or detail]. All the details use the same one.

---

[5]It is important to note that teachers provided instruction on many aspects of hypermedia composition throughout the first two documents as well, including a focus on student reflection of audience and purpose. Due to space limitations, we cannot report here all types of instructional assistance provided to students (for more on this topic, see Erickson, 1997, or Erickson & Lehrer, 1998); however, the focus on organizing information was noteworthy because it may have played a consequential role in student conceptions of links.

Amy used transition effects to signal information to the reader, an effect used by 40% of students in their compositions (e.g., a "barn door open" means the reader is in the "primary education" subtopic). This suggests that Amy, like other students, coordinated the technical means available in hypermedia (visual effects, icons, text) and consideration of purpose and audience. Furthermore, students now reported that links were necessary for structure; they provided a coherent hierarchical organization for the document. This structural function represented a change from the previous two compositions (interviews) in which links were helpful but not necessary to the document as a whole.

After revising their third composition, 90% of students asserted that links specified document-wide relationships, not simply an association between two cards. This indicates that students were considering aspects of the rhetorical problem space; one student said, "I picked these subtopics so the reader can learn about all the areas of family life." In practice, 60% of compositions showed such global connections; the other 40% displayed only local relationships. All students reported that links assisted with navigation and specified those paths for the reader. Moreover, these discussions of reader paths were now connected to a coherent structure in the document; for example, the paths were consistent with subtopics and other relationships among content.

Later, after students had completed the majority of their individual stack on culture, 60% of students explicitly discussed composing for an audience of peers, and all talked about designing for an audience after the revision period. For example, some students discussed including directions to aid the reader in their understanding of the link's function, as Amy explained:

> Interviewer: So you try to explain what the link is?
>
> Amy: Yeah . . . And I'd say, "This goes to a related topic." Something like that. I've got that at the end of every one of my subtopic fields. I think that kind of helps the reader.
>
> Interviewer: Would you design this any differently if you were working for someone who was an expert and knew hypercard already versus a new person who had never used this before?
>
> Amy: I'd probably change it a little.
>
> Interviewer: What would you change?
>
> Amy: I'd probably take out the descriptions.

Many students designed buttons that were consistent in both appearance and location on the screen to aid the reader's understanding. Links functioned to signal relationships among topic content to the reader for most students, and 80% of students reported syntactical notions of links (i.e., library of link types). Amy reported that she tried to build a library of link types for her readers, to create a syntax of icon and text types to represent particular destinations in her composition. These ideas were translated to students' compositions, with 70% of students attempting a library of link types (syntax of links) for the reader in their final compositions. For example, Fig. 7.4 illustrates the main menu screen in Amy's document, in which she used icons and text to represent submenu cards. Students stated that consistent buttons helped a reader to recognize a particular link type, and that an author should constrain the number of buttons used because too many types may confuse a reader.

Although 80% of students noted explicitly their attempts to reduce the proliferation of icons and develop a syntax of links, in practice, only 20% of the documents successfully portrayed a library of link types for the reader (a few buttons were so similar that a reader could not distinguish the type or documents were not fully consistent). The gap between intention and means reflected the difficulty students had negotiating the large number of constraints during hypermedia composition.

During the final interview, students distinguished among various functions of link types, especially in relation to potential readers. Link functions included annotation, hierarchy (links that take the user to a subtopic versus detail information), associative highlights, and navigational ease (such as return links). Two students differentiated "reader" links (most link types) from "author" links (those that would be removed or hidden from the reader and were solely to aid the author in composing). Thus, links could serve private functions as well as public ones.[6]

Most students reported that some of these link types were more important than others. Although the order varied, most students placed particular importance on links moving to the main menu ("because that's where the reader sees the choices"; "you can't have a stack without that because you need it to get to all the information"), and on the hierarchical links that moved the reader to different levels of content information (topic, subtopic, detail). In general, students explained that annotative links were

---

[6]One student used links as a mnemonic device and the other for various purposes like cutting and pasting. Perhaps this was a way to handle juggling constraints and to reduce cognitive load during hypermedia composition.

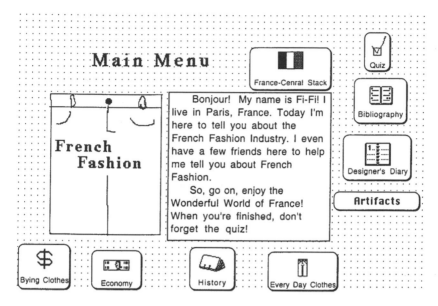

FIG. 7.4.

less important than the links moving to the main information in the stack. These results suggest that with time and experience, students had progressed from link types focused on a single dimension (where a screen is located in the stack—Interviews 2 and 3) to including multiple dimensions that reflect deeper considerations of purpose ("the reader needs to understand the information"), navigational structure ("the main menu is the most important"), and audience ("those links are to really get the reader involved").

Moreover, students designed aspects of the final composition specifically to increase audience interest and involvement. For example, each student wrote stories to "grab reader interest." Amy, in her composition about France, used a French girl named Fifi as a tour guide throughout the document, and other students used similar types of characters. Other examples included interactive quizzes developed "to gain audience involvement" and directions to the reader (e.g., "click here to find out more about . . . ").

One of the more striking examples of students' evolution toward communication and audience awareness was Amy's screen design; she used repeating, tiny versions of her link icons as a background design to communicate meaning to her audience. Figure 7.5 illustrates one screen

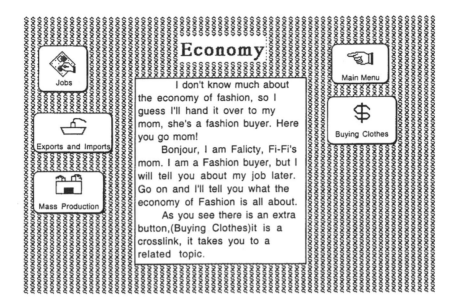

FIG. 7.5.

design in which Amy used the icons as a background design (a repeating dollar sign) to communicate information about her card topic (economy). Note however, that although Amy was trying to convey meaning to her reader, the icon that she used was inconsistent with the rest of her document; the dollar symbol was actually associated with the "Buying Clothes" subtopic, and perhaps should instead have been a dollar bill—the icon used for "Economy" in her main menu.Nevertheless, the media representation and design combinations created a host of meanings about the topic content for potential readers: The repeating icons served as semantic clues to orient potential readers as to where they were and why.

Overall, these results indicate that, like Amy, by the end of their third design effort, students were negotiating constraints of both content and rhetorical problem spaces (Scardamalia & Bereiter, 1987) and were beginning to develop a rhetoric of links. The increase in student use of rhetorical devices throughout their compositions further demonstrates that students were actively composing with both audience and purpose in mind, indicating an interaction between the rhetorical and content problem spaces. Figure 7.6 illustrates the development of rhetoric for all student participants across the school year. The graph was calculated by

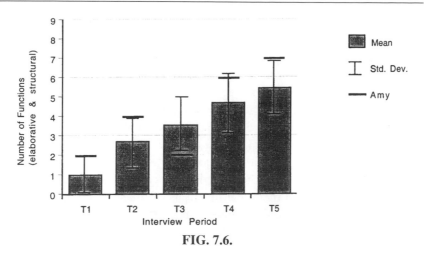

FIG. 7.6.

collapsing the elaborative and structural functions of links (because these functions suggest a consideration of the rhetorical problem space during composition) and counting the mean number of link functions reported by students during each interview.[7] Note that students moved from reporting an average of one function in the beginning of the year to reporting five and a half (of nine possible) elaborative and structural functions of links at the end of the year. The pattern displayed in Fig. 7.6 suggests the emergence and coordination of the rhetorical problem space with the content problem space (Scardamalia & Bereiter, 1987), so that by the end of the year, students were attending to multiple link functions (and negotiating multiple constraints) as they composed their hypermedia documents.

Variations in Student Conceptions of Links

Several students varied from the common development. The student who developed the least differentiation about the role of links began by reporting the "go to" and "specified destination" functions of links. However, she often reported the name of the origin card, not the destination card, and thus reduced the function to a mere move. For several interviews, she reported that the purpose of links was an alternate method of moving for the author as she composed (this author used the arrow keys to move

---

[7]There were four total elaborative functions: navigational landmark, transition in media, local similarity, and annotation. There were five structural functions: organization, clusters (threads of traversal), semantic relationship, global relationship, and syntax of links.

through the stack and therefore saw no real purpose to links). By the end of the year, however, she clearly marked the destination card (with text, sometimes icons), and specified the main menu card in her stack (landmark). Links could show local similarities between cards. In addition, she believed that links provided the reader with a choice of paths, and she considered the reader in the design of her document. There was evidence that the student was beginning to develop rhetorical awareness in her composing, demonstrated by some talk about the audience.

The student who began with the most sophisticated notions of links initially marked the destination and landmarks consistently in his stack and discussed structural and rhetorical functions of links during his interviews. He believed that links could provide "an understanding" to the reader of topic content; that is, links could help the reader understand relationships among content. Unlike Amy, he talked during his second interview about how links could present two or more views on an issue, like pro and con, within one document. For this student, links afforded multiple arguments to be sustained in the composition, as in Bolter's (1991) "multivoiced" aspect of hypermedia. The student also discussed using media (animation and sound) to annotate ideas during that second interview. By the end of the year, the student had, like Amy, developed a syntax of links for the reader. He commented that links could be used for the multitude of functions listed throughout this chapter, and incorporated aspects of his composition to facilitate reader interaction. Thus, he began with rhetorical functions of links that increased in multitude and technical expertise over the year.

FROM DECORATION TO COMMUNICATION

Over the course of the school year, students first conceived of links as local moves that served as decorations ("they looked cool!") but gradually expanded their repertoire of links to make possible substantive communication with an audience. Students made a transition from using links that marked where *they* *w*anted to go to links that communicated a host of meanings to a *reader*. Student composition began with knowledge telling, (i.e., move or "next") but the expansion of the rhetoric of links made knowledge transformation possible (i.e., the content was restructured to reflect student interest and what readers might find significant).

This expanded sense of links occurred progressively as students repeatedly designed hypermedia documents. For example, buttons initially using text to report destination later incorporated text, conventionally understood icons, and transition effects that served a variety of semantic ends, such as signaling a subtopic area or a location in the document. Links could provide multiple paths for the reader, and these paths through the document became tied to structure: Links provided both structural and communicative functions for the reader. This change demonstrated not only that students had differentiated more functions of links, but that those functions were tied to the purpose (tutorial) of the composition and to consideration of the audience. This shift suggests that students had developed and integrated the rhetorical problem space with the content problem space during the composition process (Flower, 1994; Scardamalia & Bereiter, 1987) and had developed a rhetoric or language of links with which to transform knowledge. Further evidence of this interaction between the rhetorical and content problem spaces was an increase in student attention to other rhetorical devices throughout their compositions; Amy's "French girl tour guide" is an example.

However, the connection between students' ideas about links and their compositions was not a one-to-one correspondence; students' notions about links were often in advance of composition. For example, during the second psychology composition, a majority of students mentioned that links could show similarities among ideas so that the reader could understand the topic information (global relationships), although they did not deploy them for these purposes in their documents. During the culture composition, notions of syntactical functions of links were evident in many student interviews, but they were not consistently employed in compositions for these purposes. Our speculation is that as in written composition, intentions are not always translated directly to the written text (Flower, 1994); the complexity of integrating the content and rhetorical problem spaces during hypermedia composition requires the negotiation of a large number of constraints, resulting in a heavy cognitive load. As Flower (1994, 1996) suggests, successful negotiation and incorporation of rhetorical intentions may require a variety of strategies (recall that students designed only three documents) that take much time, personal reflection, and instructional support to develop.

Students' evolving conceptions reflected teacher facilitation throughout the school year. Teachers continually asked students to justify their design choices and to consider their audience in the process of composition. Teachers scheduled whole-class and peer-critique sessions to assist students in developing critical standards (e.g., what makes a good screen design) that evolved throughout the year (Erickson & Lehrer, 1998). Students had a role in the assessment process by helping to develop an assessment rubric that was used to evaluate the stacks for a grade (Erickson, 1997).

In future studies, it would be interesting to examine the effects of other instructional approaches and other purposes of hypermedia compositions. For example, other instructional contexts might include students designing documents in a creative writing class or researching a social issue in the community and presenting a persuasive argument. Although the purpose of hypermedia documents in this study was tutorial, it would be interesting to examine rhetorical functions of links when hypermedia is used for other types of purposes, like technical reports, entertainment, or study aids. In addition, future studies might include a sample of Web page designers, as well as hypertext authors, to ascertain what stylistic and rhetorical devices may differ in that medium (if any). But whatever the rhetorical goal, students' conceptions of "what's in a link" help us to examine distinctions and similarities in rhetorical devices for hypermedia authoring and certainly play an important role in the design of appropriate pedagogy for hypermedia composition.

ACKNOWLEDGMENTS

Portions of this study were reported at the American Educational Research Association conference in New York, April 1996.

We thank Stuart Greene, Tom Romberg, Leona Schauble, and Ron Serlin for their comments on earlier drafts of this chapter. We also thank the seventh graders who participated in this study and both of their dedicated classroom teachers.

REFERENCES

Bolter, J. D. (1991). *Writing space: The computer, hypertext, and the history of writing.* Hillsdale, NJ: Lawrence Erlbaum Associates.

Brown, A. L., & Campione, J. C. (1994). Guided discovery in a community of learners. In K. McGilly (Ed.), *Classroom lessons: Integrating cognitive theory and classroom practice.* Cambridge, MA: MIT Press/Bradford Books.

Brown, A. L., & Campione, J. C. (1996). Psychological theory and the design of innovative learning environments: On procedures, principles, and systems. In L. Schauble & R. Glaser (Eds.), *Innovations in learning: New environments for education* (pp. 289–325). Mahwah, NJ: Lawrence Erlbaum Associates.

Carver, S., Lehrer, R., Connell, T., & Erickson, J. (1992). Learning by hypermedia design: Issues of assessment and implementation. *Educational Psychologist, 27*(3), 385–404.

Chi, M. (1997). Quantifying qualitative analyses of verbal data: A practical guide. *Journal of the Learning Sciences, 6*(3), 271–315.

Collins, A., Brown, J. S., & Newman, S. E. (1989). Cognitive apprenticeship: Teaching the crafts of reading, writing, and mathematics. In L. B. Resnick (Ed.), *Knowing, learning, and instruction. Essays in honor of Robert Glaser* (pp. 453–494). Hillsdale, NJ: Lawrence Erlbaum Associates.

Erickson, J. (1997). Building a community of designers: Restructuring learning through student hypermedia design. *Journal of Research in Rural Education, 13*(1), 5–27.

Erickson, J., & Lehrer, R. (1998). The evolution of critical standards as students design hypermedia documents. *Journal of the Learning Sciences, 7*(3 & 4), 351–386.

Flower, L. (1994). *The construction of negotiated meaning.* Carbondale: Southern Illinois University Press.

Flower, L. (1996). Collaborative planning and community literacy: A window on the logic of learners. In L. Schauble & R. Glaser (Eds.), *Innovations in learning* (pp. 25–48). Mahwah, NJ: Lawrence Erlbaum Associates.

Flower, L. S., & Hayes, J. R. (1980). The dynamics of composing: Making plans and juggling constraints. In L. W. Gregg & E. R. Steinberg (Eds.), *Cognitive processes in writing* (pp. 31–50). Hillsdale, NJ: Lawrence Erlbaum Associates.

Landow, G. P. (1991). The rhetoric of hypermedia: Some rules for authors. In P. Delany & G. P. Landow (Eds.), *Hypermedia and literary studies* (pp. 81–103). Cambridge: MIT Press.

Landow, G. P., & Delany, P. (1991). Hypertext, hypermedia, and literary studies: The state of the art. In P. Delany & G. P. Landow (Eds.), *Hypermedia and literary studies* (pp. 3–50). Cambridge: MIT Press.

Lehrer, R. (1993). Authors of knowledge: Patterns of hypermedia design. In S. Lajoie & S. Derry (Eds.), *Computers as cognitive tools.* Hillsdale, NJ: Lawrence Erlbaum Associates.

Lehrer, R., Erickson, J., & Connell, T. (1994). Learning by designing hypermedia documents [Special issue on hypermedia & multimedia in the schools]. *Computers in the Schools, 10*(1/2), 227–254.

Liu, M. (1998). A study of engaging high-school students as multimedia designers in a cognitive apprenticeship-style learning environment. *Computers in Human Behavior, 14,* 1–29.

Liu, M., & Rutledge, K. (1997). The effect of a "learner as multimedia designer" environment on at-risk high school students' motivation and learning of design knowledge. *Journal of Educational Computing Research, 16,* 145–177.

Perkins, D. N. (1986). *Knowledge as design.* Hillsdale, NJ: Lawrence Erlbaum Associates.

Scardamalia, M., & Bereiter, C. (1987). Knowledge telling and knowledge transforming in written composition. In S. Rosenberg (Ed.), *Advances in applied psycholinguistics* (Vol. 2, pp. 142–175). Cambridge: Cambridge University Press.

Slatin, J. (1991). Reading hypertext: Order and coherence in a new medium. In P. Delany & G. P. Landow (Eds.), *Hypermedia and literary studies* (pp. 153–169). Cambridge, MA: MIT Press.

Wilhelm, J. D., Friedemann, P., & Erickson, J. (1998). *HyperLearning: Students inquiring, learning and sharing with technology.* Columbus, OH: Stenhouse Publishers.

APPENDIX A

COGNITIVE COMPONENTS
OF HYPERMEDIA-BASED DESIGN

Design Component	Primary Skills Involved
Planning	
Define the nature of the problem	Define purpose
	Ask questions
Project management	Collaborate with team members
	Manage deadlines
Transforming	
Find information	Document search techniques
	Use keywords in electronic search
Develop new information	Interview others
	Write to an embassy
	Collect artifacts
Select information	Take notes
	Summarize information
	Distinguish relevant from irrelevant information
Organize information	Use multiple organizations for information (outlines, pyramids, issue trees, webs)

Represent information	Segment animation and sound
	Produce graphics
	Combine media to represent ideas
Evaluating	
Evaluate the Design	Articulate purpose and intentions
	Public speaking
	Use reflection and organizational tools
	Provide feedback to peers
Revising	
Revise the design	Take design as an object for thought
	Solicit feedback from peers and adults

Note. For more on this framework, see Lehrer (1993) or Lehrer et al. (1994).

APPENDIX B

CODING SCHEME OF LINK FUNCTIONS
AND EXAMPLES OF EACH CODE

Link Functions	*Example*
1. Move	"Go to."
• Speed	"It's faster."
• Efficiency (direct, easy)	"It takes you right to the card you want."
• Alternate way to move	"You could use them instead of the arrow keys to get to a card."
2. Specified destination	"Go to Sports Card."
• Navigation	"You want the user to be able to move around easily in your stack."
3. Elaborative information	
• Mark navigational landmark	"It shows you're going to the menu."
• Mark transition in media	Camera icon signals move to video.
• Signal local similarity	"Those two cards have similar topics."
• Annotation	"You can add a pop-up text field or an animation or sound."

CODING SCHEME OF LINK FUNCTIONS
AND EXAMPLES OF EACH CODE (continued)

Link Functions	*Example*
4. Structure	
• Organization	"They help organize your information, your stack."
• Signal clusters, threads of traversal	A, B, and C form a cluster of ideas; A causes B, which in turn causes C.
• Mark semantic relationships	Icon represents all links of a particular type, such as all "battle" links.
• Signal global relationships to reader	"They show the similarities and differences to help the user understand the topic."
• Syntax	"You have to be conservative in the number of buttons you make, so that a user can spot it and know it right away."

8

Employing Cognitive Tools Within Interactive Multimedia Applications

Barry Harper, John Hedberg, Bob
Corderoy, and Robert Wright
University of Wollongong, Australia

The introduction of information and telecommunication technologies into the learning process has often been heralded as the panacea for educational problems. However, like past revolutionary promises for education, these may go the way of earlier technologies, unless there are also changes to the cognitive technologies provided within or supporting complex applications (Pea, 1985). Alfred Bork (1995) argued in his critical review of the failure of computers in schools and universities that the effective use of new instructional paradigms requires software that supports the modes of instruction that cognitive scientists say are appropriate. This chapter describes the development of a learning environment that embodies solutions to these problems within computer applications. Exploring the Nardoo (*http://www.immll.uow.edu.au/immll/nardoo.htm*) provides a series of supportive cognitive tools that were designed to assist students in solving complex problems.

CHANGING INSTRUCTIONAL STRATEGIES
WITH INTERACTIVE MULTIMEDIA

Instructors have traditionally presented a linear narrative sequence, which progressively reveals the underlying structure of their ideas. This narrative was based largely on their personal understanding of the concepts and their perception of the learning environments they were generating. However, interactive multimedia technologies can represent ideas in almost any mediated form. Provided we can generate a comprehensible metaphor for organizing functional options and the underlying knowledge structures, students can roam through the multimedia resources, creating their own meanings and understandings of the phenomena they encounter. Thus they can create their own learning environment rather than one generated by their teacher or the application designer. With graphical and visual display, coupled with large databases of resources, it is possible to explore an information space in whatever sequence appeals to the user's chosen task, whether it is intentional or exploratory. Florin (1990, p. 30) saw "information landscapes . . . as virtual towns, or intellectual amusement parks." The analogy is quite intriguing and helps us to visualize many abstract concepts within a single metaphor.

This metaphorical view of multiple forms of representation of information can support students' learning architectures advocated by researchers like Schank and Cleary (1995; *http://www.ils.nwu.edu/~e_for_e/index. html*). They argued strongly for the use of information technologies to support students as they follow their own interests or seek answers to self-generated questions. This rich context enables novices to work with authentic problems and practice as if they were professional users of the same knowledge domain. Nevertheless, novices need some support to enable them to work as experts in a knowledge domain with which they are only partially familiar. Cognitive tools can assist in this transition.

SUPPORTING LEARNING
WITH COGNITIVE TOOLS

Cognitive tools that can assist learners to accomplish cognitive tasks have been described by writers such as Pea (1985), who proposed the term *cognitive technologies,* and Salomon, Perkins, and Globerson (1991), who used the term *technologies of the mind*. Jonassen (1996) described *cognitive tools* as technologies that enhance the cognitive powers of human beings during thinking, problem solving, and learning and used to term *mindtools*.

Lajoie (1993) succinctly described this theme in the educational literature and proposed that such tools can be classified according to the function they serve. She proposed that cognitive tools can assist learners when they

a) support cognitive processes, such as, memory and metacognitive processes,

b) share the cognitive load by providing support for lower level cognitive skills so that (cognitive) resources are left over for higher order thinking skills,

c) allow the learner to engage in cognitive activities that would be out of reach otherwise, and

d) allow learners to generate and test hypotheses in the context of problem solving. (Lajoie, 1993, p. 261)

More recently, Jonassen and Reeves (1996) proposed that cognitive tools are best used as reflection tools that amplify, extend, and even reorganize human mental powers in order to help learners construct their own realities and complete challenging tasks. They summarized the foundations for cognitive tools research as follows:

- Cognitive tools will have their greatest effectiveness when they are applied to constructivist leaning environments.
- Cognitive tools empower learners to design their own representations of knowledge rather than absorbing knowledge representations preconceived by others.
- Cognitive tools can be used to support the deep reflective thinking that is necessary for meaningful learning.
- Ideally, tasks or problems for the application of cognitive tools should be situated in realistic contexts with results that are personally meaningful for learners. (Jonassen & Reeves, 1996, p. 698)

If students are to create their own meanings and understandings of the phenomena they encounter, then designers need to incorporate user tools that will enable them to present their findings using the full array of resources contained in the packages. The lack of embedded support in learning environments in much of the available interactive multimedia products cannot be entirely attributed to the lack of understanding of the results of cognitive science research by developers. Few researchers have provided learning environments that model tools that support information learning processes such as information analysis, knowledge generation, and argumentation.

Some leaning environments of this type have been demonstrated. Schank and Cleary (1995) and Korcuska (1996) described a set of innovative learning architectures based on their conceptualization of realistic learning situations. They created powerful example implementations of cognitive tools where different cognitive learning strategies are built into the software and learners are encouraged to explore their ideas and solutions with differing degrees of support and advice. They illustrated their designs with specific packages: Dustin, a simulator designed to help a student learn a foreign language; Road Trip: The Geography Un-Lesson; Sounding Board, a package to brainstorm ideas; Creanimate, a case-based package for designing and creating animals; and ASK, based on the metaphor of having a conversation with an expert.

The innovative use of cognitive tools in interactive multimedia learning environments has also been demonstrated by Lajoie et al. (1995). The package Bio-World (Lajoie, 1993) is an interactive learning environment designed to support the acquisition of scientific reasoning skills in high school students and to integrate a variety of cognitive tools that scaffold scientific reasoning. Users of this package engage in explicitly justifying hypotheses with evidence; organizing, categorizing, and rating evidence; and constructing a final summary argument on the topic of bacterial and viral infections. A proposed development for this package incorporates an authoring mode for students to generate new scenarios for their peers to investigate. This in turn, will support the powerful argumentation framework design of the package.

All of these examples provide models of complex problem-solving approaches that support and scaffold the learner to work with an unfamiliar knowledge domain. Exploring the Nardoo provides another model that addresses these challenges and provides a range of information analysis and construction tools for learners.

STUDENT-DRIVEN INVESTIGATION: EXPLORING THE NARDOO

With an understanding of the shortcomings of much of the commercially generated learning packages, in the early 1990s we sought to combine constructivist learning environments, situated learning (Cognition and Technology Group at Vanderbilt, 1990), and problem-based learning (Koschmann, Myers, Feltovich, & Barrows, 1994) into rich information landscapes to form the basis for student-driven investigation. We also sought to incorporate a range of cognitive tools within each landscape and thus support learners in constructing their own realities and completing the embedded challenges and tasks.

There has been considerable controversy, which will no doubt continue to simmer, over the interpretation of the term *constructivism*. Phillips (1997, p. 85) claimed that "the situation has become so confusing that to be told that a particular individual is a 'constructivist' is to acquire no useful information whatsoever." Using the distinction that Grandy (1997, p. 44) proposed, we are referring to the concept of cognitive constructivism (as opposed to epistemic or metaphysical constructivism) when proposing our constructivist learning environments. Within this framework we have been working with what Geelan (1997) described as an emphasis on a social focus as opposed to a personal one and an emphasis on an objectivist epistemology as opposed to a relativistic view. Within this social constructivist framework, we are seeking to demonstrate support of Ogborn's (1997) argument for an insistence on active learning, a respect for each learner's own thinking, and a high priority for ideas that are taught to students to make sense.

Earlier we proposed (Hedberg, Harper, Brown, & Corderoy, 1994) that learning outcomes from our software depended on the starting points: the learning environment, the learner's view of the purpose of the task, and the motivation of the learner. Thus the process of learning involves the construction of meanings by the learner from what is said, demonstrated, or experienced. To the learner, the constructivist learning experience may not look welcoming. It may seem daunting and complex to those who feel ill prepared for such creative freedom and choice of direction. Often constructivist learning situations suddenly throw students on their own management resources, and many fend poorly in the high cognitive complexity. Cognitive support tools and the explicit acknowledgment of the double agenda of metacognitive self-management and learning can help (Hannafin & Land, 1997).

Exploring the Nardoo is a software package that provides a dense information landscape of resources based on general issues in ecology. Its purpose is to engage students in long-term studies using the skills of problem solving, measuring, collating, elaborating, and communicating. Like the Jasper project (*http://peabody.vanderbilt.edu/projects/funded/jasper/*

FIG. 8.1. *The Water Research Centre.*

Jasperhome.html), the package is based on the assumption that thinking is enhanced when learners have access to rich and complex learning environments. Exploring the Nardoo was designed for high school use, for students aged from 14 to 18 years, and is based on current Australian state and national curriculum content documents for biology and geography. A mapping of the achievable learning outcomes for these documents has been included for teachers on the CD-ROM. The package has the potential to provide extensive opportunities for students studying biology and geography to extend and consolidate their knowledge base in many critical areas. In addition, they can practice investigative, analytical, and communicative skills, as well as develop and appreciate different values and attitudes. Specifically Exploring the Nardoo provides extensive support for the study of interactions between living organisms and the physical and chemical environment in which they operate, with particular emphasis on the role and impact of the human species at both a macro- and a microlevel. The major form of assessment for each problem solved is the communication of results through a scientific report.

The information landscape uses spatial and geographic metaphors: a Water Research Centre (see Fig. 8.1) and a navigable fictitious river environment. On entry to the environment, users are challenged by three researchers in the center to help them solve problems and carry out investigations on the river. The challenge encourages active learning and supports students in constructing their ideas in teams from measurements taken, resources reviewed, maps interpreted, and data analyzed. By providing a metaphor easily linked to the real world, students are encouraged to apply scientific concepts and techniques in new and relevant situations throughout the problem-solving process. In so doing, learners are likely to become more interested in developing questions, ideas, and hypotheses about the learning experiences they encounter. The real-world representation was chosen for numerous reasons, including the reduction in learning time for the package in that the operation of many of the tools and instruments could be intuitively derived from the context and the student's knowledge of the world.

The user is presented a broad range of investigations from the investigations notice board at the back of Fig. 8.1: fish dying from pollution, weeds infesting the river, and communities discussing farming practice. In one of the investigations, weed infestations have affected the Nardoo River ecosystem:

Water Plants and Weeds

Hugh Smythe captains a riverboat that ferries passengers up and down the Nardoo River. As the river is the key to his livelihood, he has become concerned about the rampant growth of weeds and willows that have begun to obstruct parts of the river in recent months.

Your task: Investigate the extent to which the river is affected by the weed and willow growth. Keep a journal of the information that you find and try to re-organize your information to clearly recount the history of the weed problem.

To investigate such issues, students may access a rich set of resources and data that are embedded in the river environments in situ, through hot buttons, and also in the Water Research Centre through organizing interface metaphors such as books and newspaper clippings. The resources in the Water Research Centre include a book containing descriptions of all of the plants and animals of the river; lists of television and radio news reports and interviews; newspaper cuttings; a filing cabinet containing technical articles and reports on the various investigations; a "Presentation Booklet" containing support for learners in note taking, filing notes, and

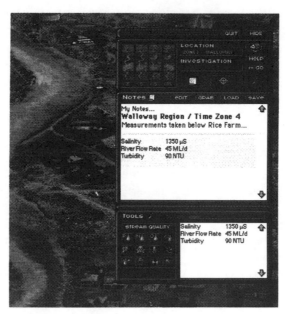

FIG. 8.2. *The personal digital assistant (PDA).*

construction of reports; and a "Text Tablet" for editing and elaborating the notes and data collected in the personal digital assistant (PDA; see Fig. 8.2). Three what-if simulators support students' investigations through helping them to identify, define, and explore cause-and-effect relationships.

Exploring the Nardoo provides students with a flexible set of tools, some of them cognitive, made available through the PDA, a multimedia notebook for collection of any of the resources in the package, including video, audio, graphics, and text; a viewer for viewing the video and graphic resources; and a set of measuring tools to take measurements on the river. It also provides user support through help file and navigation tools.

The combination of notebook and viewer equips students to view and then critically evaluate or compare different representations of the same idea. By collecting different media representations of the same topic and flipping between these representations (video to transcript) at their discretion, students have the opportunity to establish cognitive links between different media forms that complement each other and support a central theme or information focus. To facilitate the reordering or reprioritizing of information Exploring the Nardoo provides a separate, expanded form of

FIG. 8.3.   *The text tablet for restructuing and formatting notes.*

the notebook. This device, the text tablet (see Fig. 8.3), provides the editing facilities offered by the PDA, as well as other features to assist with the restructuring of notes into a form more suited to a small-group presentation or a particular style of writing genre. The text tablet provides a larger expanse of editable screen and document space into which student notes may be copied from the PDA notes module.

SPECIALIZED SUPPORT TOOLS
FOR CONSTRUCTION OF KNOWLEDGE

Exploring the Nardoo contains sets of specialized cognitive tools that can provide more extensive support for the exploration process:

- A note-taking facility to manage the collection of information and references to the variety of media forms in the package. This tool enables students to maintain links among many media forms and their context—for example, a video news clipping and other forms of textually based information on the same issue. The same tool enables collection of evidence to construct arguments for problem solutions.

- A set of nine genre templates to scaffold the elaboration process. The templates are passive models for students to compare their evidence and argument structure as they construct a response to their problem.
- A set of three interactive simulators with a guide for advice and investigation strategies. These tools have been designed to support hypothesis generation and to enable students to ask "what if" questions about ecological relationships.

A series of research projects, some complete and others continuing, have investigated the impact of these cognitive tools in Exploring the Nardoo. Initial pilot studies in classrooms and in the Interactive Multimedia Learning Laboratory have focused on the use of the genre templates to support learner elaboration of ideas, what mental models are developed through the use of the simulators, and how concept mapping tools support note taking and identify key issues.

RESEARCHING THE USE OF COGNITIVE
TOOLS BY STUDENTS

Constructivist learning environments with embedded cognitive tools make assumptions about the actions of learners. Hannafin and Land (1997) identified the lack of understanding of the problem-solving and data exploration processes that learners undertake in such environments and the motivation that they might have to complete tasks. They proposed that learners need to apply a theory-action model constantly as they investigate issues and view data; that is, they develop a theory about the solution to a problem or about data access and take action to test that theory. We sought to investigate the theory-action model through setting a structured and an ill-structured problem (Jonassen, 1997) and logging the construction of ideas by collaborative pairs of students. One investigation of the learner's understanding of the use of these tools was a study of a group of Year 9 students studying ecology as a science elective over a 4-week period. Different data-gathering methods were employed with two groups of students ($N = 10$ and 12).

The teacher presented an overview of the key features of the package and then asked the students to explore the package to ensure that they could use all of the embedded tools and access information. They were encouraged to use the help walk-through videos if they did not understand how tools worked or had trouble accessing information. After this initial period, one group was given an investigation to carry out on determining the cause of a weed infestation in part of the river and then to offer solutions (this was the structured problem). The second group was asked to investigate a location on the Nardoo River, identify a problem, and propose a solution. The second group did not have access to the investigations board and did not have a defined problem to solve (this was the ill-structured problem).

At the end of each period, students were asked to save their PDA notes and text tablet files, which were logged daily for later examination as a representation of the knowledge construction process. Additionally, students were given a paper journal to keep notes on what they had done so far and what they planned to do during their next class period.

Students in both groups perceived the tasks as being in context, motivating, and worth spending a significant amount of time to develop possible solutions to the investigations. Very little instruction in the use of the cognitive tools was needed, and students developed extended arguments with multiple solutions to the investigations undertaken. In general, the ill-structured-problem group produced more complex and complete solutions to the task. Because they did not have a defined task to solve but rather had to generate a series of hypotheses, they sought to be comprehensive and complete. More often the structured-problem group sought to answer only the questions asked of them and did not seek to find alternative explanations or other issues embedded in the investigation.

Genre Templates

As an element of the solution process, we have included genre writing templates as cognitive tools to assist learners in accomplishing writing tasks. The genre templates, based on the New South Wales (NSW) Department of School Education (1992) English curriculum documents, provide models of the variety of community discourse in the electronic notebooks of Exploring the Nardoo, and, as cognitive tools, they support the function that Lajoie (1993) described as sharing "the cognitive load by providing support for lower level cognitive skills so that (cognitive) resources are left over for higher order thinking skills" (p. 261)

Different subjects or curriculum areas may be considered as being different "discourse communities" (Christie, 1991; Swales, 1990), in which the usual members have the greatest genre-specific expertise. These members are networks or communities that work toward a common goal when they communicate with colleagues and others. "It is *this* communicative purpose, that drives the language of activities, . . . that is the criteria for genre identity . . . *and* . . . that operates as the primary determinant of task" (Swales, 1990, p. 10). The essential aim of the templates was to provide access to the different genres specific to and characteristic of the various discourse communities. In doing this, the package has strong links across the curriculum and supports initiatives in science writing. The templates also provide a means of composing meaning for both the writer and the reader or listener while providing a means of reflection, reordering, and creating new learning nodes and links between new and prior knowledge. The production of an effective piece of writing or presentation in any media can provide the student with a means of consolidating these links.

Established members of a particular discourse community are familiar and comfortable with the particular genre set characteristic of that discourse community such that they may be termed experts in that genre. "Outsiders" are novices in this genre and are consequently disempowered to varying degrees, and thus cannot communicate as successfully and effectively unless they are either trained or supported in the use of the genre being or to be used. In terms of the specific communication tasks in Exploring the Nardoo, lack of understanding of different discourses will effectively limit the quality and transmissibility to others of the student's solutions to their investigations. To address this issue, a set of genre templates, based on the on NSW Department of School Education (1992) English curriculum documents commonly used in school science discourse, were included. The nine templates were designed to scaffold learner construction of solutions to problems through reviewing, reporting, recounting, narrative, exposition, explanation, discussion, and procedure, with an additional template that supports multimedia presentation.

Using the Genre Templates

In the ongoing study we sought to determine if students who used the genre templates scored higher on learning outcome measures than students who did not. The study involved a group of students with significant experience in using computers in their school environment. The data collection occurred in the school's computer laboratories with 80 Year 10 students. The study used two randomly assigned groups of students: one that experienced the treatment Exploring the Nardoo with access to the genre template and one with no access to the genre templates. In addition to controlling for simple testing effects and the interactions between testing and treatment, no pretest was given to either group. The groups undertook the same task; the difference was the access to the discussion writing genre template (cognitive tool). The researcher gave instruction on the use of Exploring the Nardoo package to all students in the form of a verbal protocol illustrated with selected segments of the help videos provided within the CD-ROM package. Students were then allowed some time to familiarize themselves with the software package and were asked to indicate to the researcher when they felt comfortable with the material. They were then told how long they had to work on the investigation and that the aim was to carry out the task and or to learn as much as they could about the topic while producing an investigation result in the form of a report.

The data collection process included student measures with both qualitative and quantitative data on students' cognitive style, their approaches to learning, their learning outcomes (investigation results), and a posttreatment questionnaire based on genre template use. The protocol included open-ended questions that were used to elicit participants' perceptions and knowledge, as well as structured questions on template use. Learning outcomes (solution to the problem) were marked by several science educators. Elements of the student solutions assessed included style and structure, information sources, presentation, and quality of argument. Most students who had access to the templates used them and found them helpful in carrying out reporting tasks; they believed that the templates allowed them to construct better solutions to the investigations. The results endorsed the value of the templates in supporting student reporting (Gordon, 1998), but the static nature of the templates improved only the structure of the reports, not the quality of the arguments chosen. It appears that further work needs to be undertaken on the development of more context-sensitive assistance to improve reflection and assessment of the quality of the responses generated.

SIMULATORS FOR WHAT-IF ANALYSES

Simulations as learning environments have a long history of use in education and training and have been based on a variety of theoretical views of learning. Along with increasing computational power, software has increased in complexity so that object-oriented systems can now be used to simulate devices of great complexity. Bliss and Ogborn (1989) described computer-based simulations as programs in which the computer acts as an exploratory tool that supports a real-world activity while facilitating user understanding of the otherwise inaccessible processes involved in complex dynamic systems. Essentially, educational simulations are experiential exercises. They are useful wherever real objects or processes are involved in a learning task; they are less dangerous and less messy, and, if well designed, can exactly replicable real-world objects and processes. Simulations can display aggregated behavior, illustrating the interactions of objects or processes, and can also be decomposed into constituent components that can be manipulated to simulate variation in systems.

Simulations can be presented as models that represent systems as either "in-place-of" or a "bring-to-life" format. The question posed by some as to whether the terms *model* and *simulation* have similar meanings in this context may prove a pivotal point around which a better understanding of the cognitive outcomes for the users may be achieved. The in-place-of interpretation of representation applies to the standard widely accepted notion of a model. The exact nature of what constitutes a true simulation is not agreed on among researchers or designers, but we would suggest that, commonly, the goal of the simulation must be to provide interactive experiences that mimic the real-world experience closely.

Ecological processes are complex and occur over extended time frames. Developing an understanding of the processes and grasping the concepts at a more than a superficial level place a high cognitive load on learners. Three simulations were developed for Exploring the Nardoo: an algal bloom simulation; a whole catchment, water demand management simulation; and a personal home-based water use simulator. They were designed to achieve two basic outcomes:

- To allow students to observe and study firsthand in a risk-free environment complex processes that would otherwise be inaccessible to them.
- To provide students with a tool that allowed them to identify, define, and explore cause-and-effect relationships at a deep level by the manipulation of input parameters in an open-ended model.

The process in terms of both of these outcomes has been enhanced by an interface that allows students to select the most appropriate and meaningful method of displaying the output from the model. Students can view output data in any one or a combination of formats: graphical, numerical, or an animated visual representation.

Each simulation enriches the quality of the problem-solving process by providing students with unhindered access to act and become immersed in a "real" situated process, manipulating the various causal parameters and testing hypotheses without a "real" consequence or risk. For example, the

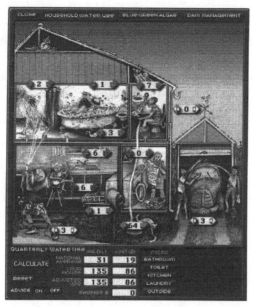

FIG. 8.4. *The personal water use simulator.*

personal water use simulator (see Fig. 8.4) supports an investigation into water rationing during a drought in the town of Pilliga Crossing. In this simulator, students can identify the use of water in their household by entering the number of baths, showers, use of the dishwasher, garden hose, car washing, toilet flushes, use of the sink, and number of people in their home. The simulator calculates the student's water use and compares it with the national average. Students can then make adjustments to their water use and implement water-saving features. Rerunning the simulation will review their water use. A guide supports the user by offering advice on how to further save water.

The simulations are cognitive tools, in terms of Lajoie's (1993) description of the types of cognitive tools in that they "allow users to engage in cognitive activities that would be out of their reach otherwise" (p. 261). They promote the student's adoption of the active learner mode and thus support the active construction of knowledge during the process of solving a problem. The simulations complement the problems embedded in a complex information landscape by providing links with the real-world experience and by creating an environment in which the user may practice skills. More able students are provided with the facility to solve problems at a deeper level through the testing of their own "what-if" scenarios. This facilitated more detailed exploration and learning by allowing users to take readings at a site and study the changes as the simulation runs and allowing the monitoring of all parameters while the simulation is running, with the aim of exploring the relationships between them (Corderoy, Harper, & Hedberg, 1993, p. 126).

The use of the simulators by students is being investigated in two ways. In this study, we are seeking to determine if there is any improvement in the process and success of formation of new knowledge links (knowledge acquisition) for students who study an ecological process (blue-green algal bloom development), using interactive multimedia-based simulations of these processes as opposed to those who study them using more traditional methods. We also are seeking to determine if there is an improvement in the level of understanding of relationships (cause and effect) for students who study the ecological process using the simulators.

The study is being conducted with two groups of university students enrolled in preservice teacher education who are studying science education. One experimental group has access to the simulators as well as all other resources provided in the Water Resource Centre to solve a set blue-green algal bloom problem. The control group has access to all of the same resources except the simulators. The combined size of the two groups is in excess of 120.

A number of instruments are being used to review the treatment effect and student perceptions of their learning experience. A knowledge acquisition schedule (comprising 24 multiple-choice questions) is being used to measure any changes in the students' knowledge base. A relationships schedule (comprising a set of cause statements that must be physically linked using lines drawn to one or more listed key effects) is being used to measure changes in the ability of students to draw or recognize cause-and-effect relationships. Additionally, a user-perceived value schedule will be administered, and tracking data will be collected. Currently the study is being run, and data are being collected.

CONCLUSION

Few interactive multimedia packages support student-driven exploration and investigation by active interventions designed by multimedia designers. Exploring the Nardoo provides a range of cognitive tools in an information landscape to support student investigation. The support has been provided through simulations and tools to support information collection and organization. These allow multimedia reporting by the students as they seek to manage text, video, audio, and other representational forms. Other tools embedded in the package scaffold effective problem solving and support the writing process. Studies have demonstrated that problem solving and student-centered learning goals are achieved in several studies based in actual classrooms. The complexity of the supportive notebook tool, which allows students to collect and report their investigation, has been found to be less a distraction to effective outcomes than previously thought.

The embedded tools enable successful multimedia reporting and support the manipulation of complex ideas, which can be represented in different visual forms. Students can manipulate the tools and extend common concepts such as copy and paste into other forms of representation of information. The several metacognitive tools that supported the writing process while enabling the students to write effective communications for specific audiences also require further development to support dynamically issues such as the quality of reasoning and argument. It was found that the passive tool improves the organization of ideas but requires a more dynamic redesign to assist students in developing their ideas into reasoned argument. This support becomes even more critical when students face ill-structured problems. Without a directed problem to solve, students believed that there were more solutions and possible problems than there were embedded in the information landscape. Thus, Exploring the Nardoo extends the range of learning environments that model tools that support information learning processes such as information analysis, knowledge generation, and argumentation. Use of the package in classrooms has supported this view.

REFERENCES

Bliss, J., & Ogborn, J. (1989). Tools for exploratory learning. *Journal of Computer Assisted Learning, 5*, 37–50.

Bork, A, (1995). Guest editorial: Why has the computer failed in schools and universities? *Journal of Science Education Research, 4*(2), 97–102.

Christie, F. (1991). Genre and curriculum. Genre approaches to literacy: theories and practices. In B. Cope & M. Kalantzis (Eds.), *1991 LERN Conference* (pp. 3–15). Sydney: University of Technology, Sydney.

Cognition and Technology Group at Vanderbilt. (1990). Anchored instruction and its relationship to situated cognition. *Educational Researcher*, *19*(6), 2–10.

Corderoy, R. M., Harper, B. M., & Hedberg, J. G. (1993). Simulating algal bloom in a lake: An interactive multimedia implementation. *Australian Journal of Educational Technology, 9*(2), 115–129.

Florin, F. (1990). Information landscapes. In S. Ambron & K. Hooper (Eds.), *Learning with interactive multimedia* (pp. 28–49). Redmond, WA: Microsoft.

Geelan, D. R. (1997). Epistemological anarchy and the many forms of constructivism. *Science and Education*, *6*(1–2), 15–28.

Gordon, J., (1998). *Learning with technology tools*. Unpublished doctoral dissertation, University of Wollongong.

Grandy, R. E., (1997). Constructivisms and objectivity: Disentangling metaphysics from pedagogy. *Science and Education*, *6*(1–2), 43–53.

Hannafin, M. J., & Land, S. M. (1997). The foundations and assumptions of technology-enhanced student-centered learning environments. *Instructional Science, 25*, 167–202.

Hedberg, J. G., Harper, B. M., Brown, C., & Corderoy, R, (1994). Exploring user interfaces to improve learner outcomes. In K. Beatie, C. McNaught, & S. Wills (Eds.), *Interactive multimedia in university education: Designing for change in teaching and learning* (pp. 15–29). Amsterdam: North-Holland, Elsevier.

Jonassen, D. H. (1996). *Mindtools for schools*. New York: Macmillan.

Jonassen, D. H. (1997). Instructional design models for well-structured and ill-structured problem-solving learning outcomes. *Educational Technology Research and Development, 45*(1), 65–94

Jonassen, D. H., & Reeves, T. C. (1996) Learning with technology: Using computers as cognitive tools. In D. H. Jonassen (Ed.), *Handbook of research on educational communications and technology*. New York: Scholastic Press in collaboration with the Association for Educational Communications and Technology.

Korcuska, M. (1996). Software factories for active learning environments. In P. Carson & F. Makedon (Eds.), *Proceedings of EdMedia 96 World Conference on Educational Multimedia and Hypermedia* (pp. 360–365). Boston.

Koschmann, T. D., Myers, A. C., Feltovich, P. J., & Barrows, H. S. (1994). Using technology to assist in realising effective learning and instruction: A principled approach to the use of computers in collaborative learning, *Journal of Learning Sciences, 3*(3), 227–264.

Lajoie, S. P. (1993). Computer environments as cognitive tools for enhancing learning. In S. P. Lajoie & S. J. Derry (Eds.), *Computers as cognitive tools* (pp. 261–288). Hillsdale. NJ: Lawrence Erlbaum Associates.

Lajoie, S. P., Greer, J. E., Munsie, S. D., Wilkie, T. V., Guerrera, C., & Aleong, P. (1995). Establishing an argumentation environment to foster scientific reasoning with Bio-World. In D. Jonassen & G. McCalla (Eds.), *Proceedings of the International Conference on Computers in Education* (pp. 8–96). Charlottesville, VA: Association for the Advancement of Computing in Education.

New South Wales Department of School Education. (1992). Metropolitan West Literacy & Learning Program (kit). Peter Knapp, Resource Book,

Ogborn, J. (1997). Constructivist metaphors of learning science. *Science and Education*, 6(1–2), 85–104.

Pea, R. D. (1985). Beyond amplification: Using the computer to reorganize mental functioning. *Educational Psychologist*, 20(4), 167–182.

Phillips, D. C. (1997). Coming to grips with radical social constructivisms. *Science and Education*, 6(1–2), 85–104.

Salomon, G., Perkins, D. N., & Globerson, T. (1991). Partners in cognition: Extending human intelligence with intelligent technologies. *Educational Researcher*, 20, 1016

Schank, R. C., & Cleary, C. (1995). *Engines for education*. Hillsdale, NJ: Lawrence Erlbaum Associates.

Swales, J. M. (1990) *Genre analysis: English in academic and research settings.* Sydney: Cambridge University Press.

9

Cognitive Tools for Medical Informatics

Susanne P. Lajoie
McGill University

Roger Azevedo
University of Maryland

As with other educational fields, medicine is looking to new technologies to facilitate instruction and improve learning. The medical academic community is witnessing a migration of traditional, instructor-led curriculum toward small-group teaching situations that include the use of interactive multimedia and computer-based learning environments (Bouchard, Lajoie, & Fleiszer, 1995). Educational applications were identified as a research field in artificial intelligence in medicine over two decades ago (Shortliffe, 1984) but with limited success. Lillehaug and Lajoie (1998) reviewed this literature and provided a plan for empowering medical personnel in problem solving through the use of technology. In this chapter, we review three such applications in terms of the cognitive tools that they provide to learners: Bio-World, a system to support scientific reasoning about disease; the SICU tutor designed to support patient assessments in a surgical intensive care unit; and the RadTutor, a system to support radiology residents in their diagnostic interpretation of mammograms.

Although each system fits within the medical informatics domain, each is disparate in terms of domain knowledge and use of technology for educational purposes. This chapter notes the need to consider the appropriate use of technology based on the domain and audience. Different learning paradigms and philosophies may be appropriate for different types of cognitive tasks within the same broad field of study.

MEDICAL INFORMATICS

Shortliffe (1984) referred to medical information science (informatics) as a science that uses system analytic tools designed to assist in the development of procedures or algorithms for management, decision making, and scientific analysis of medical knowledge. More specifically, medical informatics refers to the development and assessment of methods and systems for the acquisition, processing, and interpretation of patient data with the help of knowledge obtained from scientific research (Van Bemmel & Musen, 1997). The systems referred to in this chapter describe tools that guide medical students and practitioners in the interpretation of patient data.

THEORETICAL PERSPECTIVE

Too often the knowledge acquired in school lies inert (Whitehead, 1929) due to the lack of opportunities for using such knowledge. Current learning theories increasingly center on the learning process as it occurs within "situations," or meaningful contexts (Brown, Collins, & Duguid, 1989; Collins, Brown, & Newman, 1989; Eisner, 1993; Greeno, 1989, 1997). Situated cognition affirms that knowledge acquisition cannot be separated from the authentic settings and real-world contexts in which learning is applied. A problem-based learning approach in medicine is widely accepted (Barnett, 1995; Bashook, 1993; Friedman & Dev, 1996; Koschmann, Myers, Feltovitch, & Barrows, 1994); students are given opportunities to practice their problem-solving and hypothesis-testing skills early in their professional development. Computer-based learning environments for medical domains can be designed to provide safe practice environments for learners to develop their understanding of patient data in realistic contexts and to practice their diagnostic reasoning in medicine. By safe practice, we mean that learners can practice their diagnoses without harm to an actual patient. Simulations provide opportunities to practice new techniques and receive guidance in the context of errors without fatal consequences.

Appropriately designed computer-based learning environments can be considered as cognitive tools that aid cognition through interactive technologies that expand the mind (Jonassen, 1996; Jonassen & Reeves, 1996; Kommers, Jonassen, & Mayes, 1992; Lajoie, 1993; Lajoie & Derry, 1993; Lajoie, in prep.; Pea, 1985; Perkins, 1985; Salomon, Perkins, & Globerson, 1991). The literature suggests that cognitive tools help students during thinking, problem solving, and learning by providing opportunities to (a) practice knowledge in the context of complex activities rather than practice skills in isolation; (b) share the cognitive load by providing computer support for lower level cognitive skills so that learners have resources left over for higher order thinking skills; (c) generate and test hypotheses in the context of problem solving; (d) support cognitive processes (memory and metacognitive processes); (e) empower learners to design their own representations; (f) support cooperative learning within a problem-based learning environment; (g) scaffold learning through diagnostic feedback based on computer assessment of misconceptions or errors; and (h) reify students' problem solving through computer traces of evidence collection, data representation, interpretation, and argumentation and consequently support self-assessment.

The underlying philosophy behind the design of the computer-based learning environments described in this chapter is that there is a shared intellectual partnership between the computer and the learner (Salomon et al., 1991), where the learner is an active constructor of knowledge (Jonassen & Reeves, 1996). By performing lower level operations, the computer frees up the learners' resources, enabling them to carry out higher order thinking skills and engage in cognitive activities that would be out of their reach otherwise. Learners generate and test hypotheses in the context of problem solving, create their own knowledge representations, and reflect on their learning in the context of problem solving.

Although there are underlying similarities in the design features of the three systems we describe, each has a specific audience, curriculum, and underlying domain knowledge. Each system was designed to promote knowledge acquisition in the context of patient management problems. BioWorld, designed for students in their first few years of medical school, provides an extension of the basic science classroom to an environment where students can apply their knowledge to clinical cases. The SICUN tutor is designed for on-the-job training for individuals who are already practicing their skills in a surgical intensive care ward. The RadTutor provides radiology residents with a practice environment where they can apply their extensive medical and radiology training to diagnosing breast disease.

BIO-WORLD: EXTENDING
THE CLASSROOM

Bio-World (Lajoie, 1993; Lajoie et al., 1995; Lajoie, Lavigne, Guerrera, & Munsie, in press) was designed to situate learners in authentic problems where they would apply their schooled knowledge to realistic contexts. Students who obtain acceptable test scores in school subjects, such as science, often fail to use the learned facts and concepts on appropriate occasions in everyday (Resnick, 1987; Whitehead, 1929). Failures in conventional methods may be due to the fact that much of school learning is situated in well-structured knowledge domains as opposed to ill-structured domains (Koschmann, Myers, Feltovitch, & Barrows, 1994). Bio-World provides a mechanism for learning to solve ill-structured problems within a computer-based learning environment. Technology can improve problem-based learning in the classroom (Hoffman & Ritchie, 1997) by providing multiple modalities for representing real-world problems, the capacity for providing adequate information and advice and feedback when and where needed, and reducing the time to complete the problem by providing online resources.

Scientific reasoning involves an understanding of both declarative information and procedural problem-solving skills. In the biology classroom, students are taught declarative information about bacterial and viral infections, how infections are transmitted, how different infections affect different parts of the body, and how bodies have different defense systems to guard against certain diseases. Bio-World provides a mechanism for putting this declarative knowledge into practice by enabling students to use such knowledge in the context of realistic problem-solving tasks, such as diagnosing a disease.

Bio-World presents a hospital simulation where students learn to reason about infections. It poses realistic diagnostic scenarios, and students solve these problems by collecting evidence to confirm their hypotheses. At the completion of a problem, students justify their diagnosis by building a solid argument supported by observations and evidence. Rather than tutor students on the various types of diseases and how they are transmitted and diagnosed, Bio-World engages students in the scientific reasoning process, whereby they hypothesize about what disease a patient might have.

Through an argumentation process, students form a diagnostic hypothesis and collect evidence to confirm or disconfirm it. Toulmin (1958) describes argumentation as a process consisting of making assertions or claims and providing support and justification for these claims using accumulated data, facts, and evidence. This skillful coordination of theory and evidence is believed to be the central premise underlying scientific thinking (Kuhn, 1989). Bio-World facilitates scientific thinking through the reification of a student's argumentation skills through argumentation tools made available during problem solving (Lajoie et al., 1995). In the argumentation phase, the learner engages in explicitly justifying hypotheses with evidence; organizing, categorizing, and rating the evidence; and constructing a final summary argument. As students construct arguments to defend their hypotheses, Bio-World monitors their actions and determines the kind of advice or hints to generate in response to their requests. By making arguments visible, students can begin to monitor their own scientific thinking in the context of problem solving.

The BioWorld Environment

Problem solving within Bio-World requires a basic understanding of the respiratory, digestive, and reproductive body systems because problems are diagnosed by first identifying which body system is involved. The graphical interface is identical for each problem. Each problem begins with an initial problem statement (see Fig. 9.1) that sets the context for problem solving. The statement contains both relevant and irrelevant information. For instance, the fact that the patient was at a picnic prior to admission may be relevant to solving the case, whereas having a good weekend may not be relevant. Students read the statement and make an initial hypothesis regarding the patient's problem by selecting a hypothesis (in this case, gastroenteritis) from a pull-down menu on the left of the screen. They then enter their degree of certainty about their hypothesis into a belief meter located under their hypothesis entry. Next, students provide evidence to back up their hypothesis by selecting relevant evidence from the problem statement and entering it into their evidence table (at the left of the screen in Fig. 9.1). In Fig. 9.1 nauseous, diarrhea, and abdominal cramps are posted as evidence. The evidence table is updated dynamically as students collect data pertinent to solving the case.

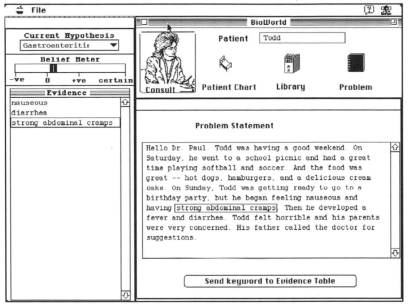

FIG. 9.1.

Subsequently, students might select the library, patient chart, or consult button, or change their hypothesis at any time. The disease library is illustrated in Fig. 9.2. Cirrhosis is the highlighted disease, with information about how it is transmitted, the symptoms associated with it, and what diagnostic tests could be ordered to identify the disease. Students who are systematic problem solvers will read about diseases in the library and decide which disease is most likely for the presenting problem. After accessing the library, students generally request the patient chart information and order the diagnostic tests as specified in the library. However, there is no set order of steps. Students may collect diagnostic tests without knowing how to interpret the results.

Once students enter a correct final hypothesis, they are asked to categorize their evidence and build a final argument as to which information was crucial to solving the problem. This phase allows time for reflection and communication among group members as to what information was most important in the problem-solving process. In Fig. 9.3 a student argument is compared to an expert argument. At the top of the screen is a "talking head" icon that the user can select to hear an expert explain his problem-solving strategy. The expert walk-through is presented as an alternative

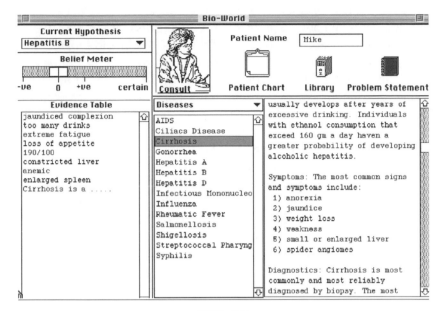

FIG. 9.2.

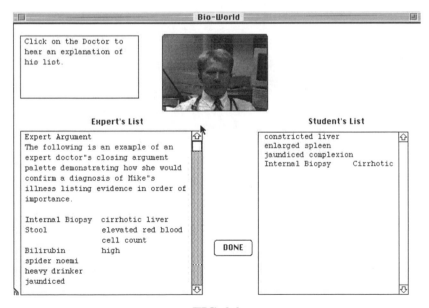

FIG. 9.3.

solution path to the one that the students provided. It helps students reflect on their actions and put the problem-solving process into perspective.

The cognitive tools underlying the design of Bio-World support cognitive processes by providing online resources, such as the library and patient chart, for students to acquire knowledge in the context of problem solving. Learning is contextualized within domain-specific problems but generalized across similar problem types within the common body system of digestion. These tools allow students to engage in real-world practice activities by supporting lower-order thinking skills and freeing up resources allocated to higher order reasoning skills. Bio-World provides safe practice of research experiences in the classroom by supporting multiple hypotheses. Students can take any number of paths to solving the problem and request assistance in the context of their problem. Assistance is dynamic and adaptive. Memory processes are supported by the evidence palette, in that students post the information that they think is most relevant to solving the problem. In addition to a memory aid, this palette facilitates metacognitive strategies and argumentation skills. Metacognition is supported since students can compare their problem-solving processes with that of an expert. Argumentation is supported because students must articulate their reasoning to each other when selecting information for the evidence and argumentation palette.

Types of Learning Situations and Assessment Possibilities

Bio-World has been tested with high school biology students and will be evaluated in medical school classrooms in the near future. It has been used in multiple types of learning situations: one-on-one tutoring, face-to-face small-group learning, and telelearning (small groups working at a distance to solve problems). The flexibility in type of pedagogical strategy provides opportunities for researchers to ask different types of questions about learning and scientific reasoning in problem-based learning situations. Both process and product assessment data are available. Process information is collected dynamically by Bio-World and stored as slime trails at the completion of each problem. The types of actions conducted throughout problem solving can be examined in the context of the exact location where students were working within Bio-World and compared with their verbal protocol data. For example, when activity is reported within the library, the verbal protocols can be examined to see how students reason with the data and decide on their hypotheses and tests of hypotheses. This type of "within-tutor" data is as important as whether students solve the problem or perform well on posttests. Different learning situations produce different outcomes and certain pedagogical strategies, such as the presence of human versus computer tutors, or the style of tutors, may be more successful than others (see Lajoie et al., in press).

THE SICUN

The surgical intensive care unit is a high-information-flow environment where medical personnel act together to care for critical care patients. SICUN (Lajoie, Azevedo, & Fleiszer, 1998) is a computer-based learning environment that was designed to assist surgical intensive care unit (SICU) medical personnel in their assessments of critical care patients. The "N" in SICUN stands for nurses, since it was piloted with nurses. This system will eventually be extended to include physicians' training.

The theoretical underpinnings of this system are similar to those of the Bio-World environment, with the exception that SICUN is designed for actual practice. Learning is situated in the context of authentic trauma cases. Clinical decision making is an advanced form of scientific reasoning, which is supported in the SICUN by online access to expert knowledge representations. These representations were obtained through a cognitive task analysis of patient assessments in the SICU. Verbal protocol analysis revealed the types of expert plans and actions needed to solve patient cases in the SICU.

An effective problem space (Lesgold, Lajoie, Logan, & Eggan, 1990) was designed that incorporated both expert and novice plans and actions needed to solve problems in this domain. Dynamic feedback was provided to the learner in the format of text and graphical representations of how a more advanced peer or expert might solve the problem. Modeling expertise in this manner can help individuals become aware of more proficient strategies for solving problems. Access to alternative strategies is crucial given the ill-structured nature of this problem-solving domain.

Guided Tour of the SICUN

The SICUN is a problem-based practice environment. Learners are presented with an initial patient case history (see Fig. 9.4). Similar to Bio-World, the patient scenario presents important clues as to the patient's problems. Information within the scenario is hypertexted so that users can

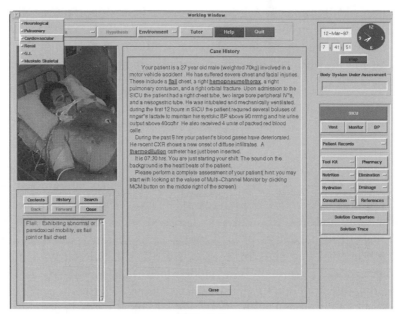

FIG. 9.4.

link to an explanation or glossary of information when they need assistance. Unlike Bio-World, there are specialized medical devices that must be monitored since patients are likely to be hooked up to various devices, depending on the problem. The right-hand side of Fig. 9.4 illustrates some of these devices (the multichannel monitor and baxter pump). It also shows a button for drainage of patient fluids, access to a pharmacy to order medications, patient charts to examine the change in patient status during the person's stay in the SICU, and a clock to indicate how long medical personnel have been working with the patient. This figure demonstrates the complexity of the high information flow that personnel face in the SICU.

Another major difference between the two environments is that clinical decision making often involves entertaining more than one hypothesis at a time. There may be more than 10 hypotheses to choose from, and the learner may post up to 3 hypotheses at a time. Figure 9.5 illustrates how differential hypotheses can be entered. The user can then rank-order her certainty about each hypothesis and can change or discard hypotheses at any time. Learners can compare their solution process with that of an expert (see Fig. 9.6) at any point in the process. This comparison allows the learner to self-assess and change strategies as necessary.

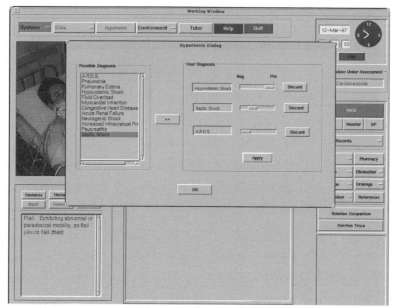

FIG. 9.5.

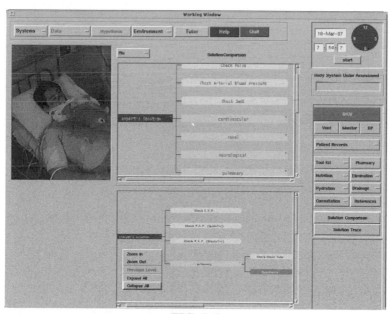

FIG. 9.6.

The cognitive tools that underlie the design of the SICUN are quite similar to those used in Bio-World. The tutoring system is designed to scaffold the acquisition of declarative knowledge through the hypertext links in the problem scenarios, as well as through the online glossaries throughout their interaction with the tutor. For example, a user who does not understand a word or procedure can look this information up and have immediate access to it. Procedural knowledge as to how to perform some action, such as how to calculate the correct dosage based on a patient's body weight and the physician's orders, is assisted through online tools, such as calculators, and equations, where the nurse can fill in the blanks and perform the calculations needed. Simulations of how to set up specific equipment, such as the intravenous baxter pump, can also be made available to learners who need that level of assistance.

The SICUN supports memory and metacognition. At any time during problem solving, students can access the "where am I" button, which will provide them with a graphical representation of their problem-solving process to that point. The representation is hierarchical in that the nurse's plans, and actions within each plan, are noted. These representations remind the nurse of the students' prior actions, thereby reducing repetition. Furthermore, these external representations help reduce the cognitive load of managing this high information-flow environment. The tutor ensures that students reflect on their plans and actions by forcing them to state explicitly whether they accomplished their goals within each plan. This helps students reflect on their actions in the context of their hypotheses. Furthermore, students can compare their problem-solving processes with those of an expert. The comparison process ensures that students assess their own plans and actions and helps them expand their repertoire of problem-solving strategies to include a model of expertise. Another important aspect of the SICUN environment is that it does not restrict hypothesis formation. Multiple hypotheses are supported through the menus of differential diagnoses, and learners can adjust these hypotheses at any time throughout the problem-solving process.

Assessment Issues

The SICUN is in the early stages of development and has only been piloted. However, we do know that in addition to helping learners assess their own performance throughout the problem-solving process, SICUN can record the types of decisions learners make, the accuracy of their diagnoses and interpretations of data, and the types of strategies they use to confirm or disconfirm their hypotheses. Furthermore, it is possible to analyze such records to determine how structured or fragmented their knowledge is and whether they respond to the cognitive tools and, in so doing, improve their performance.

RADTUTOR: A PRACTICE ENVIRONMENT FOR MAMMOGRAM INTERPRETATION

Whereas Bio-World is designed for students just entering medical school and SICUN is designed for practitioners, the RadTutor falls somewhere in between since radiology residents are applying their extensive medical knowledge and radiology training to diagnosing breast disease cases. The RadTutor is a computerized practice environment designed to train radiology residents to diagnose mammograms exhibiting breast diseases (Azevedo & Lajoie, 1998; Azevedo, Lajoie, Desaulniers, Fleiszer, & Bret, 1997). The RadTutor is described in terms of its theoretical and conceptual framework, which is based on a cognitive theory of skill acquisition and empirical findings from cognitive studies in radiology (Azevedo, 1997; Azevedo, Lajoie, Desaulniers, & Bret, 1996).

Bridging Theory, Empirical Research, and the Design of Computer Tools

The design of the RadTutor is supported by information processing theory (Anderson, 1993; Newell & Simon, 1972) that assumes that the mind is a computational system that constructs, manipulates, and represents symbols. This theoretical approach uses protocol analysis to determine how experts differ from novices in a specific domain, such as mammogram interpretation, in terms of cognitive processes (e.g., knowledge states, problem-solving operators, control processes, and types of errors). A cognitive task analysis of mammogram interpretation was conducted, resulting in a cognitive model that includes the problem-solving strategies that staff radiologists and radiology residents use, along with typical case-related errors (Azevedo, 1997).

The cognitive task analyses consisted of working with domain experts and conducting a content analysis of breast disease. Extensive interviews with domain experts determined the types of cases and sequencing of cases that would be appropriate for building knowledge about mammogram interpretation. The RadTutor's expert module was based on these interviews. The content analyses of the areas of breast disease and mammography were represented as a series of production rules underlying the domain knowledge module of the prototype.

The results of the cognitive task analysis and content analysis revealed that mammogram interpretation can be described by a seven-step sequential problem-solving model (Azevedo, 1997) which was incorporated into the RadTutor. Learners are encouraged to follow a prespecified instructional sequence: (a) reading the patient history; (b) inspecting a set of mammograms; (c) identifying and characterizing mammographic observations and findings; (d) providing a diagnosis; and (e) specifying a subsequent medical examination (if required).

The verbal protocol analysis revealed the problem-solving operators that both radiologists and residents used. These operators subsequently were used to design the instructional scaffolding provided by the RadTutor. Less skilled learners could be assisted by more expert-like strategies for solving problems. The graphical interface of the RadTutor provided opportunities for learners to use the same problem-solving operators they would turn to in the real world. For example, the interface was built to display the case history and set of mammograms and allow the user to manipulate the images for clearer feature characterization or comparison. Similarly, the system provides extensive instructional scaffolding during the hypothesis-generation phase to ensure that the user has proposed the appropriate level of hypothesis (e.g., malignant versus infiltrating ductal carcinoma).

The verbal protocol analyses indicated that diagnostic planning—proposing further medical examinations—was the most frequent control process that the subjects used. As such the interface provided opportunities for listing more than one medical examination simultaneously. An error analysis of the protocols revealed five types of errors, which are currently being formalized as production rules within the RadTutor and integrated into the expert module. That is, each error type can be identified by the RadTutor, and subsequently a specific instructional scaffolding strategy is used to remedy the error. For example, a finding mischaracterization error (e.g., characterizing a border of a mass as well defined when in fact it is only partly well defined) is associated with an instructional strategy that focuses the user's attention on the part of a mammographic finding that was mischaracterized (e.g., the border of a mass). The process of identifying error commission is facilitated by the fact that the analyses indicated errors to be case dependent. For example, cases with subtle mammographic manifestations are highly likely to produce a perceptual detection error. The RadTutor is also capable of determining if the learner is employing a data-driven or a mixed problem-solving strategy, which is extremely critical in identifying errors and providing the appropriate level of scaffolding.

Guided Tour of the RadTutor

The RadTutor's instructional features include opportunities for the residents to follow the seven-step problem-solving model. Figure 9.7 presents the interface of the mammography prototype. The interface is divided into seven components: (a) a number of pull-down menus allowing the user to select several actions (circle a region, select a region, delete a region, rectify an action, make a diagnosis, and propose subsequent examinations); (b) a clinical history box; (c) the mammogram display area; (d) the tutor's dialogue box; (e) the resident's dialogue box; (f) a list of mammogram observations, findings, and diagnoses; and (g) a differential diagnosis box.

Solving a typical breast disease case begins with the tutor's providing the clinical history. The tutor then displays the mammograms in a random order whereby a resident can reposition the images in the mammogram display area. The tutor then queries the resident if there are any significant observations to be highlighted. Depending on the resident's response and its correctness, the tutor either identifies and characterizes the observations,

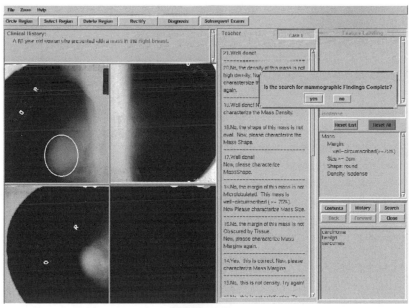

FIG. 9.7.

or bypasses these two steps and goes directly to the identification of mammographic findings. During the identification of observation phase, the resident has to highlight the observation on the mammogram; if the resident is correct, the tutor characterizes the observation by displaying a text label and arrow pointing to the area. If the resident was incorrect, the tutor highlights the correct area and displays a text label and arrow pointing to the area. If there are multiple observations, the tutor asks the resident if more observations are exhibited on the mammograms, and the cycle is repeated until all observations are identified and characterized.

The tutor instructs the resident to circle and identify the critical findings and select a diagnosis. The tutor provides the resident with feedback concerning the placement of the mammograms and prompts the resident to look for findings. The resident then has the option of selecting the critical findings from a list of features or going directly to the images and highlighting the critical features with the aid of the tools provided in the floating palette. Depending on the accuracy, the tutor will subsequently intervene by asking the resident to rectify her characterization of the mammographic feature. The resident may select a diagnosis and place it in the active diagnosis box.

The resident can select as many features from the features identification list and can highlight as many mammographic regions as she wants. At a microlevel, tutoring interventions, instructional scaffolding, and resident queries are based on one of the features identified. However, at the global level, the scaffolding and tutoring interventions are based on the number of findings selected and highlighted, the accuracy of their characterization, and differential diagnoses selected. The dialogue between tutor and resident is presented in dialogue boxes, and the termination of a dialogue sequence is represented by the dotted lines.

Cognitive Tools Underlying the Design of the RadTutor

The rationale behind the RadTutor design is based on the assumption that a learner's cognitive processes can be modeled, traced, and corrected in the context of problem solving (Anderson, Corbett, Koedinger, & Pelletier, 1995; Lajoie, 1993, in press; Shute & Psotka, 1994).

The cognitive tools embedded in the RadTutor are based on a set of instructional principles (multiplicity, activeness, accommodation and adaptation, and authenticity) that have been derived from extensive research in cognitive psychology, instructional psychology, and medical education (for an extensive review, see Koschmann et al., 1996). The principle of multiplicity is based on the concept that knowledge is complex, context sensitive, and interrelated, and thus instruction should promote multiple perspectives, representations, and strategies. This principle is based on the theory of cognitive flexibility (Spiro, Feltovich, Jacobson, & Coulson, 1991) in medicine that emphasizes the use of multiple knowledge representations and repeated exposure to instructional content. According to this principle, single mental representations and unitary learning approaches are insufficient for capturing the nature of complex instructional materials and knowledge application in ill-structured domains (such as radiology). The RadTutor provides the resident with a stock of breast disease cases that can be accessed in a structured manner according to diagnostic categories, specific mammographic manifestations, and relevant clinical history cues.

The principle of activeness is based on the concept that learning is an active process, requiring mental construction and manipulation of multiple representations (e.g., gray-scale densities exhibited on mammograms and relevant clinical history findings) that comprise the task environment. Therefore, instruction fosters knowledge construction through problem-solving activities that lead to the development of skill acquisition. This principle reflects the nature of learning through active construction of knowledge facilitated by problem-solving activities. Effective instructional methods should promote planning, reasoning, goal-directed problem solving, and reflection. This principle reflects the empirical findings in the areas of cognitive skill acquisition (VanLehn, 1996) and the development of expertise (Ericsson & Charness, 1997; Ericsson & Lehmann, 1996). In the RadTutor, instruction fosters knowledge construction through meaningful problem-solving activities that facilitate skill acquisition and the development of expertise.

The principle of accommodation and adaptation is based on the concept that the learning process is to a large degree affected by the extent of the learner's existing knowledge. As such, instruction facilitates adaptability by building on the learner's existing knowledge, monitoring learner progress and rectifying misconceptions when they arise, and fostering the development of metacognitive skills. A rule-based domain knowledge module and a student modeling approach are being constructed based on the well-constrained nature of the domain of mammography.

The principle of authenticity is based on the concept that learning is sensitive to contextual factors, which determine the usability of what is learned, and the extent of skill transfer. Therefore, instruction should provide learning activities that are required in the domain, are valued in the real-world context, and emulate the real-world environment as much as possible. In the RadTutor, the problem-solving activities resemble what is routinely encountered in a resident's work environment and also provides the tools typically used to solve mammogram cases (e.g., a magnifying glass and a ruler).

Types of Learning Situations and Assessment Issues

The RadTutor is in the early stages of development and as such is designed to be used only by single users engaged in solving breast disease cases. The focus on single users and individual cognition is critical for validating the viability of a prespecified instructional sequence and the appropriateness of the instructional interventions. Future plans include porting the tutor to the World Wide Web for increased dissemination and accessibility to residents and radiologists. Plans also include the formal development of a cognitive model of the domain of mammography based on the ACT-R/PM architecture (Byrne & Anderson, 1998). This architecture will consist of a set of modules for perception and action that are integrated in the most recent incarnation of the ACT-R theory (Anderson & Labriere, 1998) and will include both model and knowledge-tracing components.

FROM SCHOOL
TO REAL-WORLD PRACTICE

The instructional approach underlying each computer-based learning system corresponds to learner type. Bio-World, designed for more junior students, allows a lot of flexibility in how students can engage with the system. Students discover the solutions to realistic problems by engaging in evidence collection, data interpretation, and evaluation. They can receive assistance from an online coach and can compare their solutions with those of an expert at the completion of a problem. There is no specific set of procedures for scientific reasoning, but there are different levels of sophistication that can evolve with learning. This system allows students to engage in scientific dialogues about patient diseases that pertain to specific body systems. Students learn to build an argument through collecting, categorizing, and posting evidence and representing their arguments. Bio-World can also take on many pedagogical styles. For instance, if a one-to-one tutor-to-student ratio is desired, then Bio-World can be used in this fashion. If a collaborative model of instruction is preferred, small groups can work with Bio-World in either a face-to-face small-group setting or at a distance in a telelearning setting. In the latter case, through videoconferencing technologies, small groups of students in remote locations work on the same problem simultaneously and negotiate among themselves as to what plan or action they will take next. Empirical studies are underway to investigate the effects of such pedagogical changes on learners as well as specific examinations of how Bio-World fosters learning.

The SICUN environment is designed for practitioners and goes beyond the typical nursing curriculum in that it provides a platform for safe clinical practice in a setting that emulates a real SICU environment. The intended audience for this system is more sophisticated and has more background knowledge than the Bio-World students. The SICUN provides simulations that can reduce the anxiety of patient care and maximize learning opportunities in realistic contexts by providing expert advice and models of the problem-solving process when needed. Nurses can access an expert-problem-solving trace at any time during their activity. The complexity of the SICU necessitates the dynamic access to explicit knowledge representations since this is a high-information-flow environment where attention to multiple forms of data is needed. Nurses can examine their own knowledge representations and those of experts. Some of this explicit knowledge posting is available in Bio-World through the evidence palette, but comparison to an expert trace is done only at the completion of the problem. Unlike the Bio-World environment, the SICUN was designed for individual one-on-one learning situations, where nurses can assess their own problem-solving efforts by comparing their solution steps with an expert. In Bio-World, much of the scaffolding is done by peers who are working together to solve problems.

The RadTutor is designed for advanced learners who are trying to integrate specialized medical knowledge with clinical skills in mammography. A cognitive task analysis revealed that mammogram interpretation is a well-structured task, and hence a set of production rules could be developed based on the error analysis of the verbal protocols. This analysis led to a model tracing coaching that allows the RadTutor to trace the learners dynamically in the context of problem solving and provides explicit guidance in the context of problem solving. However, students can still have multiple hypotheses and be coached in the context of their hypotheses.

All three systems were described in terms of the underlying theoretical perspectives and empirical data that led to the design of specific features. The design process is often cyclical in that theory-guided design is followed by empirical evaluations of computer-based learning environments, followed by the necessary modifications. The revision cycle is complete when the learning environments demonstrate that the cognitive tools they contain provide opportunities for learning and problem solving. For instance, in BioWorld the evidence palette serves as both a memory and a metacognitive tool for learners. It contains a memory tool since the evidence that students placed in the palette is visible at all times during the solution process. It is a metacognitive aid as well since it makes thought processes visible and hence inspectable. Furthermore, students articulate their reasoning with one another and form an explicit final argument as to how they solved the problem, and they compare this argument with that of an expert at the end of the problem. The online library is a cognitive tool for scaffolding declarative knowledge. Students can look up any information required to improve their understanding of specific diseases.

The SICUN also presents cognitive tools. Prior to conducting actions, learners explicitly state multiple hypotheses, provide a confidence rating for each hypothesis, and state their specific goals. After conducting actions, they are asked whether their goals were met. In this way, the SICUN can assess learners in the context of their own hypotheses and coach them when assistance is requested. Explicit graphical representations can be viewed at all times in order for learners to compare their solution processes with an expert solution. These graphical representations are a metacognitive aid since they focus the learners' attention on the cognitive processes needed to solve the problem. Procedural knowledge is also scaffolded by online simulations of how to perform specific procedures such as calculating a dosage for a specific patient case.

The RadTutor provides a great deal of explicit perceptual scaffolding, where specific observations and findings are highlighted on the mammograms so that learners can see the critical regions needed to make a diagnosis. Textual scaffolding in the form of hints is also provided.

Important differences among the three systems lie in the type of cognitive tools to support the various levels of medical expertise required for the task. Bio-World and SICUN provide ill-structured problem-solving tasks requiring scientific reasoning and clinical decision making, respectively, and hence could fit into the discovery or guided model (or the no model or middle camp perspective described by Derry & Lajoie, 1993).

The RadTutor presents well-structured problems and hence fits a model-tracing approach to instruction based on ACT-R (the modeler camp, as described in Derry & Lajoie, 1993).

The type of research outlined in this chapter can provide detailed evidence regarding computers as cognitive tools for learning and assessment. Computer-based environments such as Bio-World, the SICUN, and the RadTutor are problem-based learning environments that provide more authentic contexts for studying scientific reasoning and clinical decision-making processes. They represent a considerable improvement over the traditional experimental paradigms using paper-and-pencil multiple-choice assessment tasks. These types of intelligent systems can observe patterns in tool use, and researchers can draw appropriate inferences regarding learner understanding from such patterns. More research using these new technologies can help answer questions about the appropriateness of instructional models and provide a window on rapid forms of decision making in more realistic settings. This allows for a new perspective on decision making. Furthermore, these environments provide rich test beds for manipulating various factors to examine how changes in pedagogical strategies may influence the problem-solving process. These rich instructional and assessment platforms, when joined with traditional cognitive methodologies of verbal protocol analyses of student dialogues, can add to our understanding of learning, reasoning, and problem-solving processes.

ACKNOWLEDGMENTS

S.P.L. gratefully acknowledges the assistance of the numerous people involved in both the Bio-World and SICUN projects. Regarding Bio-World the first author would like to acknowledge the funding agencies for promoting this research: the Canadian Social Sciences and Humanities Research Council, the Canadian Telelearning Center of Excellence Network, and the Wisconsin Alumni Research Fund at the University of Wisconsin, Madison. Bio-World was made possible due to its many supporters: Marilyn Hanson, Sue Brass, Sue Johnson, all gifted biology teachers; Richard Day and David Fleiszer, supporting physicians interested in improving instruction; and many students who have contributed to the Bio-World Project throughout the years, including Sheryl Brock, Nancy Hollar, Vicki Jacobs, Glenn Peterson, Keith Tookey, Liang Yin Yu, Paul Aleong, and Abdu Elwhidi, Steve Munsie, Claudia Guerrera, and

Nancy Lavigne. The first author would also like to extend special thanks to Jim Greer, a visiting scholar at the time of the study, for his assistance in the development of the argumentation tools. Finally, we thank Marguerite Roy for her statistical expertise.

Regarding the SICUN project, the first author would like to thank David Fleiszer, Roger Azevedo, and the other researchers and industrial partners: Claude Frasson, Jan Gecsei, Gilles Gauthier, Bernard Lefebvre, Marc Kaltenbach, Gilles Imbeau, Novasys, and Virtual Prototype. The first author also acknowledges the solid work of the programmers, Wei Gu and Xiaoyan Zhao; Robert Bouchard, a research assistant; and Julie Kinnon, our nursing expert, who has helped in all phases of this research. The SICUN project was funded by the Quebec Ministry of Industry, Commerce, Science and Technology.

The design and development of the RadTutor prototype is based on the results of the second author's dissertation and was prepared for publication while the author was working at the Department of Psychology of Carnegie Mellon University as a postdoctoral fellow, funded by the Social Sciences and Humanities Research Council of Canada (SSHRC). This project was funded by Dr. Fleiszer and McGill University's Medical Informatics Committee (Molson Project) and partial funds from a doctoral fellowship from the SSHRC also awarded to the second author. Partial funding was also provided by the Quebec government's Ministry of Industry, Science, Commerce and Technology and the SAFARI project. The authors would like to thank Xiaoyan Zhao for the development of the RadTutor prototype, Dr. Desaulniers for her expertise in the areas of mammography and breast disease, and Sonia Faremo for insightful comments and various discussions on the RadTutor.

REFERENCES

Anderson, J. R. (1993). *Rules of the mind*. Hillsdale, NJ: Lawrence Erlbaum Associates.

Anderson, J. R., & Labriere, C. (1998). *The atomic components of thought*. Hillsdale, NJ: Lawrence Erlbaum Associates.

Azevedo, R. (1997). *Expert problem solving in mammogram interpretation: A visual cognitive task*. Unpublished doctoral dissertation, McGill University, Montreal, Quebec, Canada.

Azevedo, R., & Lajoie, S. P. (1998). The cognitive basis for the design of a mammogram interpretation tutor. *International Journal of Artificial Intelligence in Education*, 9(1/2),32-44.

Azevedo, R., Lajoie, S. P., Desaulniers, M., & Bret, P. M. (1996, August). *Tutoring complex visual concepts in radiology*. Paper presented at the 26th International Congress of Psychology, Montreal, Quebec, Canada.

Azevedo, R., Lajoie, S. P., Desaulniers, M., Fleiszer, D. M., & Bret, P. M. (1997). RadTutor: The theoretical and empirical basis for the design of a mammography interpretation tutor. In B. du Boulay & R. Mizoguchi (Eds.), *Frontiers in artificial intelligence and application* (pp. 386–393). Amsterdam: IOS Press.

Barnett, O. (1995). Information technology and medical education. *JAMIA, 2,* 285–291.

Bashook, P. G. (1993). Clinical competence and continuing medical education: Lifelong learning to maintain competence. In C. Coles & H. A. Holm (Eds.), *Learning in medicine* (pp. 21–41). Oxford: Oxford University Press.

Bouchard, R. M., Lajoie, S. P., & Fleiszer, D. (1995). Constructing knowledge within the medical domain: A cognitive perspective. In K. Cox & J. Marsh (Eds.), *Proceedings of the First International Cognitive Technology Conference* (pp. 45–56). Hong Kong: City University.

Brown, J. S. Collins, A., & Duquid, P. (1989). Situated cognition and the culture of learning. *Educational Researcher, 18,* 32–42.

Byrne, M. D., & Anderson, J. R. (1998). Perception and action. In J. R. Anderson & C. Labriere (Eds.), *The atomic components of thought* (pp. 167–200). Hillsdale, NJ: Lawrence Erlbaum Associates.

Clancey, W. J. (1987). *Knowledge-based tutoring: The GUIDON Program*. Cambridge, MA: MIT Press.

Collins, A., Brown, J., S., & Newman, S. E. (1989). Cognitive apprenticeship: Teaching the craft of reading, writing, and mathematics. In L. B. Resnick (Ed.), *Knowing, learning, and instruction: Essays in honor of Robert Glaser* (pp. 453–494). Hillsdale, NJ: Lawrence Erlbaum Associates.

Derry, S. J., & Lajoie, S. P. (1993). A middle camp for (un)intelligent computing. In S. P. Lajoie & S. J. Derry (Eds.), *Computers as cognitive tools* (pp.1–11). Hillsdale, NJ: Lawrence Erlbaum Associates.

Eisner, E. (1993). Forms of understanding and the future of educational research. *Educational Researcher, 22*(7), 5–11.

Friedman, C. P., & Dev, P. (1996). Education and informatics: It's time to join forces. *JAMIA, 3,* 184–185.

Greeno, J. (1989). A perspective on thinking. *American Psychologist, 44*(2), 134–141.

Greeno, J. (1997). Response: On claims that answer the wrong question. *Educational Researcher, 26*(1), 5–17.

Hoffman, B., & Ritchie, D. (1997). Using multimedia to overcome the problems with problem-based learning. *Instructional Science, 25,* 97–115.

Jonassen, D. H. (1996). *Computers in the classroom: Mindtools for critical thinking.* Columbus, OH: Prentice-Hall.

Jonassen, D. H., & Reeves, T. C. (1996). Learning with technology: Using computers as cognitive tools. In D. H. Jonassen (Ed.), *Handbook of research for educational communications and technology* (pp. 693–719). New York: Macmillan.

Kommers, P., Jonassen, D. H., & Mayes T. (Eds.). (1992). *Cognitive tools for learning.* Berlin: Springer.

Koschmann, T. D., Kelson, A. C., Feltovich, P. J., & Barrows, H. S. (1996). Computer-supported problem-based learning: A principled approach to the use of computers in collaborative learning. In T. D. Koschmann (Ed.), *CSCL: Theory and practice of an emerging paradigm* (pp. 83–124). Hillsdale, NJ: Lawrence Erlbaum Associates.

Koschmann, T. D., Myers, A. C., Feltovich, P. J., & Barrows, H. S. (1994). Using technology to assist in realizing effective learning and instruction: A principled approach to the use of computers in collaborative learning. *Journal of the Learning Sciences, 3*(3), 227–264.

Kuhn, D. (1989). Children and adults as intuitive scientists. *Psychological Review, 96*(4), 674–689.

Lajoie, S. P. (1993). Computer environments as cognitive tools for enhancing learning. In S. P. Lajoie & S. Derry (Eds.), *Computers as cognitive tools* (pp. 261–288). Hillsdale, NJ: Lawrence Erlbaum Associates.

Lajoie, S. P., Azevedo, R., & Fleiszer, D. (1998). Cognitive tools for assessment and learning in a high information flow environment. *Journal of Educational Computing Research, 18*(3) 203–233.

Lajoie, S. P., & Derry, S. (Eds.). (1993). *Computers as cognitive tools* . Hillsdale, NJ: Lawrence Erlbaum Associates.

Lajoie, S. P., Greer, J. E., Munsie, S. D., Wilkie, T. V., Guerrera. C., & Aleong, P. (1995). Establishing an argumentation environment to foster scientific reasoning with Bio-World. In D. Jonassen & G. McCalla (Eds.), *Proceedings of the International Conference on Computers in Education* (pp. 89–96). Charlottesville, VA: Association for the Advancement of Computing in Education.

Lajoie, S. P., Lavigne, N. C., Guerrera, C., & Munsie, S. (in press). *Constructing knowledge in the context of BioWorld.* Instructional Science.

Lesgold, A., Lajoie, S. P., Logan, D., & Eggan, G. M. (1990). Cognitive task analysis approaches to testing. In N. Frederiksen, R. Glaser, A. Lesgold, & M.

Shafto (Eds.), *Diagnostic monitoring of skill and knowledge acquisition* (pp. 325–350). Hillsdale, NJ: Lawrence Erlbaum Associates.

Lillehaug, S. I., & Lajoie, S. P. (1998). AI in medical education: Another grand challenge for medical informatics. *Journal of Artificial Intelligence in Medicine, 12*(3), 1–29.

Linn, M. C., Songer, N. C., & Eylon, B. (1996). Shifts and convergences in science learning and instruction. In D. C. Berliner & R. Calfee (Eds.), *Handbook of educational psychology* (pp. 438–490). New York: Macmillan.

Olson, D. R. (1988). *Mind and the technology of communication.* Paper presented at the Australian Educational Conference, Melborne.

Pea, R. D. (1985). Beyond amplification: Using the computer to reorganize mental functioning. *Educational Psychologist, 20,* 167–182.

Perkins, D. N. (1985). The fingertip effect: How information processing technology shapes thinking. *Educational Researcher, 14,* 11–17.

Rahilly, T. J., Saroyan, A., Greer, J., Lajoie, S. P., Breuleux, A., Azevedo, R., & Fleiszer, D. (1996, July). *The InforMed professor: Clinical instruction of breast disease diagnosis and management.* Paper presented at the Third International Conference on Computer Aided Learning and Instruction in Science and Engineering, Donostia, San Sebastian, Spain.

Resnick, L. B. (1987). Learning in school and out. *Educational Researcher, 16,* 13–20.

Salomon, G., Perkins, D. N., & Globerson, T. (1991). Partners in cognition: Extending human intelligence with intelligent technologies. *Educational Researcher, 20,* 10–16.

Shortliffe, E. H. (1984). The science of biomedical computing. *Med Inform, 9,* 185–193.

Shute, V. J., & Psotka, J. (1995). Intelligent tutoring systems: Past, present and future. In D. Jonassen (Ed.), *Handbook of research on educational communications and technology* (pp. 570–600). New York: Scholastic Publications.

Spiro, R. J., Feltovich, P. J., Jacobson, M. J., & Coulson, R. L. (1991). Cognitive flexibility theory, constructivism, and hypertext: Random access instruction for advanced knowledge acquisition in ill-structured domains. *Educational Technology, 31*(5), 24–33.

Toulmin, S. E. (1958). *The uses of argument.* New York: Cambridge University Press.

VanLehn, K. (1996). Cognitive skill acquisition. *Annual Review of Psychology, 47,* 513–539.

Whitehead, A. N. (1929). *The aims of education.* New York: Macmillan.

10

Computer Tools That Link
Assessment and Instruction:
Investigating What Makes
Electricity Hard to Learn

Daniel L. Schwartz, Gautam Biswas,
John D. Bransford, Bharat Bhuva,
Tamara Balac, and Sean Brophy
Vanderbilt University

In this chapter we describe software that helps teachers and students link assessment and instruction to promote learning in science. Many researchers are exploring ways to link assessment and instruction through computer environments (e.g., Koedinger & Anderson, 1993; Lajoie & Lesgold, 1992; Levidow, Hunt, & McKee, 1991; Magnusson, Templin, & Boyle, 1997; White & Frederikson, 1998). For example, Hunt and Minstrell's (1994) program Diagnoser presents students with a physics problem. Students choose from a list of solutions and possible justifications. If they choose foils that reflect misconceptions, the system branches to an appropriate unit of instruction. In this method of joining instruction and assessment, the computer makes formative assessments that guide on-the-spot instructional decisions. This model of formative assessment reflects the explicit practices of good teachers who evaluate problem-solving accuracy to determine subsequent instructional steps.

Our investigations differ from this formative approach because we rely on a dynamic model of assessment that emphasizes students' preparedness for learning (Bransford & Schwartz, 1999). Our assessments also indicate what type of problem a student can or cannot solve but further determine whether the student is ready to learn and what format of instruction is most appropriate. In this regard, we rely on assessments that are often implicit in good teacher practices. From experience, expert teachers know which concepts are essential to future learning yet difficult to understand, and they spend more time on those concepts. Teachers also assess how well a student is prepared to learn; for example, they determine whether the student has a solid grasp of calculus or if it is necessary to rely on other methods for describing physical phenomena. Assessments that emphasize future learning are very valuable.

It is important to assess students' preparedness for future learning because knowing that a student is unable to solve a problem can simply indicate that the student needs to learn, not that the student is prepared to learn. Moreover, many assessments can be misleading with respect to how well prepared a student is to learn. Standard assessments can yield evidence of understanding that looks good until students try to learn more about a domain. For example, we found that students who explored simple data sets from memory experiments did worse on a standard true-false assessment compared to students who studied and summarized a book chapter on the same memory experiments (Schwartz & Bransford, 1998). On the basis of this static knowledge assessment, one would suppose that the students who read the chapter were better off. However, when the students were evaluated with respect to how well they had been prepared to learn, the results reversed. After completing their initial learning activities and the true-false test, both groups listened to a theoretical lecture on memory. The students who had analyzed the data sets learned much more from the lecture. The data analysis activity had prepared them to understand a theoretical explanation at a deep level. On a subsequent transfer test, the data analysis students made twice as many correct answers as the read students. We know the data analysis students learned from the lecture because another group of data analysis students never heard the lecture and did quite poorly on the transfer test. In our dynamic assessments, opportunities for learning are an integral part of the assessment process and provide valuable information on student understanding and preparedness to learn.

In this chapter, we describe several computer tools designed to elicit information about learning preparedness. Both students and teachers can use these dynamic assessment tools to help assess learning needs. Some of the tools can also be used to help assess learning relevant characteristics of a knowledge domain. For example, we describe how we assess which misconceptions in the domain of electricity are often troublesome for future learning and which misconceptions are handled more easily. Our discussion of computer tools for dynamic assessment comes in four sections.

- A discussion of why it is important to develop dynamic assessments that can evaluate students' preparedness for learning.
- The use of dynamic assessment to evaluate misconceptions as they affect future learning, or as we call it, Assessing Domain Learnability.
- The description of a software shell, STAR.Legacy, that we used to assess the learnability of the basic concepts of electrical circuits.
- A description of difficulties college students have in introductory electricity courses and a pilot study that demonstrates the value of dynamic assessments for determining which difficulties impact learning most strongly.

DYNAMIC ASSESSMENT AND THE PREPARATION FOR FUTURE LEARNING

Many approaches to assessment take what we call a sequestered problem-solving format (Bransford & Schwartz, 1999). Students are required to solve problems in isolation without the benefit of the knowledge resources that are typically available outside the testing setting such as texts, tutorials, worked examples, experts, and other students. Sequestered problem solving is often used to provide some indication of an individual's ability to perform in a future setting. The Scholastic Aptitude Test is an example. These tests, however, can be misleading. Imagine two individuals who are applying for a job that requires troubleshooting electrical circuits. Individual A, who has been trained for the circuits that appear on the test, does reasonably well and receives 60% correct on a tough entry exam. Individual B, who has had no specific training, achieves only 20%. Even so, one might prefer to hire Individual B. For example, Individual B may have a better grasp of electricity principles or may have better skills for learning from manuals and other resources. Individual B may be better prepared to learn. After 2 months on the job, Individual B might get 80% on the test, whereas Individual A might improve to only 65%. Single-shot tests of sequestered problem solving are only proxies for determining whether an individual is on a productive learning trajectory. Ideally, we should be able to assess an individual's preparedness to learn in a domain more directly.

The dynamic assessment tradition (Bransford, Delclos, Vye, Burns, & Hasselbring, 1987; Campione & Brown, 1987; Cole & Griffin, 1987; Feurestein, 1979; Lidz, 1987; Vygostky, 1978) provides a way to measure learning potential directly. In a typical dynamic assessment, an individual receives an initial test, then instruction, and then a posttest. The degree and nature of the gains from pre- to posttest provide direct information about the individual's learning potential.

Dynamic assessments can also reveal information about instructional resources that are particularly effective for an individual. Identifying appropriate resources is important because it can change an individual's future learning. For example, individual A might have learned better on the job if the initial assessment had revealed what knowledge or resources needed strengthening. The assumption of dynamic assessment is that proper assessment and instructional resources can change the course of future learning. This approach does not imply that everyone can be brought to the same level of understanding or that the benefits of assessments done in one domain easily spill into others. It simply states that learning in a domain may be enhanced by assessments that look at the ability to learn in that domain and at instructional resources that affect that ability.

We can illustrate our perspective on dynamic assessment by discussing the hypothesis visualization software (HVS) developed with Chuck Czarnik. Recently, researchers have been using computers to help students and scientists visualize data (e.g., using colors overlaid on maps to represent weather measurements; Gordin & Pea, 1995). We have found that students are good at identifying patterns in visualized data, but not very good at tying these patterns to hypotheses the way scientists do. Therefore, we created HVS simulations. An HVS simulation includes a simulated catalogue of testing equipment and overlay maps that students "order" to help complete the simulation. Figure 10.1 shows the ordering page for the maps needed to complete a simulation on river pollution. The maps suggest hypotheses for why the data take the form they do, and they help to structure further inquiry. Consider an HVS simulation we designed to help students understand how a team of scientists documented the link between paint chips and lead poisoning in children. In the simulation, the students' goal is to identify the source of health problems in a community. Students begin with a basic street map of the community. During the course of the simulation, the map automatically updates dynamic data by placing icons as markers where individuals become sick with lead poisoning symptoms. To gather data on possible sources of the illnesses, students

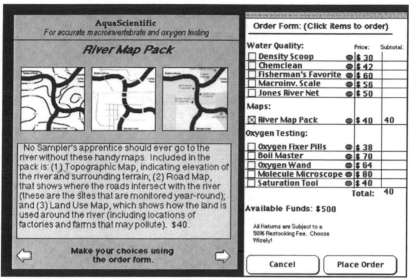

FIG. 10.1.

have a number of different tests that they can apply to the map. For example, if they use the lead testing tool to click at location X, a red or green lead symbol appears at X depending on the outcome of the test. Students cannot blindly test everywhere in the community because time is precious (children are getting sick). To help develop hypotheses about where to test and why, the students can overlay different maps—a topographic map, a map of local industries, a map showing the geographic distribution of wealth, and a map showing the average age of the houses. They can see where the data are located with respect to the regions of a map. For example, they may notice that a number of illnesses are occurring in a region of old houses, suggesting the hypothesis that housing age is causing the problem. They can evaluate this hypothesis by systematically testing for lead in neighborhoods of different ages.[1]

To tie HVS to the topic of dynamic assessment, consider what happens when students confront a map they do not fully understand; for example, a

---

[1] The opportunity to visualize hypotheses to guide data collection may have some benefits for scientific reasoning. A day after completing the lead testing simulation, middle-school students received a simple map showing two rivers feeding into a polluted lake. They were told that a scientist had proposed the hypothesis that river A is the source of the lake pollution. The students were asked to mark the location(s) they should test to evaluate the hypothesis. Of the 26 HVS students, 62% marked River B as well as River A. They were trying to falsify the scientist's hypothesis. In contrast, 24 control students took the same test and exhibited a confirmation bias. Only 36% of these students thought to test places that might falsify the hypothesis; most of them simply wanted to test River A.

topographic map. Imagine they believe that lead is flowing down a river in the community. To test the hypothesis, many middle school students choose to test a river location at the bottom of the map based on the misconception that the bottom of a map corresponds to "down." Many of these students are highly confident and do not feel the need for further learning or discussion. Other students who make wrong choices are more aware they do not know. Some, especially many older students who have been out of school for awhile, believe that they simply need to be reminded by some definitions about topographic maps; others request definitional help plus an example. Others participants cannot define the kinds of help they need in order to proceed.

Given these types of responses, we developed a tool to help students assess their preparedness for learning about a topic and to identify the most helpful types of learning events. The tool is organized around challenges like those of reading a topographic map. Users answer a question relevant to the challenge, rate their confidence, and then indicate whether they are ready to work with the original challenge or need to consult resources for solving this type of problem. If they answer correctly and confidently, they receive an additional problem. If they are again competent and confident, they can move on to the task at hand. More interesting are those who cannot initially solve the problem or have limited confidence in their answer. These participants receive feedback about their initial answers and have opportunities to access different resources to help their learning.

Depending on their self-assessment, students can access resources that vary in the prior knowledge and learning abilities they presume. The resources are accessed through a series of buttons: Definitions, Refresher Lecture, Worked out Example, Practice Problems, and Simulations. People who have the knowledge but have simply forgotten the facts may seek the help of a definition. Others may benefit from a brief lecture or text. Those who have little familiarity with the domain may select from various levels of more extended help, ranging from worked-out examples to dynamic visual events showing the flow of water. Students select their learning resources and decide for themselves when they are ready to solve another problem.

Over time, participants should require less and less assistance to complete a class of problems, like reading a topographic map. But one can imagine situations where students do not improve. They may have excessive confidence that prevents them from accessing the learning resources, students may have little experience assessing their knowledge or simply not be prepared to learn from the resource they have chosen (perhaps they choose a dictionary when they need a tutorial). Ideally, the computer tool could include an intelligent component that dynamically assesses these situations by noticing a lack of learning over time. The program would respond by taking the student to appropriate resources.

The prototype tool highlights our major commitments to dynamic assessments. Dynamic assessments involve the evaluation of learning potential in a specific domain. The assessments ideally rely on evaluating learning over time. The information gained from a dynamic assessment should help determine the most appropriate types of instruction. Sometimes hands-on activities are most appropriate, but sometimes listening quietly to a lecture can be very effective depending on an individual's preparedness to learn (Schwartz & Bransford, 1998). We believe these types of tools generate interesting information for teachers and students. Teachers who focus solely on teaching to the test may find that students have difficulty assessing their own knowledge and determining their own paths of learning. Students should learn about themselves as learners, and they should begin to differentiate cases where they need simple reminders from ones where they need opportunities for in-depth exploration. Overall, we believe that shifting away from assessments of one-shot problem-solving performance to assessments of preparedness for learning may have a profound effect on people's abilities to improve and learn (Bransford & Schwartz, 1999).

ASSESSING DOMAIN LEARNABILITY WITH DYNAMIC ASSESSMENT

Dynamic assessments typically are used to evaluate the learning profile of individuals. Individual learning abilities and knowledge states are one element of the learning story. Another important element is the profile of the domain under consideration. Some topics are more difficult to learn than others. Children spontaneously learn to add 3 and 5 by starting with the larger number 5 and counting up 6, 7, and 8 (Groen & Resnick, 1977). Yet surprisingly few adults learn that when they drop a ball from a moving car, the ball falls in a curved trajectory (McCloskey, 1983). There are many reasons why it is difficult to learn some topics. In the following sections, we explore whether dynamic assessment can be extended to develop a learning profile for a domain. Ideally, we will be able to identify features and concepts of a domain that influence its learnability, which may help us to select appropriate resources to facilitate learning. We call this task assessing domain learnability (ADL).

A large misconception literature tells us that people have certain failings, but it rarely explains how difficult it would be to correct those failings, whether different failings require different types of instruction, or how important it is to correct those failings for future learning. For example, although we have rarely seen it in the literature (Cooke & Breedin, 1994), it would be interesting to ask people to compare their confidence for answers that exhibit misconceptions relative to those that do not. We suspect that for many of the misconceptions that have been documented, people are reasonably aware that they do not know what they are talking about. For those misconceptions that are of low confidence, should we expect people to be more likely to overcome their misconceptions and learn? Can we expect them to make a reasonable estimate of how much or what type of instruction it would take for them to learn the concept to a satisfactory level? To find out these types of information, it seems appropriate to take a dynamic assessment approach: teach people to see whether and when they overcome their misconceptions and whether this learning affects their subsequent abilities to learn. By trying to remediate misconceptions, we may determine which are particularly difficult to remediate given our methods of instruction (Heller & Finley, 1992) and which understandings have the greatest impact on subsequent learning. This is the goal of ADL.

STAR.LEGACY
IN THE DOMAIN
OF ELECTRICAL CIRCUITS

The quality of ADL depends on the instructional techniques used to teach about the domain of interest. If the techniques are too narrow, it is hard to determine whether the difficulty comes from the instruction or the domain and what type of instruction is most valuable for overcoming a difficulty. A computer can be helpful; it can provide an integrated learning assessment environment for pulling together different assessments, instructional techniques, and resources. In this section, we describe a computer tool, STAR.Legacy, that was originally designed to join and organize assessment and instructional resources into an inquiry cycle (for more thorough description, see Schwartz, Brophy, Lin, & Bransford, 1999; Schwartz, Lin, Brophy, & Bransford, 1999).

Overview of the STAR.Legacy Software

STAR.Legacy is meant to serve as both a model of instructional design and a design for creating model instruction. It is an easily authored, multimedia software shell that supports development and research on complex sequences of instruction that require students to act on and evaluate their understanding. (The prefix STAR stands for Software Technology for Action and Reflection.) STAR.Legacy has grown from collaborations with teachers, trainers, students, curriculum designers, psychologists, and computer scientists. Its structure helps people organize their thinking about learning, whether they are students learning from a STAR.Legacy or teachers incorporating instructional resources into the Legacy shell. STAR.Legacy has a number of programming features for adding digitized video, audio, pictures, and text, as well as for launching to and downloading from the Web and branching to simulation programs and other types of software. These features allow designers and teachers to create or repurpose units of instruction, and it enables students to add their own "Legacy" that future students may consult. In an educational psychology course, for example, students left multimedia essays that taught the next year's cohort about important concepts (Schwartz, Brophy, et al., 1999). The prospect of leaving a Legacy can be very motivating to students, and it can help a Legacy grow and adapt to the interests and resources of the local community. STAR.Legacy is currently being used by professors in college courses ranging from audiology to psychology to business, by middle school teachers who are creating new curricula for their school district, and by instructional designers at the Learning Technology Center at Vanderbilt.

The main STAR.Legacy interface (see Fig. 10.2) is an inquiry cycle where each of the icons reflects an often implicit, yet important component of most learning events. We have organized the components into this interface because it is worthwhile for students, teachers, and instructional designers to see where they are in a complex sequence of learning events (Barron et al., 1998). The interface is a learning map that helps them understand where they should be in their knowledge development, and it helps them see that there are typical activities involved in learning, like first tries and revisions. For each STAR.Legacy inquiry cycle, students receive a challenge that creates a need to know. To meet the challenge, students move through the inquiry cycle using a variety of resources that help them develop, assess, and revise their understanding. The inquiry cycle is not meant to imply that STAR.Legacy is a rigid sequential environment that lock-steps the learner and designer. STAR.Legacy is intended as a flexibly structured tool that helps people organize and adapt instruction to their specific content and context. We expect users to navigate through the system depending on their learning needs. They may, for example, go backward in the cycle if they feel the need to review previous components, and they may choose to complete some activities and not others, depending on their knowledge state. To help people determine their learning needs, we have included multiple opportunities for assessment. This is one of the reasons that STAR.Legacy is appropriate for dynamic assessment. It integrates assessment and instruction into a single design model.

DC.Legacy

We designed a specific STAR.Legacy, DC.Legacy, to help assess domain learnability for electricity. We have chosen the domain of electricity because it is notoriously difficult to learn. Research has uncovered a variety of misconceptions. Beginners, for example, often believe that it is only necessary to hook one point of a light bulb to a circuit (Fredette & Lochhead, 1980). Evidently they think of the light bulb as a "sink" into which "energy" flows. More advanced students often exhibit an attenuation model, where current weakens or reduces in "volume" as it moves

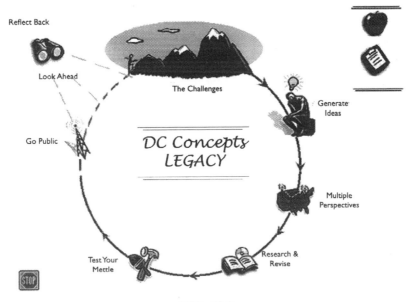

FIG. 10.2.

from one load (e.g., a light bulb) to another (Shipstone, 1988). In our own protocol work with college students, field experts, electrical engineers, and military trainees, we found these difficulties as well as others. We did not evaluate the implications of these difficulties with respect to learning. To avoid contaminating our results, we did not try to teach the students. When they exhibited misunderstandings, we simply probed further. As a result, we developed some idea of student difficulties but not an understanding for how strong these difficulties were or how to remediate them. DC.Legacy captures our movement toward an ADL approach. It includes multiple resources for trying to help students learn. DC.Legacy was not designed for students to complete on their own (although they could). Instead, it supplements a structured interview format where interviewers do their best to figure out and remediate a student's difficulties. The following sections briefly describe DC.Legacy. They are organized around the icons that represent the inquiry cycle of STAR.Legacy.

Look Ahead & Reflect Back. The Look Ahead & Reflect Back icon presents the starting and ending point of any Legacy. In line with the test-teach-retest model of dynamic assessment, students begin with a question in the Look Ahead and end with the same question when they Reflect Back after completing multiple inquiry cycles. For DC.Legacy, the question asks students to explain what happens in a simple flashlight circuit when a 5-watt bulb is replaced by a 10-watt bulb (that is, what causes the 10-watt bulb to burn more brightly and what changes occur throughout the circuit). The Look Ahead question provides the students with a view of the things they will learn about and a preassessment by revealing their abilities to notice and evaluate various aspects of the Look Ahead example. This information can help the teacher make instructional decisions and help students develop an appreciation for what they have learned when they return to the same problem when they Reflect Back. Students can recognize their learning gains (Schwartz, Brophy, et al., 1999) and reflect on the learning process (Bransford & Stein, 1993). The chance to see knowledge gains can be very valuable, especially for students who do not believe they are good learners.

Successive Challenges for Progressive Deepening. After completing the Look Ahead, students begin an inquiry cycle by clicking on one of the mountains, each representing a challenge that students need to solve. Figure 10.3 shows the challenge students receive if they click on the smallest mountain in DC.Legacy. To solve a challenge, students complete the

The Challenge

Relating Voltage, Current, Resistance, & Power

Tips

Help

Notebook

- There is a special lamp that cannot be exposed to the air for very long.

- Someone has reported that the bulb seems dim.

- You will have just a few moments to find out whether something is wrong, and if so, where the problem is.

- **How will you prepare and what will you do when you open the lamp?**

How Will You Find Out What is Wrong?

FIG. 10.3.

inquiry cycle shown in Fig. 10.2. By completing successive challenges (represented by taller mountains) and their associated inquiry cycles, students progressively deepen their understanding of a topic (Barron et al., 1998).

A Legacy challenge can take many forms, ranging from solving a video-based mathematics problem like an Adventure of Jasper Woodbury (CTGV, 1997) to preparing an oral report on infant learning. In any form, a challenge should create a mental model of a problem solving context. When knowledge is learned in the context of solving a problem, it is more likely to be useful for subsequent problem solving and less likely to remain inert (Bransford, Franks, Vye, & Sherwood, 1989).

The three Challenges of DC.Legacy were chosen on the basis of our protocol research. We found three problem situations that were particularly good at making students' thinking visible. Challenge 1 asks students to reason about the possible causes of a dim bulb. This problem is intended to emphasize Ohm's law; to help students differentiate voltage and current; to help them understand that changes in power imply two changes among current, voltage and resistance; and to give them some increased experience in the domain and its analogies. After students complete the inquiry cycle for Challenge 1, they move to Challenge 2: to design a battery-operated drill that can run at different speeds. Students must explain how connecting resistors, batteries, and fuses in series and in parallel can change the motor's RPM. In this design problem, students progressively deepen their understanding of the topics raised by Challenge 1 while adding the issues of local versus global analysis and of Kirchoff's laws. Finally, Challenge 3 brings the lessons together into a single problem. In this challenge, students reason about a flashlight that has two bulbs: one that points forward and one that points to the ground. They hear that somebody wants to change the forward bulb to a higher wattage. How will that affect the flashlight overall?

These challenges were intended to bring forward specific classes of misconceptions. At the same time, we expected the interaction of the challenges and instruction to reveal other conceptual hot spots we had not anticipated. In the following, we describe movement through Challenge 1 of DC.Legacy. Challenges 2 and 3 are structured in a similar manner, though the specific content differs.

Generate Ideas.   After reading Challenge 1, students click on the Generate Ideas icon, which takes them to the Generate Ideas page and opens Legacy's electronic notebook. They enter their initial ideas about how to prepare for testing the dim light bulb. (In a classroom setting, a teacher or student may compile ideas into a central notebook as a shared resource.) Explicitly generating and recording ideas helps students clarify their own thoughts in preparation for learning. Later, they revise and complement those initial ideas based on resources gathered throughout the Legacy. For DC.Legacy, the ideas generated in this phase of the inquiry cycle provide the interviewer with a sense of the strengths and weaknesses of the students. This helps the interviewer and student choose which of the perspectives to listen to in the next component of the inquiry cycle.

Multiple Perspectives.   After the generation phase, students are prepared to listen to Multiple Perspectives on the challenge. Typically, we use experts to provide perspectives on a challenge. There are many learning situations where multiple expert perspectives are a natural component of instruction (e.g., a conference panel). Multiple perspectives serve a number of purposes. For one, they guide students to different problem spaces or vantage points for understanding a situation (Spiro & Jehng, 1990). For another, they usually provide a contrast to the ideas the students originally generated. When the students hear experts notice aspects of a challenge they failed to generate, it helps the students "hear" what the expert has to say rather than simply glossing over it (Schwartz & Bransford, 1998).

The perspectives for Challenge 1 of DC.Legacy directly target key learning difficulties with brief videotapes of four experts. One of the experts explains that "a common mistake that people make with these problems is that they often do not realize that when the power changes, two other things in the circuit must change." Another ties the perceptual phenomena (a dim bulb) to electrical concepts by pointing out that a dim bulb means less power is being consumed. A third prepares students to differentiate voltage and current by discussing the value of using an ammeter and voltmeter rather than simply swapping components in the circuit. And a fourth, who assumes the students have learned a water analogy, tries to help students map voltage and current into the water domain.

When students listen to the perspectives, they are expected to explain whether they understand what the experts have said. This provides the interviewer with valuable knowledge about which aspects of the domain students may have trouble with. For example, some students do not know that "two things must change," whereas others may not know how to draw the analogy between water and electricity. This becomes important when the interview proceeds to Research & Revise. The student and interviewer choose which resources to work with depending on the specific knowledge gaps.

Research & Revise.   After hearing the Multiple Perspectives and gathering ideas about what they need to learn, students Research & Revise their original ideas. Depending on the students' knowledge state, interviewers can move between resources and perspectives to help probe and explain a concept. The Research & Revise component of STAR.Legacy tries to draw together many different instructional techniques, ranging from drill-and-practice to lectures to intelligent computer simulations.

Figure 10.4 shows the resources available for Challenge 1. A chalk talk on Ohm's law explains why two things (current and resistance) must change if the power changes. Another resource is a brief presentation of a mnemonic that helps students memorize that current is a "through" property, whereas voltage is an "across" property. There are multiple choice problems that allow students to practice using Ohm's law. These problems include automated feedback that states the qualitative implications of an incorrect answer. For example, one feedback comment reads, "Your answer implies that increasing the voltage across the circuit decreases current. For example, if we used a more powerful battery, the current in the flashlight circuit would decrease. Does that make sense?" This form of feedback helps students think about qualitative relationships as opposed to simply applying algebraic manipulations.

The computer environment allows us to bring together many resources that would be unwieldy to organize in other media. For example, the resource page includes connections to web sites that we have found helpful, to Legacies left by students who have completed the process and offer their thoughts about key insights that helped their learning, and to simulations and hands-on activities that others have developed (Parchman, 1997). The resource page also includes cognitive tools that are uniquely possible in a computer environment. One of the more powerful tools with potential for dynamic assessment is the interactive analogy resource (Brophy & Schwartz, 1998). Interactive analogies are pairs of parallel simulations from distinct domains. Figure 10.5 shows a water simulation of a brick thrower and an electricity simulation of a light bulb circuit. Students explore how measures of current and flow, voltage and pressure can be related and how different changes, like reducing the height of the water source or decreasing the number of batteries, affect voltage and current, and therefore power delivery. These simulations are not yoked. Students

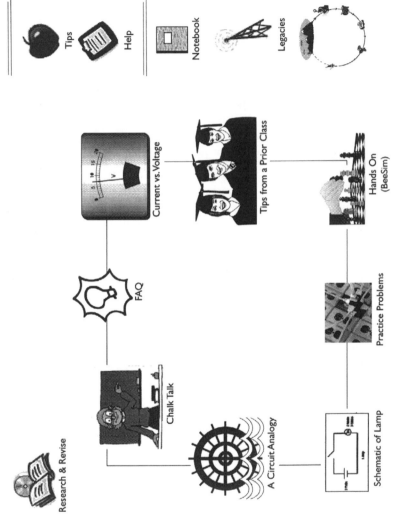

FIG. 10.4.

interact with each simulation independently as they try to map the correspondences and achieve analogous outcomes in each simulation.

Analogies often play a large role in electricity instruction, perhaps because the domain is largely invisible. In a review of beginning texts on electricity, Stocklmayer and Treagust (1994) found that nearly all texts used some form of a water analogy to explain current. In its own right, this analogy approach is not problematic in that there are proper mappings between liquid flow and current, and pressure and voltage. However, instruction often relies on analogies that can become a disservice to future understanding (Gentner & Gentner, 1983). Liquid flow is a complex domain in its own right, and analogies are rarely sufficiently developed. For example, most of the textbooks we reviewed contained water analogies that led students to infer incorrectly that current is used up (siphoned off) as it flows through a bulb.

Interactive analogies provide a complementary use of analogies and simulations; the weaknesses of one approach are handled by the strengths of the other. For example, simulations do not always provide a causal model the students understand; consequently students may flounder in trial-and-error investigations. Analogies are useful in this regard because they allow students to draw on prior knowledge from a structurally related domain. Analogies by themselves do not provide feedback that helps students progressively map structures between the two domains. Simulations provide useful feedback that allows students to test out possible relations and implications.

The interactive analogies appear to be powerful vehicles for assessing and developing understanding. As students predict and explain parallel behaviors in the two domains, they readily see where they are in their understanding. This self-assessment helps guide their inquiry of the simulation and the questions they ask of an instructor. For example, seeing the water pouring into the tank and looking at the negative lead of the batteries led some students to realize that they did not fully understand the concept of ground. To the students, the water simulation exhibited ground because the water flowed into the tank, but the electrical simulation did not because the current moved from positive to negative, not to "ground." This led to fruitful discussions about reference values and how the notions of voltage and pressure were relative. One student, for example, began to explore the idea that if the whole water system were raised or lowered, the effective pressure would still be the same, but if only the tank were raised, it would increase the pressure.

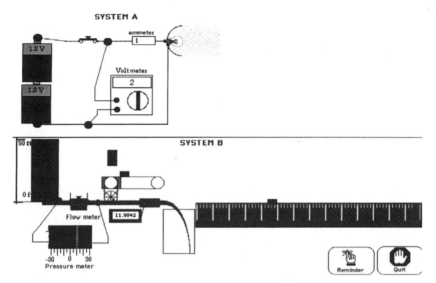

FIG. 10.5.

Test Your Mettle and Go Public. Once the students and interviewer feel that they have made satisfactory learning progress, students move to Test Your Mettle to assess the depth of their understanding. For DC.Legacy we included two questions that require students to differentiate and relate voltage, current, resistance, and power. For one question, students see a graph of voltage decreasing over time, and they generate and justify graphs for the current, resistance, and power. For the second question, students explain whether a light bulb has a resistor and justify their answer in terms of observable outcomes. We have been exploring a variety of more automated dynamic assessments for Test Your Mettle. A good example comes from a set of Wold Wide Web tools that sixth-grade students use to assess their understanding of river pollution and ecology (Vye et al., 1998). In one Test Your Mettle, students evaluate their knowledge about monitoring a river. The students "order" from a Web-based catalogue that includes a number of different tools designed to help collect macroinvertebrates, an indicator species for pollution. The students' task is to select and justify a tool, and to explain why they reject other tools. We have designed the catalogue entries so that some of the tools are bogus and reflect aspects of macroinvertebrate testing that students often do not understand. Figure 10.6 provides an example of one catalogue entry. In this example, the students have chosen the Meyer Crayfish Trap because

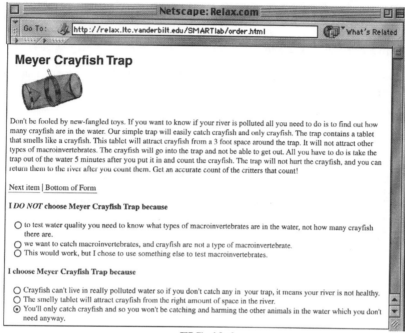

FIG. 10.6.

they do not want to hurt any of the other types of macroinvertebrates. After submitting this and other responses on the Web, the students receive feedback for each choice. Figure 10.7 shows how the feedback tries to explain where the student went wrong, and it provides guidance to helpful resources. The feedback prepares students to learn when they return to Research & Revise. After Research & Revise, the students return to the catalogues to see how well they have learned.

Test Your Mettle is meant as a formative instructional event, not a final exam. It is a chance for students to bump up against the world to see if their knowledge is up to the task. If it is not, they can return to the resources to revise their understanding. Typically Test Your Mettle is designed with specific rubrics so students can determine what type of resource would enrich their understanding. Once students pass through the gate of Test Your Mettle, they can Go Public with their work. This is intended to be a summative event in which students "officially" deliver their solution to a challenge answer for review. Public forums such as publishing to the Web or presenting to an outside audience add a high-stakes component that motivates students to do well. After presenting their work,

---

First Submission

14:53 Fri Feb 20, 1998

Please use the **Print** button on the Netscape Toolbar or **Print** under the **File** menu to print out this page. After printing, please click here for the next user to start.

1. Meyer Crayfish Trap Confirmation: You have selected Meyer Crayfish Trap. Your justification was "Won't harm unnecessary animals"

Feedback: It is good that you do not want to harm the other animals in the water, but scientists who want to test water do not try to collect just one type of macroinvertebrate from the river. So even though the Meyer Crayfish Trap might help you find out how many crayfish you have, this is not the information you need to test the quality of the water. Read the section, Using Macroinvertebrates to Test Water Quality in your Stones River Resources to learn more about macroinvertebrates and about water quality testing. Or ask someone in your class what they think.

FIG. 10.7.

students move to the next challenge. If they have completed all challenges, they return to Look Ahead & Reflect Back to evaluate what they have learned.

A Comment on Authorability

STAR.Legacy has been designed to be a flexible software shell for designing and delivering inquiry-based instruction. It includes a visual interface that presents a user-friendly theory of assessment and instruction. It includes a small set of tools, shown in Fig. 10.8, for building, adapting, or adding material to any program, including the Legacy a student might leave. This same tool set is used to add content to any screen of STAR.Legacy. There is a single tool palette, shown in the upper-right corner of Fig. 10.8, that allows people to add "action objects" and determine their look (a picture, a text field, a drawing, or a sequenced list of other action objects). The dialog window in Fig. 10.8 shows the list of actions available for an object: playing a movie, playing a sound file, or launching to additional resources. Each action has its own set of properties that control specific execution. The launch action, for example, can be instantiated in three ways, as shown in the edit window of the dialog box (i.e., launch to an external program like a simulation, launch to a Web browser, or create and launch to a new card within STAR.Legacy). We have found the small set of looks, actions, and action properties to be very accessible and

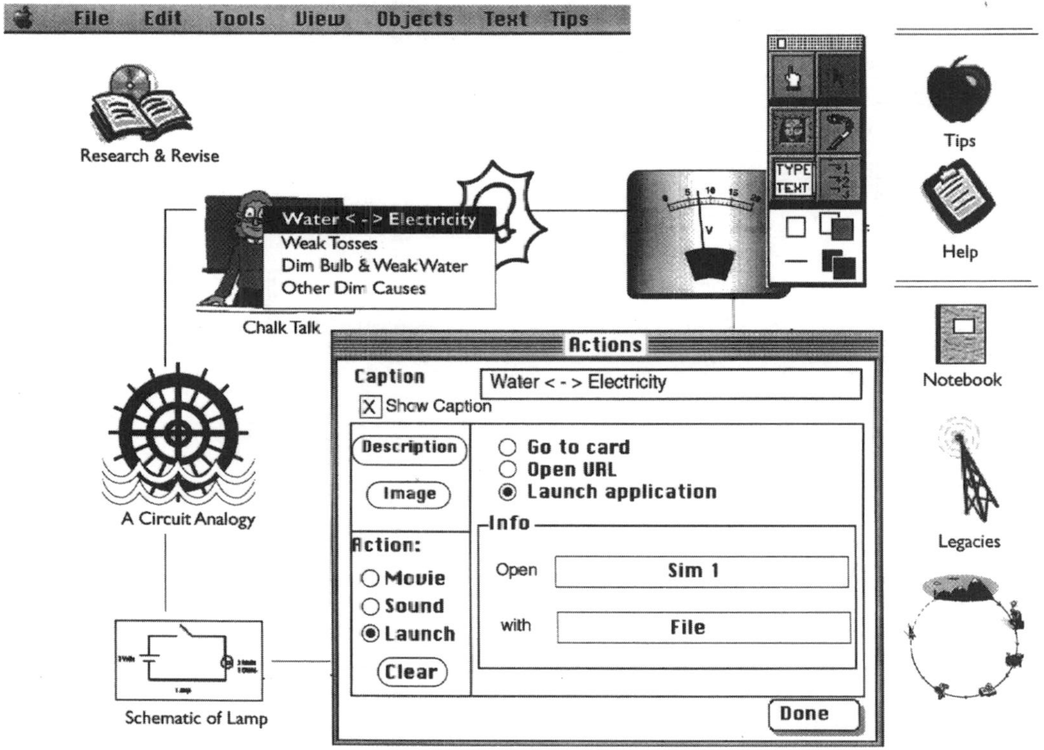
File Edit Tools View Objects Text Tips
Research & Revise
Water < - > Electricity
Weak Tosses
Dim Bulb & Weak Water
Other Dim Causes
Chalk Talk
A Circuit Analogy
Schematic of Lamp
Actions
Caption
Water < - > Electricity
Show Caption
Description
Image
Go to card
Open URL
Launch application
Info
Open
Sim 1
with
File
Action:
Movie
Sound
Launch
Clear
Done
TYPE TEXT
Tips
Help
Notebook
Legacies

FIG. 10.8.

easy to learn. Presumably, reducing the learning and programming over-head will lead more people to use STAR.Legacy and to focus on pedagogical content (Murray, 1998), and this will increase our opportunities for evaluating the integration of instruction and assessment.

A PILOT ASSESSMENT
OF DC.LEGACY AND ADL

We describe a pilot study that used DC.Legacy to explore which aspects of DC circuits are particularly hard to understand and what types of instructional resources are useful. To understand the study, it is useful to review the difficulties that we targeted with DC.Legacy. In our research on people's understanding of electricity, we have found that "knowledge is in pieces" (diSessa, 1993). There is not a single underlying theory or cognitive limitation that leads to poor understanding. Whereas people may be inclined to be naive physicists in the domain of mechanical and fluid systems (Halloun & Hestenes, 1985), they show less inclination to be naive electrical engineers. People have misconceptions, they are missing other conceptions, they know very few empirical facts, and they are simply overwhelmed by the complexity of the domain. To help communicate the nature of understanding, we describe five classes of problems that surfaced repeatedly in our protocol research. Our posttest targeted these five classes of difficulties, so it is necessary to understand them in some detail to make sense of the results.

Classes of Difficulties that Affect Learning

We organize difficulties in understanding DC circuits according to the underlying psychological phenomena that make them particularly troublesome aspects of electricity and that may have implications for the types of instruction that would be most effective.

Failure to Differentiate.   Beginners often fail to differentiate key elements of a domain (Bransford & Nitsch, 1978). In physics, for example, children do not understand the difference between density and weight (Smith, Snir, & Grosslight, 1992), and adults often conflate the notions of force, velocity, and momentum (McCloskey, 1983). In electricity, our research indicates that beginners often do not differentiate voltage from current. For example, students incorrectly state, "The voltage flows through the light bulb." Consequently, beginners often believe that if they were to measure voltage across an (idealized) open switch, the reading would be zero, but when the switch is closed, the reading would be high. This is exactly backward. The current is zero when the switch is open because it cannot flow, but the voltage drop is high. And when the switch is closed, the current is high because it can flow, but the voltage drop is zero because there is no resistance to create a potential difference between the two sides of the switch.

Incorrect Simplifying Assumptions. People often inadvertently over-simplify concepts to reduce cognitive complexity. In electricity, people make what we call, the minimum causality error. They assume that if there is a single change in outcome, there is a single change in cause (White, Frederiksen, & Spoehr, 1993). An example comes from the question of what happens to a simple flashlight circuit when a 5-watt light bulb is replaced with a 10-watt light bulb. Most people know that there will be more power consumed (light given off) by the 10-watt bulb. However, they usually assume that only one thing in the circuit has changed. For example, some people believe that the 10-watt bulb has a higher resist-ance, and this causes more "friction" (heat generation), which in turn pro-duces more light. Even college students who use Ohm's law make the mistake of thinking that only one element of a circuit changes when switching to a 10 watt bulb. They use the power equation: power equals voltage times current ($P = VI$). They infer that because P increased, the I or V must have increased. Students stop there and state that current has increased (since it is the same voltage source). They do not consider the second applicable equation: voltage equals current times resistance ($V = IR$). By this equation, if current increases and voltage stays the same, resistance must go down. The reason a 10-watt bulb is brighter than a 5-watt bulb is that it has a lower resistance which increases the current.

Overly Local Reasoning. People tend to reason about the local prop-agation of effects through a circuit, and consequently, they lose the global structure of behavior. They often think about the movement of current from point to point, and this leads them to believe that current moves sequentially through the system. For example, imagine that there is a sim-ple battery and motor circuit. Does it matter where the fuse is inserted into the circuit? Should it be placed before the incoming lead of the motor or after the outgoing lead? Many people believe that the fuse cannot be after the outgoing motor lead because the current will have already done the damage to the motor by the time it reaches the fuse. This is incorrect. Current is constant throughout the system. It is like a train that already fills the tracks. When the train begins to move, all the cars move together. Thus, a spike in the current will hit the complete circuit simultaneously; it will not move from one point to another over time as though it were a pulse or clot moving through a system. Erroneous local reasoning may have a variety of sources. People reason in sequential fashion as they trace the effect of electricity in the system. They may inadvertently map the structure of their reasoning onto the structure of the phenomenon at hand. Another contributing factor is probably the incomplete water analogy that people learn in school. The analogy is not sufficiently developed, and people may assume that the analogy is about water filling a pipe rather than about water being moved around an already filled pipe.

Bad Framing. People incorrectly generalize basic qualitative knowledge and end up framing the domain in a suboptimal manner (diSessa, 1993). We found in our investigations that field experts and electrical engineering experts do not usually have a single canonical understanding of electricity. They switch from mathematical explanations, to physics explanations, to well-known facts, to analogical models (Biswas et al., 1997). No doubt these explanations can be mapped onto one another, but the experts in our research often discover the mappings only during our interviews. Even so, they were excellent at knowing which type of explanation or model was likely to frame the problem most productively for the task at hand. Novices need to rely on framing as well, and they often frame a problem in the wrong way (Chi, Feltovich, & Glaser, 1981). An example comes from the topic of parallel resistor configurations. People have trouble understanding that two parallel resistors yield more current flow than a single resistor. Different framings may cause this problem. Gentner and Gentner (1983) show that framing the situation in terms of water flow causes problems and suggest framing it in terms of crowds passing through gates. In our work, we have found that people frame the problem as, "How can more resistors increase current? Resistors restrict current!"

A different way to frame the problem is to emphasize that a second resistor in parallel introduces a second current path. Unless the resistor has infinite resistance, the new path is going to increase the amount of current flow. The ADL question is how hard will it be to help people learn to frame electrical problems like this in a productive manner. Although the switch from an emphasis on resistors to an emphasis on paths seems simple enough, people's framings often inadvertently interact with other classes of misconception. Gentner and Gentner (1983), for example, observe that thinking of current as a crowd pushing through the gates of parallel resistors is helpful. Yet this framing may interact with people's tendency towards local reasoning. They may think of the crowds as piling up on one side of the resistors but not the other. This is a misconception in that current (the crowd) is constant throughout this circuit.

Experiential Impoverishment.   Electricity is invisible except for its end products. Consequently, people cannot rely on perception to structure their understanding. On the one hand, this may enhance domain learnability because it means that there is not a mass of perceptual intuition that needs to be overcome, as might be the case in mechanics problem solving. On the other hand, it may explain why people are so dependent on analogies, often incomplete, for understanding the domain. They do not have much perceptual experience with the basic ontology of electricity.

These five classes of difficulty—lack of differentiation, simplifying assumptions, local reasoning, bad framing, and experiential impoverishment—result from the interaction of cognitive tendencies and the domain of electricity. The question is how serious the difficulties are with respect to learning electricity. Some of the difficulties may be easily remediated with appropriate instruction, some may not. The goal of DC.Legacy is to determine which of these difficulties make the domain particularly difficult to learn and which concepts are particularly important for further understanding in the domain.

Methods

We recruited 16 undergraduates at the end of a beginning circuits course taught in the Electrical Engineering Department at Vanderbilt University. The course covered the basic DC concepts associated with resistive circuits including voltage, current, resistance, power, the laws of Ohm and Kirchoff that define the relations between these parameters, and the analysis of parallel and series circuit configurations. Half of the students completed the DC.Legacy, and half were control students. The Legacy students individually completed the dynamic assessment with an interviewer and DC.Legacy. To ensure that effects were not due to the interviewer, there were four different interviewers. The interviewers worked with two students each, one at a time. The interviewers helped the students identify and remediate their conceptual weaknesses using DC.Legacy. Because of the

TABLE 10.1. *Abbreviated Versions of Posttest Questions*

1. There is a simple circuit with a heater attached to a battery. You replace the heater with a new one that gives off more warmth. Please explain whether each of the following changes or does not change in the circuit, and explain why each does or does not change: Voltage, current, resistance, and power.

2. Sam put a fuse in a circuit to protect a lamp. It was between the negative lead and the lamp. Johnny believes the fuse is in the wrong place. He thinks it needs to be between the positive lead and the lamp. Explain what you would tell Johnny and Sam.

3. Sally explained about her DC circuit with a light bulb, "As the voltage flows around a circuit, it becomes weaker." This is not the right way for Sally to talk about this. What is the right way?

4. Five identical light bulbs are connected in a series configuration. When a DC voltage is applied to them, do they all light up at the same time? Do they all burn with the same brightness at all times? Would your answer change if an AC voltage were applied?

5. Consider a light bulb circuit with a light bulb connected to DC source. Tom adds a 3-ohm resistor to this circuit. This dims the light bulb. His curious kid brother Sam comes along and takes the circuit apart. While putting it back, he adds a second 3-ohm resistor in parallel to the first. Do you think this will make the light bulb in Sam's circuit brighter, dimmer, or the same as Tom's? Explain.

6. Without changing the voltage, a flashlight system was redesigned so that the light bulb consumes 10 watts of power instead of 7.5 watts of power. Which of the following is true?
   (a) Current and resistance both must have changed.
   (b) Only the resistance must have changed.
   (c) Only the current must have changed.

7. John is checking out a circuit in which a 120V AC source is connected to a heating appliance. He measures the current in the circuit to be 2 amps. Tom, who has been observing John, says, "Hey! Just a moment, buddy! AC current and voltage are sinusoidal. Unless you measure the voltage and current exactly at the heating element, you will not be computing the right resistance and current. You better retake the measurements." John does as Tom says. What do you think the measured values of voltage and current are in the second case? Explain your answer.

8. There is a simple AC circuit with a heater. Point A is on the left of the heater, point B is on the right of the heater, and C is to the right B. Draw the current waveforms at points A, B, and C.

individualization, not all students completed the same resources or spent the same amount of time per challenge. Moreover, interview sessions were limited to a maximum of 1 ½ hours. Therefore, the study administered a weak dosage of ADL to the students.

After completing the interview, the Legacy students took a 30- to 60-minute posttest. Ideally, we would have used a pretest–posttest format in the spirit of dynamic assessment. At the late point in the semester, however, we did not want to burden the students with nearly 2 hours of testing and only 1 hour of instruction. Therefore, we used control students as a proxy for what the Legacy students' baseline performances would have been like. The control students simply completed the posttest.

The posttest was composed of eight key questions that targeted four of the difficulties we have described. Table 10.1 provides an abbreviated version of the questions. The questions were designed to provide overlapping coverage of students' abilities to reason about the fact that two components of a circuit change at the same time (incorrect simplifying assumptions, Questions 1 and 6), to differentiate voltage and current (lack of differentiation; Questions 1 and 3), to reason about simultaneous changes in the circuit (local reasoning; Questions 2 and 4), and to reason about parallel resistors (bad framing; Question 5). We also included three questions about AC circuits to see whether the DC.Legacy had any effects on students' initial conceptions about AC (local reasoning; Questions 4, 7, and 8). Ideally, we would have tested whether the Legacy students could learn AC concepts better. This, however, would require a much larger experiment. In the meantime, we provided a few questions that we thought the students might be able to answer given their modest classroom exposure to the sinusoidal waveforms of AC voltage and current.

Results

Even for this modest intervention, the results were informative. We begin with the concepts that both the control and Legacy group appeared to understand. (There were no questions for which the control group more frequently exhibited understanding than the Legacy group.) This can tell us which concepts the students understood within the context of their regular course. (These results, of course, may not generalize to other students taking other courses.)

Students in both conditions differentiated voltage and current reasonably well. Only one student in the Legacy condition and two in the control condition stated, "As voltage flows" (Voltage does not flow; current flows.) Most students had learned that voltage provides a difference in potential energy that drives the current around the circuit. The students in both conditions also understood that parallel resistors yield less resistance than a single resistor. One student who had not covered the topic in Legacy and two students in the control condition thought that the two resistors would increase resistance. An interesting difference between the conditions was that all eight control students computed the answer using the mathematical equations they had derived in class using Kirchoff's laws, whereas Legacy students explained the increase of current in more qualitative terms (e.g., "Twice as much current will flow through the paths"). In either case, the results suggest that these students did not have trouble framing the parallel resistors and that they had learned to differentiate voltage and current.

The control students did have trouble with local reasoning and a lack of perceptual experience. Seven of the eight control students thought that the position of a fuse made a difference, and five thought that bulbs in series light one after another. Moreover, only half of the control students understood that bulbs of equal wattage in series will be equally bright. This conforms to much prior research showing that people do not understand that current is the same at all points in a series circuit. The dynamic assessment of the Legacy condition, however, showed that this misconception is not too difficult to overcome. Only one of the Legacy students thought that it mattered where one put a fuse, none thought that the bulbs would light at different times, and only one thought they would have different brightness. Moreover, the remediation that improved the Legacy students' performance on DC questions transferred to the AC questions. Students in the control condition incorrectly generalized their "filling pipe" and "using up current" models to the AC questions, whereas the Legacy students did not. Students in the Legacy condition transferred their understanding of constant current to their graphs of AC current. Six of the Legacy students created a single waveform to represent the current at all points in the series circuit, whereas six of the control students indicated that different parts of their waveform referred to different points in the circuit. Whether other questions would trip up the Legacy students and whether this new understanding would facilitate their learning of AC remains an open question.

The dynamic assessment easily helped students appreciate the constancy of current. It was not as effective at overcoming the simplifying assumption of minimum causality. We can get a sense of the basic conceptual challenge by reviewing the control students. Seven of the eight students thought that power consumption increases because the resistance of a heating element or a bulb filament increases. This is exactly backward. This confusion may derive from the faulty analogy that more friction (a resistance) generates more heat. Although many of these students relied on $V = IR$ to reason about the problem, they did not work through the causal relations implied by the complementary law, $P = VI$. Thus, they made the minimum causality error of assuming that only one thing changed (resistance). Current and resistance change together in this situation.

The Legacy students were explicitly taught about the interacting equations of $P = VI$ and $V = IR$. Moreover, they explored the idea that a higher-wattage bulb pulls more power from a constant voltage source because it has a lower resistance and therefore draws more current. Even so, their learning was not as great as one might hope for. Three of the students thought that the higher wattage heater had a greater resistance and a lower current draw. And another thought that only resistance changes when increasing the wattage of a light bulb. Thus, four of the eight students did not overcome the minimum causality error, although they had received instruction on the point.

This result says something about what makes learning difficult in electricity: when two conceptual challenges interact, students have special trouble sorting things out. Here, the interacting challenges were bad framing (a faulty analogy) and simplifying assumptions (only one thing changes). Bad framing by itself may not be too difficult to overcome. The Legacy students had little difficulty overcoming their view that current fills an empty pipe. But they did have trouble overcoming their belief that a higher resistance causes more heat. This may be because beginners have a tendency to simplify explanations to single relationships. This tendency toward minimum causality prevented the Legacy students from simultaneously considering the two equations that could have helped them see both that current and resistance must change.

People have trouble integrating multiple causes, and this is exacerbated by faulty intuitions that cause them to focus on singular causes. We suspect that most instruction does not sufficiently help students construct mental models that incorporate both the empirical reasoning of causal intuition and the helpful structure of mathematics (Schwartz & Moore, 1998). In electricity it seems particularly important to help students make sense of the mathematical formulas (qualitatively and quantitatively) so they may overcome the tendency toward minimum causality. In our protocols with college professors and field experts alike we have found that they resort to equations to solve difficult conceptual problems. And in our discussions of AC circuits, electrical engineering experts rely so heavily on mathematics that they often cannot even generate physical analogies. They are reasoning about representations, primarily mathematical; the empirical phenomena are far in the background.

In addition to helping us to assess some of the learning challenges associated with the domain of electricity, DC.Legacy led to a worthwhile experience for the students. Different students were impressed by different aspects of the program. For Research & Revise, three students found the interactive analogy of electricity and water to be particularly compelling. The parallel simulations helped one student to articulate and refine a previously vague analogy. After working through the interactive analogies, the experimenter asked the student, "Does that make sense?" The student answered, "Yeah. Now that I understand it." One student appreciated the chance to Reflect Back on the original problem of the Look Ahead to see just how much her understanding had changed. Another commented that the Multiple Perspectives feature was useful: "It helps a lot—the thought process and actually seeing it in action instead of fixing a circuit with a whole lot of mathematical computations." More generally, the students were appreciative of the chance to complete DC.Legacy and to assess dynamically and improve their understanding. Quotes from two students capture the general sentiments nicely. After expressing satisfaction at their new understanding, they continued:

> Student 1: It's hard to explain things. In class, you just do it. No one asks you why. You just do it. I mean this is scary, you know. Cause I'm not doing bad in that class. I just think I should know this. Even through the physics stuff—you should know this. I should've been able to explain this.
>
> Student 6: It's interesting to me that I've gone this far in the semester and . . . passed as far as difficulty of circuits, [to find] that there are some things in the basics that I didn't know.

Evidently the students were surprised to find out what they had not learned when placed in the context of trying to learn something new. As fits our overall story, assessments that evaluate preparedness for learning can be both revealing and instructional.

SUMMARY

We have argued for new kinds of tools that can help assess and develop preparedness for future learning. To this end, we propose a dynamic assessment approach where assessments occur in the context of trying to enhance students' preparation for learning. Our computer examples included hypothesis visualization software, faux merchandise catalogues presented over the Internet, interactive analogies, and STAR.Legacy, an instructional shell that embodies an idealized learning cycle. It is intended to be flexible and readily adapted by other instructors and researchers. To this end, it makes its learning theory manifest in its interface, and it offers a small set of programming tools that strike a balance between programmability and ease of use. STAR.Legacy has been adopted by professors, and middle school teachers, and students have used it to create model instruction.

We proposed that STAR.Legacy could be extended to help assess domain learnability. In this approach, researchers try their best to teach students. Those concepts that students still have difficulty with tell us something about the components of the domain that are particularly difficult to learn, at least with respect to the instruction that we can provide. The assessments help focus attention on concepts that are particularly problematic for future learning rather than simply making a list of possible misconceptions in a domain.

We described several classes of learning difficulties that we and others have found for the domain of electricity. We tried to organize these misconceptions according to the way they fit into basic cognitive processes: differentiation, simplifying assumptions, local reasoning, induction from empirical experience, and the need for framing. Our underlying assumption is that domain learnability is best understood as the interaction of individuals' cognitive tendencies, the demands of the domain, and instruction. We constructed a DC.Legacy that targeted these different classes of learning difficulties. Using DC.Legacy, several members of our group were able to add their own expertise to make a rich dynamic assessment environment for learning DC circuits.

In a small proof-of-concept study, we found that some commonly cited misconceptions, like the difficulty of understanding parallel resistors, are not problematic by the time students leave a typical college course in electricity. Other misconceptions, like reasoning locally about the movement of current from point to point, are not treated by our courses. However, they are easily remediated and do not have to serve as blocks to learning the domain. And we found that some aspects of the domain are difficult to learn even with special attention. In particular, people have trouble integrating interacting causes, and this is exacerbated by faulty intuitions that lead students to focus on singular causes.

In conclusion, we are using the computer as a catalyst for thinking about new methods of assessment. The computer provides ways to bring together instructional and assessment resources that have always been available but difficult to link seamlessly. The computer also presents new opportunities for designing innovative assessment-instruction tools, like interactive analogies, that are hard to imagine in any other medium. The current theorizing and the empirical results present our beginning efforts at thinking about dynamic assessment tools that can inform instruction in complex domains and prepare students for future learning. Our hope is to make computer tools that are easy to use so they may be widely adopted, modified, and evaluated. In this way, we may dynamically assess our tools and theories. Just as we argue that the best dynamic assessment presents multiple opportunities for assessment and revision, we think the best computer tool should afford the same.

ACKNOWLEDGMENTS

The work reported in this chapter was supported by ONR grant N00014–96–1–0444. The ideas expressed here do not necessarily reflect those of the granting agency.

REFERENCES

Barron, B. J., Schwartz, D. L., Vye, N. J., Moore, A., Petrosino, A., Zech, L., Bransford, J. D., & the Cognition and Technology Group at Vanderbilt. (1998). Doing with understanding: Lessons from research on problem- and project-based learning. *Journal of the Learning Sciences, 7,* 271–312.

Biswas, G., Schwartz, D., Brophy, S., Bhuva, B., Balac, T., & Bransford, J. (1997). Combining mathematical and everyday models of electricity. In M. G. Shafto & P. Langley (Eds.), *Proceedings of the Nineteenth Annual Conference of the Cognitive Science Society.* Mahwah, NJ: Lawrence Erlbaum Associates.

Bransford, J. D., Delclos, V., Vye, N. , Burns, S., & Hasselbring, T. (1987). Approaches to dynamic assessment: Issues, data, and future directions. In C. Lidz (Ed.), *Dynamic assessment: An interactional approach to evaluating learning potentials* (pp. 479–495). New York: Guilford Press.

Bransford, J. D., Franks, J. J., Vye, N. J., & Sherwood, R. D. (1989). New approaches to instruction: Because wisdom can't be told. In S. Vosdiadou & A.

Ortony (Eds.), *Similarity and analogical reasoning.* New York: Cambridge University Press.

Bransford, J. D., & Nitsch, K. E. (1978). Coming to understand things we could not previously understand. In J. F. Kavanagh & W. Strange (Eds.), *Speech and language in the laboratory, school, and clinic* (pp. 267–307). Cambridge, MA: MIT Press.

Bransford, J. D., & Schwartz, D. L. (1999). Rethinking transfer: A simple proposal with multiple implications. In A. Iran-Nejad & P. D. Pearson (Eds.), *Review of research in education* (Vol. 24, pp. 61–101). Washington, DC: American Educational Research Association.

Bransford, J. D., & Stein, B. S. (1993). *The ideal problem solver: A guide for improving thinking, learning, and creativity* (2nd ed.). New York: Freeman.

Brophy, S. P., & Schwartz, D. L. (1998). Interactive analogies. In A. Bruckman, M. Guzdial, J. Kolodner, & A. Ram (Eds.), *Proceedings of the International Conference of the Learning Sciences* (pp. 56–62). Charolttesville, VA: Association for the Advancement of Computing in Education.

Campione, J. C., & Brown, A. L. (1987). *Linking dynamic assessment with school achievement.* In C. S. Lidz (Ed.), Dynamic assessment: An interactional approach to evaluating learning potential (pp. 82-114). New York: Guilford Press.

Chi, M., T. H., Feltovich, P. J., & Glaser, R. (1981). Categorization and representation of physics problems by experts and novices. *Cognitive Science, 18,* 439–477.

Cognition and Technology Group at Vanderbilt. (1997). *The Japser project: Lessons in curriculum, instruction, assessment, and professional development.* Mahwah, NJ: Lawrence Erlbaum Associates.

Cole, M., & Griffin, P. (Eds.). (1987). *Contextual factors in education.* Madison, WI: Wisconsin Center for Education Research.

Cooke, N. J., & Breedin, S. D. (1994). Constructing naive theories of motion on the fly. *Memory and Cognition, 22,* 474–493.

diSessa, A. A. (1993). Toward an epistemology of physics. *Cognition & Instruction, 10,* 105–225.

Feurestein, R. (1979). *The dynamic assessment of retarded performers: The learning potential assessment device, theory, instruments, and techniques.* Baltimore, MD: University Park Press.

Fredette, N., & Lochhead, J. (1980). Student conceptions of simple circuits. *Physics Teacher, 18,* 194–198.

Gentner, D., & Gentner, D. (1983). Flowing waters or teeming crowds: Mental models of electricity. In D. Gentner & A. L. Stevens (Eds.), *Mental models.* Hillsdale, NJ: Lawrence Erlbaum Associates.

Gordin, D. N., & Pea, R. D. (1995). Prospects for scientific visualization as an educational technology. *Journal of the Learning Sciences, 4,* 249–279.

Groen, G., & Resnick, L. B. (1977). Can preschool children invent addition algorithms? *Journal of Educational Psychology, 69,* 645–652.

Halloun, I. A., & Hestenes, D. (1985). *The initial knowledge state of college physics students. American Journal of Physics, 53,* 1043–1055.

Heller, P. M., & Finley, F. N. (1992). Variable uses of alternative conceptions: A case study in current electricity. *Journal of Research in Science Teaching, 29,* 259–275.

Hunt, E., & Minstrell, J. (1994). A cognitive approach to the teaching of physics. In K. McGilly (Ed.), *Classroom lessons: Integrating cognitive theory and classroom practice* (pp. 51–74). Cambridge, MA: MIT Press.

Koedinger, K. R., & Anderson, J. R. (1993). Reifying implicit planning geometry: Guidelines for model-based intelligent tutoring system design. In S. Lajoie & S. Derry (Eds.), *Computers as cognitive tools: Technology in education* (pp. 15–45). Hillsdale, NJ: Lawrence Erlbaum Associates.

Lajoie, S. P., & Lesgold, A. M. (1992). Dynamic assessment of proficiency for solving procedural knowledge tasks. *Educational Psychologist, 27,* 365–384.

Levidow, B. B., Hunt, E., & McKee, C. (1991). The DIAGNOSER: A HyperCard tool for building theoretically based tutorials. *Behavior Research Methods, Instruments, and Computers, 23,* 249–252.

Lidz, C. S. (1987). *Dynamic assessment: An interactional approach to evaluating learning potential.* New York: Guilford.

Magnusson, S. J., Templin, M., & Boyle, R. A. (1997). Dynamic science assessment: A new approach for investigating conceptual change. *Journal of the Learning Sciences, 6,* 91–142.

McCloskey, M. (1983). *Naive theories of motion.* In D. Gentner & A. L. Stevens (Eds.), Mental models. Hillsdale, NJ: Lawrence Erlbaum Associates.

Murray, T. (1998). Authoring knowledge-based tutors: Tools for content, instructional strategy, student model, and interface design. *Journal of the Learning Sciences, 7,* 5–64.

Parchman, S. (1997). The Bee Sim simulator package. Available at: *http://cswww. vuse.vanderbilt.edu/~tamara/Web.1/table.htm.*

Schwartz, D. L., & Bransford, J. D. (1998). A time for telling. *Cognition and Instruction, 24,* 477–524.

Schwartz, D. L., Brophy, S., Lin, X. D., & Bransford, J. D. (1999). Software for managing complex learning: An example from an educational psychology course. *Educational Technology Research and Development, 47,* 39–-59.

Schwartz, D. L., Lin, X., Brophy, S., & Bransford, J. D. (1999). Towards the development of flexibly adaptive instructional design. In C. Reigeluth (Ed.),

Instructional design theories and models: New paradigms of instructional theory (pp. 183–214). Mahwah, NJ: Lawrence Erlbaum Associates.

Schwartz, D. L., & Moore, J. L. (1998). On the role of mathematics in explaining the material world: Mental models for proportional reasoning. *Cognitive Science, 22,* 471–516.

Shipstone, D. (1988). Pupils' understanding of simple electrical circuits. *Physics Education, 23,* 92–96.

Smith, C., Snir, J., & Grosslight, L. (1992). Using conceptual models to facilitate conceptual change: The case of weight-density differentiation. *Cognition and Instruction, 9,* 221–283.

Spiro, R. J., & Jehng, J. C. (1990). Cognitive flexibility and hypertext: Theory and technology for the nonlinear and multidimensional traversal of complex subject matter. In D. Nix & R. J. Spiro (Eds.), *Cognition, education, and multimedia: Exploring ideas in high technology.* Hillsdale, NJ: Lawrence Erlbaum Associates.

Stocklmayer, S. M., & Treagust, D. F. (1994). A historical analysis of electrical currents in textbooks: A century of influence on physics education. *Science and Education, 3,* 131–154.

Vye, N. J., Schwartz, D. L., Bransford, J. D., Barron, B. J., Zech, L. and Cognition and Technology Group at Vanderbilt. (1998). SMART environments that support monitoring, reflection, and revision. In D. Hacker, J. Dunlosky, & A. Graesser (Eds.), *Metacognition in educational theory and practice* (pp. 305–346). Hillsdale, NJ: Lawrence Erlbaum Associates.

Vygotsky, L. S. (1978). *Mind in society: The development of higher psychological processes* (M. Cole, V. John-Steiner, S. Scribner, & E. Souberman, Eds.). Cambridge, MA: Harvard University Press.

White, B. Y., & Frederiksen, J. R. (1998). Inquiry, modeling, and metacognition: Making science accessible to all students. *Cognition and Instruction, 16,* 3–118.

White, B. Y., Frederiksen, J. R., & Spoehr, K. T. (1993). Conceptual models of understanding the behavior of electrical circuits. In M. Caillot (Ed.), *Learning electricity and electronics with advanced technology.* New York: Springer-Verlag.

11

DNA: Toward an Automated Knowledge Elicitation and Organization Tool

Valerie J. Shute, Lisa A. Torreano,
and Ross E. Willis
GKIS, Inc.

The research described in the first volume of *Computers as Cognitive Tools* reflected the premise that computer power can be harnessed in multifarious ways to enhance student learning. The editors described this research as falling along a dichotomy between two camps—modelers and nonmodelers—with a third camp bridging the two. Regarding this dichotomy, then and now, our tent is pitched in the modelers' camp. This view holds that modeling the learner renders computer-based instruction more intelligent, and thus more effective (Anderson, 1993; Shute & Psotka, 1996). However, whereas the previous volume used modeling to denote the process of representing students' knowledge structures, we expand the term to include the process of representing the domain or task being instructed. Modeling in this context allows the computer to know what to teach, as well as when and how to teach it.

There are three agreed-on components that serve to make computer-assisted instruction intelligent: an expert model, a student model, and an instructor model (Lajoie & Derry, 1993; Polson & Richardson, 1988; Psotka, Massey, & Mutter, 1988; Shute & Psotka, 1996; Sleeman & Brown, 1982). Basically, the expert model represents the material that is to be instructed—the ideal representation of the domain or task. In essence, it is a blueprint of the knowledge elements and their associated structure and interdependencies. The student model represents the student's knowledge and progress in relation to this blueprint. Finally, the instructor model customizes the instructional experience for each learner based on discrepancies between the student and expert models. This is achieved by embodying theories of learning that guide the course of instruction in the program.

This chapter describes the new computer program Decompose, Network, Assess (DNA). We discuss it in conjunction with another system, called Student Modeling Approach for Responsive Tutoring (SMART; Shute, 1995), because both attempt to render computerized instructional programs intelligent. The programs work in concert, such that DNA extracts and organizes knowledge and skills from subject matter experts and SMART uses the resulting structured curriculum elements as the basis for assessment, cognitive diagnosis, and instruction. In other words, DNA provides the blueprint for instruction, obtaining curriculum elements directly from the responses and actions of multiple subject matter experts, who answer structured queries posed by the computer (Shute, Willis, & Torreano, 1998). The student modeling paradigm (SMART) assesses performance on each curriculum element by way of a series of regression equations that are based on the level of assistance the computer gives each person per element (Shute, 1995). Thus, DNA relates to the "what" to teach, and SMART addresses the "when" and "how" to teach it.

Historically, specifying what to teach has hampered efforts to develop intelligent instructional software efficiently. In fact, due to its time and resource costs, it has often been referred to as the bottleneck in the development process (Durkin, 1994; Gordon, Schmierer, & Gill, 1993; Hayes-Roth, Waterman, & Lenat, 1983). That is, the processes of eliciting and hierarchically organizing the necessary elements for an expert model involve exorbitant amounts of time to accomplish, and even then are more art than science. Despite the fact that the expert model is difficult to develop, it is often characterized as the backbone of any intelligent instructional system (Anderson, 1988). Therefore, our aim with DNA is to attempt to open up this bottleneck. We wish to increase the efficiency of developing the expert model by automating the bulk of the knowledge elicitation and organization processes. This automated approach to creating the expert model is embodied in DNA.

FOUNDATIONS OF DNA

We begin this section with an overview of the SMART framework–presented to highlight the content and structure requirements for the DNA program. Relevant cognitive analysis techniques are discussed.

The SMART Framework: Precursor to DNA

Three basic features of SMART directly influenced DNA design decisions. First, SMART requires the categorization of each bit of knowledge or skill, comprising some domain, into one of three different learning outcome categories: symbolic knowledge (SK), procedural skill (PS), and conceptual knowledge (CK). Before DNA was developed, several independent raters achieved this categorization of elements by applying well-defined operational definitions. The simplified operational definitions are: SK: knowledge of any symbol, formula, basic definition, or rule; PS: the application of a formula or rule, or performing a specific action within the tutor; and CK: the definitions of, and relations among, various concepts. Basically, this represents a slight extension of the well-established declarative-procedural knowledge distinction (see Anderson, 1983, 1993).

Second, SMART differentially instructs curriculum elements (CEs) based on these outcome types. For instance, symbolic knowledge is instructed by means of drill and practice. Procedural skill is instructed by presenting problems to solve that are specifically related to either the CEs that are currently being instructed or the CEs that were inferred as the bug in the learner's knowledge and therefore require remediation. Finally, conceptual knowledge is instructed by carefully designed analogies (Shute, 1994, 1995). This attempts to capitalize on the best aspects of a variety of theoretically grounded student modeling approaches by pairing each approach (drill and practice, problem solving, or analogies) with the most appropriate knowledge or skill type (Shute & Catrambone, 1996). Thus, instruction methods are applied differentially to distinct knowledge types to optimize learning.

Third, SMART relies on the inheritance relationship of a hierarchical structure of CEs for managing assessment and instruction. That is, the underlying knowledge base consists of CEs arrayed such that their relationships are clarified. The hierarchical structure denotes elements that are basic or prerequisite to more complex bits of knowledge. This influences instruction and assessment in that more basic, prerequisite knowledge elements are instructed prior to more complex dependent ones, and deficiencies in learner performance are inferred based on these dependency relations. For instance, one must know the individual symbols of Σ, X, and N before understanding the formula for the mean: $(\Sigma X)/N$. Therefore, these symbols would be instructed prior to the formula for the mean. In addition, if the learner's knowledge of the formula for the mean is deficient, then the hierarchical structure of CEs indicates which knowledge elements may be the source of the deficiency and therefore deserve remediation. Structurally and functionally, this knowledge structure constitutes a learning hierarchy (Gagné & Briggs, 1965).

These three basic features provide the instructional framework of SMART and define the parameters and criteria for DNA's design. Relying on SMART's framework is justified because the efficacy of this approach has been empirically validated. That is, a controlled evaluation examined learning gains between participants using one of two versions of the same tutor: with and without SMART enabled. Findings showed that learners in the non-SMART version showed impressive learning outcome scores (2 standard deviation pretest to post-test improvement). Their final post-test scores were 74.9% on average. Learners in the SMART version showed even higher gain scores: average post-test scores of 82.1%. An analysis of covariance was computed on the post-test data with pretest as a covariate and version as a between-subjects variable. Results showed a significant difference in learning outcome due to version: $F(1, 199) = 4.16$; $p < .05$, with superior outcome performance evidenced by participants in the SMART-enabled condition (Shute, 1995).

In summary, the empirical success with SMART has motivated key DNA design decisions. Specifically, we decided to require DNA to elicit and structure information so that it fits SMART's database requirements of three outcome types: SK, PS,[1] and CK. This categorization scheme allows for the analysis of a wide array of domains or tasks, rendering DNA a general-purpose tool for specifying curriculum. To accomplish this, DNA asks subject matter experts a semistructured series of what, how, and why questions—the analogues to symbolic, procedural, and conceptual knowledge. In addition, the success of the hierarchical structure of SMART's underlying knowledge base resulted in our decision to include a separate module in DNA to obtain the spatial and conceptual organization of elements needed for a sound curriculum.

Knowledge Elicitation and Organization Techniques

What is demanded of the methods used to conduct a cognitive task analysis (CTA) is jointly determined by the purpose of doing the analysis and the type of domain or topic that is to be analyzed. These two critical fac-

---

[1]Procedural knowledge (PK) is another outcome type, but it is subsumed under symbolic knowledge (SK), which can be divided into simple and complex components (for more on these knowledge types, see Shute, 1995).

tors determine what is required of a useful and appropriate knowledge structure. Traditionally the primary purpose for conducting a CTA has been to delineate an expert's performance in relation to some task, down to a fairly small grain size (e.g., elementary cognitive processes). However, given our specific interest in developing curriculum for intelligent instructional systems across a broad spectrum of topics, the analysis techniques we include in DNA must be able to apply to both domains that involve performance of a task and those that do not. These requirements guided the choice of which techniques would be appropriate to embed in DNA. Due to our goal of broad applicability of the tool, we use "cognitive task analysis" to denote any systematic decomposition of a domain in terms of constituent knowledge and skill elements.

Knowledge Elicitation. Interviews constitute a fundamental method for eliciting information from experts. The nature of the interview is typically based on a theory of expertise and is designed to fit the framework of the purpose for which the cognitive task analysis is being conducted (Ryder & Redding, 1993). In other words, the form the questions take and the order in which they are posed can vary according to the information one wishes to elicit. Interview methods can be structured or unstructured and can be concurrent or retrospective with the performance of a task being analyzed.

Our purpose for conducting cognitive task analysis is to obtain ample data on some topic or task for instructional purposes. The virtue of interview techniques lies in their flexibility and directness; thus, they can be used to analyze a wide range of topics which suit our particular goals. To obtain such data, appropriate questions embodied within the interview should probe the expert for as much information as possible per curriculum element. For instance, for procedural topics, experts should be asked to specify what actions and steps are relevant, how they are best accomplished, and why those steps are taken instead of alternative ones. For more conceptual issues, experts should be asked to specify what defining traits and examples are important, how they are related to the concept, and why they are consequential.

Knowledge Organization. After information from an expert is obtained, how is it optimally represented or arrayed? Conceptual graphs are one popular means of representing hierarchically-structured knowledge. As the name implies, conceptual graphs are the graphical representation of concepts showing, at various grain sizes, relevant concepts (nodes) and their interrelationships (arcs or links). This representation format resembles semantic networks in cognitive psychology (Collins & Quillian, 1969; Jonassen, Beissner, & Yacci, 1993). One beneficial characteristic of this type of representation is that it depicts information in such a way that allows inferences to be made. That is, the hierarchical structure between nodes provides "inheritance" information: a subordinate (or "child") node inherits the properties of its superordinate (or "parent") node. For example, if a canary is specified as a "kind of" bird, then it can be inferred that the properties and characteristics associated with "bird" also apply to the concept of canary.

Another popular form of knowledge representation is a production system framework that results from a GOMS-type analysis (Goals, Operators, Methods and Selection rules; Card, Moran, & Newell, 1983). Again, as the name suggests, this representation specifies the goals that are to be achieved, the methods or steps taken to achieve those goals, and the criterion on which alternative steps are selected. One beneficial characteristic of this representation is that it has the potential to be easily translated into an executable system. That is, condition-action pairs define what must occur in order for some action to fire (see Anderson, 1993; Gray, John, & Atwood, 1993; Newell, 1990).

Summary.   These knowledge elicitation and organization techniques have proven helpful when used for their respectively appropriate purposes and topics of analysis. Many other techniques exist and can be used collaboratively to balance each method's strengths and weaknesses. Successful elicitation techniques include document analysis, observation of experts, and protocol analysis that requires experts to "talk aloud," voicing their mental processes while performing the target task. In addition, techniques such as card sorting, ordered recall, similarity judgments, ranking, and ratings are useful techniques for eliciting and structuring knowledge. However, for our current purpose of putting the design decisions of DNA in context, we will not address these other techniques. (For good reviews of CTA methods, see Schraagen et al., 1997, and Williams, 1993. For a fuller discussion of knowledge organization and representation issues, see Jonassen & Carr, this volume.)

DESCRIPTION OF DNA

The primary goals of DNA are twofold: to maximize the range of domains that can be analyzed with a single CTA method and to optimize the cost-benefit ratio of the process. As a bonus, DNA is intended to provide a principled approach to the currently unstandardized process of knowledge elicitation and organization.

We view CTA as any systematic decomposition of a domain in terms of constituent knowledge and skill elements, whether the domain is related to task performance (e.g., troubleshooting jet engine malfunctions) or not (e.g., understanding the core concepts of religions). Therefore, to achieve the first goal's capability of this breadth of knowledge representation, we chose to create and employ a hybrid output structure involving a mixture of semantic net and production system architectures.

To optimize the cost-benefit ratio of doing cognitive task analysis, DNA is automated. The intention is to improve efficiency by decreasing the personnel resources (and, hence, time and cost) required in the analysis. Traditional CTA consists of two distinct phases: elicitation of knowledge and skills and the organization of those elements. These phases customarily occur at different points in time and often with different persons doing the elicitation and organization. For example, a knowledge engineer interviews or observes a subject matter expert (SME), while a cognitive psychologist or instructional designer takes the output and arranges it into a conceptual graph or production system. With DNA, these two phases are collapsed into a symbiotic process in order to decrease the time and cost associated with conducting two separate analyses. Thus, in DNA, the SME identifies all CEs and arrays them in a hierarchical structure.

Modules of DNA

DNA consists of a core of four interactive modules that automate the knowledge elicitation and organization processes: Customize, Decompose, Network, and Assess. The Decompose module was designed to be a running dialogue between the computer and the SME. It works by asking structured interview questions while an expert decomposes a domain using keyboard input. After decomposing a domain into individual curriculum elements, the SME networks the elements into a learning hierarchy (Gagné & Briggs, 1965). Finally, the SME's data are assessed for validity (i.e., accuracy and completeness) by distributing his or her learning hierarchy to other SMEs, who edit its structure and content.

Customize. In DNA's Customize module, the instructional designer (ID) provides information about which domain is to be decomposed. This information then goes to the SMEs. In particular, the ID specifies the ulti-

Dear [Name of Expert],   [Today's Date]

We're writing today to get your help in designing a course on Microsoft Exchange (ver. 4.0).
Before you begin working with the enclosed DNA program, please sit down and think about the
critical things that make you good at using the MS Exchange software package.

As you go through DNA and respond to our questions, try to respond in terms of how you
currently perform the job or think about the particular task. Please do not respond with how you
originally learned Microsoft Exchange; you have probably developed much better ways of
performing this task since then.

The ultimate goals of the course are for our students to:
(1) Know how to create a new email message
(2) Know how to address email
(3) Know how to send email

How specific should you get? You can presume that our students will have the following
knowledge and skills:

(1) Knowledge and skills with Windows 95
(2) Basic word processing skills

Therefore, you will not need to define knowledge or skills at a detailed level in relation to these
elements.

When answering questions during the program, please adjust your responses to fit the following
guidelines:

What box: 10%
How box: 85%
Why box: 5%

Thanks very much for your time.

Sincerely,

FIG. 11.1.

mate learning goal of the tutor to be developed, prerequisite knowledge
and skills of the learners, and the desired instructional emphasis or flavor
(e.g., primarily procedural). This information provides the SME with the
superordinate goal of the analysis and the lowest level subordinate goal, at
which point the SME should stop decomposing the domain. Using the
information provided by the instructional designer, the Customize module
generates a personalized letter explaining the purpose of the project
(which the ID can edit) and a set of floppy diskettes that will be mailed to
prospective SMEs. The diskettes contain files for a SME to install on the
computer that DNA needs to elicit and store knowledge structures.

For example, Fig. 11.1 shows a letter that was generated by the Customize module and used in a formative evaluation of the system and some
in-house SMEs analyzing the domain of Microsoft Exchange (mail software). Upon receipt of the letter and installation of the software, the SME
goes through a short (10 minutes) orientation program that provides an
overview of DNA and transitions directly into the Decompose module.

Decompose. The Decompose module consists of a semistructured, interactive dialogue between the computer and the SME. It was designed to elicit most of the explicit knowledge associated with the domain or topic of analysis. DNA uses a series of three interrogation branches to elicit knowledge from experts. The symbolic (or "what") branch elicits SK by asking experts to provide definitions of terms used in his field of expertise. The procedural (or "how") branch elicits PS by asking experts to outline specific steps, conditionals, relational connections, and subprocedures of a procedure. While responding to questions in the procedural branch, experts may also provide SK elements by defining ambiguous terms and attaching multimedia files, such as pictures, movies, and sounds. The conceptual (or "why") branch elicits CK by asking experts to delineate the important components in their domain and explain how these components are functionally related. Additional CK is derived from experts who are asked to specify their understanding of why these components are important in relation to the overall learning goal. In general, DNA utilizes the "what, how, and why" questioning procedure that has been shown to elicit knowledge from experts successfully (Gordon et al., 1993).

The questioning sequence is left to some degree to the discretion of the SME, who is allowed to decide which main question to answer. This enables the expert to decompose the domain in a breadth- or depth-first manner. For instance, an expert can begin by generating a number of higher-level goals, then proceed to describe these goals at a more specific level across the topics (breadth first). Alternatively, the expert can start by identifying a single high-level goal and then delineate its lineage (depth first). Low-level, or terminal, nodes are determined by the description of learners' incoming knowledge and skills, specified in the customized letter. This flexibility differs from more rigid cognitive task analysis approaches, like GOMS, which force an expert to decompose a domain in a breadth-first manner (Williams, 1993).

During the Decompose module, all information about evolving curriculum elements is stored in a Microsoft Access 7.0 database. Each CE receives a unique number (assigned by DNA), as well as a name and description (provided by the SME). The numbering system reflects the order in which the CEs were specified by the SME and inherently contains information about higher order relations. That is, each element is given a unique number that designates it as a main element, a step within a procedure (or subprocedure), or a definition associated with either a step or a main element. Main CEs are given a unique integer, and steps within a procedure are given a number based on the main CE number and the number of the step. For example, the third step associated with CE number 2 would be numbered 2.003. Substep numbering follows the same logic but goes out three more decimal places. This numbering scheme allows a procedure to have up to 999 individual steps. Definitions associated with steps are given the main CE number, the step number, substep numbers, and the number of the definition. For example, the ninth definition associated with step number 3 for CE number 2 would be labeled 2.003.09. This numbering system allows for 99 definitions to be associated with each step or substep.

The CE name and description are obtained directly from the SME. Additionally, the program categorizes each CE in terms of knowledge type (SK, PS, or CK) based on the type of question that elicited the CE. For example, if the SME created a new CE in response to a "What do you typically do first when you . . . ?" query, that would be classified as PS. Finally, the expert can also attach graphical or sound files to individual CEs for greater elaboration and clarification. Together these data will enable the instructional designer to develop a rich and sound curriculum.

Extensive help, either solicited by the SME or provided by the system (on a need basis), is available throughout the Decompose module. In addition to the orientation, there are many online help tools. For instance, information is always available to the SME in the form of examples and pointers. Examples of valid entries are presented from a variety of domains, as are answering pointers that guide the wording of the SME's input. Furthermore, a help screen appears for the SME whenever an interface or decision point is first encountered.

After delineating all elements related to the domain, the expert proceeds to the Network tutorial, which gives the SME a basic understanding of hierarchical structures and provides practice in arranging curriculum elements that are represented as nodes. That is, the expert is instructed on how to build a graphical representation by arranging practice nodes in a hierarchical manner, much like a conceptual graph (Gordon et al., 1993). This tutorial also teaches experts how to create new nodes and link existing ones together. This work leads directly into the Network module.

Network. The Network module (currently under development) is intended to transform curriculum elements elicited during the Decompose module into graphical nodes that experts spatially arrange and link to represent hierarchical conceptual graphs or production rules. Each node contains the name of the CE as defined during the Decompose module. Node shapes differ by SMART's learning outcome type: Rectangles represent SK, ovals are PS elements, and rounded rectangles denote CK.

To simplify viewing and editing, only main-level CEs and their first-level "children" (nodes) appear on the initial screen. "Pregnant" CEs are those that have elements embedded within them. They appear in bold type. Any pregnant element can be unpacked to expose its constituent parts by right clicking on the node and choosing the option Unpack.

Some links are already in place when the SME arrives at the Network module. These come from information provided during the Decompose module, such as higher order relations inherent in the decomposition of a procedure. Other links must be drawn and labeled. CE links may vary along three different dimensions: type, directionality, and strength of association.

The first kind of link relationship is *type*. These denote the specific kind of relationship between nodes. DNA's semantically flavored link types allow the SME to specify the relationships and interdependencies among CEs, allowing the conceptual structure of the domain to be more readily grasped, similar to semantic nets. The current options are (a) IS-A (a collie IS-A dog), (b) IS-NOT-A (a dolphin IS-NOT-A fish), (c) PART-OF (a beak is PART-OF a bird), (d) CAUSES (hunger in animals CAUSES search for food), and (e) MAY-CAUSE (predatory behavior MAY-CAUSE defensive postures by the prey). On the other hand, more procedurally flavored link types allow the SME to specify the relationships among procedural steps and substeps, similar to a production system representation. This is crucial for a full understanding of procedural knowledge that can be applied to novel situations. Procedural links include the following: (a) AND (two or more nodes related by this link must co-occur), (b) OR (the condition of "A or B but not both"), (c) OR/AND (the condition of "A or B or both"), and (d) NOT (the step cannot occur). Additional link types can specify whether steps are to be performed (e) in SERIAL order (either FIXED, where steps must be accomplished in a prescribed sequence, or ANY order, where steps may be performed in any serial order) and (f) PARALLEL order (steps that are accomplished simultaneously). Finally, in addition to the available semantic and procedural links, a user-definable link allows the SME to type in a label for a relationship not already defined.

The second link option is *directionality*. This refers to the flow of control or causation between CEs. Three options exist: unidirectional, bidirectional, and no direction. These relationships are established with arrowheads attached to the end of a line. An example of the unidirectional relation, coupled with the link type CAUSES, is *Positive reinforcement—> the frequency of some behavior to increase.* A bidirectional relationship describes a balanced, symbiotic relationship between two or more elements, such as the checks and balances within the judicial, legislative, and executive branches of the U.S. government. The no-directional option, denoted by a line without arrowheads, is used between two or more nodes that do not have a clear syntactic relationship (e.g., the link between a multimedia file and its associated step in a procedure).

The third link option defines the *strength* of association. The three values for this trait—weak, moderate, and strong—indicate the degree to which the items are related. The information on strength is accomplished by varying the width of the link line (fine, medium, and bold). To illustrate, the link between fruit and kiwi would be fine, and the link between fruit and apple would be bold (at least, within North American cultures).

In general, this hybrid graphical representation of the knowledge structure is intended to make relationships among curriculum elements salient, which can thereby serve to highlight missing knowledge components. In addition, the graphical structure specifies the hierarchical dependencies between elements that are necessary for SMART to function optimally. The Network module is similar to traditional conceptual graph analysis except that with DNA, experts generate the conceptual graphs instead of the instructional designers. It is also similar to GOMS analysis in that goals, methods, and operators are represented in DNA as procedures, steps, and their logical, functional connectors.

We speculate that DNA will enable experts readily to spot and correct inadequacies (e.g., omissions, errors) in their externalized knowledge structures. Then they have the option of rectifying problems directly in the Network module or returning to the Decompose module to update the CE record. Given the shared database underlying both modules, information is easily communicated between the two. In addition, if one SME prefers to externalize knowledge and skills graphically while another prefers a text-based decomposition, both are accommodated with DNA's design.

After SMEs complete the Network module, data are stored on a floppy diskette and returned to the instructional designer. The ID reviews the CE records and conceptual graphs for glaring omissions or ambiguities in content. If there are any problems, the ID can ask the expert to expand the inadequate CEs.

Assess.   The final module under development, will be used to validate the CE records and conceptual graphs generated by SMEs. This validation of externalized knowledge structures will be accomplished by having experts in the same domain review each other's data and graphs. That is, the conceptual graph and CE database created by one SME will be distributed to other SMEs, who will be requested to review and edit the information. Distribution may occur serially or in parallel. For serial distribution, the instructional designer will send out the DNA program to SME-1, who will complete it and return the output to the ID. The ID subsequently will send SME-1's output to SME-2, who will evaluate the content and structure of the initial output and return the (potentially modified) data to the ID. Depending on the degree of similarity, the ID could then send SME-2's output back to SME-1 or to a third SME. For parallel distribution, the ID will send the DNA program to multiple SMEs at the same time. Upon receipt of all their outputs, the ID will need to aggregate their data into a single knowledge structure or expert model (which may form the basis for some curriculum). This continues until the ID is satisfied that the final curriculum contains the appropriate amount of SK, PS, and CK for training needs.

Walk-Through of the Program

To make the program more concrete, we present a demonstrative walk-through of DNA, specifically the Decompose module, accomplished by one of the authors of this chapter (hereafter referred to as E1). The area chosen for illustrative purposes is knowledge and skills in using Microsoft Exchange (version. 4.0). The demonstration is based on the results from local experts' interactions with DNA decomposing this domain.

E1 began by reading the letter generated by the Customize module (see Fig. 11.1). This informed her that the ultimate goal was to produce a training system that teaches others how to create, address, and send an e-mail message using Microsoft Exchange, and to focus on providing mostly procedural elements. She was allowed to move freely between the DNA and Microsoft Exchange programs in order to execute the procedures she attempted to describe, thus verifying her description and refreshing her memory of the domain.

DNA started by presenting E1 with three procedural queries, generated from the Customize module and presented via the Main Question Queue, shown in Fig. 11.2. The expert always returns to this Main Question Queue window upon completing a particular path (symbolic, procedural, or conceptual) of decomposition.

E1 elected to respond to the first question related to creating a new e-mail message. Given that a procedural question was chosen, DNA invoked the Step Editor window (see Fig. 11.3). A variety of options exist

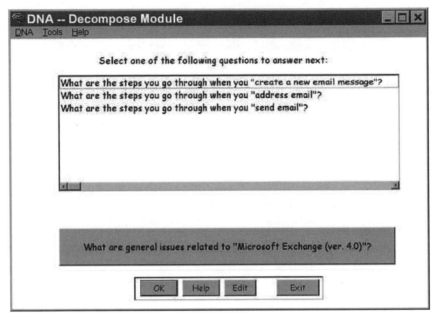

FIG. 11.2.

on the right side of the Step Editor screen for the SME to detail aspects of a procedure. Basic options are being able to add, delete, and edit steps, as well as re-order them by moving steps up and down in the Step Editor's list. Placement within the list indicates the order of execution of steps. Furthermore, because procedures can themselves be arranged hierarchically, the SME can turn a higher-level "step" into a procedure itself, with associated sub-steps, by selecting (clicking on) Sub-procedure. The Group and Ungroup options (for logically nesting steps together within a procedure) are apparent in the figure but were not operational at the time of E1's session.

Fig. 11.3 shows E1's decomposition of the procedure for creating a new e-mail message. Basically, this consists of two main steps: (a) open a new e-mail window (which can be achieved numerous ways), and then (b) compose the actual message. E1 delineated the procedure using some of the options, as well as some of the available logical operators (OR, if-then rules). For example, she outlined the multiple ways of opening a new e-mail window using if-then conditional statements, indicating three alternatives means of accomplishing the step. However, E1 described the process of composing the actual message by rendering it a sub-procedure. This is indicated by the "{more}" tag next to the last step, Compose message.

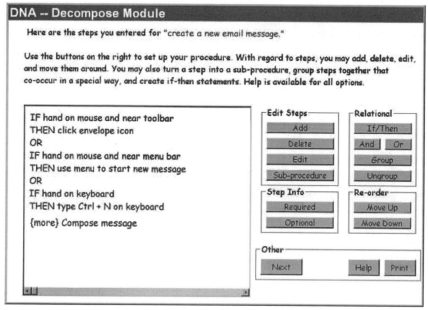

FIG. 11.3.

Figure 11.4 illustrates the interface and body of the "compose message" sub-procedure. Here, E1 indicated two steps of the sub-procedure: (a) get the cursor into the correct area (by clicking or tabbing), and then (b) compose the message (by typing, cutting and /pasting, or attaching a file). The Decompose module currently allows the expert to develop sub-procedures down two levels (to the sub-sub-procedure level).

The next two screens (see Figs. 11.5 and 11.6) illustrate the interface for creating if-then rules. This conditional was spawned from the sub-procedure "compose message" and evidences how E1 summarized two ways to get the cursor into the message area. Figure 11.5 represents the "if" part of the rule. The right-side of the screen shows one of DNA's help features—providing an example of a valid if-then input related to another domain (photography). Additional examples from other domains can be viewed by clicking the Examples button. Figure 11.6 represents the "then" part of the rule, along with another of DNA's help features (on the right). That is, pointers provide the expert with guidance on the correct way to specify input to DNA. Similar to examples, pointers are context dependent; that is, they are relevant to the current task.

After summarizing all steps and sub-steps associated with creating a new e-mail message to her satisfaction, E1 clicked the "Done" button. She

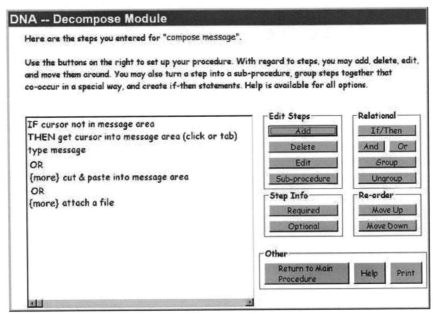

FIG. 11.4.

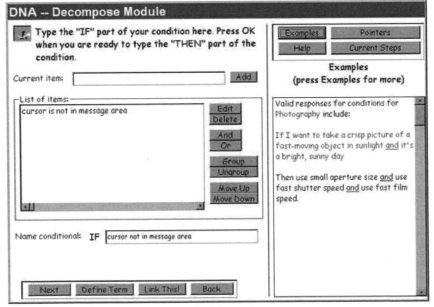

FIG. 11.5.

324

was then returned to the Main Question Queue, where she had the option to answer the remaining procedural queries, describe an alternative way of executing the procedure she had just delineated, or define some other aspect of Microsoft Exchange. She selected the third option (see Fig. 11.2), embodied by the large rectangular button at the bottom of the screen, "What are general issues related to Microsoft Exchange?" This choice invoked a new screen, shown in Fig. 11.7, that asks for additional symbolic, procedural, and conceptual knowledge using the "I know how to," "I can identify," and "I understand" template structures. E1 chose to describe her understanding of the importance of creating a good subject header, illustrated in Fig. 11.7. In contrast to the procedural questions she had previously encountered, this selection generated a new path of conceptually-based questions (CK).

The first CK screen that appeared asked about the components involved with choosing a good subject header. As shown in Fig. 11.8, E1 replied with two elements: relevance and brevity. The example on the right side of Fig. 11.8 shows the elements that are important to the area of photography conceptualizing how a picture gets onto some film.

After clicking on Next, the screen displayed in Fig. 11.9 appeared. E1's list of important items is shown, along with a question that requires her

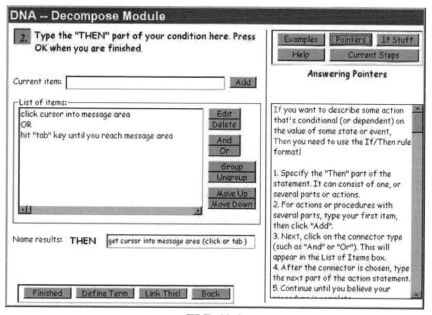

FIG. 11.6.

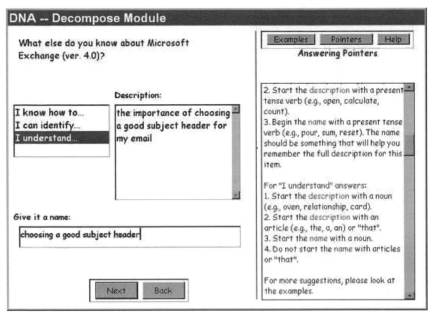

FIG. 11.7.

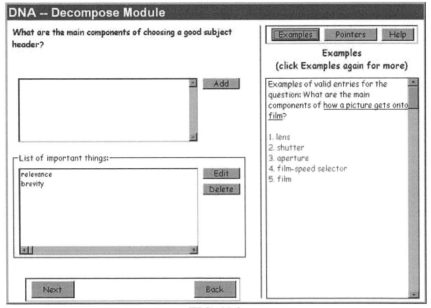

FIG. 11.8.

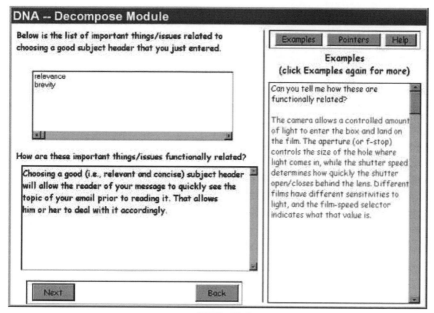

FIG. 11.9.

conceptually to "glue" the elements together in order to elaborate the current concept. The example provided to the right of the screen gives the expert an idea of what DNA seeks in the way of a response. Figure 11.9 shows how E1 wove her elements into a coherent concept. Clicking on Next took E1 to the follow-on screen (shown in Fig. 11.10), where she was asked to relate the current concept (understanding the importance of a good subject header) to the primary domain being decomposed (using Microsoft Exchange). E1's summary of the requested relationships is shown.

The last conceptually related screen (not shown) asks the expert to provide typical and atypical examples of when the current concept is useful or applicable. The expert's responses to this query can provide more information to be used by the instructional designer for developing instruction or training.

The process of answering what, how, and why questions was iterated until E1 was satisfied that all applicable questions had been answered and each higher-level goal had been decomposed into subordinate primitives. Once E1 determined she had finished decomposing her knowledge of Microsoft Exchange, she exited the Decompose module and then completed the Network tutorial before using the Network module, where she hierarchically arranged and linked the graphical nodes representing the information that she had decomposed.

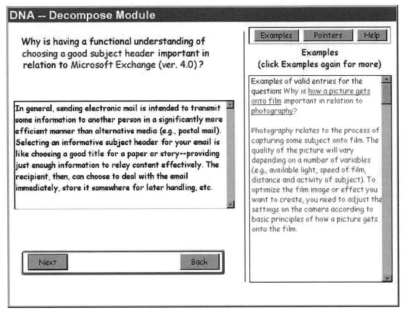

FIG. 11.10.

E1 used the Network module until she was satisfied with the labeling of the links, as well as the hierarchical and spatial arrangement of the nodes representing the CEs she had delineated within the Decompose module. This structure (in theory) would then be returned to the ID to determine whether the information elicited from the expert satisfied curriculum needs.

CURRENT DESIGN AND RESEARCH DIRECTIONS

Based on the results and feedback from a handful of experts who have interacted with DNA in formative evaluations,[2] we are changing the Decompose module's interface by redesigning the content and flow of questions and developing a way to allow experts to group steps and ideas logically together to disambiguate potentially confusing relationships.

---

[2]So far, the program has been tested out in the areas of solving linear equations, using Microsoft Exchange, waiting tables in a restaurant, and measures of central tendency, all fairly constrained and mostly procedural domains.

Flow of Questions

Originally the Decompose module asked a series of questions to elicit the rationale of each step of a procedure as it had been delineated. However, several experts noted that their train of thought was disrupted during procedural decomposition. Consequently, we now present these queries in the form of local follow-up questions after the SME has completed the delineation of a procedure into all of its constituent steps. We are also developing a series of global follow-up questions that will be presented on completion of the entire Decompose module. These questions are intended to obtain more general information about the domain, such as typical problem areas and appropriate analogies.

Local Follow-Up Questions

When implemented, local follow-up questions pertaining to each procedure will require the SME to reflect on the immediate goal being served, as well as the rationale behind the structure of individual steps that have been delineated. Examples (where X refers to the current procedure) include questions such as, Why do you do X? and What are typical and atypical situations in which you would do X? In addition, when an exclusive disjunction (e.g., "A or B") has been stipulated, the SME will be queried as to which factors influence whether A versus B would be done or occur. Similarly, when a conditional (e.g., "If A, then B") is outlined as part of a procedure, the SME will be prompted to consider its logical consequences to ensure that alternative cases have not been overlooked. Some of these questions include: When A does not hold, should one still do B? and Are there other common conditions that should trigger doing B? Thus, local follow-up questions posed when an SME finishes outlining the steps of a procedure will serve to disambiguate specifications of a given procedure, as well as elaborate symbolic and conceptual knowledge related to it.

Global Follow-Up Questions

To aid the instructional designer in generating curriculum, follow-up questions will be posed to the SME on completion of the Decompose module. They will attempt to elicit the SME's overview of the field–that is, the themes and principles of the domain being decomposed. Some global follow-up question examples include (where X is the domain being decomposed): What are some difficult areas you have encountered in the acquisition of X? What has worked for you in repairing this impasse? Can you describe a connection between this field and other domain? and What are some good analogies that help in understanding some aspect of the domain? In sum, local and global follow-up questions support DNA's effort to elicit information on which the instructional designer can generate potential examples, problem scenarios, questions, analogies, and real-world applications related to the domain to be instructed.

Grouping (and Ungrouping) Elements

The next version of DNA will incorporate changes to the Step Editor to help clarify the delineation of procedures. Specifically, experts will be allowed to group related CEs, thereby providing syntactic structure in relation to the procedure. For example, steps of a procedure such as "do A and B or C" are ambiguous unless syntactically structured to clarify whether [(A AND B) OR C] or [A AND (B OR C)] is the intended representation. These differences can be crucial in identifying the proper execution of a procedure. Once operational, the Group and Ungroup options will be available for all procedural decomposition in the Step Editor interface, as well as in the subprocedure and conditional windows. The SME will be able to left-click, and thereby highlight, steps listed in the Step Editor to identify the items to be grouped together. Once they are highlighted, the SME will click the Group button. That will result in a marker's being placed next to the selection to indicate the grouping. For example, setting up the grouping of [(A AND B) OR C] would show A and B having a "1" next to them, indicating their conjoined status at the first, most nested level.

There will be up to three levels of hierarchical grouping possible, specified from inner (most nested) to outer (most general) organizations. Ungrouping will work in the opposite manner, allowing the expert to unlink elements progressively from highest to lowest level groupings.

Summary

The local and global follow-up questions are expected to yield elaborated CEs by clarifying specific procedures and their rationales, as well as by characterizing the domain as a whole. In addition, the Grouping function will support clarification of procedures. Consequently, the instructional designer should have sufficient and rich information to facilitate curriculum development.

CONCLUSIONS

We are concerned with enhancing the development of intelligent instructional systems by focusing on, and automating, the process to obtain the "what" of these systems (i.e., expert model).

Heretofore, the practicality of using traditional elicitation and organization methods has been limited due to a number of reasons. First, traditional acquisition methods are very costly in terms of time, money, and skilled personnel resources. Second, they tend to be limited in scope of applicability. Finally, the specifications for using the various methods are largely unclear; they are more art than science. DNA can potentially deal with these shortcomings.

The costs associated with developing expert models for automated instruction can be reduced. Typically this development cycle involves a number of persons who perform different tasks across various points in time. For example, knowledge engineers elicit information through interviews, observations, and other techniques. Subsequently this information is transcribed. The transcription must then be simplified or coded into units representing discrete actions and bits of knowledge. Finally, cognitive psychologists arrange the information so that it suits the specific purpose for which the analysis was conducted—for example, expert model, cognitive simulation, or design of human–computer interface. In response to this resource–cost issue, DNA condenses these stages into one symbiotic, standardized process of eliciting and organizing knowledge. The result of this collapse is that the time overall to develop an expert model should be reduced because transcription and codification tasks are no longer necessary.

The scope of applicability of many traditional knowledge elicitation and organization methods is typically narrow. That is, many methods are designed to be domain or task specific. For example, Precursor, Action, Response, Interpretation (PARI; Hall, Gott, & Pokorny, 1995) has been shown to be useful in delineating troubleshooting procedures, particularly in relation to avionics tasks. DNA has been designed to apply to both procedural and conceptual domains. This makes it a broadly applicable tool in terms of specifying curricula for a variety of topics.

Finally, specifications for conducting analyses can be clarified. Schraagen et al. (1997) reviewed the current state of cognitive task analysis techniques and concluded, "Few integrated methods exist, that little attention is being paid to the conditions under which methods are appropriate, and that often it is unclear how products of CTA should be used" (p. 5). In response to this criticism, DNA was designed to automate and thus standardize the analysis process. This standardization is intended to reduce variance in the way that the technique is employed. However, because of inherent differences in knowledge representations, actual DNA outputs may still show variance among experts. In addition, its design is based on explicit principles of learning and instruction as embodied in SMART, a validated instructional tool. DNA's purpose is to obtain domain knowledge for intelligent instructional systems. Therefore, the use of DNA's output is readily apparent.

In addition to these features, DNA was designed to be user friendly. This extends the groups of people who can use such a tool to elicit the knowledge and skills underlying a particular domain or task. This contrasts with the few existing automated CTA programs (Hamilton, 1997; Williams, 1993; Zachary, Zaklad, Hicinbothom, Ryder, & Purcell, 1993), which typically require input by either programmers or human factors personnel.

We are well aware that DNA requires extensive empirical research. Consequently, we will be assessing its effectiveness and efficiency. Specifically, we will conduct a series of investigations, starting with basic questions: Can DNA be used to obtain meaningful data that parallel existing data in the same domain, elicited by traditional means? Our initial test of this question involves several statistics experts using DNA to decompose and network measures of central tendency. This allows us to determine the degree of similarity between an existing and effective expert model (i.e., Stat Lady, DS-2 module; Shute, Gawlick, & Lefort, 1996) and DNA-obtained data for the same topic. Preliminary data from this investigation are quite encouraging (see Shute, Torreano, & Willis, 1998).

In addition, we will investigate DNA's efficiency relative to other elicitation techniques. Specifically, can DNA obtain knowledge structures comparable to those obtained by traditional knowledge elicitation methods but more quickly? Other immediate research questions will examine the capabilities and limitations of DNA in relation to the types of domains, tasks, and purposes for which it is best suited. Some basic research questions that we will explore with DNA include examining novice-to-expert transitions within disparate domains and comparing knowledge representations underlying different levels of expertise within the same domain.

DNA promises to be a useful knowledge elicitation and organization tool for developing curriculum, representing a good first step towards opening up the bottleneck in intelligent tutoring system development as related to the expert model. Using DNA in conjunction with SMART should streamline this process. That is, DNA was developed to work in concert with SMART, deriving curriculum elements from experts that fit a particular instructional framework. This provides a rich database of underlying knowledge and skill elements that can be subsequently monitored by SMART with regard to learner's acquisition or mastery status. The degree to which this bottleneck is opened, however, will not be known until data come in from these necessary evaluations.

ACKNOWLEDGMENTS

The research reported in this chapter was conducted as part of the Air Force Research Laboratory, TRAIN Project, Brooks Air Force Base, Lackland, Texas. Funds for this research were provided by the Air Force Office of Scientific Research. In addition, this work was performed while the second author held a National Research Council AFRL Research Associateship. The opinions expressed in this chapter are those of the authors and do not necessarily reflect those of the U.S. Air Force.

REFERENCES

Anderson, J. R. (1983). *The architecture of cognition*. Cambridge, MA: Harvard University Press.

Anderson, J. R. (1988). The expert module. In M. C. Polson & J. J. Richardson (Eds.), *Foundations of intelligent tutoring systems* (pp. 21–50). Hillsdale, NJ: Lawrence Erlbaum Associates.

Anderson, J. R. (1993). *Rules of the mind*. Hillsdale, NJ: Lawrence Erlbaum Associates.

Card, S., Moran, T. P., & Newell, A. (1983). *The psychology of human-computer interaction*. Hillsdale, NJ: Lawrence Erlbaum Associates.

Collins, A. M., & Quillian, M. R. (1969). Retrieval time from semantic memory. *Journal of Verbal Learning and Verbal Behavior, 8,* 240–247.

Durkin, J. (1994). Knowledge acquisition. In J. Durkin (Ed.), *Expert systems: Design and development* (pp. 518–599). New York: Macmillan.

Gagné, R., & Briggs, L. (1965). *The conditions of learning*. New York: Rinehart & Winston.

Gordon, S. E., Schmierer, K. A., & Gill, R. T. (1993). Conceptual graph analysis: Knowledge acquisition for instructional system design. *Human Factors, 35,* 459–481.

Gray, W. D., John, B. E., & Atwood, M. E. (1993). Project Ernestine: Validating a GOMS analysis for predicting and explaining real-world task performance. *In Human-computer interaction* Vol. 8, pp. 237–309.

Hall, E. P., Gott, S. P., & Pokorny, R. A. (1995). *A procedural guide to cognitive task analysis: The PARI methodology* (Rep. No. AL/HR–TR–1995–0108). Brooks Air Force Base, TX: U.S. Air Force Material Command.

Hamilton, W. I. (1997). *Cognitive task analysis using ATLAS.* NATO-ONR Workshop on Cognitive Task Analysis, Washington, DC.

Hayes-Roth, F., Waterman, D. A., & Lenat, D.B. (1983). *Building expert systems.* Reading, MA: Addison Wesley.

Jonassen, D. H., Beissner, K., & Yacci, M. (1993). *Structural knowledge: Techniques for representing, conveying, and acquiring structural knowledge.* Hillsdale, NJ: Lawrence Erlbaum Associates.

Lajoie, S. P., & Derry, S. J. (1993). *Computers as cognitive tools.* Hillsdale, NJ: Lawrence Erlbaum Associates.

Newell, A. (1990). *Unified theories of cognition.* Cambridge, MA: Harvard University Press.

Polson, M. C., & Richardson, J. J. (1988). *Foundations of intelligent tutoring systems.* Hillsdale, NJ: Lawrence Erlbaum Associates.

Psotka, J. Massey, L. D., & Mutter, S. A. (1988). *Intelligent tutoring systems: Lessons learned.* Hillsdale, NJ: Lawrence Erlbaum Associates.

Ryder, J. M., & Redding, R. E. (1993). Integrating cognitive task analysis into instructional systems development. *Educational Technology Research and Development, 41,* 75–96.

Schraagen, J. M. C., Chipman, S. E., Shute, V., Annett, J., Strub, M., Sheppard, C., Ruisseau, J.-Y., & Graff, N. (1997). *State-of-the-art review of cognitive task analysis techniques* (Report of RSG.27 on Cognitive Task Analysis NATO Defence Research Group, Panel 8/RSG.27). (The Netherlands) TNO Human Factors Research Institute Group: Information Processing.

Shute, V. J. (1994). Learning processes and learning outcomes. In T. Husen & T. N. Postlethwaite (Eds.), *International encyclopedia of education* (2nd ed., pp. 3315–3325). New York: Pergamon Press.

Shute, V. J. (1995). SMART: Student modeling approach for responsive tutoring. *User Modeling and User-Adapted Interaction, 5,* 1–44.

Shute, V. J., & Catrambone, R. (1996, July). Unified vs. tailored analogies: Effects on conceptual knowledge acquisition. In *Proceedings of the ICLS 96 Conference.* Washington, DC: Association for the Advancement of Computers in Education.

Shute, V. J., Gawlick, L. A., & Lefort, N. K. (1996). *Stat Lady: Descriptive Statistics Module 2* [Unpublished computer program]. Brooks Air Force Base, TX: Armstrong Laboratory.

Shute, V. J., & Psotka, J. (1996). Intelligent tutoring systems: Past, present, and future. In D. Jonassen (Ed.), *Handbook of research on educational communications and technology* (pp. 57–600). New York: Macmillan.

Shute, V. J., Torreano, L. A., & Willis, R. E. (1998). DNA–Uncorking the bottleneck in knowledge elicitation and organization. In *Proceedings of the 4th International ITS 98 conference*, San Antonio, TX.

Shute, V. J., Willis, R. E., & Torreano, L. A. (1998). *DNA—Version 2.0* (Automated Cognitive Task Analysis Tool). [Unpublished computer program/prototype]. Brooks Air Force Base, TX: Armstrong Laboratory.

Sleeman, D. H., & Brown, J. S. (1982). *Intelligent tutoring systems*. London: Academic.

Williams, K. E. (1993). *The development of an automated cognitive task analysis and modeling process for intelligent tutoring system development*. Contract final report on N00014–91–J–5–1500. Manpower Personnel and Training Program, Office of Naval Research.

Zachary, W. W., Zaklad, A. L., Hicinbothom, J. H., Ryder, J. M., & Purcell, J. A. (1993). COGNET representation of tactical decision-making in anti-air warfare. In *Proceedings of the Human Factors and Ergonomic Society 37th Annual Meeting* (pp. 1112–1116). Seattle, WA. Human Factors & Ergonomic Society.

III

EPILOGUE

12

Fallible, Distractible, Forgetful, Willful, and Irrational Learners

Benedict du Boulay
University of Sussex

This chapter is about the interaction of artificial intelligence and the domain of education. From an educational point of view, the discipline of building computational theories of communication, learning, and teaching is a powerful tool in our attempts to understand educational processes. In particular, we view teaching as a specialized form of ordinary human communication. Human teachers learn their trade by extending and exploiting their existing rich stock of communicative competence, not just by applying some freestanding, self-contained body of expertise. This makes the task of understanding and duplicating this behavior all the more difficult.

In addition, the subject knowledge of human teachers (in mathematics, language, science, or other discipline) is also grounded in their everyday common sense, knowledge, and skills. Although we can now build tolerably good machine teachers for narrow domains, with limited tutorial and diagnostic abilities, such enterprises will always be limited by their lack of common sense. Trying to unpick the exact nature of this common sense is one of the goals of artificial intelligence in education.

The central problems viewed from an artificial intelligence perspective shift slightly depending on whether one's main focus of interest in education is the teacher side of the role, the student side, or the educational interaction itself and the cognitive tools that support this. Much of the work in artificial intelligence in education has concentrated on the teacher and assumed that it is the underlying goals of the teacher that shape the overall direction of the interaction with pupils. Even where the preference is that students take more responsibility for their own learning—for example, through the use of learning environments or project work—typically the teacher sets the broad parameters within which this student-centered learning takes place.

Among the plethora of issues facing teachers and designers of educational tools and environments are the following two questions:

- How can we engage and motivate students so that they are willing to attempt to learn?
- How can we ensure that what is learned during the educational interaction can be applied effectively outside that context?

A human or machine tutor that attempts a more student-centered educational strategy will also have to address such issues as these:

- How can we detect what the goals of the student are (if any) and whether they are consonant with the teaching goals of the teacher (if any)? This is a problem that can be especially hard when the student is unable to state his own goals clearly. In this case the issue may turn into that of how to help the student formulate learning goals.
- How can we make available to the student, both gracefully and effectively, the resources of the teacher, the educational environment in general (including other students), and the student himself to assist in the achievement of goals?

In concentrating on the interaction issues, the teacher needs to solve such problems as these:

- How to maintain focus and coherence in the interaction despite interruptions, asides, misunderstandings, embedded conversations, the long passage of time, and so on.
- How to play the conversational role of the teacher intelligently—for example, (a) how to make one's intentions to the learner clear, how to formulate explanations succinctly (given one's beliefs about the student's beliefs), or how to provoke the situation with an appropriate open-ended or highly specific question, when to repeat oneself and with what emphasis; and (b)

how to tease out from the student explanations, views, and beliefs when these are partially or poorly expressed.
- How to argue and convince

Finally, if one's interest is in the design of cognitive tools and educationally rich environments, the interesting problems include these:

- What makes an environment educationally rich? Is it the sparseness and versatility of (say) empty cardboard boxes? Or the richness and specificity of (say) LOGO? Or some other factors altogether?
- How does one choose what assistance might be helpful, and how does one offer that assistance in such a way so as not to undermine the student's sense of control of the interaction?

Few of these questions can be asked in a vacuum. Typically teacher and student encounter each other in an educational and cultural setting that provides institutional goals, constraints, and resources within which each is to operate. All of these resources carry with them affordances built over time and specific to a particular culture. The educational context includes other teachers (possibly other machine tutors) and other students who may in their turn frustrate or enhance the education of an individual.

Artificial intelligence in education is a broad discipline encompassing cognitive science, educational psychology, computer science, and artificial intelligence, to name but four. It includes those who wish to develop theories of human learning and their application in effective learning environments, as well as those interested in theories of teaching and their application in effective teaching systems. Clearly in many cases there is overlap between these two kinds of theories, as well as a fuzzy boundary between learning environments and teaching systems.

In many ways artificial intelligence in education is in a state of flux. People sometimes talk of one of its subfields, intelligent tutoring systems, as an outmoded technology that has in some sense "failed" (de Oliveira & Viccari, 1996). The emphasis today has shifted to exploring the possibilities of newer technologies such as virtual reality and the Internet and is particularly concerned with learning environments and collaboration. However, most of the traditional hard problems of student modeling still remain: adjusting the environment to meet the needs of the learners, determining what to say to learners and when to say it, and so on.

One aspect of the issue of teaching versus learning crystallized into the issue of whether the educational system should attempt to model the student (Lajoie & Derry, 1993). Modeling the student allows, at least in principle, the system to adjust its behavior or to react to that student as an individual, or at least as a representative of a class of individuals (see Shute, 1995). The argument for not modeling the student arises because it is hard (indeed some regard it as inherently impossible) or because it is thought unnecessary. The argument goes that if a learning environment is well designed and operated by the student within a supportive educational environment, we can rely on the students themselves to manage their own learning without having the system individualize its reactions in any way.

In some ways the heat has gone out of the debate between the modelers and the non-modelers. Although both camps have coexisted throughout the history of artificial intelligence in education, there is a stronger realization that both approaches have something useful to offer. Indeed both approaches are now sometimes to be found inside a single system, where an intelligent tutoring system of a traditional architecture may be but a single component of a more general, possibly distributed, system offering learners a variety of learning experiences from which they can choose (Mitchell, Liddle, Brown, & Leitch, 1996).

To try to get a sense of where the field is now, this chapter reviews current issues in artificial intelligence in education, drawing strongly, but not exclusively, on the fifty-nine papers presented at the Euroaied Conference held in Lisbon in September 1996. This was a gathering of researchers, drawn predominantly from Europe, who were reflecting on the field of artificial intelligence in education. The conference had an unusual structure. Prospective participants were invited to submit papers against a predefined list of questions. After refereeing, there was some recasting of the questions, and the papers were organized into sessions, each dealing with one set of questions (Brna, Paiva, & Self, 1996).

This chapter does not follow the session structure of the conference nor does it give equal weight to the papers. It represents a very personal view of what I thought was interesting, so some major pieces of work are only mentioned in passing and sometimes a minor detail of a paper is given more attention than perhaps its author might expect or wish. It represents my attempt to understand the kinds of issue on which the field of artificial intelligence in education is now concentrating, at least in Europe.

LEARNING AS A PROCESS

The main shift of focus of artificial intelligence in education has been from learning considered simply as epistemology to learning as a psychological process operating under a number of constraints. For example, there is the complex interaction between the domain presentation offered to the learner and the consequent nature of the learner's own internal representation of that domain (Scaife & Rogers, 1996). In this area computers as cognitive tools offer many possibilities for re-representing a domain. Further, there is the interaction between the learner's experience of "doing learning" and the consequent degree of reflective awareness of what he learned (Ainsworth, Wood, & Bibby, 1996; Barnard & Sandberg, 1996; Whitelock & Scanlon, 1996). Computers as cognitive tools open up new possibilities as devices to record students' actions for their later analysis.

This chapter develops the notion of learning as a process by considering five of its aspects. The first is affect: the fact that the learner's motivation (or lack of it) is a crucial factor in the learning process. The second is dialogue, now of central interest in artificial intelligence in education through its focus on collaboration. Third is knowledge organization, which splits into issues to do with context and with fragmentation. It is not just that learning always takes place in some external context that can affect the general outcome of what is learned, but that at least some of our learning (and therefore our recall) is episodic, that is, highly context specific. Moreover, our concepts in a particular domain are often unevenly developed, and we are able to tolerate gaps, discrepancies, and contradictions in what we know. Fourth is representation, both external and internal. Finally there is the issue of learning style and the way that teaching might be adapted to accommodate to (or not) the learner's preferences for particular kinds of perspectives, learning methods, approaches, and organizations of material.

Affect

The shift of emphasis from the "what" to the "how" of learning reflects an undermining of the idealization of the learner as some disembodied, entirely rational learning mechanism. A similar shift is evidenced by the willingness to acknowledge the affective dimension.

Students' motivation in learning is crucial, and some progress has been made in delineating its dimensions and describing how teaching can take account of the motivational state of the student (Keller, 1983; Lepper, 1988; Lepper & Chabay, 1988; Malone & Lepper, 1987).

One of the few systems to incorporate motivational modeling and planning into its teaching is del Soldato's MORE system (del Soldato, 1994; del Soldato & du Boulay, 1995). This system used the amount of student effort and the student's self-reported comments about her own motivation to adjust the difficulty of problems and the kind of help it offered.

Issroff and del Soldato (1996) provided an analysis of the main dimensions of intrinsic motivation, culled from the educational psychology and cognitive science literature. Del Soldato (1994) incorporated these dimensions—curiosity, challenge, confidence, and control—into MORE, which makes decisions about how to adjust the nature of learning tasks based on an explicit motivational theory. The work presented in Lisbon goes beyond the issue of how to make motivationally well-informed teaching decisions for a single learner by considering the issue of how best to motivate groups. This latter issue is concerned with how to promote collaboration within a group and how to promote competition between groups.

A very formal approach was adopted by Errico (1996), who used the situation calculus as the basis of a general-purpose student modeling system that includes primitives for reasoning about what an agent (such as the student) wants to know or is indifferent about knowing. Of course, this is a long way from the kind of experiments by Whitelock and Scanlon (1996), described later, which are a good example of the difficulties of constructing too easy an equation between what one might regard as motivating or demotivating and learning outcomes. Part of the current view of learning is the notion of sharing and the qualitatively different experience we have of undertaking a task purely privately as opposed to collaboratively. In addition, the exact nature of the collaboration can have dramatic effects. Progress in this area is slow, but motivation is now clearly on the agenda.

The notion of provoking and maintaining effective goal-directed behavior is a crucial issue and one that potentially unites the modelers and the nonmodelers in a common cause. Here the arguments are not so much whether one needs a tutor (either human or machine) to be associated with the simulation, but rather on how best to integrate tutorial capabilities in the simulation itself. While taking a weaker line on the need for integrating a tutor into a simulation-based environment, Moebus (1996) was concerned with the design principles of systems that would most effectively allow hypothesis generation and hypothesis checking by users.

A specific acknowledgment of the affective dimension in terms of systems development is found in the work of van Joolingen and de Jong (1996). They presented an authoring system to assist trainers in the design of learners' activities in simulation-based discovery environments. In some ways they provided a system that contains the means-ends rules of a classical intelligent tutoring system architecture, from which the trainer can select according to the expected training situation. Some of the attributes built into the system include such affective dimensions as "fear of failure" and "degree of motivation", whose values will have a profound effect on the success of different kinds of interaction with the system. Their concern is to stimulate goal-directed (rather than aimless) behavior on the part of the learners. In a similar vein, Forte and Forte (1996) specifically mentioned the dimension of "challenge," where the idea is not simply to provoke goal-directed behavior but to stimulate the learner's desire to learn through a challenging issue or problem to solve with the simulation system.

A similar concern with motivational issues was shown by Vassileva and Wasson (1996). Their versatile, reactive, dynamic planning system can (in principle) assess both its planned sequences and its reactions to the student based on assessments of the motivational consequences of such reactions (an issue that Issroff & del Soldato, 1996, also explore).

Lewin's (1996) work on developing an automated tutor for reading was concerned with trying to detect the child's motivational state and the child's aptitude and predisposition to use different strategies. The management of different problem-solving methods by the learner was a central issue for Lewin in her work on children learning to read, where they may use a wide variety of strategies—whole word, phonic, initial letter, context, and so on. Feedback was also a special issue for her, in that it is important to stimulate the child's interest and maintain her self-confidence, while still leaving space for her to learn from her mistakes in a productive manner.

Dialogue and Insight

"Dialogue" encompasses the internal dialogue within a single learner reflecting about learning and the external dialogue between separate individuals. Of course the two are related (Pask & Scott, 1975; Vygotsky, 1986). Born and Lusti (1996) described a blackboard architecture for tutoring systems based on a number of communicating knowledge sources. The system is designed to use the internal communication between the knowledge sources as a basis for constructing an external explanation to the learner.

Internal: Reflection. Self-explanation as described by Chi, Bassok, Lewis, Reimann, and Glaser (1989) is apparently a rather useful form of reflective or metacognitive behavior. It is an activity that good problem solvers are said to engage in, and it seems to provide a way for learners to establish more completely and more effectively what is being learned using what they already know and to explore the ramifications of the new material more fully.

So if some researchers are concerned, at some level, with ensuring that learners are properly engaged with the material, others are concerned with ensuring that the maximum gains are made by the learner as a result of that engagement. Barnard and Sandberg (1996) nicely illustrated the difficulty in practice of systematically provoking self-explanation as a reflective behavior in learners.

Barnard and Sandberg built a learning environment for the domain of tides to help students understand why, where, and how tides occur in relation to the movement of the earth, moon, and sun. Despite encouraging their students to engage in self-explanation so as to reveal areas of the tidal process that they did not understand, students were loathe to do this, and in general they had little insight into how partial their knowledge of these deceptively simple processes actually was.

The students were interested in learning the domain, and they knew how to ask themselves questions, but they did seem to demonstrate a genuine willingness to accept fragmented and nonsystematic understanding as their norm. This emphasizes the fact that learning is hard work, and self-explanation may be worth the extra effort only if the learner has some reason to believe that she will actually need the understanding for some future task. However, it leaves open the question as to whether the students knew that they had gaps and contradictions in their knowledge and did not care, or whether they did not appreciate that the gaps were there. Perhaps self-explanation is as much about motivation as it is about reasoning.

Barnard and Sandberg suggested that it is not simply a matter of showing learners how to do it. Their learners, although engaged in the task of learning about tides, showed great propensity to learn the material in a fragmented and nonsystematized way. It is clear that doing self-explanation consistently is harder work than learning piecemeal and that the issue of motivation and the reason the student is trying to learn the material at all will be of crucial importance (Laurillard, 1979).

Others working on self-explanation start from the premise that self-explanation is hard to achieve and offer technological solutions to generating the domain-specific self-explanative questions to the user in the hope that at least the learners will be exposed to these questions (at least for that domain) even if they do not learn how to undertake self-explanation as a general skill. It remains an open question as to what is the relation between offering students ready-made questions that they might ask themselves about the domain and prompting the students to generate questions for themselves about that domain. For instance, does a system that offers opportunities for reflection on past learning undermine the very skill it is attempting to foster by reducing the metacognitive agency of the learner? Barnard and Sandberg (1996) suggested that tool builders have to be open to this undesirable possibility.

Fung and Adam (1996) showed how, in principle, self-explanation questions can be generated from a domain representation based on Sowa's (1984) conceptual graphs, and Kashihara, Okabe, Hirashima, and Jun'ichi (1996) offered a system that engages users in a constrained form of concept mapping based around self-explanation.

To some extent, aspects of machine learning deal with a similar reflective process, in the sense that they are concerned with what kinds of more general hypotheses can be deduced by a student modeling system from the lower level data about the student—for instance, inducing the nature of a general misconception about Prolog from instances of individual bugs (Sison & Shimura, 1996). A lesson for intelligent tutoring system and intelligent learning environment design that seems to emerge from this is the importance for students to self-explain both correct examples and answers (Chi et al., 1989) and incorrect answers; that is, human students need to undertake the kind of self-modeling activities that would be undertaken by the student modeling component of an artificial intelligence in education system.

The educational utility of less than perfect answers was also indicated in the work of Faro and Giodano (1996). They describe a system for teaching about information systems design, one element of which is a case-based reasoning component that stores both teacher-annotated and unannotated student designs. They argue that critiquing a poor design by another student is an excellent way to learn.

Pain, Bull, and Brna (1996) were also concerned with reflection but in the narrower sense of reassessment of a view. They used a version of a student model as a "conversation piece" between teacher and student—the one to defend the model as an accurate depiction of the knowledge of the student, the other (the student) to either agree or, more often, to disagree and offer refinements. In addition to perhaps producing a more accurate assessment, it also provides a way of provoking students to think about exactly how much they have and have not learned. One could imagine such a scenario augmented with the specific self-explanatory schemas that Fung and Adam (1996) and Kashihara et al. (1996) suggested.

In a rather different stance, Swaak and de Jong (1996) argued for the value of intuitive knowledge and the utility of simulations to promote it. Intuitive knowledge is knowledge that is not verbalizable, and thus is not open so easily to a reflective internal dialogue. In some ways their argument is similar to that of Sime (1996), whose experiment suggested that learners benefited from being exposed to a qualitative before a quantitative perspective on a domain.

External: Collaboration.   One of the most important factors in the recent development of artificial intelligence in education has been the increasing interest in collaboration, normally between learners but also between teacher and learner. E-mail, computer conferencing, and the World Wide Web turn computers into cognitive tools that enable collaboration bridging space and time constraints.

The collaborative possibilities opened up by simple audio links was explored by Whitelock and Scanlon (1996). They studied collaborative learning by pairs of adults in the domain of physics problem solving. Much of the communication within each pair was concerned with the difficult task of establishing a "joint problem space" (Teasley & Roschelle, 1993). Whitelock and Scanlon (1996) adjusted the gender mix of the pairs and the mode of interaction. In one mode, pairs worked side by side, and in the other members of the pair were in separate locations with an audio link. The authors were interested in such issues as the subjects' degrees of curiosity, interest, tiredness, boredom, expectation, challenge, partnership, control, and attentiveness.

The intriguing result from the work is that the pairs linked by audio showed greater learning gains than those who had worked side by side. Moreover, these greater learning gains were achieved despite the pairs' reporting greater tiredness and greater feelings of not being on the same wavelength as their partner and (not surprisingly) reporting difficulties of shared reference. On the positive side, pairs linked by audio liked the resulting possibilities for a certain degree of autonomy in their work.

One possible explanation of the greater learning gains despite the narrower channel of communication lies precisely in that narrower channel. In order to solve shared reference problems and synchronize their problem solving (when they so wished), the participants would have had to engage in much more careful analysis of their mutual understanding. Those sitting side by side were perhaps lulled into a false sense of being on the same wavelength that did not require the same conscious attempts to maintain the mutual understanding that was needed to make the audio-only link work. In a way, impoverishing the communication link forced mutual and self-explanation to the fore.

For de Oliveira and Viccari (1996), collaboration acted as both a design metaphor for intelligent learning systems and an architectural principle. The metaphoric aspect was important to them because it signaled a shift away from the one-to-one, over-controlled, and knowledge-focused intelligent tutoring systems of the 1980s. This mixed interest in the metaphoric and the practical is also in evidence in the work of Cerri (1996) and Paiva (1996), although these two offered fairly explicit architectural details—in Paiva's case, as an attempt to make the learner modeling aspect of system design application independent.

Plotzner, Hoppe, Fehse, Nolte, and Tewissen (1996) explored the subtle interactions between representation and learning. Like Sime (1996), they were interested in qualitative and quantitative perspectives in science, and like Ainsworth et al. (1996) they were interested in multiple representations. The extra factor for them was the way that having students build concept maps supports learning and reflection when undertaken collaboratively. While the end product of building a concept map might look like a small hypermedia system, it is clear that pedagogically building a concept map is a wholly different task from exploring a ready-made map (De Vries, 1996). In an empirical study with two phases, students initially learned a topic in mechanics in either qualitative or quantitative terms. Pairs of subjects were then formed (one qualitatively trained, the other quantitatively trained), and the pairs had to cooperate on tasks that required coordinating their separate qualitative and quantitative knowledge. All subjects increased their scores following the first phase, and all subjects learned to relate the qualitative and quantitative in the second phase. However, students who had initially learned the material qualitatively gained significantly more from the second, collaborative phase than did those who had originally been exposed to the same material quantitatively. This result strongly echoed that of Sime (1996).

Plotzner et al. (1996) developed an environment that enables students both to work on their own at building concept maps *and* work cooperatively to combine such maps, for example, by adding annotations or encapsulating parts of the map in higher-level concepts. The tool and the educational methodology reifies the activity of reflection through the collaborative phase. While this tool is simply a device to build concept maps, these authors are developing a new version that contains a declarative hypertext model of the domain that will additionally enable students to undertake explorations in the style of De Vries (1996).

Another collaborative theme is that of teacher as master of ceremonies, taking part in collaborations directly or stage-managing collaborations among learners. Leroux, Vivet, and Brezillon (1996) described a multilayered model of cooperation (a weak form of collaboration) in which pedagogical assistants work with a small group of students on a micro-robot programming task, and these groups themselves interact in a reflective phase. The use of intermediaries between the teacher and the learners was also explored by Hietala and Niemirepo (1996), who described an experiment in which students learning equation solving could enlist the help of companions (distinct from the teacher) with differing degrees of expertise. Like Barnard and Sandberg (1996), they were interested in the issue of whether roles that human participants routinely play in an educational setting can be undertaken by the machine without violating the students' expectations of what are reasonable roles for a machine (du Boulay, Luckin, & del Soldato, 1999).

The question of exactly how self-questioning, self-explanation, and reflective learning can be assisted by dialogue is being explored by several researchers. Cook (1996) offered an analysis of educational dialogues and a dialogue mark-up scheme. This can be used to annotate naturally occurring dialogues as a step toward implementing computer tutors, computer peers, or indeed dialogue referees (Inaba & Okamoto, 1997) who could intervene in peer group discussions. His analysis focused on the kinds and patterns of dialogue moves that promote reflection, monitoring, reasoning, and motivation.

Pilkington and Mallen (1996) took a similar approach, but their focus was on the issue of exactly how dialogues promote learning and the roles that different participants in a dialogue play. Given the general interest in peer group learning, whether with human or machine peers, Pilkington and Mallen looked at the issue of whether more learning takes place when one member of the interactive pair takes specific responsibility for provoking reflection, that is, by acting as a teacher rather than simply a co-learner. As with Cook (1996) the analysis was seen as an initial empirical-theoretical step toward the design of effective tutors able to be interactive through dialogue. Burton and Brna (1996) were interested in building a system to take part in collaborative dialogues. As a step toward that goal, they developed a theoretical model based on Dialogue Games that attempts to allocate a dialogic role for each utterance. Their approach is an interesting contrast to that of Pilkington and Mallen (1996), who were also interested in Dialogue Games and were working at the same finely grained level but starting from naturally occurring dialogues.

A similar interest in the roles that different participants play in collaboration was explored by Issroff and del Soldato (1996). Here they were concerned about the nature of the kinds of pairings on learning outcomes and on the distribution of control of learning and the control of the tool (e.g., a keyboard) in paired problem-solving tasks. They pointed out that the way a pair works together is not just a matter of the individual capabilities of the pair but is also dependent on the social and educational context within which they are operating and the degree to which that context supports or undermines collaboration.

In addition to being interested in the fine detail of collaboration, two groups were developing interfaces to support and shape collaboration. In many ways, the work of Baker and Lund (1996) is similar to that of Plotzner et al. (1996), in that they provided an interface for students to co-construct graphical concept maps in physics. One difference is that the aspects of the interface concerned with communication between partners are given greater prominence. Baker and Lund compared two different communication interfaces. One, Chat-box, enables relatively unconstrained dialogues to occur. The other contains specific buttons to introduce different kinds of domain-level sentences associated with concept map building, such as, "What is its name?" ("it" being a chain in the concept map), as well as specific buttons to enable the participants to manage the dialogue itself, such as, "What should we do now?" In their experiment, both interfaces produced about the same ratio of dialogue to domain-level activity in concept mapping, but the dedicated interface seemed to provoke more in the way of task-specific communication than Chat-box.

Dillenbourg, Traum, and Schneider (1996) also experimented with a multimodal interface (via a shared graphical white board, a textual multi-user object-oriented environment, and an audio link), though the task was to solve a murder mystery rather than map out a subdomain of physics. Wide variations were found in the way that pairs of subjects performed the task, in particular in the way that subjects established a common understanding of some part of the problem (recall how hard this was for Whitelock and Scanlon's, 1996, audio-linked adults solving a physics problem). In particular, the experimenters found that the same subjects would use a variety of methods to establish common understanding at different points in the process and that these methods would make differential use of the available modalities.

Knowledge Organization

Many studies show that with increasing experience of a domain, intermediates and then experts structure their knowledge of that domain differently than novices do (Chi, Glaser, & Farr, 1988). It is not just that experts know more; they also know differently (see Schmidt & Boshuizen, 1993, for an example drawn from medicine). Even over the shorter term, how someone comes to (partially) understand a topic is very dependent on the idiosyncratic features of the learning experience in which they engaged. Factors that affect knowledge organization include the overall context within which the learning takes place, what learners already know, and what kinds of activity they engage in as a learning experience. An outcome is that acquired knowledge can be patchily understood and can contain gaps and contradictions; that is, it can be fragmented.

Context. The episodic nature of learning was addressed by Specht and Weber (1996). They echoed the distinction between content planning and delivery planning articulated by Wasson (1996). Specht and Weber were concerned with adaptivity in delivery, in particular in providing prompts, reminders, and explanations that refer to problems of a similar kind that the student has met before. They envisaged an interaction between a student and a learning system that would endure over many sessions and allow for references to sessions from much earlier. One can see this as a means to promote reflection in problem solving because their system specifically aimed at sensitizing the student to similarities and differences between the current problem and previous ones of a similar type.

Context specificity of a nonepisodic kind was described by MacLaren and Koedinger (1996). They explore the phenomenon that students are more reliably able to solve algebra problems when they are embedded in a story problem than when they are presented as a word equation and even better than when they are presented simply as a symbolic equation. In some ways this seems counterintuitive, since solving the symbolic equation would appear to be a subtask of solving a story problem. In their modeling work, they were interested in characterizing zones of proximal development for their domain in a way similar to Luckin's (1996) attempt to define them in the area of simple ecology. Their work supported the notion of cumulativeness offered by Akhras and Self (1996, and also this volume) in that it was the very "cumulativeness" of the story problem in the student's existing rich experience of the context of the problem that enabled the superior problem solving.

Both the problem-solving context-specific nature of learning and the way that people will often attempt to avoid learning if at all possible was addressed by Oppermann and Thomas (1996). They described how in the workplace people often prefer to ask a knowledgeable colleague rather than use a manual. They also described how casual users of a system often have to recreate the same solution to the same problem each time they meet it because little effective learning took place at the time the problem was first solved. They offered a technology, "demotheque," for an individual or a group to build up a personal or group-specific set of annotations, possibly multimedia annotation, on how to solve specific problems in a computing environment. The educational value of glossaries, and a technology to assist in the construction of glossaries, was presented by Colazzo and Costantino (1996) as a related technological fix to a context problem. They were concerned especially with ensuring that the educational context of the learner (assumed to be reading a hypertext page) is disrupted as little as possible by the method of calling up and displaying a glossary definition.

Activity. The issue of how new knowledge and skill are constructed (as opposed to the content of that knowledge and skill) was centrally addressed in the work of Akhras and Self (1996). Their concern was with the activities in which learners should engage in order that they can effectively construct their own new knowledge. Instruction in their scheme is not primarily concerned with sequencing exposure to predefined objective knowledge, but with sequencing activities or situations in which the learner can operate. They were concerned with defining a topology of situations and patterns of interaction. In particular they referred to two properties of learning processes, cumulativeness (using prior knowledge) and constructiveness (elaborating prior knowledge), which seem not dissimilar to the Piagetian terms of assimilation and accommodation. A challenging issue here is the extent to which it is possible to provide a theory of action in artificial intelligence in education terms that is more than a theory of the knowledge that the action touches on.

Akhras and Self argued that a commitment to a constructivist position on learning does not make the notion of instruction self-contradictory. Rather, instructional planning in such a rationale is no longer driven directly by the structural properties of the expert's view of the knowledge.

It is now driven by a concern to sequence the interactive activities of the learner in an effective manner such that the learner can come to construct a personal understanding that has some structural resemblance to that of the expert. Even if we allow for the infinite variety of how each one of us knows some topic, there have to be some commonalities between different ways of knowing; otherwise it is not clear how any kind of communication is possible.

The importance and value of planning, and its neutrality as an activity with respect to one's learning theory, was stressed by Vassileva and Wasson (1996) and by Wasson (1996). Wasson offered a constructivist continuum from radical through mild to instructivists. Mild constructivism seemed to be the dominant view in these papers, and this view retained a place for instruction and thus for instructional planning. (As a side issue, I find it sad that intelligent tutoring systems have come to be associated by some researchers with a nonconstructivist approach, as if a constructivist never wrote a paper or delivered a lecture. For powerful counterarguments, see Mayer, 1997, and Derry & Lajoie, 1993.)

A similar concern with action (or the "how" rather than the "what") was shown in Luckin's (1996) work, which applied a Vygotskian perspective to instruction. One focus of her work was to provide an operational definition of Vygotsky's notion of the zone of proximal development. As with Akhras and Self (1996), the idea was to reason about the sequence and character of the activities of the learner. In Luckin's case, the issue was to find the balancing point between what a child can do unaided and what he can do with expert machine teacher assistance. Luckin compared three variants of a system to teach simple ecology and found significant process and outcome differences among the subjects, depending on the way the system variant played the role of the more able partner (Luckin, 1998; Luckin & du Boulay, 1999).

Fragmentation.   The issue of the fragmented nature of learning is an ongoing issue. For instance, it figured centrally in the work of Barnard and Sandberg (1996). It also arose in the work of Karlgren and Ramberg (1996), who stressed two issues: the fragmentary nature of our own and our students' knowledge and its high context specificity and the importance of language and the use of language in coming to understand a new domain, an issue that links us via Vygotsky to Luckin (1996). To involve language is to involve the social dimension and then to open up the issue of the role that the social context plays in what we know and how we know it. Karlgren and Ramberg stressed the notion of language games and saw instruction as a process of learning how to reason and how to use the language of the new activity.

The unevenness of learning progress, or fragmentation over time, was explored by Giangrandi and Tasso (1996), who offered a logical foundation for modeling the evolving beliefs of the student and the evolving beliefs of the tutor about the student's belief. Their scheme allowed for the essentially nonmonotonic nature of both these processes; they had a nice example of a Socratic dialogue produced as a sequence of formulas in their calculus. The passage of time during learning was also an issue raised by Issroff and del Soldato (1996), who were concerned with the way that affective issues have some kind of time profile that needs to be taken into account. This is reminiscent of the work of Specht and Weber (1996), who described a mechanism for reminding the student of the context of earlier problem-solving episodes.

Some domains are, in principle, "neat" and yet lead to fragmented and contradictory learning; others are inherently "scruffy." Two papers considered the issue of ill-structured (scruffy) domains from rather different perspectives. De Vries (1996) explored the issue of the nature of the links in a hypermedia system (it is described later in this chapter). A more student-centered approach was adopted by Schroeder, Moebus, and Thole (1996) who described a system for medical diagnosis to build diagnostic models of complex medical domains. In some ways the idea is for the student doctors to impose some neatness and structure on what otherwise would be a fragmented set of individual items of knowledge. Here the links that the student doctors build are links in a (hidden) bayesian network rather than a hypermedia network, but one could imagine the two technologies coming together to provide an interesting simulation environment.

Presentation and Representation

An ongoing issue in mathematics, science, and engineering education is finding the right balance between developing students' qualitative reasoning and understanding about some phenomenon, as well as extending their ability to deal with the same issues in quantitative terms. This is an instance of the provision and exploration of multiple models of a particular domain (see White & Frederikson, 1987, for an elaboration of this issue for tuition in electricity). For example, students with well-developed intuitions about the qualitative aspects of a process (say) can conduct an internal conversation in the style described by Chi et al. (1989) about whether the answer to a quantitative problem that they have solved makes sense. A similar issue occurs in early arithmetic education where some children are willing to offer clearly nonsensical answers to sums they have worked symbolically or on calculators because the semantics of the calculation are not (able to be) considered.

Sime (1996) described the results of an experiment in engineering where there was an attempt to get novice and nonnovice students to view and experiment with the same topic from each of three different perspectives. The students approached each of these perspectives in both a quantitative and a qualitative manner, that is, 3 × 2 views—the belief being that expertise is associated with versatility of approach. An issue that immediately arises is the order in which the different perspectives should be sequenced in learning.

The system in question was a model switching process rig demonstration, a dynamic physical system. The system could be studied through a model of the heat transfer process, a model of the gas flow process, and a combined model. Sime was attempting to find evidence in support of a hypothesis derived from cognitive flexibility theory (Spiro, Coulson, Fletovich, & Anderson, 1988), which predicted that the highest learning gains would be achieved if the sequence through the perspectives obeyed the constraint that perspective n should differ from perspective $n - 1$ by only a single dimension in the 3 × 2 space. That is, a student could move in one jump from qualitative heat flow to qualitative gas flow, or from the quantitative combined model to its corresponding qualitative view, but not from qualitative gas flow to quantitative heat flow.

Contrary to her expectations, Sime found that the greatest learning gains arose for students who were exposed in general to qualitative before quantitative models. This produced slightly better learning gains than the more selective method that traversed the 3 × 2 matrix by changing only a single dimension at a time. One possibility is to see the result as an indication of the need for the students to grasp the subject in its entirety in qualitative terms before attempting to deal with some particular aspect using quantitative methods. Another explanation might be that the shift in perspective between qualitative and quantitative is cognitively more costly than that between different aspects of the domain (e.g., heat flow and gas flow), in which case making the shift once only would be beneficial.

Sime had a further interesting negative result in that the novice group, who were exposed to quantitative before qualitative perspectives, had lower posttest than pretest scores and so seemed to have gained little from the interaction. Sime pointed out that in many engineering curricula, the quantitative tends to precede the qualitative, and therefore they may be organized nonoptimally for the novices they are educating.

Ainsworth et al. (1996) were interested in the issue of developing children's ability to undertake numerical estimation of sums that they were unlikely to be able to compute exactly in their heads, for example, 84×44. They were also interested in the development of children's ability in prediction, by which they meant the ability to judge the accuracy of an estimation: Is it an overestimate or an underestimate? Is it likely to be wide of the mark or close to the accurate answer?

They conducted an experiment to examine the effect of multiple representations in the interface of a computer-based tool on children's ability to estimate, where the representations provided varying means of displaying the accuracy of the estimate. The system offered tools to help undertake the estimation where the degree of assistance could be faded with increasing expertise, as well as a means for the children to record results. Children were encouraged as part of the interaction to reflect on the relative accuracy of different kinds of estimation methods.

For example, a child working on the problem of estimating 387×123 might be helped to go through the following steps (Ainsworth et al., 1996, p. 338):

1. Produce the intermediate solution:
—round to 400×100
2. Predict the accuracy of the estimate based on the intermediate solution:
—not very close to the exact answer
—lower than the exact answer
3. Produce the estimate:
—4,000
4. Compare how well the answer matched the prediction.

Each child's predictions and comparisons were displayed using a pair of representations: one showing the magnitude of the deviation of the prediction from the true answer categorically and the other showing both the magnitude and direction of the deviation as a continuous value. The children were intended to learn how to estimate better and learn how to predict the accuracy of their estimates, by observing the size and nature of the deviation of their estimate from the true answer via the given representations.

Each of these representations was offered in mathematical form, as a histogram and a numeric display, or in pictorial form, as an archery target and a "splat wall." Children in the experiment worked with two mathematical representations, or with two pictorial representations, or with mixed representations consisting of one mathematical (numeric display) and one pictorial (archery target).

Ainsworth and her colleagues looked at two measures. One was the change in the children's ability to make accurate estimations—that is, how near to the true answer was their estimate. The other measure concerned the children's insight into the quality of their estimate—their prediction about the accuracy of the estimate. For example, we can imagine a situation where the child estimates that 84×44 is equal to roughly 3,200 on the grounds that the product is close to 80×40. Now, this is not a bad estimate, but the child may believe incorrectly that it is a very accurate estimate. So she would score fairly well on estimation but not so well on prediction.

All of the children in the experimental groups learned to estimate better over the period of the experiment compared to a control group. However, when it came to predictive accuracy, children who had worked with either two mathematical representations or two pictorial representations improved, whereas children who had worked with mixed representations did not.

One possibility is to regard the two tasks, estimation and prediction, as relatively independent and assume that the extra work in dealing with mixed representations reduced learning performance in the prediction task. Certainly the result underlines the issue of the sensitivity of problem-solving performance to changes in representation, as already indicated in the section on Sime's (1996) work.

Another possibility is to see this as an intriguing finding, indicating a situation in which a skill, estimation, had been improved, but insight, prediction, of the learner into that skill had not improved in tandem. If this were the case, one would need to investigate why the mixed representations were poorer specifically at supporting reflection compared to the coordinated representations, an issue that reminds us of Barnard and Sandberg's (1996) students' problems with self-explanation.

The work of Ainsworth et al. (1996), Sime (1996), and De Vries (1996) illustrates how sensitive learning is to choices of representation. In these cases, the alternative representations were offering different perspectives on the subject matter, but at essentially the same level of granularity. The issue of combining representations was also tackled, for modal logic by Oliver and O'Shea (1996) and for Prolog by Good and Brna (1996). Good and Brna explored the possibility that a particular kind of representation may be needed only as a transitional device to help students at a particular stage in their learning; thereafter it can be largely dispensed with as too cumbersome to reason with.

It is often the case that during problem solving or design, one needs to tackle a problem at very different levels of generality at different stages of the process. An intelligent system to teach such a process would therefore itself need to be able to represent and discuss the evolving solution or design at whatever was the most appropriate granularity for that stage. This kind of multilevel approach was adopted by Mayorga and Verdejo (1996) in their analysis of the design cycle involved in authoring systems. A similar acceptance of the need to work at different levels of granularity at different stages was taken by Pemberton, Shurville, and Sharples (1996) in their analysis of the tools needed to support the process of writing.

With the rise and rise of the World Wide Web and the improvement in quality of virtual reality technology, the educational aspects of the representations that they afford are of considerable interest.

World Wide Web.   Work in artificial intelligence in education has been influenced by the increasing use of hypermedia and the World Wide Web (Brusilovsky, Ritter, & Schwarz, 1997). One of the areas of interest is the degree to which a system can intelligently adjust the links available to the learner in a given hypermedia system. An ongoing issue both within and outside artificial intelligence in education concerns navigation—that is, providing an effective means of constraining useful paths to follow, determining one's current position in the network, or revisiting past pages of interest.

De Vries (1996) explored the issue of the nature of the links in a hypermedia system. Her experiments compared two hypermedia systems with link types defined in different ways, where the actual nodes of information so linked were identical. She was interested in the structure of these systems. She produced two systems. In each case, the nodes consisted of descriptions of concrete objects or events in the domain of energy and energy transfer (e.g., a turbine) in physics. In one system (the network structure) the links were based on an energy-theoretic conceptual analysis of the domain, for example, in terms of energy transformers, reservoirs, and transfer. In the other system (the index system), the overall structure was provided using an index node that gave the titles of all the available nodes and through which all internode movement had to pass. Although the energy-theoretic terms were mentioned in the node titles, they did not of themselves form the basis of the linkage as in the network structure version. The comparison was therefore between a multiply connected (though not a hierarchic) network whose very structure was determined by energy concepts and a network with a rather looser, radial structure centered on an index node.

In one of her experiments, students were invited to explore both hypermedia systems in order to select three nodes according to a given criterion and then later solve an energy problem. Because the hypermedia system was implemented in Hypercard, the nodes were referred to as cards. The card (node) selection task existed in two forms. The first was conceptual and invited students to select three cards according to a criterion related to the basic concepts of the domain—for example, "Select three cards that display objects producing heat." By contrast, a superficial task of the same surface form invited subjects to select cards according to some incidental common feature—for example, whether the card featured something using water.

De Vries was interested in the degree of exploration of the 54 cards of each network and in the outcomes of the card-selection and problem-solving tasks. She found that many more cards were visited by subjects using the network structure version of the hypermedia system compared to the index version. (Whether one agrees with De Vries that this is a good outcome is, of course, open to question.) This differential exploration was true for both the superficial and the conceptual card selection tasks. In nearly all cases, the selection tasks were completed correctly. Contrary to her expectation, performance on the problem-solving task was the same for both hypermedia systems.

Of course, it is possible to critique the methodology and the results of this experiment: Was there a ceiling effect in the card selection task or a floor effect in the problem-solving task? Were there both semantic and organizational differences in the structure of the two systems? Were the results significant? What exactly was the nature of the problem-solving task? However, there are intriguing issues here. The domain-specific link types encouraged roughly double the amount of exploration of the domain. However, the learning outcomes on the problem-solving task, which should have been improved by this exploration, were no better. By the same token, the domain-specific links were less efficient in helping the students solve the given card selection problems, in the sense that they chose to look at more cards in order to solve those problems.

Virtual Reality. A careful analysis of the potential values of virtual reality technology, especially in the area of conceptual learning, was provided by Whitelock, Brna, and Holland (1996). Taking a more evangelistic line, Roussos, Johnson, Leigh, Vasilakis, and Moher (1996) illustrated some of the potential problems of high-fidelity representations especially when entertainment and education are intermixed without due care (emphases in the following quotation are mine):

> The main constructive activity is to build and develop small local ecosystems on the bare parts of the island. . . . Various seeds for planting garden vegetables and trees are stored in crates and serve as starting points for building micro-ecosystems on the island. *Additionally, the child can elicit the assistance of several genies, such as a cloud genie to provide rain, or the fire-flies to illuminate the vast underground expanse.* Our immediate plans are to have the genies make their actions explicit, in the case where the child cannot perceive the cause and effect right away. When the user drops a seed on the ground, the corresponding plant, flower or tree will start to grow. The pace in which this happens can be predetermined; we may choose to see the system grow very quickly, or, *in the case of a school project, extend it over the period of a semester.* The tomatoes, carrots, pumpkins and other plant objects contain a set of characteristics that contribute to their growth. They all have values for their age, the amount of water they hold, the amount of light they need, their proximity to other plants of their kind. . . . Visual cues aid the child in determining the state of the plant or flower. *When the cloud has been pouring rain over it for too long, the plant opens an umbrella; when the sunlight is too bright, it wears sunglasses.* (Roussos et al., 1996, p. 132)

There seem to be two potential difficulties here. First is the issue of whether the system is supposed to be teaching science or providing entertainment; of course, the two are not mutually exclusive, but there do seem to be mixed messages here about which parts of the simulation are intended to be taken seriously by the child as a model of the world and which parts are there for fun. The second difficulty is concerned with the value of simulations versus the real phenomenon; my vote would be for growing real seeds in real earth if a whole semester is available.

While virtual reality heads toward high-fidelity landscapes, there still remain many subtle issues to examine concerning the conventions of graphic output and learners' understanding and misunderstanding of simple diagrams. On the first issue, given the many possibilities for high-quality graphical output in educational systems, the system designer needs guidelines (and ideally a theory) to assist in the choice of which kind of graphical convention to use for what kind of purpose in which kind of context. Some very interesting principles of visual communication have been developed by Percoco and Sarti (1996) together with a number of useful rules of thumb. On the second issue, Laborde (1996) was concerned with learners' reasoning about geometric properties from figures and constructions as compared to reasoning from symbolic representations of geometric objects. The very concreteness of the figure and its possible accidental alignments and other visual properties are both a support for reasoning and a source of misreasoning. Laborde's (1996) careful analysis of how visual perception can sometimes get in the way of reasoning is a useful counterargument to those who argue that more graphics and more virtual reality *must* be better.

Style

The variability of preferred learning styles was an issue for some researchers. The idea is usually to vary the availability of learning resources in general, the sequencing of the specific material, and, possibly, the nature of the learning activities to suit the predisposition of the learner. Of course, one could argue that this adjustment might be just the wrong thing to do consistently in that it might be a recipe for not provoking reflection and self-explanation (but that is purely speculation).

Kommers and Lenting (1996) provided a high-level model of educational interaction and argued for the versatility of "telematic supported cooperative learning" to support a wide variety of learning styles and educational needs. Dobson and McCracken (1996) adopted a position based loosely on conversation theory (Pask & Scott, 1975) and offered a means, also in the context of distance-learning technology, to allow for learners with either "holist" or "serialist" tendencies. Like Cook (1996) and Pilkington and Mallen (1996) they were also working toward capturing the essence of naturally occurring dialogue interaction, but in the context of remotely situated partners rather than face-to-face partners, as in the other studies. So for them there were several extra dialogue issues to worry about concerning the effective maintenance of shared common work space and view of problem at hand, one of the problems that Whitelock and Scanlon (1996) addressed.

The more radical, and indeed versatile, suggestions for capturing learning style and personality issues and then tailoring the following educational interaction accordingly were provided by Du Plessis and De Kock (1996). Their idea was to make the student undertake a battery of pretests and then use the scores to adjust the kind of interaction that the system offered the student. The following paragraph gives a flavor of the kind of analysis that their system will undertake, using fuzzy logic to tie together pretest scores to educational treatments:

> A typical engineering student may have been classified as a converger by Kolb's LSI, as an introvert/sensory/thinking/judging type by a MBTI test and a Mel[ancholic] phleg[matic] by La Haye's temperament test. . . . This student prefers sensory information, a deductive approach to learning, a good mixture of both actual and reflective processing of information, and a structured learning environment. His temperament blend suggests that he may need help in goal setting, and that he may be gifted and therefore needs special and extra explanatory material. . . . It continues to specify specific presentation elements that can be used to support these goals . . . mind maps, descriptions, explanations, examples, demonstrations, diagrams, flow and step charts, drill and practice exercises, step by step tutorials, the oretical and practical readings, case studies and teaching games. (Du Plessis & De Kock, 1996, p. 178)

In a way, one can view this as attempting to perform a similar kind of analysis as Akhras and Self (1996), but at a coarser level of granularity, though the relationships embodied between personality variables and activity types are perhaps more ad hoc in Du Plessis and De Kock's (1996) case.

MODELING

Given the state of artificial intelligence in education, researchers are attempting reflection on various subfields. For example, Whitelock et al. (1996) delineated the potential for virtual reality in conceptual learning; Fenley (1996) undertook a similar task for multimedia; Salles, Pain, and Muetzelfeldt (1996) compared different kinds of qualitative reasoning schemes in terms of their utility for modeling ecological processes.

One of the most ambitious synthesizing projects was that of Mizoguchi, Sinitsa, and Ikeda (1996). They embarked on the task of con-structing an ontology for artificial intelligence in education. This can be seen as preliminary to the development of a versatile authoring system able to reason about different kinds of educational interaction and their probable outcomes. In some ways the goal is a more general version of what Errico (1996) attempted with the situation calculus, in that it was attempting to model not only the student's possible changes of state of knowledge but also all the other aspects of educational interactions.

Sometimes it seems hard to make substantive progress. For example, Desmoulins and van Labeke (1996) described a logic programming–based system for critiquing students' geometric constructions, much in the style of classical work by Goldstein (1975). Despite the overall change of emphasis in the field, many standard modeling problems have emerged, though sometimes stated in different terms.

The Student

It is clear that shifting the focus of instructional planning toward planning the nature of the educational interactions rather than planning the traversal of the experts' view of the domain does not make the problem of student modeling go away; it just changes it. In such a system the student modeling issue will be concerned with exactly the extent to which a particular activity may or may not be, or may not have been, successfully cumulative. So the focus of student modeling shifts into a model of how the student learns and away from what the student learns.

Even in simulation-based environments, there will be a need to try to relate explanations from the system to the goals of the student and to interpret actions on the simulation or hypotheses about the behavior of the simulation in terms of what the student knows and does not know.

A striking example of the tension that can be provoked by the phrase *student modeling* was shown by Forte and Forte (1996). They linked a pedagogical hypertext to a simulation system augmented by a mechanism to propose specific activities to the student: typically to find a route within the simulation, from a given start state to a given goal state. For them the "classical" notion of a student model was "useless," but they had a means to select preferred routes through the pedagogical hypertext for different purposes, and they wished to discriminate between different classes of student, in terms of their conceptual gaps, in order to select the most useful of the preferred routes. This may not be classic student modeling, but it seems to me that it is still student modeling.

The Domain

A classic issue that has driven the evolution of most systems is that of modeling the domain of interest explicitly. A recurrent theme has been the fact than an intelligent learning environment has modeled some domain, D, where the learner is supposed to be learning a higher-level domain, *Dprime*. For example, the early Sophie system provided an interactive learning environment for electronic troubleshooting, where the learner made measurements and replaced components in a simulated circuit (Brown, Burton, & de Kleer, 1982). The system could report the effects (and the utility) of these changes but could not directly engage the learner in a discussion about troubleshooting per se. Here the domain D was the behavior of the circuit under various conditions, but the domain of interest, *Dprime*, was the higher-level skill of troubleshooting. Later versions of Sophie addressed this issue. A similar evolution occurred in the development of Guidon, where the initial domain, D, was based on a diagnostic expert system where the diagnostic theory, *Dprime*, was implicit within the system. In order to engage the learner in activities that focused on diagnosis itself, it was important to reengineer the system in such a way that *Dprime* was modeled explicitly and was not just an emergent property of D.

This tension between D and *Dprime* is still in evidence. I already noted the issue in relation to a concern as to whether systems that prompted students with questions about a domain (Fung & Adam, 1996) would teach the skill of self-explanation itself. In a similar vein, Auzende (1996) described a simulation of a complex electrical supply system. It has a clever mechanism to generate an explanation of the behavior of the system consequent on certain changes (D) but cannot, I believe, interact with the user at the level of *Dprime*, that is, fault diagnosis. By contrast, in the work of de Koning, Bredeweg, and Breuker (1996) one can see something like a Socratic dialogue emerging semiautomatically from the model of the beakers on a balance that they used. Augmenting an expert system–based trainer with a hypertext system is another way of helping the student deal with a domain at different levels of generality. Reinhardt (1996) integrated two such systems to provide an environment in which students could learn how to classify flowers and be critiqued on their classification expertise as well as on their ability to deal with realistic visual data.

The D and *Dprime* issue was explored by Mitchell et al. (1996) in the area of industrial training, where the typical high-fidelity simulation (e.g., a flight simulator) operates at the D level and a human tutor is required in order to get the student to focus at the *Dprime* level. Proponents of the value of virtual reality in education tend to stress immersion at the D level and assume that reflection on the experience will happen on its own. One of the constructive lessons of the years of work on LOGO was that the subjects' explicit attention needed to be focused on problem solving rather than LOGO as such in order to bring about improvements at the *Dprime* level. Indeed the very immediacy of the experience of producing interesting visual effects could act as a hindrance to generalization. We are in danger of repeating this kind of mistake if we accept uncritically all the promises about the educational value of virtual reality systems.

The Teacher

A standard methodology in artificial intelligence in education is to observe skilled human teachers and then try to formalize their skills in machine teachers—for example, when to take charge, when to withdraw, when to help, and so on (Lajoie & Lesgold, 1989). But an issue that arises immediately is whether techniques that work for human teachers (Lepper, Woolverton, Mumme, & Gurtner, 1993) will also work for machine teachers, especially when the techniques are concerned with motivation. Del Soldato (1994) found that students were rather surprised when *the machine* refused to help when requested or told them it was too soon to give up on a problem. A similar point was made by Barnard and Sandberg (1996) while investigating the promotion of student self-explanation. They argued that strategies that can be adapted by a human teacher to provoke reflection and self-explanation may not work when the teacher is known to be a machine.

CONCLUSION

In part the argument between the modelers and the nonmodelers can be seen in terms of the different motivations that drive researchers to work in the field of artificial intelligence in education. One motivation is a worthy interest in improving education. With this motivation in mind, people rightly point out that better educational outcomes do not necessarily stem from a technically more complex (intelligent) educational system compared to a simpler system (see Larkin & Chabay, 1992, for a collection of papers exploring this question). For some of them, the manifest difficulties of modeling can seem counterproductive when equally good (or even better) education can be achieved without modeling. Another motivation stems from an interest in a particular technology and a belief that this technology offers something of potential value in education. Proponents of hypermedia, the Internet, or virtual reality fall into this camp. For them, the issue of modeling can be a distraction from the technology of interest. Yet another motivation is an interest in trying to understand the processes of learning and teaching as fascinating phenomena in their own right, irrespective of whether the research has immediate educational applications. For these people, especially in the context of artificial intelligence in education, modeling is at the heart of the enterprise, as it is their method of reifying and testing their theories. For them the notion that intelligent tutoring systems (say) might have "failed" is the wrong kind of criticism. The question for them should rather be, "How good a model of teaching does such a system offer?" or "How good a model of learning underpins the system?" If the models are impoverished and inadequate, how are they so, and how can they be improved?

The perspective I offer in this chapter is much colored by the third motivation—learning and teaching are fascinating phenomena in their own right. Indeed some of the intriguing empirical results could perhaps be summed up under the slogan that educational outcomes are hard to predict from experimental conditions.

The field of artificial intelligence in education has gained much from its roots in artificial intelligence, but it has perhaps been overly influenced by a view of learning dominated more by epistemology than by genetic epistemology. The strength of this particular reflective event, and perhaps the strength of the field of artificial intelligence in education in Europe, is its concern with learning as it actually occurs—not an idealization of learning.

ACKNOWLEDGMENTS

I thank Rosemary Luckin and Susanne Lajoie for reading various drafts of this chapter and making many useful and insightful comments.

REFERENCES

Ainsworth, S., Wood, D., & Bibby, P. (1996). Co-ordinating multiple representations in computer based learning environments. In P. Brna, A. Paiva, & J. Self (Eds.), *Euroaied: European Conference on Artificial Intelligence in Education* (pp. 336–342). Lisbon: Edicoes Colibri.

Akhras, F. & Self, J. (1996). From the process of instruction to the process of learning: Constructivist implications for the design of intelligent learning environments. In P. Brna, A. Paiva, & J. Self (Eds.), *Euroaied: European*

Conference on Artificial Intelligence in Education (pp. 9–15). Lisbon: Edicoes Colibri.

Auzende, O. (1996). Explaining the evolution of a simulated system. In P. Brna, A. Paiva, & J. Self (Eds.), *Euroaied: European Conference on Artificial Intelligence in Education* (pp. 59–65). Lisbon: Edicoes Colibri.

Baker, M. J., & Lund, K. (1996). Flexibly structuring the interaction in a CSCL environment. In P. Brna, A. Paiva, & J. Self (Eds.), *Euroaied: European Conference on Artificial Intelligence in Education* (pp. 401–407). Lisbon: Edicoes Colibri.

Barnard, Y. F., & Sandberg, J. A. C. (1996). Self-explanations, do we get them from our students? In P. Brna, A. Paiva, & J. Self (Eds.), *Euroaied: European Conference on Artificial Intelligence in Education* (pp. 115–121). Lisbon: Edicoes Colibri.

Born, A., & Lusti, M. (1996). An architecture for knowledge based tutoring systems in algorithmic domains. In P. Brna, A. Paiva, & J. Self (Eds.), *Euroaied: European Conference on Artificial Intelligence in Education* (pp. 291–297).

Brna, P., Paiva, A., & Self, J. (Eds.). (1996). *Euroaied: European Conference on Artificial Intelligence in Education*, Lisbon. Edicoes Colibri.

Brown, J. S., Burton, R. R., & de Kleer, J. (1982). Pedagogical, natural language and knowledge engineering techniques in SOPHIE I, II and III. In D. Sleeman & J. S. Brown (Eds.), *Intelligent tutoring systems*. Orlando, FL: Academic Press.

Brusilovsky, P., Ritter, S., & Schwarz, E. (1997). Distributed intelligent tutoring on the web. In B. du Boulay & R. Mizoguchi (Eds.), *Artificial intelligence in education: Knowledge and media in learning systems* (pp. 482–489). Amsterdam: IOS.

Burton, M., & Brna, P. (1996). Clarissa: An exploration of collaboration through agent-based dialogue games. In P. Brna, A. Paiva, & J. Self (Eds.), *Euroaied: European Conference on Artificial Intelligence in Education* (pp. 393–400). Lisbon: Edicoes Colibri.

Cerri, S. A. (1996). Cognitive environments in the STROBE model. In P. Brna, A. Paiva, & J. Self (Eds.), *Euroaied: European Conference on Artificial Intelligence in Education* (pp. 254–260). Lisbon: Edicoes Colibri.

Chi, M., Bassok, M., Lewis, M., Reimann, P., & Glaser, R. (1989). Self-explanations: How students study and use examples in learning to solve problems. *Cognitive Science, 13*, 145–182.

Chi, M., Glaser, R., & Farr, M. (1988). *The nature of expertise*. Hillsdale, NJ: Lawrence Erlbaum Associates.

Colazzo, L., & Costantino, M. (1996). Using multi-user hypertextual glossaries in multimedia-based learning. In P. Brna, A. Paiva, & J. Self (Eds.), *Euroaied:*

European Conference on Artificial Intelligence in Education (pp. 142–149). Lisbon: Edicoes Colibri.

Cook, J. (1996). Knowledge mentoring: Towards a framework for linking dialogue analysis to teaching agent design. In P. Brna, A. Paiva, & J. Self (Eds.), *Euroaied: European Conference on Artificial Intelligence in Education* (pp. 199–205). Lisbon: Edicoes Colibri.

de Koning, K., Bredeweg, B., & Breuker, J. (1996). Interpreting student answers: More than diagnosis alone. In P. Brna, A. Paiva, & J. Self (Eds.), *Euroaied: European Conference on Artificial Intelligence in Education* (pp. 233–239). Lisbon: Edicoes Colibri.

de Oliveira, F. M., & Viccari, R. M. (1996). Are learning systems distributed or social systems? In P. Brna, A. Paiva, & J. Self (Eds.), *Euroaied: European Conference on Artificial Intelligence in Education* (pp. 247–253). Lisbon: Edicoes Colibri.

De Vries, E. (1996). Educational multimedia for learning and problem solving. In P. Brna, A. Paiva, & J. Self (Eds.), *Euroaied: European Conference on Artificial Intelligence in Education* (pp. 157–163). Lisbon: Edicoes Colibri.

del Soldato, T. (1994). *Motivation in tutoring systems* (Tech. Rep. No. CSRP 303). School of Cognitive and Computing Sciences, University of Sussex.

del Soldato, T., & du Boulay, B. (1995). Implementation of motivational tactics in tutoring systems. *Journal of Artificial Intelligence in Education, 6*(4), 337–378.

Derry, S. J., & Lajoie, S. P. (1993). A middle camp for (un)intelligent instructional computing. In S. P. Lajoie & S. J. (Eds.), *Computers as cognitive tools* (pp. 1–11). Hillsdale, NJ: Lawrence Erlbaum Associates.

Desmoulins, C., & van Labeke, N. (1996). Towards student modeling in geometry with inductive logic programming. In P. Brna, A. Paiva, & J. Self (Eds.), *Euroaied: European Conference on Artificial Intelligence in Education* (pp. 94–100). Lisbon: Edicoes Colibri.

Dillenbourg, P., Traum, D. R., & Schneider, D. K. (1996). Grounding in multimodal task-orientated collaboration. In P. Brna, A. Paiva, & J. Self (Eds.), *Euroaied: European Conference on Artificial Intelligence in Education* (pp. 415–425). Lisbon: Edicoes Colibri.

Dobson, M., & McCracken, J. (1996). Resolution of instructional conversation breakdowns with the Distance Learning Toolkit. In P. Brna, A. Paiva, & J. Self (Eds.), *Euroaied: European Conference on Artificial Intelligence in Education* (pp. 220–225). Lisbon: Edicoes Colibri.

du Boulay, B., Luckin,, R. & del Soldato, T. (1999). The plausibility problem: Human teaching tactics in the 'hands' of a machine, in S. P. Lajoie & M. Vivet (Eds.) *Artificial Intelligence in Education. Proceedings of the International*

Conference on Artificial Intelligence in Education. (Pp. 225–232). Le Mans. IOS Press.

du Boulay, B., & Mizoguchi, R. (Eds.). (1997). *Artificial intelligence in education: Knowledge and media in learning systems.* Amsterdam: IOS.

Du Plessis, S., & De Kock, H. (1996). A fuzzy expert and decision-making system to individualize computer-based tutoring. In P. Brna, A. Paiva, & J. Self (Eds.), *Euroaied: European Conference on Artificial Intelligence in Education* (pp. 177–183). Lisbon: Edicoes Colibri.

Errico, B. (1996). Student modeling in the situation calculus. In P. Brna, A. Paiva, & J. Self (Eds.), *Euroaied: European Conference on Artificial Intelligence in Education* (pp. 305–312). Lisbon: Edicoes Colibri

Faro, A., & Giodano, D. (1996). Story telling reasoning to learn information system design. In P. Brna, A. Paiva, & J. Self (Eds.), *Euroaied: European Conference on Artificial Intelligence in Education* (pp. 101–107). Lisbon: Edicoes Colibri.

Fenley, S. (1996). Strategies for the integration of design structures and learning environments in multimedia software. In P. Brna, A. Paiva, & J. Self (Eds.), *Euroaied: European Conference on Artificial Intelligence in Education* (pp. 164–170). Lisbon: Edicoes Colibri

Forte, E. N. & Forte, M. W. (1996). Goal oriented vs free simulation: Feasibility of automatic hyperhelp links—results from the HIPOCAMPE project. In P. Brna, A. Paiva, & J. Self (Eds.), *Euroaied: European Conference on Artificial Intelligence in Education* (pp. 66–72). Lisbon: Edicoes Colibri.

Fung, P.-W., & Adam, A. (1996). Questioning students on the contents of example solutions. In P. Brna, A. Paiva, & J. Self (Eds.), *Euroaied: European Conference on Artificial Intelligence in Education* (pp. 108–114). Lisbon: Edicoes Colibri.

Giangrandi, P., & Tasso, C. (1996). Modeling the temporal evolution of student knowledge. In P. Brna, A. Paiva, & J. Self (Eds.), *Euroaied: European Conference on Artificial Intelligence in Education* (pp. 184–190). Lisbon: Edicoes Colibri.

Goldstein, I. P. (1975). Summary of MYCROFT: A system for understanding simple picture programs. *Artificial Intelligence, 6,* 249–288.

Good, J., & Brna, P. (1996). Novice difficulties with recursion: Do graphical representations hold the solution? In P. Brna, A. Paiva, & J. Self (Eds.), *Euroaied: European Conference on Artificial Intelligence in Education* (pp. 364–371). Lisbon: Edicoes Colibri.

Hietala, P., & Niemirepo, T. (1996). Studying learner-computer interactions in agent-based social learning situations. In P. Brna, A. Paiva, & J. Self (Eds.), *Euroaied: European Conference on Artificial Intelligence in Education* (pp. 386–392). Lisbon: Edicoes Colibri.

Inaba, A. & Okamoto, T. (1997). Negotiation process model for intelligent discussion coordinating system on CSCL environment. In B. du Boulay & R. Mizoguchi (Eds.), *Artificial intelligence in education: Knowledge and media in learning systems* (pp. 175–182). Amsterdam: IOS.

Issroff, K., & del Soldato, T. (1996). Incorporating motivation into computer-supported collaborative learning. In P. Brna, A. Paiva, & J. Self (Eds.), *Euroaied: European Conference on Artificial Intelligence in Education* (pp. 284–290). Lisbon: Edicoes Colibri.

Karlgren, K. & Ramberg, R. (1996). Language use and conceptual change in learning. In P. Brna, A. Paiva, & J. Self (Eds.), *Euroaied: European Conference on Artificial Intelligence in Education* (pp. 45–51). Lisbon: Edicoes Colibri.

Kashihara, A., Okabe, M., Hirashima, T., & Jun'ichi, T. (1996). A self-explanation assistance with diagram tailoring. In P. Brna, A. Paiva, & J. Self (Eds.), *Euroaied: European Conference on Artificial Intelligence in Education* (pp. 122–128). Lisbon: Edicoes Colibri.

Keller, J. M. (1983). Motivational design of instruction. In C. M. Reigeluth (Ed.), *Instructional-design theories and models: An overview of their current status.* Hillsdale, NJ: Lawrence Erlbaum Associates.

Kommers, P., & Lenting, B. (1996). Telematic learning support and its potential for collaborative learning with new paradigms and conceptual mapping tools. In P. Brna, A. Paiva, & J. Self (Eds.), *Euroaied: European Conference on Artificial Intelligence in Education* (pp. 408–414). Lisbon: Edicoes Colibri.

Laborde, C. (1996). Towards a new role for diagrams in dynamic geometry? In P. Brna, A. Paiva, & J. Self (Eds.), *Euroaied: European Conference on Artificial Intelligence in Education* (pp. 350–356). Lisbon: Edicoes Colibri.

Lajoie, S. P., & Derry, S. J. (Eds.). (1993). *Computers as cognitive tools.* Hillsdale, NJ: Lawrence Erlbaum Associates.

Lajoie, S. P., & Lesgold, A. (1989). Apprenticeship training in the workplace: A computer-coached practice environment as a new form of apprenticeship. *Machine-Mediated Learning, 3*(1), 7–28.

Larkin, J. H., & Chabay, R. W. (Eds.). (1992). *Computer-assisted instruction and intelligent tutoring systems: Shared goals and complementary approaches.* Hillsdale, NJ: Lawrence Erlbaum Associates.

Laurillard, D. (1979). The processes of student learning. *Higher Education, 8,* 395–409.

Lepper, M. R. (1988). Motivational considerations in the study of instruction. *Cognition and Instruction, 5*(4), 289–309.

Lepper, M. R., & Chabay, R. (1988). Socializing the intelligent tutor: Bringing empathy to computer tutors. In H. Mandl & A. Lesgold (Eds.), *Learning issues for intelligent tutoring systems* (pp. 242–257). New York: Springer-Verlag.

Lepper, M. R., Woolverton, M., Mumme, D. L., & Gurtner, J.-L. (1993). Motivational techniques of expert human tutors: Lessons for the design of computer-based tutors. In S. P. Lajoie & S. J. Derry (Eds.), *Computers as cognitive tools* (pp. 75–105). Hillsdale, NJ: Lawrence Erlbaum Associates.

Leroux, P., Vivet, M., & Brezillon, P. (1996). Cooperation between a pedagogical assistant, a group of learners and a teacher. In P. Brna, A. Paiva, & J. Self (Eds.), *Euroaied: European Conference on Artificial Intelligence in Education* (pp. 379–385). Lisbon: Edicoes Colibri.

Lewin, C. (1996). Improving talking book software design: Evaluating the supportive tutor. In P. Brna, A. Paiva, & J. Self (Eds.), *Euroaied: European Conference on Artificial Intelligence in Education* (pp. 269–275). Lisbon: Edicoes Colibri.

Luckin, R. (1996). TRIVAR: Exploring the "zone of proximal development." In P. Brna, A. Paiva, & J. Self (Eds.), *Euroaied: European Conference on Artificial Intelligence in Education* (pp. 16–22). Lisbon: Edicoes Colibri.

Luckin, R. (1998*). "ECOLOAB" : Explorations in the zone of proximal development* (Tech. Rep. No. CSRP 386). Sussex: School of Cognitive and Computing Sciences, University of Sussex.

Luckin, R. & du Boulay, B. (1999). Ecolab: The development and evaluation of a Vygotiskin Design framework. *International Journal of Artificial Intelligence in Education, 10.2*, 198–220.

MacLaren, B. A., & Koedinger, K. R. (1996). Towards a dynamic model of early algebra acquisition. In P. Brna, A. Paiva, & J. Self (Eds.), *Euroaied: European Conference on Artificial Intelligence in Education* (pp. 38–44). Lisbon: Edicoes Colibri.

Malone, T., & Lepper, M. R. (1987). Making learning fun. In R. Snow & M. Farr (Eds.), *Aptitude, learning and instruction: Conative and affective process analyses.* Hillsdale, NJ: Lawrence Erlbaum Associates.

Mayer, R. E. (1997). Learners as information processors: Legacies and limitations of educational psychology's second metaphor. *Educational Psychologist, 31*(3–4), 151–161.

Mayorga, J. I., & Verdejo, M. F. (1996). Authoring systems revisited: The software design cycle metaphor. In P. Brna, A. Paiva, & J. Self (Eds.), *Euroaied: European Conference on Artificial Intelligence in Education* (pp. 319–328). Lisbon: Edicoes Colibri.

Mitchell, J., Liddle, J., Brown, K., & Leitch, R. (1996). Integrating simulations into intelligent tutoring systems. In P. Brna, A. Paiva, & J. Self (Eds.), *Euroaied: European Conference on Artificial Intelligence in Education* (pp. 80–86). Lisbon: Edicoes Colibri.

Mizoguchi, R., Sinitsa, K., & Ikeda, M. (1996). Knowledge engineering of educational systems for authoring system design—a preliminary result of task ontology design. In P. Brna, A. Paiva, & J. Self (Eds.), *Euroaied: European Conference on Artificial Intelligence in Education* (pp. 329–335). Lisbon: Edicoes Colibri.

Moebus, C. (1996). Towards an epistemology of intelligent design and modeling environments: The hypothesis testing approach. In P. Brna, A. Paiva, & J. Self (Eds.), *Euroaied: European Conference on Artificial Intelligence in Education* (pp. 52–58). Lisbon: Edicoes Colibri.

Oliver, M., & O'Shea, T. (1996). Using the model-view-controller mechanism to combine representations of possible worlds for learners of modal logic. In P. Brna, A. Paiva, & J. Self (Eds.), *Euroaied: European Conference on Artificial Intelligence in Education* (pp. 357–363). Lisbon: Edicoes Colibri.

Oppermann, R., & Thomas, C. (1996). Supporting learning as a process in a social context. In P. Brna, A. Paiva, & J. Self (Eds.), *Euroaied: European Conference on Artificial Intelligence in Education* (pp. 150–156). Lisbon: Edicoes Colibri.

Pain, H., Bull, S., & Brna, P. (1996). A student model "for its own sake." In P. Brna, A. Paiva, & J. Self (Eds.), *Euroaied: European Conference on Artificial Intelligence in Education* (pp. 191–198). Lisbon: Edicoes Colibri.

Paiva, A. (1996). Learner modeling agents. In P. Brna, A. Paiva, & J. Self (Eds.), *Euroaied: European Conference on Artificial Intelligence in Education* (pp. 261–268). Lisbon: Edicoes Colibri.

Pask, G., & Scott, B. (1975). CASTE: A system for exhibiting learning strategies and regulating uncertainties. *International Journal of Man-Machine Studies, 5,* 17–52.

Pemberton, L., Shurville, S., & Sharples, M. (1996). External representations in the writing process and how to support them. In P. Brna, A. Paiva, & J. Self (Eds.), *Euroaied: European Conference on Artificial Intelligence in Education* (pp. 343–349). Lisbon: Edicoes Colibri.

Percoco, G., & Sarti, L. (1996). On the usage of graphics in ICAI systems. In P. Brna, A. Paiva, & J. Self (Eds.), *Euroaied: European Conference on Artificial Intelligence in Education* (pp. 313–318). Lisbon: Edicoes Colibri.

Pilkington, R., & Mallen, C. (1996). Dialogue games to support reasoning and reflection in diagnostic tasks. In P. Brna, A. Paiva, & J. Self (Eds.), *Euroaied: European Conference on Artificial Intelligence in Education* (pp. 213–219). Lisbon: Edicoes Colibri.

Plotzner, R., Hoppe, H., Fehse, E., Nolte, C., & Tewissen, F. (1996). Model-based design of activity spaces for collaborative problem solving and learning. In P.

Brna, A. Paiva, & J. Self (Eds.), *Euroaied: European Conference on Artificial Intelligence in Education* (pp. 372–378). Lisbon: Edicoes Colibri.

Reinhardt, B. I. (1996). Expert systems and hypertext for teaching diagnostics. In P. Brna, A. Paiva, & J. Self (Eds.), *Euroaied: European Conference on Artificial Intelligence in Education* (pp. 298–304). Lisbon: Edicoes Colibri.

Roussos, M., Johnson, A. E., Leigh, J., Vasilakis, C. A., & Moher, T. G. (1996). Constructing collaborative stories within virtual learning landscapes. In P. Brna, A. Paiva, & J. Self (Eds.), *Euroaied: European Conference on Artificial Intelligence in Education* (pp. 129–135). Lisbon: Edicoes Colibri.

Salles, P. S., Pain, H., & Muetzelfeldt, R. I. (1996). Qualitative ecological models for tutoring systems: A comparative study. In P. Brna, A. Paiva, & J. Self (Eds.), *Euroaied: European Conference on Artificial Intelligence in Education* (pp. 226–232). Lisbon: Edicoes Colibri.

Scaife, M., & Rogers, Y. (1996). External cognition: How do graphical representations work? *International Journal of Human-Computer Studies, 45,* 185–213.

Schmidt, H. G., & Boshuizen, H. P. (1993). On acquiring expertise in medicine. *Educational Psychology Review, 5*(3), 205–221.

Schroeder, O., Moebus, C., & Thole, H.-J. (1996). Acquiring knowledge from linguistic models in complex, probabilistic domains. In P. Brna, A. Paiva, & J. Self (Eds.), *Euroaied: European Conference on Artificial Intelligence in Education* (pp. 206–212). Lisbon: Edicoes Colibri.

Shute, V. J. (1995). SMART: Student modeling approach for responsive tutoring. *User Modeling and User-Adapted Interaction, 5*(1), 1–44.

Sime, J.-A. (1996). An investigation into teaching and assessment of qualitative knowledge in engineering. In P. Brna, A. Paiva, & J. Self (Eds.), *Euroaied: European Conference on Artificial Intelligence in Education* (pp. 240–246). Lisbon: Edicoes Colibri.

Sison, R., & Shimura, M. (1996). The application of machine learning to student modeling (a 1996 perspective): Towards a multistrategy learning student modeling system. In P. Brna, A. Paiva, & J. Self (Eds.), *Euroaied: European Conference on Artificial Intelligence in Education* (pp. 87–93). Lisbon: Edicoes Colibri.

Sowa, J. (1984). *Conceptual structures: Information processing in mind and machine.* Reading, MA: Addison-Wesley.

Specht, M., & Weber, G. (1996). Episodic adaptation in learning environments. In P. Brna, A. Paiva, & J. Self (Eds.), *Euroaied: European Conference on Artificial Intelligence in Education* (pp. 171–176). Lisbon: Edicoes Colibri.

Spiro, R., Coulson, R., Fletovich, P., & Anderson, D. (1988). Cognitive flexibility theory: Advanced knowledge acquisition in ill-structured domains. In *10th*

Annual Cognitive Science Conference (pp. 375–383). Hillsdale, NJ: Lawrence Erlbaum Associates.

Swaak, J., & de Jong, T. (1996). The assessment of intuitive knowledge acquired in simulation-based discovery environments. In P. Brna, A. Paiva, & J. Self (Eds.), *Euroaied: European Conference on Artificial Intelligence in Education* (pp. 31–37). Lisbon: Edicoes Colibri.

Teasley, S. D., & Roschelle, J. (1993). Constructing a joint problem space: The computer as a tool for sharing knowledge. In S. P. Lajoie & S. J. (Eds.), *Computers as cognitive tools* (pp. 229–258). Hillsdale, NJ: Lawrence Erlbaum Associates.

van Joolingen, W., & de Jong, T. (1996). Supporting the authoring process for simulation-based discovery learning. In P. Brna, A. Paiva, & J. Self (Eds.), *Euroaied: European Conference on Artificial Intelligence in Education* (pp. 73–79). Lisbon: Edicoes Colibri.

Vassileva, J., & Wasson, B. (1996). Instructional planning approaches: From tutoring towards free learning. In P. Brna, A. Paiva, & J. Self (Eds.), *Euroaied: European Conference on Artificial Intelligence in Education* (pp. 1–8). Lisbon: Edicoes Colibri.

Vygotsky, L. (1986). In A. Kozulin (Ed.), *Thought and language.* Cambridge, MA: MIT Press.

Wasson, B. (1996). Instructional planning and contemporary theories of learning: Is this a self-contradiction? In P. Brna, A. Paiva, & J. Self (Eds.), *Euroaied: European Conference on Artificial Intelligence in Education* (pp. 23–30). Lisbon: Edicocs Colibri.

White, B. Y., & Fredcrikson, J. R. (1987). Qualitative models and intelligent learning environments. In R. W. Lawler & M. Yazdani (Eds.), *Artificial intelligence and education: Learning environments and tutoring systems* (Vol. 1, pp. 281–305). Norwood, NJ: Ablex.

Whitelock, D., Brna, P., & Holland, S. (1996). What is the value of virtual reality for conceptual learning? towards a conceptual framework. In P. Brna, A. Paiva, & J. Self (Eds.), *Euroaied: European Conference on Artificial Intelligence in Education* (pp. 136–141). Lisbon: Edicoes Colibri.

Whitelock, D., & Scanlon, E. (1996). Motivation, media and motion: Reviewing a computer supported collaborative learning experience. In P. Brna, A. Paiva, & J. Self (Eds.), *Euroaied: European Conference on Artificial Intelligence in Education* (pp. 276–283). Lisbon: Edicoes Colibri.

13

It Won't Happen Soon: Practical, Curricular, and Methodological Problems in Implementing Technology-Based Constructivist Approaches in Classrooms

Ellen B. Mandinach
Educational Testing Service, Princeton, New Jersey

Hugh F. Cline
Columbia University

The leitmotif of this chapter is aptly stated in the title: "It Won't Happen Soon." Although all of the projects reported in this book, as well as those included in its predecessor (Lajoie & Derry, 1993), describe powerful vehicles for effectively reforming and vastly improving teaching and learning activities in a wide variety of educational settings, we are certain that it will be many years before such innovations are widely implemented. In other words, do not expect to see any of them in your local schools in the near future.

In one respect this chapter is similar to the discussant essay written by Chipman (1993) near the end of Lajoie and Derry (1993). After reviewing the many intriguing projects reported in that book, Chipman concluded with a plea to both developers and users of computer-based systems to work together to produce curricular innovations that will be widely used. We strongly agree with Chipman: "The challenge is to develop innovative instruction that is actually used in the nation's schools and has a significant positive effect on the learning of a significant number of students." This same plea recently was reiterated in a meeting of projects funded by the National Science Foundation (Center for Innovative Learning Technologies, 1998), indicating that little progress has been made in the past five years toward the practical, widespread implementation of technology in classroom settings. There continues to be an abyss between research and development projects and actual classroom practice. In our view three main types of issues preclude the more widespread dissemination and utilization of computers as cognitive tools: a dearth of adequate evaluation research designs, a paucity of appropriate measures of cognitive activity, and a plethora of financial and practical problems.

BACKGROUND

How extensively are computers deployed in the nation's schools? The simple answer is that there are many more computers in classrooms now than there used to be. For example in 1984, there was one computer for every 125 students; in 1997 there was one computer for every 9 students (CEO Forum, 1997). This decrease in the ratio over the past 13 years is nothing short of phenomenal. Another recent survey estimates that 98% of the nation's schools have at least one computer (Coley, Cradler, & Engel, 1997). It can reasonably be anticipated that this growth trend will continue. The prices of computers continue to decline, and the power and memory of these machines seem to double every few years.

As is often the case with trends in technology development, there is both good and bad news. The proliferation of computers in schools is really good news. However, national survey data indicate generally low levels of student use, particularly applications that require high-level cognitive skills. For example, the 1994 National Assessment of Educational Progress (NAEP) reported that among 4th-, 8th-, and 11th-grade students, 60%, 50%, and 33%, respectively, never use a computer (Coley et al., 1997). These same data show that the ways in which computers are being used in the schools do little to promote cognitive development among the students. The most common use of computers among students in the fourth and eighth grades was to play games, and the most common use among students in the eleventh grade was word processing. It is clear that these applications are much less demanding than those discussed in this book and certainly do not encompass using computers as cognitive tools. Although we have come a long way in expanding the use of computers in schools, these data show just how much further we must go before realizing their potential for facilitating cognitive development.

Another perspective that can be used to examine how computers are being used in schools was provided by the researchers at the Cognition and Technology Group at Vanderbilt University (CTGV, 1996). Their selected review and discussion of technology and education research was organized around a framework they call LTC: *l*ooking at *t*echnology in the *c*ontext of learning theory and educational practice. They created a two-dimensional matrix. The first dimension consists of three categories representing the educational setting in which the research project occurs: in a laboratory, in an individual classroom, or in multiple classrooms or schools participating in the same project. The first dimension then represents the extent to which the project has progressed from a laboratory setting to approximating an actual school environment, such as a district or larger educational unit.

The second dimension also consists of three categories. This dimension corresponds to a conception of pedagogy known as constructivism, and the categories represent a progression from traditional models of education in which an active teacher transmits knowledge to passive, receiving students to a model in which the teacher helps students learn by constructing their own knowledge. This chapter is not the place for a full explication of constructivist pedagogy, for the literature is replete with such treatments (e.g., Brown & Campione, 1996; CTGV, 1992). Furthermore, CTGV (1996) provided for a complete description of the LTC matrix. For the purpose of this chapter it is sufficient to point out that cognitive demands on students increase as the learning environment becomes more constructivist.

An examination of the contents of the nine cells formed by the two dimensions of the LTC matrix makes it clear that most of the research projects reported in the CTGV (1996) review, and for that matter in the educational research literature at large, fall in the upper left corner of the matrix. These are the efforts that are closer to the laboratory setting and the transmission mode of pedagogy. There are far fewer cases to report in the lower right corner, the more widely connected and constructivist-oriented projects. This observation from the LTC matrix confirms the NAEP data finding that the current uses of technology in schools are a far cry from effectively using computers as cognitive tools.

ISSUES IN IMPLEMENTING TECHNOLOGY

Research Design Problems

It is inevitable that the funding agencies and the taxpayers, who are providing the monies for all the new computers that are appearing in schools, soon will ask for some convincing evidence that the substantial resources that are being expended thus far are producing some positive results. It is our contention that educational researchers will have great difficulty in producing such evidence in a timely fashion, and one of the reasons is that prevalent evaluation research designs are not adequate for the task of producing this kind of evidence. Fundamental to all attempts to assess the effects of any innovation in psychological and educational research is the concept of the experiment. An experiment is designed to verify one hypothesized causal relationship and eliminate other possible explanations. Drawing from the successful experiences of colleagues in the physical and natural sciences, researchers in the social and behavioral sciences have attempted to create an analogue of the scientific laboratory experiment. Infield, as contrasted with laboratory, research, it is virtually impossible to control for all possible contaminating influences. For example, in a classroom there are countless possible confounding influences that might affect a curriculum innovation. Therefore, a quasi-experiment is frequently used to approximate the laboratory setting.

By randomly assigning subjects or students to experimental and control groups and administering a stimulus to only one group, an investigator hopes to uncover evidence that will support a claim that a specific stimulus or innovation causes a particular outcome. In the case of research evaluating the use of computers as cognitive tools, the stimulus might be a new computer-based instructional program; the outcome might be scores on a test of higher order problem-solving skills. The random assignment of students to the experimental and control groups theoretically eliminates other confounding factors. However, the implementation of the quasi-experimental design in classrooms is severely compromised by the problems accompanying the timely administration of the stimulus to only the experimental group (Newman, 1990).

The use of computers in classroom settings comprises a complicated sequence of events: (a) the selection, acquisition, and installation of hardware; (b) accompanied by the selection, acquisition, and installation of appropriate software; (c) the training and ongoing support of the teachers who will participate in the field experiment; (d) enlisting the support, encouragement, and participation of students, other teachers, administrators, school board members, and parents; and (e) the actual classroom implementation, which can last anywhere from one day to several school years.

Almost all the steps in this sequence take a very long time to accomplish. It is really quite unreasonable to expect that one could arrange these complicated activities in such a way that only students in the experimental classes are exposed to the stimulus or treatment of the computer-based cognitive tools. Most schools are vibrant social organizations. Many individuals—students, teachers, administrators, board members, and frequently parents or involved community members—are intensely interested and well informed about what of importance is happening in their environments. Therefore, it is quite naive to assume that anyone could conduct a quasi-experiment in schools that employed computers as cognitive tools. In practice, such a quasi-experiment is impossible, and the results of such efforts should be interpreted with utmost caution (Cline & Mandinach, in press). Salomon (1991, 1996) distinguishes between analytic and systemic perspectives in studying learning environments. The analytic is appropriate for the quasi-experiment. Therefore we propose that the systemic is more appropriate for the questions raised by the policymakers who control resources for educational research and development. We acknowledge that there may be occasions for which the analytic approach could be appropriate, but in dealing with technology implementations, we think the systemic approach is correct.

On the other hand, the need for accountability in the use of any resource is real and must be addressed. If the field-based quasi-experiment is deficient for this purpose, how can the accountability issue be addressed? The short answer to this question is, "With great difficulty." There is no one research method or design that will provide the definitive answer to the question of whether the innovation was successful in enhancing learning. It is necessary to employ a number of research strategies asking different but related questions, all concerned with various aspects of the effect of the innovation.

We have found it useful to think of three aspects of research design that can shed light on the outcomes of a computer-based curriculum innovation project (Mandinach & Cline, 1994). That design is an amalgam of multiple methods examining outcomes at multiple levels at multiple points in time, congruent with procedures advocated in the National Council of Teachers of Mathematics (NCTM) (1995) standards for assessment. The multiple methods refer to gathering, analyzing, and interpreting data collected in a wide variety of ways and from a wide variety of sources: classroom observations; interviews with teachers, students, and relevant others; scores on examinations, quizzes, and homework assignments; performance on standardized achievement tests; results from assessment instruments especially created to measure the intended outcome of the innovation; and many of the data items routinely generated in the operation of any school, such as grade point averages, course-taking patterns, participation in extracurricular activities, attendance, tardiness, disciplinary actions, and dropout rates.

Obviously it is not possible to collect and analyze all of these data and combine the results into one conclusive statement of the outcome of the innovation. Rather, a consistent pattern of findings across the data sources indicating that the innovation is producing positive changes would be highly convincing. However, the results of social and behavioral science research are rarely consistent, and the complex patterns of somewhat convincing outcomes are often not sufficient to persuade skeptical policymakers to continue to provide support for the innovation. Perhaps the second relevant aspect of research design, multiple levels, will provide some further evidence of outcomes.

The phrase *multiple levels* refers to the fact that curriculum innovations take place in schools, which are complex organizations with several levels of social structure or hierarchy. We are simply pointing out that students are enrolled in courses or classes, which are taught by teachers, who are usually assigned to some type of department structure within a school building, which is part of a district that is subject to certain constraints imposed by county, state, and federal agencies. Schools are multilayered organizations, and all activities, including curriculum innovations, take place in the context of the various levels. Research designed to shed light on the effect of any innovative effort must look concurrently at the various relevant levels.

In the case of the curriculum innovation project (Mandinach & Cline, 1994), we concentrated on three levels of analysis: the student learning outcomes, the dynamics of classroom activities and interactions, and the structural and functional changes in the school as an organization. In our view any research designed to shed light on the effect of a curriculum innovation must look at all the relevant levels of organization that may influence or be influenced by the reform activities. Anything less will be ignoring the systemic nature of the change and the organization. The long list of failed educational reform efforts is eloquent testimony to the perils of ignoring the systemic perspective in attempting to introduce change in schools.

The third relevant aspect of the research design concerns the need for gathering information over multiple time points. Cognitive development may occur in many different patterns and at different rates. There may be substantial growth at some times and long periods of minimal development at others. Cognitive scientists frequently refer to this kind of uneven or episodic development as transferring large bodies of knowledge or skills very rapidly to an existing structure of growing expertise. The occurrence and rate of transfer vary greatly among students and subjects. Consequently, a research design that takes one measure of all students in a class prior to administering a stimulus or innovation and one measure after is likely to reveal a pattern that shows very little change. However, there may be substantial changes occurring that are canceling each other out in the aggregation. What is needed is a longitudinal design that collects data at many points in time over an extended period. Indeed, what is really called for is an ongoing, continuous research effort.

Summarizing all our observations concerning the inadequacy of existing research designs for assessing the impact of curriculum innovations that use computers as cognitive tools, we recommend that multiple methods be employed at multiple levels in the schools on a continuous basis. This is a large order for evaluation research and would require what most would feel is an exorbitant amount of effort and monies to complete. Yet anything less will not produce compelling evidence that an innovation is worth pursuing. How is this dilemma to be resolved? A radical resolution would be to expand the role of classroom teachers to include the collection and analysis of such data as a regular part of their professional activities.

Paucity of Cognitive Measures

The second set of issues that preclude evaluation research from producing useful evidence of the effects of using computers as cognitive tools in schools is the difficulty of creating good outcome measures. The problems of developing valid and reliable measures of academic aptitude and achievement tests are well known. After many decades of instrument development and administration, the testing industry is widely accepted as producing useful standardized tests. There remains considerable controversy about the ways in which test results are used or misused. Nevertheless, the assessment of academic aptitude and achievement is widespread, and there is some support for a set of national tests for the elementary and secondary schools. Regardless of the outcome of that particular proposal, the use of standardized tests is clearly increasing. The recent development of computer-adaptive tests has added new dimensions to the problems of potential bias and equity.

The development of measures of cognition that can be economically administered on a large-scale basis is more of a challenge than a reality.

There is little consensus in the field as to what could and should be taught and assessed to promote more advanced cognitive performance. There are some who argue that cognitive development cannot be separated from the acquisition of content knowledge in both teaching and testing. Others claim that there are metacognitive skills, such as problem solving, self-regulation, and transfer, that can be learned and measured independently of substantive areas (Corno, 1992; Corno & Mandinach, 1983; Schunk & Zimmerman, 1994; Winne, 1995, 1997; Zimmerman & Schunk, 1989).

To complicate matters further, many of the projects described in this book and elsewhere in the cognitive science literature focus on a constructivist approach, whereas others espouse cognitive or situative perspectives (see Anderson, Reder, & Simon, 1996, 1997; Donmoyer, 1997; Greeno, 1997; Greeno and the Middle School Mathematics Through Applications Project Group, 1998). For the purposes of the discussion, a constructivist environment enables the learner to create or construct his or her own learning experiences. Teachers provide the guidance in using computer-enriched environments, but students take, or at least share, the initiative and responsibility for their learning. The claim is that learning that takes place in this constructivist manner is more effective, in the sense that it is deeper or more fundamental, lasts longer, and is more readily applied in new contexts (CTGV, 1992). However, the problems of assessing constructivist learning complicate the task of evaluating the use of computers as cognitive tools.

If the cognitive development that takes place in a constructivist manner is independent of any specific content area, then the assessment of that development should entail some type of performance that demonstrates a level of mastery that is not based on a substantive expertise. In recent years, for this as well as other reasons, performance assessment has enjoyed a resurgence of interest and activity. In much of the testing that is done in the areas of academic aptitude and achievement, the items are constructed to represent knowledge or mastery in recalling from memory and using content knowledge in the resolution of certain types of tasks, such as reading comprehension, mathematical reasoning, and quantitative or symbolic problem solving.

On the other hand, performance assessments usually involve complex, multistep tasks that are much like real-world problems. It is expected that students will react with more enthusiasm and involvement to problems that resemble the kinds of situations or dilemmas that they are likely to encounter routinely in their daily lives. However, recent work in developing performance assessment standards and procedures has made it clear that this type of measurement is time-consuming and very expensive (Sheingold, Heller, & Paulukonis, 1994). It typically involves the active collaboration of teachers in developing criteria, and it is reported to be a profound professional development experience by the participants (Sheingold, Heller, & Storms, 1997). Nevertheless, the expenses are enormous, and we are a long way from having readily available performance assessments that can be employed to answer questions concerning the efficacy of using computers as cognitive tools.

One further complication in evaluating computer-based curriculum innovations derives from a fact already mentioned. For the foreseeable future it is unlikely that many schools will have one computer for each student. Therefore, students working on computers in groups of two or more will be the prevailing pattern. Although there has been a great deal of speculation about how to assess group performance and whether it is possible to separate out individual contributions, we are just beginning to unravel these issues. Some combination of individual and group scores seems appropriate for many settings, but the rationale and procedures for such assessments are in the early stages of development.

Financial Issues and Practical Problems

The sad stories of many failed school technology projects reveal the peril of ignoring some very practical issues when introducing change. Unless such practical issues are readily resolved, the widespread use of computers as cognitive tools will not occur in the near future.

Financing Technology. Despite the decreasing costs of computers, funding educational technology is still a very difficult problem. There are many pressing demands that face schools and districts as they plan for the acquisition of computers. The financial problems are exacerbated by the increasing rates of change in both hardware and software, as well as the need to update the curriculum and provide professional development opportunities for teachers and staff.

Glennan and Melmed (1996) have examined the costs of implementing technology in schools. They reviewed a wide range of technology implementations ranging from one or two computers per classroom or school to environments that are saturated with information systems. Our focus is on the former, although the ultimate goal is the latter. Glennan and Melmed reported that approximately $3 billion was spent on educational technology during the 1994–1995 academic year. The authors estimated that half

of those dollars were spent for the purchase of hardware. Software acquisition accounted for another 25%, and the remaining quarter went for networking, personnel, training, and other costs. These figures translate into
an average annual per student expenditure of only $70. Because the total
average educational expenditure per pupil for 1994–1995 was $5,623,
only 1% was devoted to technology. Of course, these figures vary widely
across states, districts, and schools. Nevertheless, it is clear that only a
tiny proportion of educational expenditures is directed to technology.

Hardware and software account for 75% of the cost of financing technology. These are considered front-end expenditures. Ongoing expenses
include the upkeep of technology through technical support, preventive
maintenance, and repair. Teacher time is an issue that often is overlooked
and underestimated. Substantial resources need to be made available for
staff development on a continuous basis, not just at a one-time session.
Teachers need to be trained through in-service programs as well as contin-
uing-education courses. These professional development activities need to
reflect a clear vision of why technology is being used and how it can
strengthen teaching and learning activities. Increasingly and with encouragement from the White House, more schools and districts are connecting
to the Internet. Consequently, telecommunications is another area of cost.
Schools need to pay for initial connections, telephone lines, lines for local
area networks and Internet service providers, usage fees, and other wiring
costs. They also have to deal with changes to the existing school physical
plant, such as the increased need for electrical power, air-conditioning,
and security. The extent of these costs depends on the type of implementation model a school employs (see Coley et al., 1997, for an extended discussion).

A further challenge is the need for quality software to take advantage of
the power of the hardware. Most schools cannot afford to spend large
amounts of money on software. They tend to focus on applications rather
than content software. There are issues about how best to integrate either
type of software into the curricula. However, as Glennan and Melmed
(1996) note, there is a distressing lack of good and appropriate content
software that can be readily integrated into curricula. Further, for much of
the software to run effectively, schools need to purchase multiple copies,
obtain site licenses, run networked versions, and prevent illegal copying.
Software often needs to be updated frequently with new releases that keep
pace with upgrades to the hardware. All of these issues present considerable financial challenges to schools. As Glennan and Melmed (1996) conclude, little progress will occur in schools until the public and the

educational communities are convinced that technology is essential to meet its educational objectives.

Technology Acquisition, Installation, Security, and Other Related Issues.

Related to the financial issues are a number of necessary physical resources that make the implementation of technology in schools possible. They too require the outlay of funds and substantial planning for integration into the infrastructure of the school, in both the physical plant and the curriculum. These four issues are important and interrelated and include: the actual acquisition of hardware and software, the installation of technology with respect to its location as well as the requisite changes to the curriculum, security, the need to provide teachers with dedicated computers, and support issues.

It is critical for school districts to have a coherent and well-considered plan for the purchase and use of technology to support educational objectives. Despite the decreasing cost of technology, the outlay of money for a critical mass of hardware remains substantial. Often older machines suffice. However, this depends entirely on the applications and software that will be implemented. Many computers still in schools are virtually obsolete, yet they can be used effectively for certain applications.

There is a delicate balance that must be struck concerning the purchase of machines, the obsolescence factor, the constantly changing world of hardware and software development, and a school's educational objectives. Much so-called cutting-edge technology is too expensive and impractical for many school districts. A great deal depends on financial resources and educational goals. As Redfield and Steuck (1991) insightfully noted, there are major differences between the technology that researchers use and the technology that is readily available and practical for school settings. Another issue that faces schools is hardware platform dependence; that is, software packages are designed for use on one platform and do not readily translate to others. As Greer et al. (this volume) and Sugrue (this volume) have shown, the increasing use of the World Wide Web as an instructional tool may reduce some of the problems and issues associated with platform dependence.

Once the decision to acquire computers is made, schools must plan how best to install them, in what configurations, and with what necessary changes to the physical plant. First, a school must decide where to install the technology—for example, across classrooms, in a central laboratory, or in some combination. According to Becker (1991), there is no one right answer with respect to how technology should be configured within a school. Much depends on the school's educational goals and curricular integration. However, there is a pressing need to retrofit the classrooms in which the technology is situated to accommodate the increased need for electrical power, ventilation, and security. Classrooms often need to be redesigned to accommodate group learning activities and the need for additional work space. The traditional row-by-row configuration of students at single desks usually does not work. Perhaps most important is the provision for adequate security, in either individual classrooms or laboratories. Computers can easily be carried out the door if proper measures are not taken. A teacher who leaves his or her classroom unattended is asking for trouble; trackballs, modems, and other peripherals can fit easily into backpacks and exit the room. The issue of security should not be overlooked.

Teachers should not have to compete with students for the use of computers at school. They need dedicated machines that are available wherever they do the majority of their work: teaching, counseling, course preparation, and grading. Ideally, there should be machines in each teacher's classroom and home, as well in several public locations. Mandinach and Cline (1994) found substantial payoff by providing each teacher participating in their research and development project a dedicated machine that was situated in the most convenient location for that individual.

Other problems that are likely to arise concern the need for technical support and expertise as well as maintenance. Technology breaks down. Software malfunctions. Teachers need immediate assistance on how to handle problems as they occur. If the district takes several weeks to repair a faulty technical problem, that is one less computer available for student use. Furthermore, a well-planned lesson can easily blow up if there is an unexpected malfunction. Technical expertise needs to be made available for emergencies. Teachers are not computer experts, nor are they software gurus. Sometimes they can rely on other teachers and, increasingly, on knowledgeable students to troubleshoot problems. Often there are simple questions about a software command or function that technical expertise can solve. Running into such problems in a classroom when there is an audience of 30 or more students is a daunting challenge for most teachers. We cannot expect teachers to become all-knowing experts about every facet of hardware and software operation.

The resolution of the methodological and practical problems that make it difficult to implement and evaluate curriculum innovation projects that employ computers as cognitive tools requires resources, wisdom, and, above all, patience. It is incumbent on both the developers and users of such innovative instructional projects to convince policymakers that it takes time to produce definitive evidence—something like, "Rome was not built in a day."

CURRICULAR
AND PROFESSIONAL REFORM

We now turn to the implications of using computers as cognitive tools on the curriculum and the teachers who are responsible for ensuring that their students achieve according to the standards prescribed by their state, county, and district. Using computers to facilitate cognitive development clearly places the emphasis in teaching and learning on the mastery of certain thinking skills, and this immediately promotes a potential clash in goals and objectives. Most curriculum standards are written stressing what knowledge and skills students should master by the time they are promoted to various grades. However, educational researchers are fairly adept and confident about assessing the knowledge components of the standards. But we are less certain that we can validly and reliably measure thinking skills. In fact, there are many quite vocal parent, community, political, and religious groups that adamantly insist that they do not want the schools to teach their children how to think. These people do not want children exposed to ideas, only to facts (Berliner & Biddle, 1995). Coupling that resistance with the fact that we can more readily measure knowledge acquisition, it would not be surprising to find some resistance to introducing computers as cognitive tools among the teaching profession as well. That resistance may be particularly strong in the secondary schools, for teachers at that level are trained and evaluated on their expertise to instruct students in their subject areas of English, history, physics, or mathematics.

In order to use computers as cognitive tools effectively in classrooms, it obviously is necessary to change the curriculum, especially at the secondary level. However, most high school teachers find it difficult to change their courses. This is particularly true in schools where students are intending to go to college, and they and their parents want to be certain that their high school courses cover all the material necessary to prepare them adequately for college admissions testing and their postsecondary academic work. A teacher in our computer simulation project reported to us that he would be delighted to introduce some new material involving computer models *after* the first Saturday in May, the day his students would be taking the Advanced Placement calculus examination (Mandinach & Cline, 1994). Prior to that time, he could not afford to give up a single class period for anything that would not be included in the test. Changing the curriculum is a zero-sum game; if you add something, you must take something else out. This is a dilemma for most teachers and curriculum coordinators.

Even if we could achieve some consensus about altering the curriculum, introducing computers as cognitive tools is not a simple matter of replacement. Teachers need to learn how to use these new curriculum units. For many teachers, this may be their first experience in using computers in teaching. Most uses of computers in schools involve application programs such as word processors or spreadsheets. Few teachers are using computers directly to enhance the teaching of specific subject matter. As computers become more ubiquitous, we can expect that it will be rare for a teacher not to be at least minimally experienced with technology by the time they enter the profession. However, it will be many years before we can assume that most teachers will not require special instruction in computer uses.

Perhaps more problematic is the requirement for providing training and support for teachers as they begin to use these new tools. A number of projects have been developed that provide ongoing teacher training and professional development with various tools (CTGV, 1997; Mandinach & Cline, 1994), technical perspectives (David, 1996; Sandholtz, Ringstaff, & Dwyer, 1997; Yocum, 1996), and increasingly with a focus on the use of the Internet (Derry, Schlager, Gance, & Gance, this volume; National Semiconductor, 1998; Stanford University, 1998). We know from our experience in assisting teachers to use computers for modeling and simulation in science and mathematics classes that it takes three to five years for them to integrate such activities into their curriculum in a way that they feel is effective (Mandinach & Cline, 1994). Undoubtedly, with experience, this time to become proficient in using new materials and techniques can be reduced, but it will always be a substantial cost in any curriculum innovation project.

In a more general sense the use of computers as cognitive tools in classrooms portends a pervasive transformation of the means by which teaching and learning occur in schools. Indeed, in our view it suggests a rather radical change in the nature of learning and potentially a redefinition of the teaching profession. A number of investigators have suggested that the use of computers in the classroom and the proliferation of constructivist learning environments are changing the behavior of teachers. Rather than standing in front of the class lecturing and disseminating facts, the teacher is facilitating the self-directed learning activities of many small groups of students. This transformation has been referred to as the teacher playing the role of the "guide on the side" rather than the "sage on the stage." From a broader perspective, the function of teaching should be to prepare students to be lifelong, independent learners rather than to prepare them to pass a particular test or gain admission to a particular postsecondary institution.

This role for the teacher of tomorrow will likely be quite different from that of today. It will be very important for teachers to be competent in cognitive development, particularly as it relates to helping students gain mastery in specific content areas. A critical skill for teachers to develop is be the capacity for intellectual empathy. By this we mean that teachers need to be able to detect the extent and nature of each individual student's knowledge and competence in a subject so that they may help that learner move ahead in developing independent mastery. There are very few, if any, opportunities for teachers to develop such skills in either preservice or in-service training programs. This suggests that the curricula of our teacher training institutions need to be reviewed for appropriate changes, for the capacity of intellectual empathy will be required of all teachers in future.

If this description of the function, role, and necessary skills of the teacher of tomorrow is accurate, it suggests a number of important consequences for the profession. In addition to changes in the programs of teacher training institutions, the criteria for admission, certification, and the attainment of senior status in the profession should include the dimensions of cognitive development and intellectual empathy. Furthermore, the means of evaluating teacher performance and the criteria for rewards and promotion also need to be modified. Finally, it might make sense to change the support systems for teachers to incorporate these new dimensions of professional practice. A study of the activities of teachers in constructivist environments might reveal some activities that would be more efficiently accomplished by paraprofessionals. The full explication of the implications of these changes should be the object of another and more extensive inquiry. It is our hope that this chapter will stimulate thinking on these aspects of the development and utilization of computers as cognitive tools.

CONCLUSION

It is quite possible that the readers might conclude that we are hiding a negative bias toward the use of computers in education. It might be suspected that we are in fact disguised Luddites operating undercover in a pro-computer rally. This would be a totally incorrect conclusion. We believe strongly that when appropriately implemented, computer-based curricular innovations can markedly improve cognitive performance and, subsequently, achievement on standardized tests. Furthermore, we know from our own experiences that engaging and cognitively demanding computer-based curricula can promote academic achievement among many students who are currently not served well by our schools. We have seen such programs completely turn around high school students who were about to drop out. Many of those same students subsequently graduated from high school and went on to become science, mathematics, and engineering majors in college.

Our convictions are based on decades of observing the field as well as managing a large-scale project that employed computer-based modeling and simulation to enhance teaching and learning of science and mathematics at the secondary school level. However, even in that project, which continued over 10 years, we are just beginning to develop adequate measures that documented the cognitive performance of the students. To realize the enormous potential benefits for millions of our nation's future workforce in combining the recent advances in cognitive and computer science, we need resources from funding agencies; diligence and hard work from scientists; an appreciation of the importance of technology by teachers, curriculum coordinators, and administrators; and, perhaps most important, patience from all involved parties.

REFERENCES

Anderson, J. R., Reder, L. M., & Simon, H. A. (1996). Situated learning in education. *Educational Researcher*, *25*(4), 5–11.

Anderson, J. R., Reder, L. M., & Simon, H. A. (1997). Rejoinder: Situative versus cognitive perspectives: Form versus substance. *Educational Researcher*, *26*(1), 18–21.

Becker, H. J. (1991). How computers are used in United States schools: Basic data from the 1989 I.E.A. computers in education survey. *Journal of Educational Computing Research, 7*, 385–406.

Berliner, D. C., & Biddle, B. J. (1995). *The manufactured crisis: Myths, fraud, and the attack on America's public schools.* Reading, MA: Addison-Wesley.

Brown, A. L., & Campione, J. C. (1996). Psychological theory and the design of innovative learning environments: On procedures, principles, and systems. In L. Schauble & R. Glaser (Eds.), *Innovations in learning: New environments for education* (pp. 289–326). Hillsdale, NJ: Lawrence Erlbaum Associates.

Center for Innovative Learning Technologies. (1998, January). *Visualization and modeling workshop*. University of California, Berkeley, School of Education, Berkeley, CA.

CEO Forum. (1997). Report '97. Available at: *www.CEOForum.org.*

Chipman, S. F. (1993). Gazing once more into the silicon chip: Who's revolutionary now?. In S. P. Lajoie & S. J. Derry (Eds.), *Computers as cognitive tools* (pp. 341–367). Hillsdale, NJ: Lawrence Erlbaum Associates.

Cline, H. F., & Mandinach, E. B. (in press). The corruption of a research design: A case study of a curriculum innovation project. In R. Lesh & E. Kelly (Eds.), *Designing research for reform in mathematics and science education*. Mahwah, NJ: Lawrence Erlbaum Associates.

Cognitive Technology Group at Vanderbilt. (1992). The Jasper series as an example of anchored instruction: Theory, program description, and assessment data. *Educational Psychologist, 27*, 291–315.

Cognitive Technology Group at Vanderbilt. (1996). Looking at technology in context: A framework for understanding technology in education. In D. C. Berliner & R. C. Calfee (Eds.), *Handbook of educational psychology* (pp. 807–840). New York: Simon & Schuster Macmillan.

Cognitive Technology Group at Vanderbilt. (1997). *The Jasper project: Lessons in curriculum, instruction, assessment, and professional development*. Mahwah, NJ: Lawrence Erlbaum Associates.

Coley, R. J., Cradler, J., & Engel, P. K. (1997). *Computers and classrooms: The status of technology in U.S. schools*. Princeton, NJ: Educational Testing Service, Policy Information Center.

Corno, L. (1992). The best-laid plans: Modern conceptions of volition and educational research. *Educational Researcher, 22*(2), 14–22.

Corno, L., & Mandinach, E. B. (1983). The role of cognitive engagement in classroom learning and motivation. *Educational Psychologist, 18*, 88–108.

David, J. L. (1996). Developing and spreading accomplished teaching: Policy lessons from a unique partnership. In C. Fisher, D. C. Dwyer, & K. Yocum (Eds.), *Education and technology: Reflections on computing in classrooms* (pp. 237–250). San Francisco: Apple Press.

Donmoyer, R. (1997). Introduction: This issue: Refocusing on learning. *Educational Researcher, 26*(1), 4, 34.

Glennan, T. K., & Melmed, A. (1996). *Fostering the use of educational technology: Elements of a national strategy*. Santa Monica, CA: Rand.

Greeno, J. G. (1997). Response: On claims that answer the wrong questions. *Educational Researcher, 26*(1), 5–17.

Greeno, J. G., and the Middle School Mathematics Through Applications Project Group. (1998). The situativity of knowing, learning, and research. *American Psychologist, 53*, 5–26.

Lajoie, S. P., & Derry, S. J. (Eds.). (1993). *Computers as cognitive tools*. Hillsdale, NJ: Lawrence Erlbaum Associates.

Mandinach, E. B., & Cline, H. F. (1994). *Classroom dynamics: Implementing a technology-based learning environment*. Hillsdale, NJ: Lawrence Erlbaum Associates.

National Council of Teachers of Mathematics. (1995). *Assessment standards for school mathematics*. Reston, VA: Author.

National Semiconductor. (1998). *Global connections: Making the most of the Internet in the classroom*. Unpublished teacher training materials, Sunnyvale, CA.

Newman, D. (1990). Opportunities for research on the organizational impact of school computers. *Educational Researcher, 19*(3), 8–13.

Redfield, C. L., & Steuck, K. (1991*)*. The future of intelligent tutoring systems. In H. Burns, J. W. Parlett, & C. L. Redfield (Eds.), *Intelligent tutoring systems* (pp. 265–284). Mahwah, NJ: Lawrence Erlbaum Associates.

Salomon, G. (1991). Transcending the qualitative-quantitative debate: The analytic and systemic approaches to educational research. *Educational Researcher, 20* (6), 10–18.

Salomon, G. (1996). Studying novel learning environments as patterns of change. In S. Vosniadou, E. DeCorte, R. Glaser, & H. Mandl (Eds.), *International perspectives on the design of technology-supported learning environments* (pp. 363–377). Mahwah, NJ: Lawrence Erlbaum Associates.

Sandholtz, J. H., Ringstaff, C., & Dwyer, D. C. (1997). *Teaching with technology: Creating student-centered classrooms*. New York: Teachers College Press.

Schunk, D. H., & Zimmerman, B. J. (Eds.). (1994). *Self-regulation of learning and performance: Issues and educational applications*. Hillsdale, NJ: Lawrence Erlbaum Associates.

Sheingold, K., Heller, J. I., & Paulukonis, S. T. (1994). *Actively seeking evidence: Teacher change through assessment development*. Princeton, NJ: Educational Testing Service, Center for Performance Assessment.

Sheingold, K., Heller, J. I., & Storms, B. (1997, March). *On the mutual influence of teacher professional development and assessment quality in curricular reform*. Paper presented at the meeting of the American Educational Research Association, Chicago.

Stanford University. (1998). *Stanford institute for educational leadership through technology*. Stanford, CA.

Winne, P. H. (1995). Inherent details in self-regulated learning. *Educational Psychologist, 30*, 173–187.

Winne, P. H. (1997). Experimenting to bootstrap self-regulated learning. *Journal of Educational Psychology, 89*, 397–410.

Yocum, K. (1996). Conversation: An essential element of teacher development. In C. Fisher, D. C. Dwyer, & K. Yocum (Eds.), *Education and technology: Reflections on computing in classrooms* (pp. 265–279). San Francisco: Apple Press.

Zimmerman, B. J., & Schunk, D. H. (Eds.). (1989*). Self-regulated learning and academic achievement.* New York: Springer-Verlag.

IV

DISCUSSION

14

What Are the Tools For? Revolutionary Change Does Not Follow the Usual Norms

Alan Lesgold
University of Pittsburgh

The chapters in this book are the latest contributions to a ritual that has been under way for close to four decades. The ritual has two parts. In the first part, visionary authors examine new tools from the cognitive and information sciences, notice the substantial and ever-increasing penetration of the home market by computers, and propose revolutionary approaches to learning that take advantage of the new affordances of the information age. In the second part, reflective authors point out how little these visionary ideas have been implemented and show how the visions have failed to take account of the ways in which educational practice is taught, evaluated, and paid for. Many authors have played both the visionary and the reflective roles. Both are mostly on target in their assertions.

The information age is truly revolutionary. It is a major disjunction from earlier times. This makes it very unlikely that the practices and opportunities that develop from it will fit neatly with practices of the past. Consider past educational revolutions. Prior to the 15th century, codified knowledge was extremely rare. The artifacts used to capture it were not easily reproduced. Direct discussion with a wise person was a primary way of gaining knowledge, but there were other ways as well. The stained glass windows of the cathedral at Chartres tell the stories of the Bible, and the carvings in the Kailash Temple in Ellora, India, tell the story of the Ramayana. Troubadours carried stories from one place to another in the form of epic songs. And, of course, there was the book.

The book was expensive and not easily replicated. For this reason, schooling often had the form of a reading of a book by one person, sometimes even titled a "reader," to a group of students. Because of the high cost of reproducing a book, emphasis was placed on accuracy of reproduction, not on innovation. What validation there was of the effectiveness of this form of education was informal and embedded in the culture. The good reader not only read the lesson but offered elaborations and interpretations as well. Perhaps he answered questions. His suitability for the role was determined mostly by his peers, who accepted him if he fit into the social niche they jointly occupied. No one asked whether there was a discernible connection between the way a reader read the lesson and handled any discussion of it and the subsequent success of the students in later roles they filled.

With the development of printing, a revolution in learning took place, though it took almost 400 years to occur. Very quickly, certain key books were reproduced widely, including Bibles. This allowed the central institution of learning to be supplemented by many local centers of learning. It also allowed for a specialization of the "value added" by the reader. At one extreme was the acknowledged leading scholar. He had the most to say about a particular book; indeed he wrote some of the books himself. The most able students were sent to him, so they could take advantage of his special insights. The local scholars, often parish clergy, were valued because they spoke the language of the common folk. An average student might even prefer the increased sensitivity and less challenging ideas of a nearby teacher to that of the world expert off in the distance. And, of course, a new opportunity became available: those who were literate could read the book and draw their own conclusions.

A few vestiges of the era before movable type remain today. Teachers still often speak from a lectern, though they usually substitute personal notes for the rare volume from which they once read. The very title of *reader* remains in some universities. More important, memorization remains a key part of organized schooling. This made great sense when books were rare. One way to have control of a body of knowledge when one did not own a book was to memorize it. To this day, elementary education in some traditional Islamic schools focuses on memorization of the Q'uran.

Once books became ubiquitous, memorization no longer was needed for the purpose of knowledge preservation. Still, there remained a sense that memorization might somehow be important because of the facility it conferred, a belief that remains with us—probably correctly in part—to this day. Many schools continue to be conservative in moving even from memorization of important texts to accessing those texts in libraries and focusing learning on skills of interpretation and application of the wisdom embodied in literature. For at least some people, the ability to recite Shakespeare is more noteworthy than the ability to discuss the plot of a particular play.

It would be possible to argue that this remaining, though highly diminished, tendency to demand memorization of material that is readily accessible should be treated as a characteristic of schools that should be accommodated, especially for schools with inadequate libraries. However, few of us, even those of us who believe that some students need a base of overlearned knowledge, would argue that the conservatism of schools with respect to memorization or the lack of library funds justifies sticking to memorization-based curricula. Indeed, we have reached the point where we tend to feel that a school that focuses strongly on memorization and does not attend sufficiently to interpretation and use of information is in need of major restructuring.

The information age is still too new for us to be quite as certain in our demands on schools. We know that just as the book removed some of the need for memorization as a force for knowledge distribution, so the computer removes some of the need for overlearning of routine information processing procedures, since these can now be accomplished by computers. Many of us question, for example, whether algebra students should spend long periods learning to factor polynomials when symbolic manipulation programs can do this for us. But we also legitimately wonder whether we fully understand the extent to which overlearning of expression factoring skills helps or hinders deeper understanding and use of mathematics.

As Perfetti and I (Lesgold & Perfetti, 1978) suggested more than 20 years ago for reading, there are a number of possible trade-offs of facility in basic word recognition, domain-specific knowledge, and higher-level comprehension skills in supporting overall reading expertise. For example, one student might absorb a text because he has good word recognition and higher order skills, while another leverages superb background knowledge relevant to the content of the text. At least some students have much better prospects in reading if they get extended practice on some of its basic strokes. Perhaps the same is true in mathematics, where lots of number facility might provide a stronger base of "mathematical intuition" for a student who has trouble following extended sequences of mathematical reasoning. Overall, there is room for extended practice, breadth of knowledge, and specific "higher order thinking skills" training in a number of school subject areas. One role that extended practice might play is to mediate which brain processes are engaged when attempting various intelligent actions; there is some indication that part of what changes with practice is the relative dominance of recognition and other processes in overall cognition.

Clearly, at least a number of schools are ready for educational technology that supports practice on basic components of intelligent activity. This kind of technology fits the traditional view—still held by many parents, teachers, and political leaders—that practice of the basics is the most important part of schooling. So far, it is these tools that have been most readily adopted by schools, along with some of the tools of modern information age life like word processing (though at least some people believe that it is bad to use some of the standard office tools like spreadsheets, symbolic mathematics systems, and even calculator programs).

Schools have also proved ready to adopt relatively complete systems that handle a specific problem. An example is the collection of intelligent tutors for algebra and geometry that have been developed by John Anderson, Ken Koedinger, and Al Corbett at Carnegie Mellon University and are now being sold by Carnegie Learning (*http://www.carnegielearning. com/*; Koedinger, Anderson, Hadley, & Mark, 1995). To market this system, the Anderson team needed to develop complete curricula, including lesson plans, extra activities, and worksheets, even though the tutors address learning goals that are universal in algebra and geometry courses. However, part of the implicit contract that society makes with school teachers is that they will not have to spend significant time deciding what and how to teach unless they choose to do so or are separately engaged in a district curriculum development effort. Indeed, school systems often severely limit the variations in content and even teaching methods that teachers can use. Because of this built-in resistance to change, materials developed to add a new dimension to current instruction or to afford opportunities for learning content not currently taught are difficult to introduce.

We need to be sure that we separate excessive use of a learning tool from limited and more reasonable use. For example, phonics drill can be helpful to reading competence when we have clear goals for reading, but it can also have a negative effect if it becomes a major curricular goal on its own. Similarly, drill in basic number facts is a reasonable part of an effective scheme to teach students how to use mathematical techniques to represent and make sense of their world. Still, it is not my intention to support the conservative view that only technologies that schools are ready for should be developed. Nevertheless, we do need to find ways in which new technologies for new learning can be introduced successfully.

The problem we face in inserting new technologies into education is that they partly represent new ways of teaching and partly represent new content that ought to be taught now. We need to understand the extent of revolutionary content in new learning technologies (i.e., content not currently the focus of instruction) and to allocate resources to the curriculum development and teacher professional development that will be needed for the new technologies to be deployed and to achieve their goals.

NEW LEARNING REQUIREMENTS IN THE INFORMATION AGE

Let me consider a few examples of thinking about, and sometimes acting on, new competences that students need to acquire to do well in the information age. One person who has thought about this is Tom Hill, chief executive officer of @learning Corporation. Hill (1998) has suggested that part of modern life is being able to learn continuously and often on one's own. Further, he argues, students need to become facile with exactly those technologies that allow them to acquire the following attributes:

- Skill in designing and constructing new knowledge.
- Ability to structure and self-publish knowledge without an intermediary.
- Ability to process knowledge recursively.
- Perceived self-efficacy for learning.
- Self-monitoring competence.
- Conscious competence—a continual state of personal development as an active undertaking.

He then focuses his attention on technologies that will help students acquire these capabilities. Some of those technologies may push the social or infrastructural envelope of the current school world, but this is, I would argue, justified because some of the needed new curriculum is necessarily dependent on such technologies.

Another example is the work of Uri Wilensky (Wilensky & Resnick, 1999). Wilensky noted that high-powered computer systems allow the development of parallel models that can sometimes be more easily understood by students. For example, the statistical nature of AIDS infections may be easier to understand by building a model that has separate representations of each of a large number of people. This makes it possible both to look at the overall infection rate in the population and track the experience of individuals. For example, if 50% of a population with 1% AIDS infection uses condoms and the members of the population average x sexual encounters per month, then the population will, after 10 years, have y% of themselves infected, where y is a function of the proportion of people infected, the mean number of new contacts per person per month, the probability of disease transmission per sexual episode, and the mean number of sexual episodes per partner per month. The numbers, although large, will still not be staggering. On the other hand, if students follow a few selected individuals who do not use condoms, they will see specific instances of an individual being lucky some number of times but eventually being infected. The group average game is, in many conceptual ways, different from the individual game of "eventually you'll be hit." In the group view, the relevant measure is a group summary, but in the individual view, infection will eventually occur; the only thing to measure is how long it takes for this to happen. By looking at both views, students can get a much better appreciation of what the population statistics are summarizing.

As it happens, Wilensky was by no means the first person to model both individuals' and groups' AIDS experience as a function of preventive practices, promiscuity, and rate of encounters. José Gonzalez (personal communication, 1995) of Agder College of Engineering in Grimstad, Norway, developed such a simulation earlier, but the limitations on computing at the time made it less able to present multiple levels of aggregation clearly in a simulation. Now that the tools exist, Gonzalez has become part of a company called PowerSim that builds simulation tools and templates that facilitate modeling complex systems by defining their components and how those components interact. Earlier classroom research (e.g., Mandinach & Cline, 1994) suggests that such tools can have powerful effects, though it is not clear how well these effects continue once researchers and other support are withdrawn from the school.

Simulation tools are becoming commonplace in management and planning situations, and there are many indications that life in the information age will include the use of such tools in many areas of our society. This is clear partly because there is ample evidence that such tools and the thinking associated with them are very much needed. Dörner (1989/1996) used a simple simulation game much like Sim City to study human ability to manage complex environments. A basic scenario Dörner used was to manage the evolution of a small village into a city or to introduce cattle into the food mix of a developing country. Inevitably, people focused on too small a portion of the overall system and encountered disasters as the simulation unfolded. They had only the macromodel of the system to manipulate and examine, and that was not enough to support their limited ability to deal with complex systems.

So, learning on one's one and understanding and interacting with large systems are two important examples of new capabilities that are important for success in the information age. To get these capabilities taught in schools, we need to develop a clear and socially shared sense of what these new capabilities are and to teach teachers and school leaders how they can be taught. We also need to develop the tools for this professional development work. Since the need for these new competences was produced by the information revolution, we can assume that teaching them requires the use of some of the new information technologies. Almost every strong idea presented in this book has potential for helping in this new enterprise, though a focus on tools aimed specifically at the new curricular areas will likely be beneficial.

This suggests one possible resolution to the conflict between giving schools what they can use and giving them the most exciting new tools. When aiming at the traditional subject areas, it is especially important to fit new tools to the best existing approaches to teaching, even if there is a delay in introduction of some of the most exciting features. When aiming at the newly needed information age competences, part of the role of the technology is to produce revolutionary change in what is taught. This means that some amount of provocation might be helpful and that complete and immediate success in getting the new tools adopted may not be a feasible goal, especially if it means softening the message implicit in the new media. It also means that new learning tools are not complete until they are part of a systematic package that can support the institutional and professional development changes that are required in order for the new content those tools support to be merged into existing schooling goals.

A major characteristic of the list of capabilities that Hill suggests is their lack of close ties to a single school subject. Rather, Hill is concerned with broad skills of learning, self-management, and complex problem solving. These are skills much in demand, but they do not tie directly to any specific subject matter. This ensures that learning tools aimed at these new information age skills will not fit well into current schools unless some kind of restructuring of those schools takes place. Again, the problem is not that learning tools aimed at Hill's list of new skills are less desirable than tools for conventional curriculum. Rather, it is that we must specify clearly the additional resources needed before the new learning tools can be successfully deployed.

TEACHING TEACHERS COMES
BEFORE TEACHING STUDENTS

One interesting property of these new learning tools is that often they can be used to change teachers' views about content, just as they can be used to change student thinking and performance. Indeed, this may turn out to be the vehicle by which information age skills become part of the curriculum. If our primary concern is to produce change in schools so that they become able to teach new skills, then the first target for cognitive tool software might be teachers. Once new self-managed schemes for continual learning are embedded in the school culture, it is likely that they naturally will come to be used for teaching students as well. Our experience has been that creative teachers routinely repurpose software and other tools to help achieve their educational goals; the problem is getting the right set of goals to be adopted.

Basically, I am suggesting that the problem of getting powerful new learning tools to be adopted and used should be partitioned into two parts. First, the goals of school systems and teachers need to be shaped to include the kinds of capabilities that Hill listed, along with deeper levels of understanding of certain key pieces of science and technology. This will prepare teachers to use new cognitive learning tools in their teaching. The second step, which will then be more readily achieved, will be to take some of the same cognitive tools used for organizational transformation and use them instead for student learning.

ONE STEP IN THIS DIRECTION

In the work my colleagues and I have been doing with cognitive tools for argumentation (Cavalli-Sforza, Lesgold, & Weiner, 1994; Suthers, 1999), we came to this conclusion indirectly. First, we built a set of tools to support argumentation activities by students over networks. These tools, which we named Belvedere, worked quite well, and innovative teachers were able to use them. However, in a larger sense, our development efforts were not entirely successful; schools do not seem able to keep using the tools over extended periods once we bow out of the developer role. Although it is likely that further support of the schools already using our tools would eventually result in a school-based capability to use them without support, it is certainly clear that scaling up our intervention would not be easy. We built our tool to support activities that teachers envision in their long-term thinking about education but that they are not fully prepared to implement once the tools arrive.

We are now turning the same kinds of capabilities we built for students into tools for teachers. Just as we made tools that would help students keep track of what they read as they browsed a set of pages about a complex scientific topic, we now are building tools to help teachers keep track of their thinking and investigations as they study examples of classroom practice and student products and relate what they see to a set of emerging new goals for schooling. The tools allow both professional development specialists and teachers to examine and annotate video and still images and to connect segments of those images to various concepts that have been emerging in a discussion. As we refine these materials, we find ourselves building in many of the capabilities and approaches discussed in this book.

The cognitive tools described in these chapters work; they foster a higher level of engaged, self-managed learning and thinking. These tools can indeed change education and make it more suitable for the information age. In addition, they can stimulate organizational learning by school systems that will lay a foundation for an information age curriculum. With that foundation, these tools will indeed be used by schools, and to good effect.

REFERENCES

Cavalli-Sforza, V., Weiner, A. W., and Lesgold, A. M. (1994). Software support for students engaging in scientific activity and scientific controversy. *Science Education, 78,* 577–599.

Dörner, D. (1989/1996). *The logic of failure: Recognizing and avoiding error in complex situations.* Reading, MA: Addison-Wesley.

Hill, T. (1998, December 9). *Dimensions of the Workforce 2008: Beyond training and education, toward continuous personal development.* Presentation at workshop conducted for the Office of Science and Technology Policy (Executive Office of the President). Alexandria, VA: Institute for Defense Analyses. Available from: *http://www.learningnetwork.com/Dimensions2008/Dimensions2008c.htm.*

Koedinger, K. R., Anderson, J. R., Hadley, W. H., & Mark, M. A. (1997). Intelligent tutoring goes to school in the big city. *International Journal of Artificial Intelligence in Education, 8,* 30–43.

Lesgold, A. M., & Perfetti, C. A. (1978). Interactive processes in reading comprehension. *Discourse Processes, 1,* 323–336.

Mandinach, E. B., & Cline, H. F. (1994). *Classroom dynamics: implementing a technology-based learning environment.* Hillsdale, NJ: Lawrence Erlbaum Associates.

Suthers, D. D. (1999, January 5–8). Representational support for collaborative inquiry. In *Proceedings of the 32nd Hawaii International Conference on the System Sciences* (HICSS–32), January 5–8, 1999. Maui, Hawaii: Institute of Electrical and Electronics Engineers.

Wilensky, U., & Resnick, M. (1999). Thinking in levels: A dynamic systems approach to making sense of the world. *Journal of Science Education and Technology, 8,* 3–19.

Author Index

�֍ �֍ ✖

Subject Index

❄ ❄ ❄